# Thinking with Bruno Latour in Rhetoric and Composition

# Thinking with BRUNO LATOUR in Rhetoric and Composition

Edited by
**Paul Lynch** and
**Nathaniel Rivers**

Southern Illinois University Press • *Carbondale*

Printed in the United States of America

18 17 16 15 4 3 2 1

*Cover illustration*: "Wooden Pillar, Welsh Assembly."
Photograph by Steve Mosley, cropped.

Library of Congress Cataloging-in-Publication Data
Thinking with Bruno Latour in Rhetoric and Composition /
Edited by Paul Lynch and Nathaniel Rivers.
p. cm
Includes bibliographical references and index.
ISBN 978-0-8093-3393-6 (paperback)
ISBN 0-8093-3393-7 (paperback)
ISBN 978-0-8093-3394-3 (ebook)
1. Rhetoric. 2. Latour, Bruno—Intellectual life. I. Lynch, Paul, 1971–
editor. II. Rivers, Nathaniel A., editor. III. Latour, Bruno, honouree.
P301.T488 2015
808—dc23 2014026164

The paper used in this publication meets the minimum
requirements of American National Standard for Information
Sciences—Permanence of Paper for Printed Library Materials,
ANSI Z39.48-1992. ∞

*For our parents,*
*Philip and Mary Lynch*
*Thomas and Nancy Rivers*

# Contents

# Acknowledgments

We first thank those who introduced us to Latour: Patricia Sullivan, Thomas Rickert, and Michael Salvo.

Many thanks as well to the SLU Latour Reading Group: Ruth Evans, Jennifer Rust, Rachel Greenwald Smith, Patrick Brooks, Chris Dickman, Abigail Lambke, and Katie Zabrowski. Our gratitude also goes to our colleagues in the Department of English at Saint Louis University.

Thanks to Thomas Rivers for his insightful comments on the introduction. We are also grateful to Kristine Priddy of Southern Illinois University Press for her consistent encouragement of this project, and we also extend our gratitude to Mary Lou Kowaleski, an extraordinarily careful copy editor.

Thanks to all the contributors who made this collection possible.

Most important, we are always and forever grateful to our spouses, Melody Gee and Jodi Rivers, and our children, Beatrice Lynch, Josephine Lynch, and Will Rivers.

# Abbreviations

## Books

| | |
|---|---|
| *Aramis* | *Aramis, or the Love of Technology* |
| *LL* | *Laboratory Life* |
| *MC* | *On the Modern Cult of the Factish Gods* |
| *ML* | *The Making of Law* |
| *Modern* | *We Have Never Been Modern* |
| *PF* | *Pasteurization of France* |
| *PH* | *Pandora's Hope* |
| *PN* | *Politics of Nature* |
| *PW* | *The Prince and the Wolf* |
| *RS* | *Reassembling the Social* |
| *SA* | *Science in Action* |

## Essays

| | |
|---|---|
| "Critique" | "Why Has Critique Run Out of Steam? From Matters of Fact to Matters of Concern" |
| "Dingpolitik" | "From Realpolitik to Dingpolitik or How to Make Things Public" |
| "Interobjectivity" | "On Interobjectivity" |
| "New Method" | "A New Method to Trace the Path of Innovations: The Sociotechnical Graph" |

# Thinking with Bruno Latour in Rhetoric and Composition

# 1. Introduction: Do You Believe in Rhetoric and Composition?

Paul Lynch and Nathaniel Rivers,
*Saint Louis University*

> "I have a question for you," he said, taking out of his pocket a crumpled piece of paper on which he had scribbled a few key words. He took a breath: "Do you believe in reality?"
>
> "But of course!" I laughed. "What a question! Is reality something we have to believe in?"
>
> —Bruno Latour, *Pandora's Hope*

"Wait, don't tell me," we hear the reader. "*Another* French theorist to rescue rhetoric and composition from its intellectual doldrums." It is a fair complaint about work in rhetcomp. Call it the Ikea approach: insert critical theorist A into disciplinary gap B and *voila!* (as Bruno Latour might say) you have another piece of cheap academic furniture that will last until you settle down and start antiquing. Given the sprawl of our discipline—whose "House of Lore" rivals an Ikea's size—acquiring another avant-garde European is about as hip as buying a futon. Worse still, Latour joins a long line of scholars who have "rediscovered" rhetoric. Examining Colin Powell's infamous Iraq War UN presentation, Latour concludes that we need better public deliberation: "eloquence, or more pejorative, rhetoric, or, even more derogatory, sophistry [. . .] are just the labels that we might need to rescue from the dustbin of history" ("Dingpolitik" 8–9). Uh, yeah. Meanwhile, he has produced a "compositionist's manifesto" in which he suggests that composition might qualify as an intellectual project. Shall we be relieved or annoyed? It's nice to have friends in high places—Latour ranked number 10 on the *Times Higher Education Supplement*'s 2007 list of the humanities' most cited authors—but there is something humiliating in being seduced simply because "rhetoric" and "composition" have passed someone's lips. Do we need to be told that a healthier rhetorical culture would lead to a healthier political culture? That writing is a technology that restructures thought? Is it anti-intellectual xenophobia to wonder whether we can finally just go ahead and believe in rhetoric and composition?

Of course, we believe that rhetoric and composition exists. The professors, graduate programs, journals, students, papers, books, adjuncts, conferences, endowed chairs, and Listservs (oh, the Listservs) are all testament to that. We're asking whether we can import yet another "outside" scholar without implying that we still cannot drink from our own wells. Legitimation by association is a benefit of "doing theory" in our field, but it sometimes suggests that we do not quite believe in our own enterprise. Yet, the problem with the question is deeper. In asking, "Do you believe in . . . ?" we seem to mimic the assumptions behind the question, "Do you believe in reality?" That implies an unbridgeable gulf between words and things, the very gulf that has undermined rhetoric and infantilized composition. Fortunately, that is not the only way to think about belief. "Belief," Latour insists, "is not a state of mind but a result of relationships" (*MC* 2). If that is the case, then, perhaps believing that Latour has something to offer—believing, that is, *with* Latour—need not occasion a crisis of faith in which we feel compelled to justify the ways of rhetoric to (French)men.

But a relationship with Latour will occasion some struggle. Latour himself argues that the most important rule of rhetoric "is to ask the (imaginary) reader what sort of trials it will require before believing the author" (*SA* 53). Each of the following seventeen chapters in this volume conducts such a trial. Though it seems rude to invite a guest in order to test him, our guest seeks such tests: "The text builds a little story in which something incredible (the hero) becomes gradually more credible because it withstands more and more terrible trials" (53). Our two heroes are Latour and rhetcomp, and our text recounts a series of trials through which they put each other. But our story begins long before our discipline or its potential ally arrived on the scene; it begins back in the agora, where our forebears insisted that rhetoric was something in which we could believe.

## Do You Believe in Rhetoric? Toward a Strange Defense

Rhetoric reading Latour is like remembering something we thought we always knew, like a not-quite-repressed memory edging forward in our minds. Though we sometimes privilege the human and the symbolic, Latour returns us to the barnyard, teeming with nonhumans, where mud and words are flung together. Repeatedly in his work, Latour relies on rhetoric to articulate his notion of knowledge making. His articulations of rhetoric are inclusive and robust—strong defenses, as Richard Lanham has called them in "The 'Q' Question," where he names our discipline's greatest foe: "the weak defense." "The Weak Defense," explains Lanham, "argues that there are two kinds of rhetoric, good and bad. The good kind is used in good causes, the bad kind in bad causes. Our kind is the good kind; the bad kind is used by our opponents" (155). The gist of the weak defense is that outside of rhetoric there sits an arhetorical measuring stick we can and should use to assess our rhetoric and, hence, adjudicate our strife. The weak defense postpones difficult questions about the good or the true by placing them beyond our reach. Rhetoric remains the surly teenager in need of adult supervision. The weak defense, simply put, does not believe in rhetoric. "The Strong Defense," on the other hand, "assumes that truth is determined by *social dramas*, some more formal than others but *all man-made*. Rhetoric in such a world is not ornamental but determinative, essentially creative" (156; emphasis added). Rhetoric is no longer subject to the good and the true; the good and the true are subject to rhetoric. We articulate the good and the true through political strife, human interaction, and social drama.

There is, nevertheless, a worrying rub. What does Lanham count as a "social drama"? It seems to be a human and discursive affair. The truths produced via these dramas are "all man-made." This opens the strong defense to the charge of being a kind of social constructionism: the world as "we" know it is made through symbolic projections, and reality is an effect of the collective *human* imagination. Against an untenable realism that pictures a world full of static objects, Lanham's social constructionism projects an equally untenable idealism that imagines a world controlled exclusively by language.[1] The world is either ready-made or made-to-order; human rhetoric is either powerless or omnipotent.

Latour provides the balm for this rub. In Latour, the social drama includes both humans *and* nonhumans. People are not the only actors who "wield" rhetoric; so, too, do objects: "For scientific, political, and even moral reasons it is crucial that enquirers do not in advance, and *in place* of the actors, define what sorts of building blocks the social world is made of" (*RS* 41). Those building blocks include language but alongside all the objects with which language (as an object itself) might collide. Not words *or* things; words *and* things. Lanham's *strong* defense becomes Latour's *strange* defense. Where Lanham bets on human rhetoric alone, Latour dramatically increases the number and kind of deliberators. The truth is made but not solely by humans. In Latour's agora, *everything* is nervously loquacious. There is not a "society" but rather a "collective" "defined as an exchange of human and nonhuman properties inside a corporate body" (*PH* 193).

As Latour argues with respect to intelligence, so must we for rhetoric: "To be *intelligent*, as the word's etymology indicates, is to be able to hold all these [human and nonhuman] connections at once" (*PH* 90). Such is the intellectual work of the strange defense of rhetoric: escaping the constraints of binaries we neither created nor honor, rhetoric must mutate beyond the human/nonhuman divide: "Was it one thing to persuade a minister to provide a stock of graphite, and quite another to persuade a neutron to slow down enough to hit a uranium atom so as to provide three more neutrons? Yes and no" (*PH* 89–90). His strange idea is that we owe it to the neutron to speak of it the same way we speak of the minister. If we are alarmed by this idea, Latour offers a paradoxical defense: "tell the humanists that *the more nonhumans share existence with humans, the more humane* a collective is" (*PH* 18; original emphasis). To believe in rhetoric is to admit this strangeness into our propositions and our parliaments.[2]

Unfortunately, rhetoricians sometimes count only the human, symbolic, and discursive. But when Latour admonishes sociologists, engineers, and scientists to account for the missing masses, he implicitly encourages rhetoric to account for the nonhuman, the nonsymbolic, and the nondiscursive. Instead of mere representation as signification, we need ways to re-present—to make present again and again—the nonhuman in collectives. In "Dingpolitik," Latour argues, "[E]ach object gathers around itself a different assembly of relevant parties" (5). Objects aren't simply talked about; they coproduce the occasions for talking. Rhetoric's new thing is, in fact, *things*, and Latour prods us toward recognizing that the work of rhetoric gets stronger as it gets stranger.

Rhetoric has already begun this turn to objects. Reading new media through Martin Heidegger, Jennifer Bay and Thomas Rickert describe, "Learning to dwell with new media and its technologies entails a harkening to their ontological weight and rhetorical agency" (213).[3] In other words, there is rhetoric produced *through* new media and rhetoric produced *by* the media themselves. Jenny Edbauer Rice encapsulates this investment: "If we dismiss this technical work as rote mechanics, we risk calcifying a distinction between the *production work* of texts (including the operations of buttons, cords, and wires that cut and record texts) and the produced texts themselves" (367–68). Following Latour, we can avoid this self-defeating distinction. The fully suasive act will gather human and nonhuman in a stronger—and stranger—articulation. "Even the best mechanic," Latour argues, "will find it difficult to regulate the machine—check the wind, mend the sails, enforce the law—so that all the allies stay content" (*SA* 130). Where Latour points to the nondiscursive components of persuasion, we find a range of mechanical or manual elements and activities that intensify and redistribute rhetoric: "In order to argue, we would now need the manual skills required to handle the scalpels, peel away the guinea pig ileum, interpret the decreasing peaks, and so on" (*SA* 67). The techno- and socio- are not two distinct realms but different elements of collectives that range across humans and nonhumans. (In the Latourian parlor, we worry about the furniture as much as the conversation.) Indeed, the world can be productively understood as a *rhetorical machine* fueled by both persuasion and technology, each shaping the other. Successful scientists and engineers keep their rhetoric strong and their projects alive by moving between the human and nonhuman allies.

The agency of objects unconceals a fundamental concern. This strange defense of rhetoric inevitably leads us to agency, that thing that matters so much to rhetoric. A basic question is repeatedly asked of approaches that distribute agency: how do we hold people accountable? But the question is zero-sum: if some strange force or network is responsible for our actions, then we as individuals are not. "Deeds are always done by someone, and replacing the doer of the action, the agent, with an amorphous force [. . .] leaves us with no basis for assigning responsibility" (Cooper 438). This worry likewise haunts our pedagogical mission. As Cheryl Geisler argues, "only if we can assent to the role of the rhetor producing efficacious action can we as a discipline have a mission to educate such rhetors to have agency" (13). Like the subject/object and science/politics binaries, this is a distinction that rhetoric should no longer recognize. "To use the word 'actor,'" writes Latour, "means that it's never clear who and what is acting when we act since an actor on stage is never alone" (*RS* 46). Agency is not something we own. Latour's treatment of actors dovetails with contemporary rhetorical theorists who likewise distribute or otherwise complicate agency. The "understanding of agency as a possession," argue Christian Lundberg and Joshua Gunn, "is central to reproducing the humanist model of the intentional agent who owns the capacity to make agential choices" (89). Lundberg and Gunn suggest a different kind of possession. For them, the Ouija board is a model for thinking about rhetorical agency because it fosters "an uncertain posture towards the flows of agency and agents implied by an open disposition toward the séance" (86). Though they do not summon Latour, their idea of agency suggests his strange notion of allies—not just the humans and their fingers but also the nonhumans, including the board, the planchette, and perhaps something more.

Perhaps the most familiar invoking of the humanist notion of agency is the old National Rifle Association defense: guns don't kill people, people kill people. For Latour, however, the gun is not a passive receptacle of human motives—any more than it is the direct cause of them. It is rather that a gun being held and a person holding a gun are distinct from an unarmed person and an unheld gun. Latour contends, "It is neither people nor guns that kill. Responsibility for action must be shared among the various actants" (*PH* 180). The act of shooting, made strange, is rather like moving a planchette on the Ouija board. Human hands manipulate and are manipulated. This is not some amorphous force but, rather, a partially discernable—though mysterious—network. It is a different game, but it is one in which we are no less responsible though being a different sort of actor. All parties, all actants, can be put on trial: the person, the gunman, the gun, the gun manufacturer, the bullet (see comedian Chris Rock), the bullet maker, gun laws, gun shops, saltpeter, and many, many other actors. If more responsibility is what we want, then we need more litigation. We need to follow the actors, trace all translations, and hire a damn good attorney. We don't need less-complex notions of agency; we need bigger courtrooms for a judicial rhetoric in which human and nonhuman actors face ever-stranger trials of strength. To believe in rhetoric, then, is not to assert anything but, rather, to commit to seeing things through, to go all the way in following the networks.

## Do You Believe in Composition? A Manifesto of Our Own

If the participation of nonhuman actors distinguishes Latour's notion of rhetoric, his rejection of representation distinguishes his notion of composition. The scientists he describes in *Laboratory Life* are upset to find that Latour is more interested in the fact of their writing than its content. Surely, the important thing is the substance (53). But truth production, Latour insists, is always a matter of writing, no matter the field: "All of us who sit down in front of a computer keyboard know that we find out what we think about things by reading what we are writing" (*MC* 22). This attitude makes Latour especially important at this moment in composition. Raúl Sánchez argues that the field is still too invested in the idea of representation: "We firmly believe, despite our postmodern claims, in the presence of something else beyond the veil of language" (10). The "hermeneutic disposition" reduces writing to "a notation system of experience" (4, 47). But writing is an experience in and of itself.

When Latour describes himself as a teacher of writing, he reveals himself to be the sort of teacher Sánchez imagines. Latour recounts a dialogue with a graduate student who insists that writing is a notation system for his study of organizations. Latour rejects this claim rather forcefully: "you are being badly trained!" (*RS* 149). For Latour, writing is not a means but a mediator. But writing, the student insists, is only a tool. To this, Latour replies, "There is no tool, no medium, only mediators. A text is thick. That's an ANT tenet, if any" (*RS* 148). *ANT* is the acronym for actor-network-theory,[4] the idea most closely associated with Latour and "a name that is so awkward, so confusing, so meaningless that it deserves to be kept" (*RS* 9). Like Frankenstein's monster, ANT is an idea that only its author could love. Latour himself is ready to chuck it until he is reminded that it spells A-N-T, "perfectly fit for a blind, myopic, workaholic, trail-sniffing, and collective traveler" (*RS* 9).

To do ANT is to be an ant, particularly of the sort recounted in a story of Daedalus's brilliance. King Minos, in search of the escaped inventor of the labyrinth, offers a reward "to anyone who could thread the circumvoluted shell of a snail" (*PH* 175). Unable to resist the challenge, a disguised Daedalus ties a thread to an ant and lets it wend its way through. (King Minos immediately recognizes his quarry, only to lose him again when Daedalus reroutes the king's plumbing and scalds him to death in his own bath. Moral of the story? Don't mess with the IT guy.) Daedalus's ant embodies ANT: the practice of tracing networks of humans and nonhumans through various forms of inscription, including writing. Not discerning the social but the "tracing of associations" (*RS* 5): "ANT does not tell anyone the shape that is to be drawn—circles or cubes or lines—but only how to go about systematically recording the world-building abilities of the sites to be documented or registered" ("On Recalling" 21). The text does not simply record knowledge; it (re)mediates knowledge into its next needful iteration—that is, text and knowledge create each other.

The image of an ant may not prove attractive to composition, already burdened by an inferiority complex. Every well-mannered member of our field knows to be embarrassed by the ugly Latinate compound that names it. Is the word "composition" not just the sort of faux sophistication that George Orwell warned us against in "Politics and the English Language" (which may, coincidentally, reign as comp's most widely assigned essay)? Some would prefer "writing studies," a phrase that does seem to add a touch of class. Even Geoff Sirc, once described as "the most dangerous man in composition," is feeling glum: "Until other departments are willing to take ownership for teaching students to do the writing in their field [. . .], it seems composition programs will remain a compromised, scapegoated service unit" (518). Meanwhile, Sidney Dobrin says that we are *Postcomposition* (a title which, at the very least, should tell us that we need more responsible stewardship of our prefixes). Composition suffers, Dobrin states, from a "neurosis of pedagogy [and] must escape the shackles of classrooms, students, and management" (28). No students, no classrooms, no programs, no university, and no composition—just writing.

In a compelling reading that is Latourian in spirit, Jeanne Gunner observes that in postcomposition, "writing is purified of all but itself" (624). Postcomposition is composition "pared down and cryonically preserved in . . . boutique humanities departments" (626). Gunner finds the counterpart purification in the work of Stanley Fish, who has famously argued that writing teachers should just teach grammar, a stance that purifies the field "of theoretical, historical, and pedagogical content" (620). From Dobrin to Fish, composition moves from boutique to big box, but this is a distinction without a difference. Together, Fish and the fisherman gut composition of both teaching and scholarship. This is what a crisis of belief looks like: two—and only two—bad choices.

Reading Plato's *Gorgias*, Latour asks, "Is there really no other way? Is it really impossible to build up other reflexes, other intellectual resources?" (*PH* 218). Is it possible, in other words, to maintain both the bureaucratic and the imaginative? What would that composition look like?

> Even though the word "composition" is a bit too long and windy, what is nice is that it underlines that things have to be put together (Latin *componere*) while retaining their heterogeneity. Also, it is connected with composure; it has clear roots in art, painting, music, theater, dance, and thus is associated with choreography and scenography; it is not too far from "compromise" and "compromising," retaining a certain diplomatic and prudential flavor. Speaking of flavor, it carries with it the pungent but ecologically correct smell of "compost," itself due to the active "de-composition" of many invisible agents. ("Attempt" 473–74)

This comes in Latour's "An Attempt at a 'Compositionist's Manifesto,'" a title that should have already appeared in the pages of *CCC*. It is unsettling that someone outside our field has captured composition's conflicting projects: beautiful writing, diplomacy, and our work in large institutions. Moreover, Latour's composition allows for compromise and decomposition, which suggest the sort of impurity one might expect from a "compromised, scapegoated service unit" (Sirc 518). If writing isn't compromised—perhaps even scapegoated—then it may not be accomplishing anything.

Latour might not see himself as a "compositionist," but his pursuit of truth production always works according the maxim "*Follow the writing.*" Latour—playing the role of anthropologist in a laboratory—observes that the work of science is the work of writing. Scientists "are compulsive and almost manic writers," and their laboratory begins "to take on the appearance of a system of literary inscription" (*LL* 48, 52). "Even insecure bureaucrats and compulsive novelists are less obsessed by inscriptions than scientists" (*LL* 245). Latour's books are loaded with images of this inscription: stuffed manila folders, stacks of notebooks, printers, desks, paper—these technologies assemble truth. Truth production is a process of sentence production. A fact is a sentence bolstered by other sentences (*SA* 25). The emergence of a fact relies on rhetoric *and* composition: "this operation draws upon activities of persuasion (agonistic) and of writing (construction) in order to increase the signal to noise ratio" (*LL* 241). Persuasion and writing produce a truth that is no less true for having been produced. What critics of Latour often miss—and what leads to the question, "Do you believe in reality?"—is his insistence that truths are more true because they have been so forcefully argued and carefully scripted.

## Res Rhetorica

Latour reminds us that "thing" derives from the word "ding," which designates not an object but "a certain type of archaic assembly" ("Dingpolitik" 12). The Icelandic parliament, for example, is still called Althing. In other words, the "banal term we use for designating what is out there unquestionably, a thing, [. . .] is also the oldest word we all have used to designate the oldest of the sites in which our ancestors did their dealing and tried to settle their disputes" ("Critique" 233). In many corners of the field, this assembly has already begun. Scholars in scientific and technical communication, perhaps not surprisingly, were the first to put Latour to the test.[5] Since then, the Latourian thing has gathered even more interest from the wider fields of rhetoric and composition.[6] As the collection's title suggests, we wish to think with Latour, neither to praise nor to bury him.

Before the thing begins in earnest, we have to constitute the assembly in which the dealing and dispute settling are going to happen. If we're going to bring into our parlor this visitor we've been nodding to in the hallways, we have to set out some chairs (or assemble them out of a cardboard box with an Allen wrench). Our first section, "Constituting Assemblages," begins the diplomatic work of hearing what Latour wants to say and articulating what's at stake in offering our assent. The key to this encounter is symmetry. As Clay Spinuzzi explains in the opening essay, "Symmetry as a Methodological Move," symmetry is the condition of possibility for a Latourian rhetoric. Symmetry asks only this: if we see a human actor acting, look for the nonhuman actors, as well. Understanding what Latour might offer rhetoric requires an understanding of this fundamental concept. Until now, we have treated Latour's thought as a fulsome worldview; Spinuzzi pursues symmetry in particular as a methodology, which allows him to reckon the risk and reward of engaging Latour in rhetorical studies.

Carl G. Herndl and S. Scott Graham continue the diplomatic formalities in their "Getting Over Incommensurability: Latour, New Materialisms, and the Rhetoric of Diplomacy." Herndl and Graham argue that his work might offer us a way to back out of the dead end of incommensurability, which troubles both the rhetoric of science, specifically, and the project of diplomacy, more generally. By imagining a flat ontology—in which subject and object, the *polis* and the *pagus*, are not incommensurable—Herndl and Graham expand the range of rhetoric's topography. Marc C. Santos and Meredith Zoetewey Johnson close these opening remarks with "From Constituting to Instituting: Kant, Latour, and Twitter." For them, Latour's critique of what he calls the "Modern Constitution" provides ways to reimagine the university as an institution open—rather than vulnerable—to the public sphere. The Latourian university would welcome politicians, businessmen, neighbors, and citizens.

If part one treats Latour in his own terms, part two treats him in ours. In "Conceiving Assemblages," our authors imagine how Latour's work reassembles various *agons* within rhetoric and composition: arguments over *techne* and *physis*, artistic and inartistic proofs, agency and subjectivity. Scot Barnett's "Rhetoric's Nonmodern Constitution: *Techne*, *Phusis*, and the Production of Hybrids" rereads Aristotle's descriptions of *techne* against the historical grain. Taking seriously Latour's claim that we have never been modern, Barnett argues that a move to Latour does not necessarily represent a radical departure from rhetoric's supposedly modernist past (or present). Barnett suggests that rhetoric may not have an affinity for Latour so much as Latour has an affinity for rhetoric, which has always been nonmodern. Joshua Prenosil, likewise, revitalizes the artistry and usefulness of the *atechnic* in his "Bruno Latour Is a Rhetorician of Inartistic Proofs." Though the inartistic proofs have often been placed outside of human rhetorical intervention, Prenosil reminds us that at least one—torture—is actually an activity confined to the human species. Furthermore, Latour tends to see knowledge production as a torturous affair, full of struggles and trials and punishments among and between people and things. This view of human and nonhuman networks reminds us that we cannot finally separate artistic (or "human") proofs from nonartistic (or "nonhuman") proofs. In "Is No One at the Wheel? Nonhuman Agency and Agentive Movement," Ehren Helmut Pflugfelder articulates what Latour brings to rhetoric's vigorous and ongoing discussion of agency. Attending to kinesis provides insights into the distributed nature of agency across human and nonhuman assemblages. Taken together, these contributions suggest that rhetoric has always been a nonmodern activity that, therefore, builds theory and tells history without the division between people and things.

A welcome having been offered, part three begins the back-and-forth of diplomacy, which continues through parts four and five. The assembly having being convened, the remaining authors join Latour in composing the common world. "Convening Assemblages" invites our French ambassador to help us renegotiate some of rhetoric's most long-standing conventions. In "The Whole of the Moon: Latour, Context, and the Problem of Holism," Thomas Rickert complicates Latour's criticism of "context." Though Rickert finds Latour's criticism productive for rhetorical theory, he insists on the need for some notion of a whole, coextensive with—but also in excess of—action. Collin Gifford Brooke's "Bruno Latour's Posthuman Rhetoric of Assent" examines Latour's more "philosophical" turn by comparing the arc of Latour's work and that of a project considered within the disciplinary boundaries of rhetoric, Wayne Booth's *Modern Dogma and the Rhetoric of Assent*. The chapter assembles the two in order to complicate Booth's primarily discursive rhetoric with Latour's empirically grounded connection of *res* and *verba*. Working from the same empirical grounding, Jeremy Tirrell's "Latourian *Memoria*" articulates the ways Latour's critical framework intensifies theoretical and pedagogical implications of memory in digital culture. Latour agrees that memory exists but as a Thing, an irreducible composition of disparate elements.

In part four, "Composing Assemblages," our authors take seriously Latour's claim to be a compositionist, which Latour uses in the most diplomatic sense. A compositionist is someone who engages writing's many qualities, aesthetic, material, prudential, and ecological. Latour believes in writing, as do the authors of this section. Marilyn M. Cooper's "How Bruno Latour Teaches Writing" works through Latour's idea that knowledge is not so much a possession as it is a "mode of existence." She develops a Latourian approach to pedagogy in which writing is central to the work of composing provisional truths. Writing, thereby, becomes the production of the new rather than the reporting of the old. Casey Boyle continues this line in "An Attempt at a 'Practitioner's Manifesto.'" Since Stephen M. North's *Making of Knowledge in Composition*, many have been ambivalent about the field's relationship with practice. Following Latour—who argues, "It's practice all the way down"—Boyle articulates writing as an "ontological practice": writing does not merely record; it creates. Mark A. Hannah continues this conversation with "Flexible Assembly: Latour, Law, and the Linking(s) of Composition," where he wades into composition's persistent argument about argument. Working from Latour's demanding *The Making of Law*, Hannah suggests that the real problem with argument in composition is that the field has not articulated how argument is composed. Composition plays some role in the management of conflict; the question is whether composition knows how to set the stage for conflict.

Finally, the diplomats of "Crafting Assemblages" construct methodologies that reveal the common worlds composed with Latour's most (in)famous idea: actor-network-theory (ANT). These chapters show "Latour in Action." These deployments, however, are not without qualification. Jeff Rice's "Craft Networks" traces the craft-beer movement but with the added wrinkle that he is himself an actor within the network, which is a move beyond Latour's description and practice of ANT. Qualifying ANT in this way, Rice is able to trace how networks and participants are coextensive. In her "Making a Thing of Quality Child Care: Latourian Rhetoric Doing Things," Sarah Read remains resolutely focused on tracing the paths of the various actants who have gathered together to articulate quality child care as a (Latourian) Thing. Her field study reflects Latour's famous mantra: "describe, write, describe, write" (*RS* 149). W. Michele Simmons, Kristen Moore, and Patricia Sullivan follow this same advice in their "Tracing Uncertainties: Methodologies of a Door Closer." Their study of a diverse trio of field sites suggests that Latour does not offer an approach so much as the questions that unsettle approaches. Simmons, Moore, and Sullivan discern ways to remain productively uncertain in their own work. There may be method in Latour, but the most important thing is the madness.

Laurie Gries's "Dingrhetoriks" argues that Latour's vision of the Thing can push rhetorical studies away from its long-standing orientation toward representation. This movement would be especially fruitful in the study of images, which are too often treated as objects to be interpreted rather than as Things that occasion. If rhetorical scholars finally give images "their due," they will better understand the full reach of visual rhetoric. James J. Brown Jr. and Jenell Johnson's inventive "Symmetry" brings us full circle to Spinuzzi's overture. Their work of scientifiction, a mode of investigation they adapt from Latour's *Aramis*, confronts the full implications of symmetry. Tracing the debate over machine- or computer-graded student writing, Brown and Johnson allow everyone to speak: students, instructors, administrators, and, of course, the robo-grader itself, a move that performs the symmetrical assembly that this collection promotes.

As with any assemblage, our arrangements are provisional and partial: we hope future scholarship addresses these limitations. This hope is itself Latourian. In *Politics of Nature*, Latour describes the role of the "moralist," who attends to "the defects of composition of the collective, to all that it has externalized" (245). As editors of this collection, we are certainly aware of our own defects. Why, for example, have we gathered an assembly that has a ratio of eight female authors to sixteen male? Why is the racial makeup of our assembly so white? It would be easy for us to pass this off on Latour himself, as he does not write about issues of gender and race. But our present assemblage is also a product of our own particular networks. Like ANTs, we traced this collection myopically. Our first encounters with Latour happened in graduate school, where we read *We Have Never Been Modern* and *Politics of Nature*. As Latour became part of our research ecology, we began to produce scholarship inspired by Latour.

Yet, it seems obvious to us that the networks we traced—which began in graduate school, continued with the link between our offices, and now reach across the field—have not yet extended far enough. We expect—in fact, we hope—that there are moralists out there ready to critique this collective and add new delegates to our assembly. The Latourian thing is always under construction, most often by Latour himself. As we were gathering the final revisions for the present collective, Latour published two new books, *An Inquiry into Modes of Existence* and *Rejoicing, or the Torments of Religious Speech*. *AIME* is both the culmination of the anthropology of the moderns he has been developing his entire career and a companion for researchers who wish to push this anthropology into new territory. If *We Have Never Been Modern* tells us what we're not, *AIME* begins to tell us what we are and what we can do. The multiplicity of modern modes of existence—science, religion, politics, law, economy, fiction—is neither good news nor bad. These domains are not reducible to some epistemological Esperanto, but that does not mean diplomats can't learn other languages. And that is what Latour calls us to do: to detect different modes while respecting their integrity and to offer new accounts of these encounters. "Nothing," Latour insists, "prevents readers who have now become coinvestigators from proposing to restitute experiences and link values in ways that differ completely from my own" (*AIME* 480).

Meanwhile, *Rejoicing* recounts Latour's attempt to rearticulate religious experience, specifically his own. While most of his work has positioned Latour as an investigator, *Rejoicing* positions him as an informant. (This observation occasions Rice's chapter, which recounts Rice's participation *within* a network.) Latour is not here simply to investigate religion; he is also here to recount his own religious experience. It's clear that he struggles with this new role. At one moment, he appears to adopt his familiar function as researcher, even regarding himself: "It's a twisted situation: he is ashamed of what he hears on Sunday from the pulpit when he goes to mass; but ashamed, too, of the incredulous hatred or amused indifference of those who laugh at anyone who goes to church" (1). But this third-person stance is not sufficiently "inside" to offer the riskiest account. If he is going to articulate the felicity conditions of religious speech, he has to get close enough to the experience, an experience that is for him an ordeal. He asks, "I've accounted for my uneasiness, my confusion, and for your uneasiness, your embarrassment, when so many words of salvation ring out so falsely, haven't I? And yet I go, I stay, I keep trying, yes, I persist, I even stick to my pew" (57). The struggle between his own uneasiness and that of his imagined interlocutor recalls his central analogy for religious speech: a lover's dialogue. "Imagine a lover who answered the question 'Do you love me?' with this sentence: 'Yes, but you already know that, I told you so last year'" (25). With this comparison, Latour reminds us that the religious mode of existence requires not that we speak *about* religion but speak religiously, just as the political mode of existence requires us to speak not *about* politics but politically, not *about* science but scientifically.

It is for this reason that rhetoric and composition can claim Latour as a kindred spirit who might reassure our field about our intellectual project while also challenging us to take it in new rhetorical directions. Latour suggests that modes of existence are defined not by their substance but, rather, by the ways in which they subsist, which he describes as a kind of tonality. Like Oscar Wilde, Latour reminds us that in matters of grave importance, style, not sincerity, is the vital thing. But this claiming of Latour is not meant to shore up our belief in rhetoric and composition but is rather the act of believing itself. After all, "[b]elief is not a state of mind but a result of relationships among peoples" (*MC* 2). To believe in rhetoric and composition, then, is to continue to extend invitations and assemble collectives. We hope that the present assemblage will inspire many more.

## Notes

1. This binary is usually the other way around, with the philosopher as lofty idealist and the rhetorician as hard-bitten realist. That is certainly what Lanham implies when he talks about Quintilian's "inventively adapted Platonism" (155). We mean to suggest that the strong defense simply reverses the binary. Now, rhetoric can do whatever it will, and the good and the true wait to be shaped by discursive action. This reversal is no more persuasive than the original.

2. We would be remiss if we did not acknowledge critiques of Latour from within his own field(s). Latour has been accused of rejecting what is called—in an uncanny coincidence—the "Strong Program" of the sociology of scientific knowledge (SSK). Key to the Strong Program is the "symmetry postulate," which holds "rational and irrational ideas, in as far as they are collectively held, should all equally be the object of sociological curiosity" (Bloor 84). That is, the bad ideas of Lysenko are to be studied in the same way as the good ideas of Mendel. Latour, however, finds the Strong Program limiting in that it replaces an objective approach with a social constructivist approach. In this, he seems to be right. David Bloor argues that SSK already knows that nature "will always have to be filtered, simplified, selectively sampled, and cleverly interpreted to bring it within our grasp" (90). H. M. Collins and Steven Yearley add that in the Strong Program, "[s]ymmetry between the true and the false requires a human-centered universe" (311). Latour, however, no longer wants to see humans as the center of the universe. Thus, he extends his symmetry principle to nonhuman actors, and he therefore calls all actors—human and nonhuman—actants. For Latour's critics, this is merely "prosaic." "The language changes," they write, "but the story remains the same" (Collins and Yearley 315). In response, Latour and Michel Callon insist that *language matters* if, finally, we wish to circumvent the "Great Divide" between words and things, subjects and objects (354). Only then can one have true symmetry. The idea is not "that scallops have voting power and will exercise it, or that door closers are entitled to social benefits and burial rites, but that a common vocabulary and a common ontology should be created by crisscrossing the divide by borrowing terms from one end to depict the other" (Latour and Callon 359).

3. Bay and Rickert are far from the only ones engaging objects in this way. See Barnett, "Toward an Object-Oriented Rhetoric"; Fredal, *Rhetorical Action*; Gries, "Iconographic Tracking"; Marback, "Unclenching the Fist"; Swarts, "Information Technologies"; Weber, "Ironically, We Dwell."

4. Latour himself is inconsistent in the way he punctuates this phrase. Sometimes he hyphenates it, sometimes not. We have decided to hyphenate it in order to resist the idea that ANT is "theory," which can be "applied" to various situations. In "Actor-Network Theory: Sensitive Terms and Enduring Tensions," Annemarie Mol argues that ANT is not a theory inasmuch as it does not offer a framework but, instead, operates as "an adaptable, open repository. A list of terms. A set of sensitivities" (253). Though the English translation of Mol's title does not hyphenate, the original German does.

5. See Graham, "Agency"; Mara and Hawk, introduction; Miller, "What Can Automation Tell Us"; Spinuzzi, *Network*; Winsor, "Engineering Writing," "Rhetorical Practices," "Learning to Do Knowledge Work," and *Writing Power*.

6. See Barnett, "Toward an Object-Oriented Rhetoric"; Beard, rev. of *Pandora's Hope*; Brooke and Rickert, "Being Delicious"; Cooper, "Rhetorical Agency"; Hawk, "Reassembling Postprocess"; J. A. Lynch, "Articulating Scientific Practice"; P. Lynch, "Composition's New Thing"; Marback, "Unclenching the Fist"; Pflugfelder, "Texts of Our Institutional Lives"; Jeff Rice, "Networked Assessment"; Rivers, "Rhetorics of (Non)Symbolic Cultivation."

## Works Cited

Barnett, Scot. "Toward an Object-Oriented Rhetoric." *Enculturation* 7 (2010): N. pag. Web. 15 Feb. 2011.

Bay, Jennifer, and Thomas Rickert. "New Media and the Fourfold." *JAC* 28.1–2 (2008): 209–244. Print.

Beard, David. Rev. of *Pandora's Hope: Essays on the Reality of Science Studies*, by Bruno Latour. *Rhetoric Society Quarterly* 30.2 (2000): 104–7. Print.

Bloor, David. "Anti-Latour." *Studies in the History of the Philosophy of Science* 30.1 (1999): 81–112. Print.

Brooke, Collin, and Thomas Rickert. "Being Delicious: Materialities of Research in a Web 2.0 Application." Dobrin, Rice, and Vastola 163–179.

Collins, H. M., and Steven Yearley. "Epistemological Chicken." Pickering 301–326.

Cooper, Marilyn. "Rhetorical Agency as Emergent and Enacted." *CCC* 62.3 (2011): 420–449. Print.

Dobrin, Sidney I. *Postcomposition*. Carbondale: Southern Illinois UP, 2011. Print.

Dobrin, Sidney I., J. A. Rice, and Michael Vastola. *Beyond Postprocess*. Logan: Utah State UP, 2012. Print.

Fredal, James. *Rhetorical Action in Ancient Athens: Persuasive Artistry from Solon to Demosthenes*. Carbondale: Southern Illinois UP, 2006. Print.

Geisler, Cheryl. "How Ought We to Understand the Concept of Rhetorical Agency? Report from the ARS." *Rhetoric Society Quarterly* 34.3 (2004): 9–18. Print.

Graham, S. Scott. "Agency and the Rhetoric of Medicine: Biomedical Brain Scans and the Ontology of Fibromyalgia." *Technical Communication Quarterly* 18.4 (2009): 376–404. Print.

Gries, Laurie. "Iconographic Tracking: A Digital Research Method for Visual Rhetoric and Circulation Studies." *Computers and Composition* 30.4 (2013): 332–348. Web. <http://www.sciencedirect.com/science/article/pii/S8755461513000613>.

Gunner, Jeanne. "Disciplinary Purification: The Writing Program as Institutional Brand." *JAC* 32.3–4 (2012): 615–643. Print.

Hawk, Byron. "Reassembling Postprocess: Toward a Theory of Public Rhetoric." Dobrin, Rice, and Vastola 75–93.

Lanham, Richard. *The Electronic Word: Democracy, Technology, and the Arts.* Chicago: U of Chicago P, 1993. Print.

Latour, Bruno. *Aramis, or, the Love of Technology.* Cambridge: Harvard UP, 1996. Print.

———. "An Attempt at a 'Compositionist Manifesto.'" *New Literary History* 41.3 (2010): 471–490. Print.

———. *An Inquiry into Modes of Existence: An Anthropology of the Moderns.* Trans. Catherine Porter. Cambridge: Harvard UP, 2012. Print.

———. "From Realpolitik to Dingpolitik, or How to Make Things Public." *Making Things Public: Atmospheres of Democracy.* Ed. Latour and Peter Weibel. Cambridge: MIT P, 2005. 4–31. Print.

———. "On Recalling Ant." *Actor Network Theory and After.* Ed. John Law and John Hassard. Oxford: Blackwell, 1999. 15–25. Print.

———. *On the Modern Cult of the Factish Gods.* Durham: Duke UP, 2010. Print.

———. *Pandora's Hope : Essays on the Reality of Science Studies.* Cambridge: Harvard UP, 1999. Print.

———. *Reassembling the Social: An Introduction to Actor-Network-Theory.* New York: Oxford UP, 2005. Print.

———. *Rejoicing: Or the Torments of Religious Speech.* London: Polity, 2013. Print.

———. *Science in Action: How to Follow Scientists and Engineers through Society.* Cambridge: Harvard UP, 1987. Print.

———. *We Have Never Been Modern.* Trans. Catherine Porter. Cambridge: Harvard UP, 1993. Print.

———. "Where are the Missing Masses? The Sociology of a Few Mundane Artifacts." *Shaping Technology: Building Society Studies in Sociotechnical Change*. Ed. Wiebe E. Bijker and John Law. Cambridge: MIT P, 1992. 225–258. Print.

———. "Why Has Critique Run Out of Steam? From Matters of Fact to Matters of Concern." *Critical Inquiry* 30 (2004): 225–248. Print.

Latour, Bruno, and Michel Callon. "Don't Throw the Baby Out with the Bath School! A Reply to Collins and Yearley." Pickering 343–368. Print.

Latour, Bruno, and Steve Woolgar. *Laboratory Life : The Construction of Scientific Facts*. Princeton: Princeton UP, 1986. Print.

Lundberg, Christian, and Joshua Gunn. "'Ouija Board, Are There Any Communications?' Agency, Ontotheology, and the Death of the Humanist Subject, or, Continuing the ARS Conversation." *Rhetoric Society Quarterly* 35.4 (2005): 83–105. Print.

Lynch, John A. "Articulating Scientific Practice: Understanding Dean Hamer's 'Gay Gene' Study as Overlapping Material, Social, and Rhetorical Registers." *Quarterly Journal of Speech* 95.4 (2009): 435–456. Print.

Lynch, Paul. "Composition's New Thing: Bruno Latour and the Apocalyptic Turn." *College English* 74.5 (2012): 458–476. Print.

Mara, Andrew, and Byron Hawk. Introduction. "Posthuman Rhetorics and Technical Communication." *Technical Communications Quarterly* 19.1 (2010): 1–10. Print.

Marback, Richard. "Unclenching the Fist: Embodying Rhetoric and Giving Objects Their Due." *Rhetorical Society Quarterly* 38.1 (2008): 46–65. Print.

Miller, Carolyn R. "What Can Automation Tell Us about Agency?" *Rhetoric Society Quarterly* 37 (2007): 137–157. Print.

Mol, Annemarie. "Actor-Network Theory: Sensitive Terms and Enduring Tensions." "Koordination und Ordnungsbildung in der Akteur-Netzwerk-Theorie." *Kölner Zeitschrift für Soziologie und Sozialpsychologie* 50.1 (2010): 253–269. Print.

Pflugfelder, Ehren Helmut. "Texts of Our Institutional Lives: Translucency, Coursepacks, and the Post-historical University: An Investigation into Pedagogical Things." *College English* 74.3 (2012): 247–267. Print.

Pickering, Andrew, ed. *Science as Practice and Culture*. Chicago: U of Chicago P, 1992. Print.

Rice, Jeff. "Networked Assessment." *Computers and Composition* 28.1 (2011): 28–39. Print.

Rice, Jenny Edbauer. "Rhetoric's Mechanics: Retooling the Equipment of Writing Production." *CCC* 60.2 (2008): 366–387. Print.

Rivers, Nathaniel A. "Rhetorics of (Non)Symbolic Cultivation." *Ecology, Writing Theory, and New Media: Writing Ecology*. Ed. Sid Dobrin. New York: Routledge, 2012. 34–50. Print.

Sánchez, Raúl. *The Function of Theory in Composition Studies*. Albany: State U of New York P, 2005. Print.

Sirc, Geoffrey, "Resisting Entropy." *CCC* 63.3 (2012): 507–519. Print.

Spinuzzi, Clay. *Network: Theorizing Knowledge Work in Telecommunications*. New York: Cambridge UP, 2008. Print.

Swarts, Jason. "Information Technologies as Discursive Agents: Methodological Implications for the Empirical Study of Knowledge Work." *Journal of Technical Writing and Communication* 38.4 (2008): 301–329. Print.

Weber, Ryan. "Ironically, We Dwell." *JAC* 31.3–4 (2011): 441–471. Print.

Winsor, Dorothy A. "Engineering Writing/Writing Engineering." *CCC* 41.1 (1990): 58–70. Print.

———. "An Engineer's Writing and the Corporate Construction of Knowledge." *Written Communication* 6 (1989): 270–285. Print.

———. "Learning to Do Knowledge Work in Systems of Distributed Cognition." *Journal of Business and Technical Communication* 15.1 (2001): 5–28. Print.

———. "Rhetorical Practices in Technical Work." *Journal of Business and Technical Communication* 12.3 (1998): 343–370. Print.

———. "What Counts as Writing? An Argument from Engineers' Practice." *JAC* 12.2 (1992): 337–347. Print.

———. *Writing Power: Communication in an Engineering Center*. Albany: State U of New York P, 2003. Print.

# Part One. **Constituting Assemblages**

# 2. Symmetry as a Methodological Move

Clay Spinuzzi, *University of Texas at Austin*

One of the most recognizable and controversial aspect of Bruno Latour's work is his methodological commitment to *symmetry*, the principle that human and nonhuman actants are treated alike when considering how controversies are settled (*SA* 144). As Latour argues, symmetry involves "keep[ing] constant the series of competences, of properties, that [human and nonhuman] agents are able to swap by overlapping with one another," and he insists that we should examine these competencies before delineating "subjects and objects, goals and functions, form and matter" (*PH* 182). That is, Latour is wary of classic sociological explanations that presume human agency and social structures and use them as ready-made explanations for observed phenomena; he prefers a relativist sociology in which neither is presumed (*Aramis* 199–200).

Many find this methodological stance counterintuitive, and critics often read Latour as embracing a pantheistic or anthropomorphized view of the world: some imagine him conversing earnestly with doors or arguing with seatbelts. To these critics, symmetry seems foreign and perhaps even dehumanizing—particularly in humanistic disciplines, such as rhetoric and composition, that are grounded in classical thought and that emphasize human agency and discourse. Complicating the issue is the fact that such critics often read symmetry as a totalizing worldview rather than a methodological move.

In this chapter, I explain symmetry as a methodological move that makes sense for some investigations, even inherently humanistic investigations. First presented are two commonsense illustrations that show how symmetry can be a bounded methodological move rather than a totalizing worldview. Next, I move to more specific illustrations based on actual studies and will examine how symmetry can be productively applied to cognition, agency, and power. I apply these lessons to recent work in rhetorical genre studies, addressing recent criticisms of genre studies by emphasizing the methodological assumptions of this work. Finally, I draw methodological boundaries for applying symmetry in rhetoric and composition studies.

## Symmetry Is Not Radical

> This circulating gene entangles patients and researchers as it goes along. . . . We see that the gene is domesticated, tamed, and integrated into a collective that holds it and is held by it. It is a civilized and civilizing gene, performing the collective and performed by it. And this integration into the society of the gene, or insertion into the genetics of society, would have been impossible without a starting point: the parity, the symmetry between the complementary forms of knowledge that constitutes the foundations of this collective. (Callon and Rabeharisoa 201)

This quote from your graduate theory class echoes through your head as you walk down Austin's Sixth Street on a beautiful spring day. Michel Callon and Vololona Rabeharisoa are talking about a collaboration between research scientists and the French Muscular Dystrophy Association, which was clear enough, but in the latter half of the paper, they make this assertion, consistent with the principle of symmetry that actor-network-theory (ANT) embraces. This is the same ANT codeveloped by, and largely synonymous with the work of, Bruno Latour, a French sociologist of science whose writings have intrigued and infuriated scholars in the sociology of science, in science and technology studies, and in various other fields, including your own field of rhetoric and composition.

Personally, you are not intrigued but rather infuriated by ANT. Symmetry seems ridiculous to you. What's the point of pretending that genes, stars, and rat kidneys are actors in the sense that people are? Why apply the same language to both? Maybe this is one of those "critical theory" moves you've heard people talking about. To you, it seems more like attention seeking. Latour likes to say that symmetrical language is not metaphorical but that he isn't engaging in anthropomorphism either. Obviously, he's trying to have it both ways.

Enough. It's spring break. The South by Southwest Interactive Festival is winding down, but SXSW Music is just ramping up. You walk past the back of a club, where roadies are struggling to move a ton of sound equipment. It's going to be an exclusive show, evidently, because fourteen undernourished hipsters have already lined up at the front of the club; they're thumbing their iPhones and checking out each other's ironic T-shirts. A little farther on, seven well-nourished tourists on Segways ride along the sidewalk in a neat line, like ducks. And as you pass Jim-Jim's Water Ice, you see a mounted policeman on one horse, holding another horse's reins. The other policeman is in line getting a snow cone. Ah, Austin.

But you don't have time to enjoy the scenes. You hurry on toward the Driskill Hotel, where a temporary job awaits you. When you get there, you find out that the job is pretty easy.

"See this elevator?" your supervisor asks. "It's old. It has a maximum capacity of two thousand pounds. *Max*. But people try to overload it all the time. Your job is to make sure they don't." He turns on his heel and walks away.

Easy, you think. But then you wonder: about how much is two thousand pounds?

Let's see, you reason to yourself. Two thousand pounds is a ton. Like a ton of sound equipment, you think whimsically, remembering your walk.

But how many people? Maybe thirteen or fourteen people—like those fourteen undernourished hipsters in front of the club. Or seven well-fed tourists on Segways, you think, imagining the line riding into the elevator. Or two horses and a police officer. Any of these combinations would come out to about two thousand pounds. You resolve that whatever combination of humans and nonhumans might come through the door, if they are above two thousand pounds, they can't ride together.

Humans and nonhumans? You laugh a little, thinking back to the notion of symmetry. What if the hipsters argued, "But we're not horses! Hello? Do horses have an encyclopedic knowledge of craft brews? Did horses listen to Mumford and Sons long before they were cool? Do horses have iPhones? Of course not! Horses don't even have thumbs!" And you imagine yourself retorting, "Maybe that matters if you're trying to get backstage. But not here. All that matters is how much you weigh."

You don't believe for a minute that hipsters are the "same" as horses, that sound equipment is the same as overfed tourists, or that policemen are the same as Segways. But *for the purposes of your job*, they are judged by exactly the same criteria.

Four hours later, it occurs to you that you are indeed performing a kind of symmetric analysis.

More than that: if you don't, the elevator will.

As I've defined it elsewhere, a *methodology* is "the theory, philosophy, heuristics, aims, and values that underlie, motivate, and guide [a] method" (*Tracing* 7). In this sense, Latour's principle of symmetry can be considered a methodological *move*, a limiting assumption, a premise that is provisionally accepted to better align the methodology with its methods.

In this case, symmetry is a deceptively simple move: it is the principle that human and nonhuman actants are treated alike when considering how controversies are settled (Latour, *SA* 144). As Latour argues, symmetry involves "keep[ing] constant the series of competences, of properties, that [human and nonhuman] agents are able to swap by overlapping with one another," and he insists that we should examine these competencies before delineating "subjects and objects, goals and functions, form and matter" (*PH* 182). That is, Latour is wary of classic sociological explanations that presume human agency and social structures and use them as ready-made explanations for observed phenomena; he prefers a relativist sociology in which neither is presumed (*PH* 199–200), a sociology that (as we'll see later) focuses on the relationships of mutually defined actors, which can be human or nonhuman.

The principle of symmetry dates back to a 1972 epiphany Latour had on the road from Dijon to Gray, an epiphany that he describes in his short treatise "Irreductions," typically appended to *The Pasteurization of France*.[1] Latour realizes that "nothing can be reduced to anything else, nothing can be deduced from anything else, [and] everything must be allied to everything else" (*PF* 163). This assertion became a "new principle of philosophy" for Latour, a principle that led to four premises: "the world is made up of actors or actants"; "no object is inherently reducible or irreducible to any other"; "the means of linking one thing to another is translation"; "actants gain in strength only through their alliances" (13, 14–15). Latour also "rejects the rift between an inner substance and its trivial exterior" (17). Latour doesn't reduce truth to human power games, he accepts nonhumans as actors and measures reality in terms of how connected an actor is (19). Harman adds, "Any attempt to see actants as the reducible puppets of deeper structures is doomed to fail" in this understanding (21).

Latour has since deployed symmetry in all of his studies, using it to avoid simplistic arguments resting on human agency. As I note elsewhere, "it's an attempt to avoid Cartesian dichotomies by applying the same concepts and vocabularies across the entire actor-network" (Spinuzzi, *Network* 41). Yet, by applying the same concepts and vocabularies to both humans and nonhumans, Latour and others using actor-network-theory have tended to use the literary device of personification: texts, technologies, money, and humans all "persuade" each other (Callon, "Techno-Economic"), mass transit systems yearn to be realized (Latour, *Aramis*), scallops "vote" (Callon, "Some Elements"), rat kidneys resist the interpretations that scientists attempt to apply to them (Latour, *SA*), and political action is extended to a parliament of things (Latour, *PN*). This broad use of personification, unfortunately, creates the *appearance* of pantheism (Star) or fairy stories (Latour, *PN* 67). But its *intent* is to disrupt the assumption that only human beings have agency, acting on an inert world—an assumption that Latour considers to be, more or less, a shell game.

As a methodological move, as a limiting assumption, symmetry does have some virtues. So let's travel down this path of symmetry just a little—no commitments involved, just provisionally, just for the sake of argument. Like the scientists that Latour likes to study, we'll artificially purify the phenomenon just a bit: just as a computer scientist might start with "let $x = 10$," or an endocrinologist might maintain a sterile lab to avoid confounding influences from outside, or a physicist might use the simple formula $f = ma$ unconfounded by environmental conditions.

Let's pursue that last one further.

## Symmetry Is Not Totalizing

The formula $f = ma$ describes Newton's second law of motion: if a force acts on an object, it causes the object's acceleration. Here, $f$ is the force (measured in newtons), $m$ is the mass, and $a$ is the acceleration. This formula assumes that everything else is equal, which it often isn't: for instance, $f = ma$ does not do a good job of predicting how hard a feather hits the ground when it is dropped in an atmosphere, but it does a great job when the feather is dropped in a vacuum. (Forgive me for oversimplifying here.) In fact, if you drop *any* object from high enough in the atmosphere, it will eventually reach terminal velocity, in which the drag of the atmosphere equalizes the downward force of gravity, causing the acceleration to be zero. That is, $f = ma$ is not totalizing, applicable exactly in the same way under *all* conditions—other conditions complicate this artificially purified picture—but it is very useful and applicable under *most* conditions.

Like $f = ma$, symmetry is a methodological stance meant to get at certain things and not others.

Let's pursue this line further by performing a thought experiment. I emphasize that this is *just* a thought experiment for reasons that will become clear below.

Aristotle believed and taught that heavy objects fall faster than light ones in direct proportion to their weight. Galileo disagreed and described a classic experiment in which he stood at the top of the Leaning Tower of Pisa with two balls of different weights and dropped them, and they hit the ground at the same time. (It's unclear whether Galileo actually performed the experiment.)

Suppose you want to perform a similar experiment. Since I work at the University of Texas campus, let's imagine that you ascend UT's Tower to the observation deck. You bring a one-pound weight and a ten-pound weight.

(NOTE: You can only do this as a thought experiment. The observation deck is inaccessible due to various tragic incidents, except during guided tours. Also, dropping weights from the observation deck is a misdemeanor. Obviously, I do not endorse actually performing this experiment.)

Leaning over the railing, you drop the two weights at the same time. Not surprising, you discover that Galileo was right and Aristotle was wrong. The ten-pound weight does not fall ten times faster than the one-pound weight; they hit the ground at roughly the same time. In fact, you can even calculate the force by which each hits the ground, using the formula $f = ma$.

Interesting, you think. And then you decide to try a second variation of the experiment. You ascend the tower again, this time with a one-pound weight, a ten-pound weight, and a 150-pound hipster.

(NOTE: Again, you can only do this as a thought experiment for obvious legal, moral, and ethical reasons.)

When you reach the observation deck, you repeat the experiment, this time dropping all three objects at the same time. It turns out that no matter how ironically the hipster falls, in terms of gravity, he behaves exactly as the other weights do. You can even use $f = ma$ on this human being just as you used it with the nonhuman weights. For the purposes of the experiment, the hipster is exactly the same as the other two weights; you treat them symmetrically, and so does $f = ma$, and so does gravity.

But when you descend the elevator to the bottom of the tower, you discover that what is treated as symmetrical in one network of meaning is not treated as symmetrical in other networks. Dropping the weights is a misdemeanor. Dropping the hipster is a felony. The law of gravity treats them as symmetrical, but state and federal law do not.

When Latour describes humans and nonhumans as symmetrical, he means that differences among actants (both human and nonhuman) are generated within a given actor-network rather than preexisting them; we can't presuppose those differences (Callon, "Techno-Economic"). Consider Galileo's experiment as well as the previous illustration of elevator capacity: in these narrowly defined situations, humans and nonhumans act in exactly the same way. (If the tower experiment were a physics problem, you wouldn't even specify the materials, you'd just plug in the weight values into $f = ma$ to get the force.) But, of course, these networks of meaning are always entangled with other networks, as they *should* be. There are many good reasons why you would never actually perform this experiment, and they go beyond trouble with the law to basic questions of empathy and morality, questions that apply to all people, few, if any, artifacts, and to some extent to nonhuman animals. In the networks of law and morality, we find sharp differentials.

That's not to say that the role of morality disappears in a symmetrical analysis. Quite the opposite! And everyone knows this: we all know that good fences make good neighbors, that speed bumps cause people to follow the law, and that the safety features on a food processer keep us from losing fingers (Spinuzzi, *Network* 191; Latour, *PH*). In fact, part of what makes the tower experiment a *mere* thought experiment is the fact that few people could carry it out successfully: even in the absence of guards, I couldn't get to the top of the tower (because of gates and a locked elevator), nor could I drop objects or hipsters off the tower in the event that I *could* get up there (due to fences ringing the observation deck). These safeguards were developed over time, in response to a famous school shooting and, later, a rash of suicides—incidents that were and are morally objectionable and are now impractical because of the *moral* influence of nonhumans. The actor-network—the interrelated set of actors—can and usually does imply a morality.

But Latour talks about situations in which *people* are actually interacting: scientists, technologists, the public. Aren't these social rather than technical? And in social situations, don't we have to treat humans and nonhumans differently?

The answer is: it depends on your methodological aims. Even in terms that we consider very human—cognition and persuasion—it sometimes makes sense to take a symmetrical viewpoint in one's methods.

## Symmetry Is Not (Necessarily) Anticognition

Up to this point, I've used commonplace examples to demonstrate how, rather than being a form of pantheism or an antihumanist sociology, symmetry is simply a way of getting at certain relationships that are often overlooked or even buried in other approaches. When we examine these relationships in fairly restricted ways—weight requirements in elevators or falling bodies—symmetry makes a great deal of sense. But when we move to phenomena that are more complex, symmetry seems like a dicier proposition.

For instance, let's consider cognition.

Latour famously proposed in *Science in Action* that we institute a ten-year moratorium on cognitive explanations of science and technology. Kai Hakkarainen criticized in "Can Cognitive Explanations Be Eliminated?" this moratorium, complaining that Latour mentions this moratorium every so often, always extending it for ten years. This moratorium came out of Latour's observations of scientific work, in which he noticed that scientists would assemble a large array of nonhumans and humans—instruments, procedures, lab techs, and so forth—to perform science and then attribute the results to cognition. Without all of these nonhuman and human intermediaries, Latour argued, *cognition could not have provided an adequate explanation.*

Let's use an analogy. Suppose that as you walk home, you spot your neighbor on the roof. Do you think to yourself, "I am amazed that my neighbor can jump so high!"? Or do you look for a ladder? Analogically speaking, *Latour always looks for the ladder*. He sees the alternate explanation—based entirely on human ability—as rather implausible. Yes, it's always a possibility, but (Latour might say) let's look for the ladder first.

This does not mean that actor-network-theory is anti-cognition, as Hakkarainen and others have interpreted it to be. ANT is no more anticognition than a fork is antisoup.

No better demonstration of this point exists than Latour's positive review of Edwin Hutchins's 1995 book *Cognition in the Wild*, a superlative study in which Hutchins examines the remarkable feats of cognition that are regularly performed on a US Navy vessel—feats that are clearly beyond the capabilities of the individual sailors. Latour declares,

> The results of Hutchins' inquiry are as devastating for psychology as the results of sociology were for epistemology or those of Shirley Strum for primatology. Everything that was crammed inside the mind of individuals is deployed outside and shared collectively with the culture, through the social connections and with the many cognitive artifacts the group has been able to devise. ("Review" 55)

To put it another way: Hutchins, like Latour, looks for the ladder.

But more than that, Hutchins refuses to separate cognition from mediating artifacts. In Hutchins's account, "cognition" is not confined to what happens inside the skull but is instead distributed across a given environment. Cognition is not the domain of the individual sailors but what happens when sailors, artifacts, and practices are interrelated across the vessel. Latour summarizes the central claim of the book.

> Cognition has nothing to do with the minds nor with individuals but *with the propagation of representations through various media, which are coordinated by a very lightly equipped human subject working in a group, inside a culture, with many artefacts and who might have internalized some parts of the process.* ("Review" 56; original emphasis).

To understand what's happening here, let's dive into Hutchins's book itself. Here's what he says about cognition in chapter 2.

> Having taken ship navigation as it is performed by a team on the bridge of a ship as the unit of cognitive analysis, I will attempt to apply the principal metaphor of cognitive science—cognition as computation—to the operation of this system. In so doing I do not make any special commitment to the nature of the computations that are going on inside individuals except to say that whatever happens there is part of a larger computational system. But I do believe that the computation observed in the activity of the larger system can be described in the way cognition has been traditionally described—that is, as computation realized through the creation, transformation, and propagation of representational states. (49)

So Hutchins approaches the notion of cognition by defining it narrowly, as computation. In committing to this computational account, Hutchins takes a radically symmetrical perspective. Rather than drawing lines between what transpires inside and outside one's head, he examines computation—and, thus, propagation of representational states—wherever it happens. (I hasten to add that this approach doesn't mean *ruling out* individual cognition but rather recognizing that individual cognition is both inaccessible to our methods and insufficient for explaining the interpersonal feats of cognition that Hutchins describes.) Hutchins brilliantly demonstrates that much of what we might have assumed was expertise or intelligence is instead attributable to how these representational states propagate. For instance, he argues that by all rights the sailors he studied should not have had the depth of experience needed to perform the navigational feats they performed, but these feats are attributable to the entire system of sailors plus other computational media.[2]

To get at what Hutchins is trying to say, let's leave the ship for a moment and look at what he says late in the book about Searle's Chinese Room thought experiment. Imagine, he says, a room in which John Searle sits. Outside the room, people bring slips of paper on which they have written questions in Chinese. One by one, each person passes her or his slip of paper through a slot in the door; a few moments later, the person receives a reply, also written in Chinese.

Does Searle know Chinese? Perhaps. Let's suppose that in one scenario, Searle does, indeed, know how to read and write Chinese and is composing answers on the fly. In a second scenario, Searle doesn't know Chinese but has several baskets of Chinese characters plus a rulebook that tells him how to combine them to respond to certain strings of characters.[3] In the second scenario, Hutchins argues, Searle doesn't know Chinese, but (for our purposes) *the room does.* Or to put it another way, the "cognitive properties of the sociocultural system" are different from "the cognitive properties of a person who is manipulating the elements of that system" (362). Cognition, in the narrowly defined sense that Hutchins uses the term, is stretched across the human agent and the environment, resulting in accomplishments that could not have resulted from the human agent alone. Searle has a ladder.

And with that, we can see why Latour does something that critics, such as Hakkarainen, haven't caught. *He lifts the moratorium on cognitive explanations.*

> When I published *Science in Action* in 1987, I proposed a "moratorium" on cognitive explanations, which had been so freely and cheaply entertained by epistemologists. . . . I did not know that I would be able to safely lift the ban, less than 10 years later, since in the meantime, cognitive explanations would have been dissolved past recognition [by Hutchins]. ("Review" 62)

Here, we start to see some payoff in adopting symmetry as a methodological move, as opposed to a bedrock worldview. For Hutchins—and, I think, for Latour—symmetry is a methodological move in that it allows us to set aside long-held assumptions and ask, "What if we view it this way instead?" And what we find in *Cognition in the Wild* and elsewhere, I think, is that it allows us to look at phenomena from very different angles and investigate very different components of a phenomenon. A scale and a spectrometer give very different data, but that doesn't mean one is more truthful than the other. Similarly, these theoretical "instruments" let us get at different phenomena that we normally might not consider. Like a scale and a spectrometer, these are not exclusive, nor are they irreconcilable.

In Hutchins's case, this methodological move allowed him to get at what he *could* study, rather than speculating about internal mental states that he couldn't. He could examine interpersonal and tool-mediated activity in concrete, observable terms, rather than speculating about what goes on inside the skull—and engaging in the shell game of attributing agency and morality to this unobservable internal cognition.

But as we consider this case, we may wonder whether symmetry does its work by sweeping away an understanding of the social, focusing simply on observable representational states. Is symmetry the equivalent of looking for one's keys under the lamppost simply because the light is better there? I argue that it's not. To understand why, let's consider a final, more common example of mediated activity.

## Symmetry Is Not Asocial

Is there a difference between hitting a nail *with* and *without* a hammer?

This is one of the provocative questions that Latour asks in *Reassembling the Social* (71). The question, of course, is rhetorical: of course, there's a difference. Using the hammer remakes (perhaps I should say *makes*) the activity in a very fundamental way. Perhaps holding a hammer makes every problem look like a nail, but similarly, a nail poses a very different problem when one doesn't have a hammer.

Yet, Latour charges, classical sociology has tended to ignore the hammer and other material objects when it examines human activities. These material objects are often seen as incidental, he says, to what classical sociologists see as their real focus: social constructs, social structures, social contracts, social forces, and so on. As Latour argues in his book *Aramis,* classical sociology sees through actors to the social structure, scrutinized through fixed frames, such as norms, reason, logic, and common sense (199–200). It assumes "a stabilized state of affairs, a bundle of ties that, later, may be mobilized to account for some other phenomenon" (*RS* 1). It posits "the existence of a specific sort of phenomenon, variously called 'society,' 'social order,' 'social practice,' social dimension,' or 'social structure'" (*RS* 3). This social "context" "can be used as a specific type of causality," that is, it causes people to act in various ways (*RS* 3–4). So, Latour claims, classical sociology *begins* with society or social aggregates; sociologists then study the *effects* of these causes (*RS* 8).

Latour does not necessarily think this is a problem.

In fact, Latour says, classical sociology is like Newtonian physics. In most ordinary cases, when change happens slowly, it's fine to use a fixed frame of reference. When you're trying to determine with what *force* an object (e.g., a weight, a hipster) will hit the ground, knowing only the object's *mass* and rate of *acceleration,* it's fine to use Newtonian physics ($f = ma$). And if you're studying fixed social situations, such as traditional craftwork, a fixed-frame approach, such as classical sociology, is A-OK in Latour's book—literally his book: *Reassembling the Social* (12).

But in other cases, we need a relativist frame. If you want to understand why atomic clocks run more slowly on commercial jetliners than they do at the US Naval Observatory, Newtonian physics will not get you very far; you need a relativist physics. And if you want to study situations in which "things accelerate, innovations proliferate, and entities are multiplied," Latour says you need a relativist sociology (*RS* 12)—one with no fixed frames or metalanguage (*Aramis* 200).

In this alternate, relativist view, "'social' is not some glue that could fix everything including what the other glue cannot fix; it is *what* is glued together by many *other* types of connectors" (*RS* 5). It's not the cause but the *consequence* of the assemblage (8); the social is what you get when you associate various things. Thus, in this relativist sociology, you can't understand the social until you trace the associations among things (5). The things themselves aren't social; what's social is *how they are shuffled together* (64).

Let's try this out with some examples.

*Situation 1.* Suppose you're visiting a carpenter and his apprentice in their workspace. They're familiar and comfortable with their tools (hammers, saws, miter boards, etc.) and with each other, and they're doing work with which they are very familiar. Their hands are sure, and their movements are smooth, as you might expect from experienced people performing familiar tasks. In activity theory's terms, their work is largely *operationalized* (Spinuzzi, *Tracing*), habituated to a degree that they hardly have to think about it, leaving them free to talk baseball and politics. The details and tools of their craftwork may not be nearly as interesting as other things you might be able to investigate in this fixed frame: how they bond through talk, how they represent themselves in topics, how the carpenter retains or fails to retain social dominance over the apprentice.

*Situation 2.* But now let's suppose we visit a middle-aged college professor. He's at home, working at his kitchen table, surrounded by books and papers. The window is open, letting in a breeze that repeatedly moves the papers. Suddenly he gets up, fetches a hammer from the kitchen counter, and puts it on top of a page.

Now, that's not a completely novel use for a hammer, but it is certainly not what the hammer was designed to do. And this use snaps our attention to what we might stuffily call "the materiality of writing"—a broad set of different things (materials, artifacts, practices, people) that become associated in order for the professor to do his work. Without some of these associations, the work doesn't turn out the same way or perhaps at all. These different things all contribute somehow. Sometimes it's through direct problem solving, as in the maps and hoeys that Hutchins describes. Sometimes it's through mediations that make the problem space more tractable, like using a hammer as a paperweight. Any thing might be an actor—"*any thing* that does modify a state of affairs by making a difference," Latour says (*RS* 71). So the operative question is, "Does it make a difference in the course of some other agent's action or not?" (71).

Or as I asked at the beginning of this section: is there a difference between hitting a nail with or without a hammer?

When Latour uses symmetry, it's as a methodological move that focuses us on the associations among various humans and nonhumans. This move distinguishes relational sociology from classic sociology, just as relativist and classical physics use different assumptions to tackle different problems. And since the associations themselves are the focus, the things they associate fade into the background. It's not that nonhumans become humans or vice versa, it's that *these differences in qualities are no longer what we're investigating*. Hipsters and horses are different, but those differences don't matter to an elevator or gravity. Professors and papers are different, but that difference isn't the focus of Latour's methodology.

## Symmetry Is Not Incompatible with Rhetoric and Writing Studies

> Rhetoric is the name of the discipline that has, for millennia, studied how people are made to believe and behave and taught people how to persuade others. Rhetoric is a fascinating albeit despised discipline, but it becomes still more important when debates are so exacerbated that they become scientific and technical. (Latour, *SA* 30)

Now let's connect this discussion to something closer to home. Earlier I mentioned the materiality of writing, something I've been studying for the last fifteen years. One of my first moves—conducted after reading Hutchins but before reading Latour—was to begin describing and examining *genre ecologies* (Spinuzzi, *Tracing;* Spinuzzi and Zachry), which are (loosely speaking) associations of text types used in people's work. This move was, like Latour's, a methodological move, meant to help me focus on a specific issue: how people were solving problems by using available texts in their environments. This issue became very important to me during my first set of observations, when I discovered something that (when you think about it) should be blindingly obvious: *people don't just read one text at a time*. They string together lots of texts, sometimes surprisingly large gobs of wildly heterogeneous texts related in very different ways. Some of these are things that we would not normally consider texts at all.

My focus, that is, *shifted toward the associations* among the genres I saw being used in these observations, which I mapped using basic network diagrams, characterized based on qualitative data (observations, interviews, artifact collection), and compared between participants and observations. Rather than asking, "How does this person read and write?" I began asking questions, such as "What combinations of texts do people need in order to get work done?" "When and why do people innovate new texts to include in these combinations?" "How do they associate these texts?" "When is one association substituted for another?" "Around which associations do people encounter the most disruptions?" (e.g., Spinuzzi, *Tracing;* Spinuzzi and Zachry; Spinuzzi, Hart-Davidson, and Zachry). Others have similarly asked such questions (e.g., Gygi and Zachry; Sherlock; Slattery; Swarts).

The analytical construct of the genre ecology helped me get at questions such as these, methodologically, by helping me to focus away from individual expertise, interpretation, cognition, and vaguely defined social forces and instead focusing on the associations that held these texts together (part of what distinguishes the construct of the genre ecology from other understandings of genre assemblages, such as genre sets, systems, and repertoires[4]). At the same time, this methodological move forced me to demand specific evidence for each association.

That's not to say that genre ecologies are symmetrical in the way that Latour's actor-networks are. Genre ecologies model associations among texts, not all kinds of entities, and those associated texts collectively mediate human activity rather than enfolding human beings into the collective activity of a system. That is, genre ecologies are still conceived within a writing, activity, and genre research (WAGR) framework, based in a synthesis of activity theory and genre theory (see Russell). But, methodologically, they constitute a similar move, one that has paid dividends for me (and, I hope, for others in my line of work).

And that's where I want to leave this chapter. When Latour proposes that we study humans and nonhumans symmetrically, when I propose that we study genres in ecologies, when Newton proposes that force can be considered mass times acceleration for any mass in a fixed frame, these are not all-encompassing propositions. They are deployed only when they make methodological sense. Physicists, I'm assured, don't look at their loved ones and see kilograms (unless, perhaps, when they're worried about the elevator breaking down). Similarly, Latour doesn't talk to doorknobs—unless he needs to apply that methodology to solve a particular kind of problem.

## Notes

1. For a longer discussion, see Harman, *Prince of Networks: Bruno Latour and Metaphysics.*

2. As a side note, this book had a deep impact on me as I was planning the study for my doctoral dissertation. For instance, as I was developing the notion of the genre ecology in my own work, I ran across Freedman and Smart's 1997 article "Navigating the Current of Economic Policy," in which they coined the term "genre ecology" and modeled it after Hutchins's concept of "tool ecology" in his book. After reading their article, I picked up Hutchins's book, and its influence was key to my understanding of genres as comediating each other. More on that later.

3. The second scenario is very similar to that of Fred Saberhagen's first story, "Without a Thought," in *Berserker.*

4. See Spinuzzi, "Four Ways."

## Works Cited

Callon, Michel. "Some Elements of a Sociology of Translation: Domestication of the Scallops and the Fishermen of Saint Brieuc Bay." *Power, Action and Belief: A New Sociology of Knowledge?* Ed. John Law. Boston: Routledge, 1986. 196–233. Print.

———. "Techno-Economic Networks and Irreversibility." *A Sociology of Monsters: Essays on Power, Technology and Domination.* Ed. John Law. London: Routledge, 1991. 132–165. Print.

Callon, Michel, and Vololona Rabeharisoa. "Research 'in the Wild' and the Shaping of Social Identities." *Technology in Society* 25 (2003): 193–204. Print.

Freedman, Aviva, and Graham Smart. "Navigating the Current of Economic Policy: Written Genres and the Distribution of Cognitive Work at a Financial Institution." *Mind, Culture, and Activity* 4.4 (1997): 238–255. Print.

Gygi, Kathleen, and Mark Zachry. "Productive Tensions and the Regulatory Work of Genres in the Development of an Engineering Communication Workshop in a Transnational Corporation." *Journal of Business and Technical Communication* 24.3 (2010): 358–381. Print.

Hakkarainen, Kai. "Can Cognitive Explanations Be Eliminated?" *Science & Education* 12 (2003): 671–689. Print.

Harman, Graham. *Prince of Networks: Bruno Latour and Metaphysics.* Melbourne: Re.press, 2009. Print.

Hutchins, Edwin. *Cognition in the Wild.* Cambridge: MIT P, 1995. Print.

Latour, Bruno. *Aramis, or the Love of Technology.* Cambridge: Harvard UP, 1996. Print.

———. "Morality and Technology: The End of the Means." *Theory, Culture & Society* 19.5 (2002): 247–260. Print.

———. *Pandora's Hope: Essays on the Reality of Science Studies.* Cambridge: Harvard UP, 1999. Print.

———. *The Pasteurization of France.* Cambridge: Harvard UP, 1988. Print.

———. *Politics of Nature: How to Bring the Sciences into Democracy.* Cambridge: Harvard UP, 2004. Print.

———. *Reassembling the Social: An Introduction to Actor-Network-Theory.* New York: Oxford UP, 2006. Print.

———. "A Review of Ed Hutchins Cognition in the Wild." *Mind, Culture, and Activity* 3.1 (1996): 54–63. Print.

———. *Science in Action: How to Follow Scientists and Engineers through Society.* Philadelphia: Open UP, 1987. Print.

Russell, D. R. "Uses of Activity Theory in Written Communication Research." *Learning and Expanding with Activity Theory.* Ed. Annalisa Sannino, Harry Daniels, and Kris D. Gutiérrez. New York: Cambridge UP, 2009. 40–52. Print.

Saberhagen, Fred. *Berserker.* 1967. New York: Ace, 1999. Print.

Sherlock, Lee. "Genre, Activity, and Collaborative Work and Play in World of Warcraft: Places and Problems of Open Systems in Online Gaming." *Journal of Business and Technical Communication* 23.3 (2009): 263–293. Print

Slattery, Shaun. "Undistributing Work through Writing: How Technical Writers Manage Texts in Complex Information Environments." *Technical Communication Quarterly* 16.3 (2007): 311–326. Print.

Spinuzzi, Clay. "Four Ways to Investigate Assemblages of Texts: Genre Sets, Systems, Repertoires, and Ecologies." *ACM SIGDOC 2004: Proceedings of the 22nd Annual International Conference on Design of Communication:*

*The Engineering of Quality Documentation, October 10–13, 2004, Memphis, Tennessee, USA*. Ed. Scott Tilley and Shihong Huang. New York: Assoc. for Computing Machinery, 2004. 110–116. Print.

———. *Network: Theorizing Knowledge Work in Telecommunications*. New York: Cambridge UP, 2008. Print.

———. *Tracing Genres through Organizations: A Sociocultural Approach to Information Design*. Cambridge: MIT P, 2003. Print.

Spinuzzi, Clay, and Mark Zachry. "Genre Ecologies: An Open-System Approach to Understanding and Constructing Documentation." *ACM Journal of Computer Documentation* 24.3 (2000): 169–181. *ACM*. Web.

Spinuzzi, Clay, William Hart-Davidson, and Mark Zachry. "Chains and Ecologies: Methodological Notes toward a Communicative-Mediational Model of Technologically Mediated Writing." *ACM SIGDOC 2006: Proceedings of the 24th ACM International Conference on Design of Communication: October 18–20, 2006, Myrtle Beach, South Carolina, USA*. Ed. Robert A. Pierce and John Stamey. New York: Assoc. for Computing Machinery, 2006. 43–50. Print.

Star, Susan Leigh. Introduction. *Ecologies of Knowledge: Work and Politics in Science and Technology*. Albany: State U of New York P, 1995. 1–35. Print.

Swarts, Jason. "Mobility and Composition: The Architecture of Coherence in Non-Places." *Technical Communication Quarterly* 16.3 (2007): 279–309. Print.

———. "Recycled Writing: Assembling Actor Networks from Reusable Content." *Journal of Business and Technical Communication* 24.2 (2009): 127–163. Print.

# 3. Getting Over Incommensurability: Latour, New Materialisms, and the Rhetoric of Diplomacy

Carl G. Herndl, *University of South Florida*
S. Scott Graham, *University of Wisconsin–Milwaukee*

Bruno Latour's work grasps scientific practice as a social enterprise without it being either a fictitious construction or a narrowly humanist activity. He provides a materialist theory of agency and politics without being reductive. He rescues the much-tortured question of reference from semiotic critique and grounds it in a nonsaltatory movement from world and word. And he offers a fine-grained analysis of conflict and disciplinary change without resorting to incommensurability and the debilitating wrangles over the nature and possibility of epistemology. Throughout this nonmodern analysis of scientific practice, Latour rarely mentions rhetoric. His most extended discussion of rhetoric is the reading of Plato's *Gorgias* in *Pandora's Hope*, where he argues that scientific discourse recapitulates Plato's metaphysics driven by the same fear of mob rule. Like Richard Bernstein, Latour argues that the modern theory of scientific discourse has a debilitatingly narrow conception of rationality. Both Bernstein and Latour suggest that rationality is more flexible and comprehensive than the binary figure of science inherited from Plato and institutionalized by René Descartes. Yet, for all that, Latour has been taken up by rhetoric only very recently. Latour's few explicit references to rhetoric have been uneven at best. Further, the new philosophical and political materialism with which Latour's work is allied is itself often explicitly arhetorical, rejecting the textual/semiotic/rhetorical turn in favor of a shift from human speaker/agent to vibrant object, thus reducing the scope of rhetoric (Sayre).

The question that drives our work in this chapter is this: "what do Latour and new materialisms offer to rhetoric?" Roughly the first half of Latour's work traces the practice of science as he develops the distinction between science in the making and ready-made science. And Latour articulates the programmatic implications of this in *We Have Never Been Modern*. Beginning with *Pandora's Hope*, however, Latour's central concern becomes the failure of political ecology to fashion pragmatic public policy in the face of what he calls the impending ecocide. In the final chapters of *Pandora's Hope*, in *Reassembling the Social*, in *Politics of Nature*, and in essays like "Why Has Critique Run Out of Steam?" and "An Attempt at a 'Compositionist Manifesto,'" Latour commits himself to the problem of building a more robust civic deliberation over the questions of science policy. In this later work, Latour argues that the modern constitution he dismantles in *We Have Never Been Modern* creates a political form of Cartesian anxiety even more dangerous than the epistemological anxieties over certainty that plague scientific theory. Like the arhetorical consequences of Kuhnian incommensurability (see Walser and Gross), the modern separation of nature and culture reduces the possibility of productive civic deliberation in the "collective." Latour argues that with the invention of modern science with its facts and transcendent Nature, we lost "the capacity to debate the common world, the capacity to reach agreement by closing discussion" (*PN* 223). His efforts to address this loss offer rhetoric the beginnings of a nonmodern, materialist rhetorical theory.

In what follows, we locate Latour's work in the emerging new materialism and distinguish it from more arhetorical strains of materialism, such as object-oriented ontology. We then describe how Latour adapts Martin Heidegger's theory of the "thing" to develop his conception of "matters of concern" that avoid the practical incommensurability of science and politics inherited from modern metaphysics. Finally, we outline a materialist rhetoric of diplomacy that animates Latour's Parliament of Things.

## New Materialism and Object-Oriented Ontology

There are many varieties of new materialism. One prominent strand emerges from immanentist materialism of Brauch Spinoza, Gilles Deluze, and Félix Guattarri, and Louis Althusser's posthumous aleatory materialism. Recent works in cultural anthropology (Kosek), geopolitics (Meehana, Shawb, and Marston), feminist theory (Fausto-Sterling), and body studies (Braidotti) have all begun to rely on materialist approaches to investigate the agentive matter of their fields.[1] While not hostile to these other materialisms, the formulation of new materialism we address below emerges from science studies and the conversation between the work of Latour and contemporary political theory.

Within science studies' new materialism is a response to the science wars of the 1980s and 1990s. Latour explicitly positions *Pandora's Hope* as a response to the widespread misperception that science studies denies reality and espouses a radical form of social construction. Latour's argument for the historicity of things, his concept of the "factish," and his theory of circulating reference—itself a synecdoche for the method of actor-network-theory (ANT) as he explains it in *Reassembling the Social*—all articulate a materialist alternative to the failures of modern positivism and what he calls the "hell" of social construction. Latour's nonmodern materialism provides a model of reality that escapes the twin errors of positivist objectivity and any correspondence theory of truth or reference, on the one hand, and the postmodern reactions of social construction and deconstruction, on the other. What gathers these materialist orientations together is a whole-scale rejection of the Cartesian and Kantian legacy of modernism and a profound sense that what Latour calls the modern constitution has bequeathed us an impending ecocide and an impotent political ecology. The two founding critical moves of this new materialism are a rejection of the modern distinction between subject and object and, second, rejecting epistemology and turning to ontology.[2]

In its broadest sense, the materialist move away from the grounding modern distinction between subject and object follows from Latour's argument in *We Have Never Been Modern* that nature and society are artificial purifications of the quasi-objects and quasi-subjects that proliferate in what he calls the "zone of translation" otherwise known as the "real" world. This programmatic rejection of purified ontological zones follows from his early studies of scientific practice and his contrast between a mythic "ready made Science" of cold knowable objects, and the lively "science in the making" of laboratory practice (*SA*). This contrast marks Latour's move away from what traditional philosophy of science refers to as the "context of justification"—an epistemological project—to the "context of discovery"—an ontological project.

When Latour takes up the political consequences of this modern bifurcation, his work becomes especially productive for rhetoric by explaining why contemporary civic deliberations over science policy fail so often and setting the grounds for an alternative rhetorical practice. In *Politics of Nature*, Latour projects the metaphysical purification of Nature and Society onto the field of public life, or what he calls the task of assembling the collective. Here, Latour's empirical argument against the Cartesian dichotomy becomes a political and ethical argument whose goal is to avoid the "civil war" between the incommensurable houses of science and politics. The distinction between subjects and objects makes it impossible to pursue real politics understood as "the progressive composition of a common world" (Latour, *PN* 47) because the authority of a purified, transcendent "Nature" has always foreclosed public discourse by acting as an incontrovertible ground for knowledge and action. Latour argues: "'subject' and 'object' are the names given to forms of representative assemblies, so that they can never bring themselves together in the same place and proceed together" (*PN* 72). By distributing science and politics to separate spheres populated by facts and values, respectively, the modern constitution makes productive civic deliberation over phenomena like climate change all but impossible. Here, the classic problem of incommensurability between competing scientific paradigms appears as a more localized case of the incommensurability between science and politics writ large.

The unproductive politics of Nature in which the appeal to transcendent objects and facts trump all other argumentative grounds leads Latour and materialist political theory to redefine the political within the posthuman problematic. Politics has traditionally been understood as a *human* field of action in which material things were figured as merely the *conditions* of human action (Bennett, *Vibrant* 54), and political theory was thought to "begin with the purification of human society from the material world" (Braun and Whatmore, xiv). Bruce Braun and Sarah J. Whatmore articulate the basic political question of new materialism: "What happens to politics—indeed to the 'political' as a category—when we begin to take this *stuff* of politics seriously" (ix; see also Roe; Marres and Lezaun). What happens when the "propensities, affordances and affectivities of nonhumans" are included in the action of assembling our collective common world? The new political materialism with its interest in "stuff" is a response to the intense focus on the question of the subject and of subjectivity over the past forty years. As Bill Brown suggests, much of the new materialism is "*avowing* the force of questions that have been too readily foreclosed by more familiar fetishizations: the fetishization of the subject, the image, the word" (7).

This reaction against the traditional definition of politics with its exclusive attention to human action produces a return to materialist politics that tries to avoid the reductive failure of older materialisms (see Bennett, *Enchantment*; Bennett, *Vibrant*; Connolly). Modern forms of materialism are descended from Descartes, who defined matter as corporeal substance, extended in space and without its own motive power. As Diana Coole and Samantha Frost point out, this matches our intuitive sense of a real world of mute objects that occupy space and "whose movements and behaviors are predictable, controllable and replicable" (8). For some reductive forms of materialism, all action, including human behavior, can be reduced to the effects of material determination. Such might be the genetic determinism of the sociobiologists for whom the amino acid pairs in DNA determine everything about human life (Wilson). Alternatively, because the behavior of a passive natural world of inert matter can be carefully calculated, traditional materialism also produces the modern myth of man's mastery of the natural world. These are political avatars of Descartes's dualism. To a considerable extent, new materialisms are motivated by a recognition of the unfortunate consequences of this modernist myth of mastery and the accompanying rhetoric of certainty and a political and ethical irresponsibility. As Latour argues, our modern crime, like Victor Frankenstein's, is not creating heterogeneous creatures or things but disowning and abandoning them. By including *things* in the active constitution of our "common world," new-materialist theory redefines politics in something like Latour's definition of politics as "the management, diplomacy, combination, and negotiation of human and nonhuman agencies. Who or what can withstand who or what?" (*PH* 290; see Pels, Hetherington, and Vandenberghe).

Perhaps because of his experience in laboratory studies, Latour proposes a materialist politics that is somewhat more moderate than Bennett's vibrant materialism or the immanent materialism of critics, such as William Connolly, with its "emergent causality" (Connolly 179). Anxious to avoid both the traditional humanist error and the extremes of contemporary reactions, Latour proposes a "pluriverse" populated not by subjects and objects but by "propositions," the neutral term he borrows from Alfred North Whitehead. These propositions are all equally actors or actants if they can "modify other actors through a series of trials that can be listed thanks to some experimental protocol" (Latour, *PN* 75). The scientific and political realm of Latour's materialism is the metaphorical "flatland" that he describes in *Reassembling the Social*, where human and nonhuman actants that have neither essential identity nor agentic privilege form new relationships as they are articulated in heterogeneous assemblages. In this political and ontological flatland populated by propositions, subject and object coexist, science and politics are no longer incommensurable, and a transcendent Nature no longer closes off civic deliberation.

## From Epistemology to Ontology

The second grounding philosophical move that Latour shares with the new materialism is a programmatic rejection of epistemology in favor of ontology.

As with the great bifurcation of subject and object, Latour both shares a great deal with the materialist critique of epistemology and offers a distinctively different alternative. Latour's critique of epistemology emerges from the study of situated scientific practice, what Annemarie Mol calls praxiography. The ontology he develops also departs from that of other new materialisms, especially the contemporary philosophical movement known as object-oriented ontology (OOO). The new object of OOO retains a metaphysics of substance that gives the substance an identity that supersedes activity and recedes from perception. Latour's ontology is more radical, as we will see in the next section. Latour's object or "thing" has an inessential identity that admits of multiplicity and changes through activity, collapsing the traditional distinction between substance and accident.

In *Pandora's Hope*, Latour characterizes the task of modern epistemology as the "brain-in-a-vat" subjectivity completely separate from the objective world, yet required to have certain knowledge of that exteriority. In *Politics of Nature*, Latour returns to the original avatar of the brain-in-a-vat and presents an extended reading of Plato's Cave, in which the Cartesian dichotomy presents us with things as they are—traditional, modern objects—and our representations of them—the corrupt and corrupting activity of subjects. Rather than rehearse the traditional skepticism of epistemology, however, Latour focuses on its political and rhetorical consequences. In Latour's reading, Plato's metaphysics allows science both access to the transcendent world of objects outside the cave of social representation and the ability to return to the cave with the good news from the outside. Like the philosopher before him, the scientist is unique in being able to move back and forth between the two worlds. This "double break" allows the scientist to return to the cave of the social world "to bring order to it with the incontestable findings that will silence the endless chatter of the ignorant mob" (Latour, *PN* 11). This allows Science to short-circuit the "due process" of civic deliberation through which we might compose our common world. In rhetorical terms, Latour has articulated the genealogy of the problem of trust (Jasanoff) and the difficulty contemporary science has in negotiating the questions of certainty, uncertainty, and authority in contemporary public deliberation.

Like Latour and other new materialists, OOO rejects epistemological inquiry and locates the object outside (or prior to) the sphere of representation. But here the two varieties of new materialism part ways. Where Latour and science studies stubbornly trace the situated practices of multiple ontologies (Mol) or the associations of actor-network-theory (Latour), Levi Bryant and

Graham Harman each launches a defense of metaphysics grounded on what Bryant calls "the subjectless object." Bryant identifies the typical location of the object in dialogue with the subject as the "epistemic fallacy."

> What the epistemic fallacy identifies is the fallacy of reducing ontological questions to epistemological questions, or conflating questions of *how* we know with questions of what beings *are*. In short, the epistemic fallacy occurs whenever being is reduced to our access to being. (60)

Whether or not OOO successfully escapes the epistemic fallacy comes down to the definition of "reducing." That is, the object of OOO Bryant and Harman articulate does not reduce the object solely to its relationship with a subject—to mere sensations, talk, or signs—but neither does their object entirely escape subjectivity. Specifically, the object of OOO maintains sensual relations with subjects as an essential feature of its being, sensual relations with subjects (other objects).[3]

In developing his notion of the subjectless object, Bryant articulates his theory of the "virtual proper being of an object." Here, virtual does not refer to illusion or simulacrum but rather to a form of power.

> The virtual proper being of an object is what makes an object properly an object. It is that which constitutes an object as a difference engine or a generative mechanism. However, no one nor any other thing ever encounters an object qua its virtual proper being, for the substance of an object is perpetually withdrawn or in excess of any of its manifestations. . . . When I refer to manifestation, I am not referring to givenness to a subject, but rather to actualization within a world. (88)

Thus, the virtual proper being or substantiality of an object is tied directly to its powers of manifestation but, again, not manifesting *for* any subject. Elaborating this notion, Bryant argues, "My thesis is that the substantiality of objects is not a bare substratum, but rather an absolutely individual system or organization of powers. Powers are the capacities of an object or what it can do" (89). Substance as doing in the world: here, we have something rather like the more pragmatically oriented new materialisms, something more like actor-network-theory. Unfortunately, the promise of substance-qua-power does not live up to Bryant's ontological demands on a subjectless object. Bryant's exegesis of the power/substance of a subjectless object examines a simple, blue coffee mug. Bryant walks the reader through a serious of different situations in which one could experience the color of the cup. He points to the current blueness, the different blueness of the cup in a different light source, the blackness of the cup in darkness. In so doing, Bryant works to distance his subjectless object from the sensual quality of blueness and towards the substantive power of coloring. The mug colors. That is one of its doings in the world and, therefore, part of its virtual proper being. But a sensing being with color vision is required for the cup to manifest its coloring power. Indeed, Bryant recognizes this issue directly in his discrimination between exo-qualities and endo-qualities.

> Exo-qualities are qualities that can only exist in and through a set of exo-relations to other objects. Color, for example, seems to be a quality of this sort. Color is an event that only takes place through a network of exo-relations between the molecular endo-composition of the object, particular wavelengths of light, and a particular neurological structure in an organism. (120)

This recognition offers a serious challenge to Bryant's claim for the subjectlessness of OOO's object. Furthermore, it is a criticism to which he never really offers a satisfactory reply.

The distinction between endo-qualities and exo-qualities in Bryant's and Harmon's metaphysical substance is precisely the kind of metaphysical quandary Latour wants to escape. The subjectless object of OOO does not, finally, escape the metaphysical double bind of Plato's cave that Latour recognizes as fatal to political ecology and the civic deliberation of the collective. The difference between the two positions and the stakes involved are clear in the friction between Latour and Harmon in their dialogue in *Prince and the Wolf*, where Latour steadfastly refuses Harmon's metaphysical gambit. Harmon and Bryant want to salvage metaphysics. Latour wants to salvage civic deliberation.

While many new materialists reject epistemology and representation, Latour rejects metaphysics altogether and argues for an ontology without metaphysics.

> To go from metaphysics to ontology is to raise again the question of what the real world is really like. As long as we remain in metaphysics, there is always the danger that deployment of the actors' worlds will remain too easy because they could be taken as so many representations of what the world, in the singular is like. (*RS* 117)

The "subjectless object" of OOO preserves metaphysics but returns us to the politics of Nature that forecloses civic deliberation. To provide an ontology outside metaphysics and a quasi-object that supports public deliberation, Latour takes up Heidegger's concept of the "thing."

## From Objects to Things

In "The Thing," Heidegger articulates his famous distinction between objects and things. The first move of this distinction involves Heidegger's choice of *Gegenstand* over *Objekt,* both viable options for "object." *Gegenstand* (literally, that which stands against) highlights an object's necessary positioning vis-à-vis a subject. It is relational. In contrast, Heidegger's "thing" is akin to Bryant's virtual proper being or Harman's real object in that it recedes from contact with other objects. It is resistant and recalcitrant.

Heidegger's distinction between thing and object is most often understood through his notion of tool-being. In *Being and Time* Heidegger distinguishes between *vorhanden* (present-to-hand) and *zuhanden* (ready-to-hand). In the famous example of the hammer, a perfectly functioning hammer articulated into the praxis of carpentry is zuhanden. It is unremarked as a hammer, and its being recedes from notice. However, it is still implicated in the activity, a regime of practice, that of carpentry. If the hammer breaks, however, it becomes vorhanden because the carpenter must assess and then fix or replace the hammer. For Heidegger, things are zuhanden, and objects are vorhanden. In other words, to be an object, to be *vorhanden* is to stand against a subject in the order of representation (Gegenstand).[4]

Latour, on the other hand, is more than ready to embrace the object, or at least, the thingyness of objects. In "Why Has Critique Run Out of Steam?," Latour takes up Heidegger's distinction between objects and things to articulate the difference between "matters of fact" and "matters of concern." Matters of fact are enlightenment objects, grasped in the representational idiom and subject to unending epistemological and metaphysical questions of truth and reference. Matters of concern, by contrast, are nonmodern hybrids that arise in practice. Latour collapses Heidegger's distinction applying to seemingly uninteresting objects like a Coke can, the descriptive language Heidegger developed to explore the "things" with which he was fascinated. As Latour comments later, Heidegger's "mistake is not to have treated the jug [Heidegger's example of a thing "cradled in the respectful idiom of art craftsmanship and poetry"] too well, but to have traced the dichotomy between *Gegenstand* and *Thing* that was justified by nothing except the crassest of prejudices" ("Critique" 234).[5] Latour wants to use the same language and enthusiasm with which Heidegger described *things* to explore the artifacts of science and technology. Like the jug, the artifacts of science and technology combine both facts and values; they are both "in a sense, objects out there" and are issues formed through the gathering of values and people. In moving from object to thing, Latour is repeating in philosophy what he had done in *Pandora's Hope* with his analysis of black boxing. When a machine runs perfectly or a matter of fact becomes "settled," the distributed agency, labor, and complexity of the machine or fact are lost to consciousness, the "joint production of actors and artifacts is entirely opaque" (Latour, *PH* 183). As he opens black boxes, Latour traces the network of associations and transformations that link humans and nonhumans, facts, and values in the circulatory system of science that fabricates a machine or fact or object. Treating objects as things opens them to deliberation and dispute and returns us to the possibility of a viable political ecology.

The clearest distinction between Latour's "things" and the "objects" of critics, such as Bryant and Harmon, appears in *Politics of Nature*. In place of "real," essential, and receding objects of Harman's metaphysics that he calls "smooth " or "risk-free" objects, Latour describes "tangled objects" that circulate in his metaphorical flatland of distributed agency. The smooth objects of metaphysics have "clear boundaries, a well-defined essence" (Latour, *PN* 22). These objects "brought with them" intended and unintended consequences, but like the ideals that descend into Plato's cave from the otherworldly realm, the identity of these risk-free objects is unaltered by these consequences because they occur in a world "lacking any common measure" with that of the human world in which political, economic, or social consequences matter. The short phrase "lacking common measure" is the core of the original mathematical definition of incommensurability and the root of Latour's objection to a metaphysics of substance.

By contrast with the smooth objects of the old metaphysical constitution, Latour's tangled objects, or "quasi-objects," do not have an impact of the social or political world in the sense that they affect it from without; they are themselves, as Latour argues in *Reassembling the Social*, part of that new sociality. More significant for distinguishing Latour's materialism from that of others like Bryant and Harmon, the very identity of these quasi-objects is changed through their interaction with the other actants or propositions in the collective. That is, their identity is transformed by the unintended consequences of their associations. In making this argument, Latour rejects the metaphysics built upon the distinction between substance and accident, between an essential identity and a changing or phenomenal manifestation. For Latour, manifestation matters. And not as a power but as identity. As he argues in part two of *The Pasteurization of France*, titled "Irreductions," no entity in the world can be reduced to some metaphysically prior essence. Latour presents this as an absolute:

"nothing is, by itself, either reducible or irreducible to anything else" (*PF* 158). To reduce reality to the product of inaccessible causes or transcendent entities like the concept of "Nature" silences politics and eviscerates the civic sphere of deliberation. And this, we believe, is why Latour's adopts the Heideggerian "thing" in his political manifesto "Why Has Critique Run Out of Steam?" The theory of the object explicated by the modern constitution is broken. Like the broken hammer of tool use, it has become vorhanden, present-to-hand. The modern purification of quasi-objects into separate ontological categories along with the myth of control over nature has produced a proliferation of hybrids that rebound on the collective like the return of the repressed.

## Rhetoric as Diplomacy

While we support Latour's recourse to the thing, it is not merely for the philosophical or ontological reasons outlined in our critique of OOO's latent metaphysics. Although rhetorical studies has moved past the hyphenated locution of Robert Scott's rhetoric-as-epistemic, epistemological inquiry continues to permeate and ground rhetorical studies. Thus, the rejection of epistemology as a fundamentally failed enterprise is no mere philosophical problem but rather has the potential to transform rhetorical scholarship and pedagogy. Thus, we argue, the move from objects to things not only makes philosophical sense but it also allows for a more robust rhetorical activity. Nowhere is this more evident than in Bryant's description of communication, which essentially extends the transmission model while cutting off nearly any possibility for comprehension.

> [I]nformation is non-linear and system specific, existing only for the system in question and as a function of the organization or endo-structure of the object. In saying that information is non-linear, my point is that it is an effect of the endo-structure of the object as it relates to its environment and how the endo-structure resonates within the field of differential relations that define that structure. Information is not in the environment, but a product of the system perturbed by its environment. (166)

Thus, under Bryant's model, communication is an event wherein one object that happens to have the requisite communicative endo-structure perturbs its environment, and a second object with the appropriate endo-structure receives this annoying stimuli, and due to the accidents of the second object's endo-structure, the perturbation is interpreted as information. Bryant explains this model referring to his cat, but the same model applies equally to humans communicating with humans.

> This sort of selectivity is true not only of relations with objects between different sorts, but also of relations between objects of the same sort. Many, I'm sure, have experienced and been baffled by conversations with others from very different theoretical backgrounds and orientations. In such discussions, points and claims you take for granted as obvious seem not even to be registered or noticed by the interlocutor when made. (174)

Essentially, OOO presents a model of hyperincommensurability where communication as we know it is impossible and insofar as it is possible is merely the lucky accident of a well-timed perturbation landing on an object with an appropriate endo-structure. A rhetorical theory grounded in OOO cannot move one iota beyond the ludic postmodernism that new materialisms aim to reject. Indeed, new materialisms have been celebrated for their utility in rhetorical theory precisely because they constitute a viable alternative to incommensurability (Graham and Herndl).

For new materialisms, the crucial questions are questions of "doing" rather than "knowing." For scholars like Latour, Annemarie Mol, and Andrew Pickering, epistemology is a form of perspectivalism that seeks to adjudicate claims about the correspondence of statements to a unified and unchanging Nature. With the concept of assemblages and the performative nature of fabrication, these critics instead talk about the *enactment* of multiple ontologies. For Mol, for example, there are multiple arterioscleroses enacted in medical practice, each with a different location, set of figures and topoi (*Body Multiple*). Latour captures the shift from epistemology to ontology as the shift from a multiculturalism and a mononaturalism to a monoculturalism and a multinaturalism. This chiasmus captures his critique of social construction as a form of epistemic multiculturalism grounded in a modern faith in a single, transcendent Nature. Latour replaces this with an ontological monoculturalism that enacts many different natures each with a history of change and articulation.

Latour's, Mol's, and Pickering's focus on doing and the performative both embrace the zuhandenheit of the thing and coordinate wonderfully with performative notions of rhetoric like speech-act theory. A thing-oriented ontology inquiry from representation, epistemology, and correspondence toward action, performance, and a pragmatist sense that "essence is existence, and existence is action" (Latour, *PH* 123).

Latour's notion of the thing as a matter of concern stages an ontology intimately grounded in the activity of civic deliberation. Where Heidegger's objects are the subject of theoretical reflection, Latour's things are the subject of ethical and pragmatic concern. To accomplish this reversal of the Heideggerian categories, Latour resorts to the etymology of "thing" as a "quasi-judiciary assembly" ("Critique" 232–33). As Latour points out, a "thing" has always been a place or event where people gather to deliberate over matters that affect the public or the collective. This reading of a thing as brought to consciousness as a matter of concern through some kind of failure—a failure of modernism to deal with ecocide, a failure of science to embrace politics—returns us to a sphere of civic deliberation.

Latour's project of rediscovering a truly political ecology that negotiates the shifting relations of human and nonhumans, and the uncertain membership in any collective is an attempt to reinvigorate the rhetorical deliberations of civic life. In place of the deadly stalemate between science and politics, facts and values, Latour proposes the metaphor of a parliament of things and the figure of the diplomat. Like Isabella Stengers, Latour understands the proper activity of the civil assemblage considering matters of concern as the work of diplomacy, a negotiation of a common world undertaken without any guarantee of a solution. The diplomat's work in the parliament of things is a return to sophistic rhetoric. Latour explains,

> The external enemy, for good reason, terrifies those who imagine that what defines their essence is going to be torn away: barbarians frighten barbarians. But the enemy that the diplomat accompanies does not put the collective in danger in the same way, since he is the bearer of a peace proposal that goes far beyond mere compromise: "Thanks to you, we are going to understand the difference between our essential requirements and their temporary expressions." Finally, we are going to know what we want and what this "we" is that says it is endowed with a will. The diplomat recalls that *no one who does not lend himself to this work of negotiation can invoke the unity of the collective.* (*PN* 217; original emphasis)

The diplomat is committed to the uncertainty of the collective and eschews the assurances of nature and matters of fact to adjudicate the disputes. As Stengers argues, the art of diplomacy, which we understand as sophistic rhetoric, requires a "hesitation" that depends on engagement rather than rules, and the diplomat recognizes an "obligation" to all members of the collective. For Stengers as for Latour, the diplomatic engagement in parliamentary debate demonstrates no underlying truth, merely the very fact of its achievement. Learning what we want and who this "we" is emerges not from appeal to fact, modest witnesses, or Nature but from the practical work of negotiation facing humans and nonhumans in the uncertain flux of unfolding events. And the issue at hand is not a fact but a thing, the membership in the collective and what the collective "good" is.

The stakes in this shift from epistemology to diplomacy, from metaphysics to matters of concern appears most clearly in Latour's reading of the *Gorgias* and its reincarnation in modern (nonpolitical) science. Toward the conclusion of his analysis of the dialogue, Latour argues that the felicity conditions for successful modern science with its certainty and pure rationality do not correspond to the felicity conditions in the agora. The mathematical reasoning that allows Socrates to vanquish the straw Calicles is not part of this world but the possession of the newly dead. Latour quotes the *Gorgias*.

> They [the souls] better be judged *naked, stripped* of all this clothing—in other words, they have to be *judged after* they have died. If the assessment is to be *fair*, the judge had better be naked as well—which is to say dead—so that with an *unhampered soul* he can scrutinize the *unhampered soul* of a freshly dead individual who isn't *surrounded by his friends and relatives*, and has left those *trappings* behind in the world. (*PH* 246; original emphasis)

As Latour comments, this macabre scene of last and certain judgment is beautiful but has nothing to do with politics: "Politics," or a rhetoric of diplomacy, "is not about 'freshly dead' people, but about the living; not about ghoulish stories of the afterworld, but about gory stories of this world" (*PH* 246). All those trappings and attachments that "hamper" the soul are the vascular system of science and its hybrid creations. These are what "oblige us to pass judgment *now*, in the bright sun of Athens, not in the crepuscular light of Hades" (*PH* 246–47; original emphasis). Maintaining the separation of science and politics retards decision making.

Latour closes his discussion of democracy and diplomacy with an appeal to the capacity of the sophistic rhetor as diplomat: "the *logos* can find no help except in turning to the frail parliamentarians" (*PN* 220). Latour's theory and his hopes for a science free from the disciplining and disabling politics of modernity depend on the answer to his odd question, "Can we learn to like scientists as much as politicians so that *at last* we can benefit from the Greeks two inventions: demonstration and democracy?" (*PH* 265; original emphasis).

Put differently, can we agree to like rhetoric as much as science and even politics? This would be a seismic shift in Western philosophy. And it will require concerted effort by rhetoricians to develop the materialist rhetoric Latour and others have marked out. Developing a materialist rhetoric capable of engaging the challenges of science and policy is not a new topic for rhetoric. But Latour's outline of a nonmodern materialist rhetoric of diplomacy does offer us a new opening for our collective work.

## Notes

1. Useful synopses of the various genealogies of materialism and, more specifically, the twentieth-century theory of "things" appear in Brown, "Thing Theory," and the preface to Bennett, *Vibrant Matter*. Thus, the "new materialism" is not altogether new but, perhaps, "resurgent," and Latour's interest in the "thing," while relatively unique, is part of a well-established thing.

2. Readers may wonder at this supposed innovation in new materialisms. For, certainly, poststructuralisms and postmodernisms have famously rejected modernist and/or Cartesian binaries. However, following Latour, we argue, "Postmodernism is a symptom [of modernism], and not a fresh solution. It lives under the modern Constitution, but it no longer believes in the guarantees the Constitution offers" (*Modern* 46). In short, despite the rhetoric of rejection, postmodernisms tend to reify the Cartesian divide while reversing it. In rejecting the old reductivist materiality of positivism, postmodernism and poststructuralism invert the reduction, privileging the cultural especially the linguistic over the natural. As Bill Brown argues in his essay "Thing Theory," materialist fascination with "things"—Heideggerian, Deweyian, Latourian, or otherwise—comes as an explicit alternative to the semiotic and linguistic deconstruction of the subject in recent decades. New materialisms, therefore, embrace Latour's call to supplant the symptom of postmodernism with a solution in nonmodernism.

3. This continued relationship can be seen clearly in Harman's articulation of the quadruple object. For Harman, the object of OOO consists of the reciprocal relations among real objects, real qualities, sensual objects, and sensual qualities. To be clear, these are not four different objects but rather four essential aspects of each object. Harman clarifies, "The metaphysics presented in this book lays great stress on several key tensions between objects and their qualities" (*Quadruple* 26). Furthermore, "although we never touch real objects, we always touch sensual objects. Sensual objects would not even exist if they did not exist for me, or for some other agent that expends its energy in taking

them seriously" (Harman, *Quadruple* 74). This necessary "for me" is what Bryant rejects in this description of the epistemic fallacy.

4. Harman glosses this from "Technology, Things, and Objects in Heidegger" (*Quadruple*): "External representation of things never gives us their true inner life, which partly withdraws from every human grasp. This holds even for the vaunted achievements of science: 'science always encounters only that which its type of representation permits in advance as the object that is possible for it'" (8–9). In short, science reduces the thing to a present-at-hand caricature by replacing it with a set of tangible properties through which it is modeled. Indeed, "science annihilated the things as things long before the atom bomb exploded. This explosion is only the crudest of all crude confirmations of the annihilation of the thing that transpired long ago: that the thing as thing remains null and void" (9). But it is not just science that is found guilty of doing so. The entire history of philosophy revolves around presence (i.e., false nearness) no less than science does. In Heidegger's blunt words, "Plato, who represents the presence of that which is present by way of its outward look, thought the essence of the things as little as Aristotle and all ensuing thinkers" (7; emphasis added).

Although Harman ultimately rejects the thing in favor of objects in his larger work, he consistently recognizes the value of a Heidegger's thing in accounting for that part of reality that retreats from representation.

> To oppose the arrogant pretensions of theory, the tool-analysis shows us that the being of an apple, hammer, dog, or star is not exhausted by its presence in consciousness. No sensual profile of these things will ever exhaust its full reality, which withdraws into the dusk of a shadowy underworld. (42)

5. The "crassest prejudice" of Heidegger's distinction between the artistic jug and the banal object is revived in Benjamin's theory of the originary "aura" of the work of art in contrast to the product of mechanical reproduction.

## Works Cited

Bennett, Jane. *The Enchantment of Modern Life: Attachments, Crossings and Ethics*. Princeton: Princeton UP, 2001. Print.

———. *Vibrant Matter: A Political Ecology of Things*. Durham: Duke University Press, 2010. Print.

Bernstein, Richard. *Beyond Objectivism and Relativism: Science, Hermeneutics, and Praxis*. Philadelphia: U of Pennsylvania P, 1983. Print.

Braidotti, Rosi. *Metamorphoses: Towards a Feminist Theory of Becoming.* Cambridge: Polity, 2002. Print.

Braun, Bruce, and Sarah J. Whatmore. *Political Matter: Technoscience, Democracy, and Public Life.* Minneapolis: U of Minnesota P, 2010. Print.

Brown, Bill. "Thing Theory." *Critical Inquiry* 28.1 (2001): 1–22. Print.

Bryant, Levi. *The Democracy of Objects.* Ann Arbor: Open Humanities, 2011. Print.

Connolly, William. "Materialities of Experience." Coole and Frost 178–200.

Coole, Diana, and Samantha Frost, eds. *New Materialisms: Ontology, Agency, and Politics.* Durham: Duke UP, 2010. Print.

Fausto-Sterling, Anne. *Sexing the Body: Gender Politics and the Construction of Sexuality.* New York: Basic, 2000. Print.

Graham, S. Scott. "Agency and the Rhetoric of Medicine: Biomedical Brain Scans and the Ontology of Fibromyalgia." *Technical Communication Quarterly* 18.4 (2009): 376–404. Print.

———. "Dis-ease or Disease? Ontological Rarefaction in the Medical-Industrial Complex." *Journal of Medical Humanities* 32.3 (2011): 167–187. Print.

Graham, S. Scott, and Carl Herndl. "Multiple Ontologies in Pain Management: Towards a Postplural Rhetoric of Science." *Technical Communication Quarterly* 22.1 (2013): 103–125. Print.

Harman, Graham. *Prince of Networks: Bruno Latour and Metaphysics.* Melbourne: Re.press, 2009. Print.

———. *The Quadruple Object.* Winchester: Zero, 2011. Print.

Heidegger, Martin. *Being and Time: A Translation of Sein und Zeit.* Albany: State U of New York P, 1996.

———. "The Thing." *Poetry, Language, Thought.* Trans. Albert Hofstadter. New York: Harper, 1971. 163–182. Print.

———. *What Is a Thing?* Trans. W. B. Barton Jr. and V. Deutsch. South Bend: Regnery, 1967. Print.

Jasanoff, Seila. *Designs on Nature: Science and Democracy in Europe and the United States.* Princeton: Princeton UP, 2005. Print.

Kosek, Jake. "Ecologies of Empire: On the New Uses of the Honeybee." *Cultural Anthropology* 25.4 (2010): 650–678. Print.

Latour, Bruno. "An Attempt at a 'Compositionist Manifesto.'" *New Literary History* 41.3 (2010): 471–490. Print.

———. "Love Your Monsters: Why We Must Care for Our Technologies as We Do Our Children." *Breakthrough Journal.* 2012. Web. 3 Sept. 2014.

———. *Pandora's Hope: Essays on the Reality of Science Studies.* Cambridge: Harvard UP, 1999. Print.

———. *The Pasteurization of France*. Cambridge: Harvard UP, 1988. Print.

———. *Politics of Nature: How to Bring the Sciences into Democracy*. Cambridge: Harvard UP, 2004. Print.

———. *Reassembling the Social: An Introduction to Actor-Network-Theory*. Oxford: Oxford UP, 2005. Print.

———. *Science in Action: How to Follow Scientists and Engineers through Society*. Cambridge: Harvard UP, 1987. Print.

———. *We Have Never Been Modern*. Cambridge: Harvard UP, 1991. Print.

———. "Where Are the Missing Masses? The Sociology of a Few Mundane Artifacts." *Shaping Technology/Building Society: Studies in Sociotechnical Change*. Ed. W. E. Bijker and J. Law. Cambridge: MIT Press, 1992. 225–258. Print.

———. "Why Has Critique Run Out of Steam? From Matters of Fact to Matters of Concern." *Critical Inquiry* 30.2 (2004): 225–248. Print.

Latour, Bruno, and Steve Woolgar. *Laboratory Life: The Construction of Scientific Facts*. Princeton: Princeton UP, 1986. Print.

Latour, Bruno, Graham Harman, and Peter Erdélyi. *Prince and the Wolf: Latour and Harman at the LSE*. Washington: Zero, 2011. Print.

Marres, Noortje, and Javier Lezaun. "Materials and Devices of the Public: An Introduction." *Economy and Society* 40.4 (2011): 489–509. Print.

Meehana, Katharine, Ian Shawb, and Sallie Marston. "Political Geographies of the Object." *Political Geography* 33 (2013): 1–10. Print.

Mendelson, Michael. *Many Sides: A Protagorean Approach to the Theory, Practice, and Pedagogy of Argument*. Dordrecht: Kluwer, 2002. Print.

Mol, Annemarie. *The Body Multiple: Ontology in Medical Practice*. Durham: Duke UP, 2002. Print.

———. "Ontological Politics. A Word and Some Questions." *Actor Network Theory and After*. Ed. John Law and John Hassard. Oxford: Blackwell, 1999. 74–89. Print.

Norton, Bryan. *Sustainability: A Philosophy of Adaptive Ecosystem Management*. Chicago: U of Chicago P, 2005. Print.

Pels, Dick, Kevin Hetherington, and Frédéric Vandenberghe. "The Status of the Object: Performances, Mediations, and Techniques." *Theory, Culture, and Society* 19.5–6 (2002): 1–21. Print.

Pickering, Andrew. *The Cybernetic Brain: Sketches of Another Future*. Chicago: U of Chicago P, 2010. Print.

———. *The Mangle of Practice: Time, Agency, and Science*. Chicago: U of Chicago P, 1995. Print.

Roe, Emma. "The Ontology of a Visceral-Object: Notes on Commercial (or Cosmercial) Practices in the Meat Industry." Nonhuman Turn Conference, Milwaukee. 3 May2012. Reading.

Sayre, Nathan. "The Politics of the Anthropogenic." *Annual Review of Anthropology* 42 (2012): 51–70. Print.

Scott, J. Blake. "Extending Rhetorical-Cultural Analysis: Transformations of Home HIV Testing." *College English* 65.4 (2003): 349–367. Print.

Stengers, Isabella. "Including Nonhuman in Political Theory: Opening Pandora's Box?" *Political Matter: Technoscience, Democracy, and Public Life*. Ed. Bruce Braun and Sarah J. Whatmore. Minneapolis: U of Minnesota P, 2010. 3–33. Print.

Walser, Arthur, and Alan Gross. "Positivists, Postmodernists, Aristotelians and the Challenger Disaster." *College English* 56.4 (1994): 420–433. Print.

Wilson, E. O. *Sociobiology: The New Synthesis*. Cambridge: Harvard UP, 1975. Print.

# 4. From Constituting to Instituting: Kant, Latour, and Twitter

Marc C. Santos and Meredith Zoetewey Johnson,
*University of South Florida*

For the past two decades, Bruno Latour has critiqued the separation of academics from politics, arguing that this separation has led us to a crisis of global proportions. In his *Politics of Nature*, Latour proposed a nonmodern constitution that would reintegrate academics—both humanists and scientists—into the agora. Latour was correct that the ideal modern constitution—the absolute separation of nature and culture, human and nonhuman, science and the humanities—never actually reflected the reality in which we live (*Modern* 46–48). However, we need to recognize that the modern institution, grown from Immanuel Kant's distinctions between public and private uses of reason and between the high and the lower university faculty, has thrived and continues to thrive, despite postmodern proclamations to debunk its mission (e.g., Lyotard, *Postmodern Condition*) or declare it in ruins (e.g., Readings, *University in Ruins*). While poststructuralism and postmodernism might have destabilized the modern research university's ontological and epistemological foundations, the modern institution remains committed to the production of abstract, disciplinary knowledge. What Jean-François Lyotard identifies as its metanarratives remains intact (*Postmodern* 34–37); though theoretically dismantled, the university does the same things in its everyday operations. For nearly two centuries, we have researched and taught within this institution dedicated to the creation of objective knowledge and founded upon disciplinary autonomy. This is especially true of internal, institutional processes—specifically, tenure and promotion.

We stress the issue of disciplinarity here because it lies at the heart of Latour's diagnosis. Academics are too concerned with talking to each other and too little invested in talking with the (messy) outside world. Latour's works share a central commitment to reversing the modern separation of academics and politics underwriting what he calls the modern constitution. We champion this cause. However, we believe dreaming of a progressive constitution promises to remain ineffectual if we do not scrutinize and revise the limitations imposed upon us by modernist institutional frameworks. We argue that realizing Latour's nonmodern constitution requires scholars to recognize the extent to which our contemporary research institutions remain systemically routed in the very modernism Latour works to reject. Contemporary expectations for tenure and promotion, the example this chapter works through, remain committed to Kantian epistemology and the institution that grows from that epistemology. We argue that the university cannot enact Latour's nonmodern constitution without *both* reconsidering its commitment to Kant's resolutions *and* rewarding the role digital technologies could play in inviting dialogue between academics and the public.

## To Think *and* Disobey

At the same time, however, Latour and those committed to his goals need to recognize the political hazards that arise as one dismantles the separation of school and state. Kant's modern constitution, developed in intellectually dangerous times, sacrificed public participation in order to secure political protection. While we agree with Latour that the time has come to reinvest in politics, we want to stress that given the increasing impingement of conservative economic and political influence on education, academics need to tread carefully. Below we document this impingement, attempting to argue that it both creates an exigency academics can ill-afford to ignore and requires a rhetorical rethinking of tenure and promotion. In short, realizing Latour's nonmodern ambitions will require that academics trade lifelong job security to sustain political protection. We must be free to think *and* disobey.

This chapter begins by briefly unpacking Latour's nonmodern constitution, tracing its development through his earlier writings to its explication in *Politics of Nature*. We then review two of Kant's critical pieces on the role and scope of higher education: his early essay "An Answer to the Question: What Is Enlightenment?" and his later and more controversial manuscript *Conflict of the Faculties*. Our analysis contextualizes Kant's call for the separation of public and private duty in light of the snarly religious and political field of late eighteenth-century Germany. Then, we detail contemporary politics' increasing encroachment upon curriculum and funding across all levels of education. While contemporary scholars might not face the same "unpleasant measures" that Kant did, there are clear risks associated with reintegrating academic labor into the public sphere. However, despite these risks, academics must commit themselves to political action. Academics cannot remain idle; they must act before it is too late.

We close by offering strategies and tactics for instituting Latour's nonmodern constitution. As a strategy, we present the University of South Florida's recently approved Patel College of Global Sustainability, an interdisciplinary college dedicated to increasing scientific knowledge's impact in the public sphere. The Patel College's guidelines for tenure and promotion soften the importance of disciplinary knowledge and insist upon interdisciplinary and civic participation for tenure. Institutionally strategic initiatives such as this one take time. In the meantime, while more universities develop these kinds of interdisciplinary, public initiatives, we offer the example of how Meredith and her class used Twitter to participate in the debate surrounding the creation of Florida's twelfth public university, Florida Polytechnic. We argue that social media, such as Twitter, afford tactical methods to interrupt political encroachments on academic autonomy and power. Both of these examples demonstrate how rhetoric and composition is well poised to enact Latour's project to reintegrate academics back into civic life.

## Latour's Call to Arms

In "Irreductions" Latour indicts academics for desiring an "escape from politics. . . . We would like there to be somewhere, a way of knowing and convincing which differs from compromise and tinkering: a way of knowing that does not depend upon a gathering of chance, impulse, and habit" (215). In *We Have Never Been Modern*, Latour identifies Modernity's desire for purification, a preference for abstraction that led it to divide knowledge into discrete, autonomous disciplines, each with its own bounded purview. We have never been modern precisely because we have never lived in such an abstracted world. The real world is a collection of "hybrids," material and cultural combinations that reject the fundamental binaries of modern epistemology and ontology (nature/culture, subject/object. human/object, cause/effect, and so on). Below, we trace this dividing back to Kant's strategic solution to the conflict of the faculties, which is the tension between political power and academic labor. Here, we emphasize the extent to which this epistemological division underwrites the institutional framework in which contemporary academics research, teach, publish, and administer. While *we* might have never been modern, *academics* continue to work modern every day.

*Pandora's Hope* emphasizes the need for academics, scientists, in particular, to reintegrate themselves back into politics, to replace the modern desire for purification of knowledge with a nonmodern appreciation for the noisy yet essential cooperation of politics. Latour argues that "if scientists want to bridge the two-culture divide for good, they will have to get used to a lot of noise and, yes, more than a little bit of nonsense" (17). He advocates in favor of working with (rather than dictating to) the body politic. Though scientists are the focus of *Pandora's Hope*, they are not Latour's only target. In his essay "Why Has Critique Run Out of Steam?" published the same year as *Pandora's Hope*, Latour took aim at humanists, questioning their dedication to established critical methods despite their questionable impact on politics or society.[1]

In *Politics of Nature* Latour advocates for a new politics dedicated to "the progressive composition of a common world" shared by humans and nonhumans in which each are given equal voice. Latour reiterates that academics will have to sacrifice the epistemological purity of the lab or office for the noisy, messy, cantankerous and at times irrational clamor of what Kenneth Burke so famously identifies as our "human barnyard" (23).[2] We argue that shifting to a nonmodern constitution and returning academics to the agonistic, political sphere require more than the sacrifice of epistemological purity. They require a radical transformation of how we conceptualize our work, organize ourselves, and credential our professionals. As currently constituted, the tenure process, our chief concern in this chapter, is dominated by disciplinarity. A candidate for tenure must demonstrate affiliation through proper publication in field-specific journals. Further, tenure cases are evaluated by other established, in-field experts. Latour's ambitious political ecology requires academics invest themselves less in specialized circles and more in the composition of one common, public sphere. A Latourian university would be wary of the esoteric. Tenure cases would be vetted by extradisciplinary participants. A successful candidate for tenure would demonstrate civic relevance and publish across disciplinary lines. In this next section, we explicate the extent to which the academy's Kantian heritage impedes Latour's vision.

## Kant's "Public" Concession

On its surface, Kant's 1784 essay "An Answer to the Question: What Is Enlightenment?" is a call for self-reliance. Kant implores the educated to throw off the twin yokes of laziness and cowardice that shackle mankind. Kant charges that governments often made their domestic animals stupid and carefully prevented these placid creatures from daring to take even one step out of the leading strings of the cart to which they are tethered, they show them the danger that threatens them if they attempt to proceed on their own. (58–59)

Beneath this revolutionary rhetoric, however, there is a cautious appeal to Frederick the Great, the tolerant king of the Prussian states who supported the growth of the Enlightenment. Kant appeals to Frederick's tolerance while cognizant of the threat that reason might pose to regal political power. As a result, Kant sophistically frames two different uses of reason: public and private. This distinction, while it sanctions intellectual research, also expatriates intellectuals from the political agora. They are left to themselves in a transcendental conversation of (hu)mankind beyond the pale of worldly concerns. The resonances between Kant's modern scholar and Plato's Socrates, who casts off mere human politics at the conclusion of the Gorgias dialogue, the Socrates Latour condemns, should not go unnoticed here. However, it is important to emphasize the historic, contextual factors that led Kant to endorse this distinction—to tear academics from entering into agonistic struggles or claiming political power.

Kant identifies the duties prescribed to citizens under the laws of the state as private reason. Scholarly work located within disciplinary boundaries constitutes a public use of reason. This distinction between public and private, however, comes after Kant glowingly acknowledged Frederick's mandate: "*Argue*, as much as you want about whatever you want, *but obey!*" (133; original emphasis). Kant calls for the primacy of the abstract, theoretical realm as a sober and sophistic response to the harsh political realities of the late eighteenth and early nineteenth centuries. Writing under the auspices of the "liberal" Frederick the Great, Kant felt optimistic that the government might sanction and support the development of reason and knowledge *if* scholars agreed to provide the government complete autonomy over what knowledge reached the people. Any such optimism, however, was quickly crushed once Frederick's successor, Frederick William II, took the throne. Unlike his predecessor, Frederick William II was a staunch religious conservative. He quickly appointed people to power who were, to put it gently, deeply suspicious of the Enlightenment (Gregor). *Conflict of the Faculties* reflects Kant's struggles to publish during Frederick William's reign. Kant's preface documents how his treatise *Religion within the Limits of Mere Reason* earned him a letter from Johann Christoph Woellner, Frederick's minister of justice and head of Germany's departments of church and schools. The letter urges Kant to submit his energies to his majesty's "paternal purpose" and concluded with a warning that "failing this, you must expect unpleasant measures for your continuing obstinacy" (*Conflict of the Faculties* 11). One hardly has to strain the imagination to wonder what comprised unpleasant measures in late eighteenth-century Germany.

After he challenged the authenticity of the charges, Kant ultimately conceded not to publish during Frederick William II's lifetime. What is significant here are the grounds on which his defense rests.

> Again, as a *teacher of the people*—in my writings and particularly in my book *Religion Within the Limits etc.*—I have not in any way offended against the highest paternal purpose, which I know: in other words, I have done no harm to the public *religion of the land*. This is already clear from the fact that the book in question is not at all suitable for the public: to them it is an unintelligible, closed book, only a debate among scholars of the faculty, of which the people take no notice. (*Conflict* 15; original emphasis)[3]

Kant's defense rests on his elitist (Platonic) disdain for the multitude, whom he characterizes as lazy, thoughtless, incompetent, ignorant animals. In *Conflict of the Faculties*, Kant contends, "The people want to be *led*, that is (as demagogues say), they want to be *duped*" (51; original emphasis).

In *Conflict*, Kant doubles down on the distinction between private and public reason by introducing a distinction between "lower" and "higher" faculty. Lower faculty, such as the philosophy faculty, argues only with each other and reports their findings directly to the higher faculty. The higher faculty, composed exclusively of three disciplines, theology, law, and medicine, are responsible for judiciously disseminating the findings of the lower faculty to the general public. This movement creates a political choke point in that the higher faculty act as the agents of the government: hence, all research dissemination is government sanctioned. In exchange, Kant argues for the lower faculty to have complete autonomy over the course of their research.

Of course, Kant's promise that the public will take no notice of academic research is built on a contemporary impossibility. Today's literacy rates and social/new media exponentially amplify the rate with which knowledge spreads. However, there are more pressing questions to consider. Where, in the contemporary university, is the agency responsible for reporting scholarly findings to the government? Where, in government, is the authoritarian power necessary to act upon these findings? Latour's nonmodern constitution seeks to answer these questions by increasing the impact academics have on the political process. Latour's vision requires that all academics in the lower faculty participate in disseminating research: faculty in the contemporary institution must become an amalgam of Kant's higher and lower orders. In section 5, we document how the University of South Florida's (USF) recently developed Patel College of Global Sustainability addresses these questions by insisting upon integration and application as core components of a tenure candidate's creative and scholarly endeavors. First, however, we highlight the exigency for abandoning the modern contract and reforming the institution by documenting the extent to which contemporary conservative politics has impinged upon the territory of Kant's lower faculty.

## A Treaty Broken

One might argue that academics should remain committed to knowledge for knowledge's sake and maintain the Kantian contract. After all, what expertise do academics have that encourages or even permits them to interfere in the realm of politics (with the exception of a few political science scholars and historians)? But this hesitancy fails to acknowledge the increasing extent to which politics encroaches upon academics. This section documents but a small sample of recent encroachments on knowledge making in an effort to stress that academics must push past inertia and even discomfort to adopt Latour's nonmodern proposition if they wish to continue making some kinds of knowledge at all.

The dissolution of the Kant's contract puts many contemporary disciplines at political risk, but it seems the humanities are in a particularly vulnerable position nationwide. In his "Open Letter to the People of Purdue," Mitchell E. Daniels Jr., Republican, former Indiana governor, and Purdue University president since 2013, condemned professors for "spending too much time 'writing papers for each other,' researching abstruse topics of no real utility and no real incremental contribution to human knowledge or understanding." Our most generous interpretation of Daniels's comments would suggest that he shares Latour's goal to reprioritize the audience for academic work from each other (disciplinarity) to the public sphere.[4] More likely, his letter is just another condemnation of the humanities, albeit more subtle and implicit. A less subtle instance would be the 2012 Texas Republican Party platform's direct objection to teaching critical thinking, a practice they see as "challenging the student's fixed beliefs and undermining parental authority." The Lone Star state has inordinate influence over education in the United States; textbook publishers, in pursuit of the state's tremendous market share, often tailor their nationally distributed materials in response to Texas's curricular guidelines. As Gail Collins explains, curricular changes approved in Texas in March 2010 are particularly troubling. These approved changes include minimizing the historic importance of Thomas Jefferson and his personal convictions toward rejecting the First Amendment's separation of church and state (McKinley). Beyond the accuracy of these arguably appalling changes, what should concern academics is who is making them: "There were no historians, sociologists or economists consulted at the meetings" (McKinley). Two hundred–plus years later, Kant's lower faculty is no longer consulted; the curriculum was authorized by the Texas State Board of Education, a fifteen-member panel of elected officials, and every vote on every amendment followed straight party lines (ten Republicans, five Democrats).

In our home state, Governor Rick Scott (R) and the Florida state legislature have cultivated a climate that is hostile to higher education, in general, and the humanities, in particular. While Daniels subtly avoided naming names, leaving readers to infer which disciplines he found irrelevant, Scott took an even less subtle approach than the Texans. Scott told radio host Marc Benier.

> We don't need a lot more anthropologists in the state. It's a great degree if people want to get it, but we don't need them here. I want to spend our dollars giving people science, technology, engineering, and math degrees. That's what our kids need to focus *all* their time and attention on, those types of degrees, so when they get out of school, they can get a job. (Lende; emphasis added)[5]

In December 2012, Scott further marginalized the humanities when he announced his plan to steer college students towards STEM (science, technology, engineering, and mathematics) disciplines by freezing tuition for "job-friendly" majors like engineering (Travis). Those disciplines that emphasize critical thinking and provide no "real" benefit to human knowledge would become more expensive. It's a counterintuitive move given the lower projected incomes for those students majoring in history, psychology, and so on. But counterintuitive moves seem to be the order of the day when it comes to Florida, the state legislature, and the university system (more on that later).[6]

Scott has also proposed a "10k bachelor's degree challenge," a move that feeds STEM education initiatives, again at the expense of the humanities. On its surface, Scott's proposal reads like an egalitarian one. A similar initiative has led to the Texas Science Scholar Program. This program targets top high school juniors, through dual enrollment that ensures little, if any, exposure to humanities classes (Hamilton) and requires students to major in chemistry, computer science, geology, information systems, or mathematics. Only the very best students are eligible to participate, though, so the cheapest degree may be out of reach for those who need it most (Seligman; Hamilton). These examples testify to the exigency in which academics must acknowledge Latour's call.

The modern university never cashed in on academics' potential to participate in the civic sphere. The modern constitution, which also underwrites the university, was never ideal. But if left alone, scholars could toil away indefinitely. These contemporary intrusions of conservative politics into academia demonstrate that scholars are no longer alone. Academics must engage. As the following two sections demonstrate, rhetoric and composition is well situated to help spur this engagement. We look to our own place of employment, the University of South Florida, to present both a strategic and tactical means for moving toward a nonmodern university.

## Patel College of Global Sustainability as Strategy

The proposal for the Patel College of Global Sustainability (PCGS), USF's newest academic unit, was presented to the University of South Florida faculty senate for approval on November 14, 2012. Written by Lautorian Carl G. Herndl, the proposal's introduction stressed the extent to which contemporary problems are no longer the purview of any single discipline. Rather, responding to the challenges of globalization and urbanization requires coordinated, interdisciplinary partnership, not only between academic disciplines but also among "universities, NGO's, governments, and international companies" (Herndl 1). The proposal stresses that universities were not designed to handle interdisciplinary challenges, arguing that the original Kantian structure of the university now constrains future progress. Herndl insists, "If sustainable urban development does not stop at the city limits, it does not stop at narrow disciplinary limits either" (6). This means, of course, that the knowledge PCGS faculty produce will not reflect disciplinary boundaries either, creating challenges to traditional measures for tenure and promotion. In addressing these challenges, Herndl and the PCGS opened avenues for academics to invest themselves in political (in addition to interdisciplinary) modes of research and communication.

Anticipating the tenure and promotion challenges such a unique approach presents, the PCSG Evaluation, Tenure, and Promotion Guidelines identify three familiar categories for evaluation: scholarly and creative activity, teaching, and service.[7] However, scholarly and creative activity, the most heavily weighted category, deviates from conventional form by breaking into three parts: integration, discovery, and application. We argue that two of these parts, integration and application, move toward a nonmodern university by insisting upon interdisciplinary scholarship and civil/political engagement for promotion and tenure, respectively. Consider the category of integration.

> The scholarship of integration typically occurs at the boundary of disciplines or in intellectual spaces where multiple disciplines converge. Integration places new knowledge in meaningful context, interprets new discovery in broad or non-traditional frames, communicates new knowledge to non-specialists. [. . .] While this work often takes the form of academic publication in refereed journals, edited collections and monographs, it can also occur in non-academic venues in a variety of media. (Herndl 2)

It is important to highlight the intentional ambiguity here. "Meaningful contexts" cannot be decided in advance; they cannot be calculated according to impact factor. This is a subtle but important challenge to the modern research institution. Herndl and the PCSG bolstered their position by reframing service as well.

> Application: The scholarship of application is typically reduced to the anemic category of "service," usually understood as membership on university committees. A rigorous understanding of application requires that professional practice within or outside the university be directly related to the practitioner's academic expertise, both apply and contribute to knowledge, and address the serious challenges of sustainability in local, national, and international communities. Application enacts the value of useful knowledge that can be used to make a difference in the lives of individuals and communities. (2)

Clearly, the PCGS is dedicated to the public sphere *and* challenged traditional disciplinarity. Tenure and promotion in the PCGS *require* that a candidate's scholarship demonstrate interdisciplinary or transdisciplinary significance. In their public, nonmodern university, visibility becomes a critical ground for promotion.

Perhaps unsurprising to those familiar with academic institutional bureaucracy, the Patel College received some fierce opposition from USF's faculty senate. However, the opposition failed to recognize the truly radical challenge the Patel College presents to one of the (modern) university's most cherished foundations: the disciplinary basis for tenure and promotion. Furthermore, the ambiguity in the guidelines surrounding tenure and promotion for the Patel College allows administrators to move tenure and promotion increasingly toward civic projects rather than traditional research. USF's faculty senate simply could not see beyond the strain PCGS might put on an already limited pool of resources. Their shortsightedness is somewhat understandable, though, given the budget crisis that has hobbled higher education in Florida.

## Twitter as Tactic: The Budget Cuts Are Too Damn High

Consider the controversy surrounding the creation of the state's twelfth public university, Florida Polytechnic University, formerly USF's satellite campus in Lakeland, Florida. Serving somewhere between sixteen hundred and forty-eight hundred students—depending on who's counting—this unlikely site found itself at the center of a budget battle that made international news.[8] Our participation in the controversy surrounding Florida Polytechnic University illustrates social media's potential to aid academics in enacting the "public scholar" called for by Latour's nonmodern constitution.

State senator J. D. Alexander, Republican, as the chair of the Budget Committee and Joint Legislative Budget Commission, exerted considerable influence over economic flows in state politics well before he launched his campaign to fund the creation of Florida's twelfth state university. Alexander's proposal to divert more than $30 million in funds for this purpose came after five years of catastrophic cuts to the eleven extant Florida universities, cuts that brought about a 26 percent reduction in state spending per student. Almost immediately after taking office, Scott delivered on his campaign promises to keep the state university system in his crosshairs, cutting another $300 million in 2011 alone (Alvarez, "Florida Set"). With Scott's support, Alexander's audacious budget proposal would launch Florida Polytechnic, Alexander's legacy project, before the senator stepped down due to term limits. In keeping with the trends we previously identified, this proposed university would focus on STEM education, diverting more resources and students away from the humanities.

There is some dispute as to whether Alexander stands to personally benefit from Florida Polytechnic's creation, as he had from the creation of Florida Gulf Coast University decades earlier. In the early 1990s, Alexander's family donated the land on which Florida Gulf Coast University was ultimately built, making millions selling surrounding property for hotels, restaurants, and other businesses (Hundley and Wilmath, "USF Lakeland," "USF Poly"). Alexander claimed to own "no property closer than 10 miles away" from USF Polytechnic

(Hundley and Wilmath, "USF Poly"). However, issues of ownership are made murky by the complexity of Alexander's vast familial holdings that date all the way back to his grandfather, citrus magnate Ben Hill Griffin Jr. Alexander may or may not have positioned himself for considerable, financial gains from Florida Polytechnic, but he definitely did his best to ensure that the University of South Florida had the most to lose. Senator Alexander's budget proposal to fund Florida Polytechnic impacted USF disproportionately by slashing its budget by 58 percent, the largest cut to any of the eleven in-state universities already operating with skeleton crews fighting over meager rations. This move was openly discussed by the press as retaliation for USF's hesitation to quickly surrender the Lakeland campus (Alvarez, "Florida Higher").

As news of the proposed cuts spread, Marc took to his blog, "Insignificant Wrangler," and crafted a thoughtful response to the budget proposal. He linked to press coverage and the university's official response. He suggested the possibility that the 58 percent figure might be inflated to make a lesser but still substantial cut look like a compromise down the road. Marc's roughly five-hundred-word post traveled a familiar circuit that included Facebook friends, colleagues, graduate students, and a few random readers. It drew one comment.

Meredith took her opposition to Twitter. Meredith (@Meredothra) had tweeted roughly five hundred times before the Lakeland controversy, a very casual engagement compared to her Facebook presence. She remained largely indifferent to the platform until a (then) recent tweet brought about in less than fifteen minutes what several transatlantic phone calls and e-mails over the course of weeks could not: customer service. The day the budget news broke happened to be the same day Meredith met with her students for a graduate seminar in professional and technical communication theory. She and her graduate students spent an impromptu class session off script, crafting pointed tweets and drawing up various memes hashtagged "#saveUSF," a label that eventually came to define the crisis on Twitter and in the press.

Meredith and her class retweeted press coverage from the university newspaper and the local press until a graduate student suggested we hail journalists and news sources directly to encourage coverage, for example, "@chronicle: Looking forward to your response re: cutting funding to #USF. Would like to know your position on the proposed cuts." Colleagues from other universities were quick to reply, responses ranging from outrage, as @sophist_monster tweeted to @Meredothra, "This shit is crazy! I'm raising an army of Jesuits and marching due south tomorrow!" to curiosity, as @MichaelPennell1 asked of @Meredothra, "Are you to blame for blitz of USF-related activity in my feed?!" Locals, including Meredith and her graduate students, galvanized their resistance, encouraging each other through retweets and calls to action, such as from Meredith: @Meredothra, "Tweet. Write your reps. Call your parents. Protect public education and the 3rd largest employer in Tampa #SaveUSF." Public officials were praised and damned in turn as they claimed their turf and staked their positions.

It was a lively class meeting from the get-go, but it really picked up speed once the class began making memes distributed via Twitter. @ParkeDixon used the meme generator http://cheezburger.com/ to tweak a classic (see fig. 4.1). @LauraAHennessey used http://www.quickmeme.com/ to play on the "Embarrassed Walrus at School" trope (see fig. 4.2).

Meredith declared that budget cuts were "too damn high!" (see fig. 4.3).

It would be impossible, of course, to concretely demonstrate that the activities of Meredith and her graduate students directly influenced mainstream media coverage or that they even originated the #saveUSF hashtag, as it spread quickly and widely. But we can demonstrate that Meredith's and her students' very public participation in the debate traveled a much different path than Marc's blog post. Blogs and tweets are both inherently public rhetorics. And

*Figure 4.1. @ParkeDixon: I can haz bugit bak? #saveUSF.* Cheezburger. http://t.co/bE6JxDPW, http://t.co/bE6JxDPW.

*Figure 4.2. @LauraAHennessey: I WANTS MY BUGIT BAK! #SAVEUSF.* http://t.co/H08AUKKK. @LauraAHennessey used http://www.quickmeme.com/to play on the "Embarrassed Walrus at School" trope.

blog posts can be shared easily enough through links posted to Facebook, Twitter, or another online space. As microrhetorics, however, tweets have the added advantage of built-in portability; the message itself does the traveling. The movement of the #SaveUSF tweets and memes embodies the hypercirculatory nature of writing Jenny Rice and others have cited in their calls for a closer examination of rhetorical ecologies.

The next day, Marc made his perfunctory angry phone call to an elected official and was summarily thanked for his input. So perfunctory, in fact, that he can no longer recall the name of the official he attempted to contact. Meredith also made calls to elected officials, most memorably to Republican state

*Figure 4.3. Budget cuts are too damn high! #saveUSF.* Cheezburger. http://t.co/t2iCKWbo.

senator Jim Norman to thank him for his very public opposition to Alexander's budget. Meredith introduced herself to the receptionist and was immediately transferred to Norman's aide. He startled Meredith by revealing that Norman's office had been following her Twitterstream (unofficially) for the last few days. Meredith admitted to the aide that she was a registered member of the other party. Once again, the aide startled Meredith by adding, "Oh, we looked you up days ago. We know." Recalling our comments on potential transformations to tenure, here is a testament not only to academics' increased ability to impact political process but also the necessity of shielding them from political retribution. Becoming political activists will *require* political protection.

The #saveUSF campaign may have contributed to the eventual 25 percent reduction to the original proposed 58 percent cut. It may not have. We still wonder if a 33 percent cut was the goal all along and if the higher figure was initially put forth to make the actual desired cut seem more palatable. Once again, USF limped away hemorrhaging. And in July 2012, Florida Polytechnic was signed into law. We won neither the battle nor the war.

This anecdote is hopeful, though, in that it demonstrates how new communications technologies can extend rhetoric and composition's reach beyond its traditional boundaries, our closed circles of journals, colleagues, and friends. By tapping into a technology her students already embraced enthusiastically,

Meredith opened up new paths for critical disobedience. To the extent that technologies, such as blogs and tweets, violate the Kantian contract, they provide a possibility for realizing the Latourian university: a university that leverages all available means of persuasion to connect intellectual work to civic duty and political decision making. Combined with the Patel College of Global Sustainability's inclusion of integration and application in tenure requirements, this story shows how smaller changes in daily practice could incrementally build a nonmodern university—one in which Meredith's accomplishments would count for more than just anecdotal evidence in an academic chapter but as grounds for tenure and promotion.

## Notes

1. The essay refined Latour's aggressively pejorative read of postmodernism in *We Have Never Been Modern*. In short, we argue that Latour's reading of postmodern theory is reductively productive (see Santos, "Uncrossing God").

2. Latour would likely add that the barnyard is stuffed full of nonhumans, too, even if we have to labor to translate their protestations.

3. Kant reiterates this position in his discussion of conflict between the philosophy and theology faculty.

> The higher faculties, in other words, must answer to the government only for the instruction and information they give their businessmen to expound to the public; for these circulate among the people as a civil community and, because they could impair the government's influence over it, are subject to sanction. On the other hand, the teachings and views that the faculties, as theorists, have to settle with one another are directed to a different kind of public—a learned community devoted to the sciences; and since the people are resigned to understanding nothing about this, the government does not see fit to intervene in scholarly discussions. (*Conflict* 57)

4. The irony should be noted here: just as conservatives were able to appropriate critiques of scientific certitude in an effort to squelch concern over global warming, academics should be careful to track how contemporary critiques of the university are repurposed in the public sphere.

5. These comments were a follow-up to previous statements offered at a Northwest Business Association luncheon, at which Scott asked, "Do you want to use your tax money to educate more people who can't get jobs in anthropology? I don't" (qtd. in Deslatte).

6. The ultimate irony here is that the employment statistics upon which Scott makes his case for the inutility of anthropology were likely compiled by sociologists and cultural anthropologists. As Lende documents, Scott's comments incited quite a storm of responses defending anthropology's social and economic benefits.

7. We thank Carl G. Herndl for generously sharing with us an early draft of these guidelines.

8. Marshall Goodman, USF Poly's regional chancellor, has vacillated between claiming more than four thousand and "approximately" forty-eight hundred students at the Lakeland campus, depending on his audience, reserving higher figures for potential investors. However, for the 2010–11 academic year, less than seventeen hundred students reported USF Poly as their home (Hundley and Wilmath, "USF Lakeland).

## Works Cited


Alexander, Kate. "Social Studies Standards Win Early Board Approval." *Statesman.com.* 12 Mar. 2010. Web. 9 Apr. 2013.

Alvarez, Lizette. "Florida Higher Education May Face Big Budget Cuts." *New York Times.* 6 Mar. 2012. Web. 9 Apr. 2013.

———. "Florida Set for New Cut in Spending on Colleges." *New York Times.* 20 Feb. 2012. Web. 9 Apr. 2013.

Burke, Kenneth. *A Rhetoric of Motives.* Berkeley: U of California P, 1969. Print.

Collins, Gail. *As Texas Goes . . . : How the Lone Star State Hijacked the American Agenda.* New York: Liverlight, 2012. Print.

Daniels, Mitchell E., Jr. "An Open Letter to the People of Purdue." *Purdue University Office of the President.* 18 Jan. 2013. Web. 9 Apr. 2013.

de Certeau, Michel. *The Practice of Everyday Life.* Berkeley: U of California P, 1984. Print.

Deslatte, Aaron. "Scott: Anthropology and Journalism Don't Pay, and Neither Do Capes." *Orlando Sentinel.* 11 Oct. 2011. Web. 9 Apr. 2013.

Florida Blue Ribbon Task Force. "Florida Blue Ribbon Task Force on State Higher Education Reform." *Florida Gulf Coast University.* 6 Nov. 2012. Web. 9 Apr. 2013. < http://www.fgcu.edu/FacultySenate/files/2-22-2013_Resolution_Supplement_3.pdf>.

Gregor, Mary. Introduction. *The Conflict of the Faculties.* By Immanuel Kant. Lincoln: U of Nebraska P, 1992.

Hamilton, Reeve. "Texas State University System Has $10,000 Degree Plan." *Texas Tribune.* 12 Jul. 2012. Web. 9 Apr. 2013.

Herndl, Carl G. *Proposal for Patel College of Global Sustainability*. November 2012. TS. Submitted to the USF Faculty Senate.

Hundley, Kris, and Wilmath, Kim. "USF Lakeland Campus' Independence Has a Champion in State Sen. J. D. Alexander." *Tampa Bay Times*. 11 Sep. 2011. Web. 9 Apr. 2013.

———."USF Poly Could Be State Sen. J. D. Alexander's Legacy College." *Tampa Bay Times*. 18 Sep. 2011. Web. 9 Apr. 2013.

Kant, Immanuel. "An Answer to the Question: What Is Enlightenment?" Trans. and ed. James Schmidt. *What Is Enlightenment?* Berkeley: U of California P, 1996. 130–143. Print.

———. *The Conflict of the Faculties (der Streit Fakultäten)*. Trans. Mary J. Gregor. Lincoln: U of Nebraska P, 1979. Print.

Latour, Bruno. *Pandora's Hope: Essays on the Reality of Science Studies*. Cambridge: Harvard UP, 1999. Print.

———. *Politics of Nature: How to Bring the Sciences into Democracy*. Trans. Catherine Porter. Cambridge: Harvard UP, 2004. Print.

———. *We Have Never Been Modern*. Trans. Catherine Porter. Cambridge: Harvard UP, 1993. Print.

———. "Why Has Critique Run Out of Steam? From Matters of Fact to Matters of Concern." *Critical Inquiry* 30.2 (2004): 225–248. Print.

Lende, Daniel. "Florida Governor: Anthropology Not Needed Here." PLOS blogs. *Public Library of Science*. 11 Oct. 2011. Web. 9 Apr. 2013.

Lutz, Frank. *Words That Work: It's Not What You Say, It's What People Hear*. New York: Hyperion, 2007. Print.

Lyotard, Jean-François. *The Postmodern Condition: A Report on Knowledge*. Trans. Geoff Bennington and Brian Massumi. Minneapolis: U of Minnesota P, 1984. Print.

McKinley, James C., Jr. "Texas Conservatives Win Curriculum Change." *New York Times*. 12 Mar. 2010. Web. 9 Apr. 2013.

Readings, Bill. *The University in Ruins*. Cambridge: Harvard UP, 1996. Print.

Rice, Jenny. "The Ecology of the Question: Reading Austin's Public Housing Debates, 1937–1938." *Ecology, Writing Theory, and New Media: Writing Ecology*. Ed. Sid Dobrin. New York: Routledge, 2012. 180–194. Print.

Santos, Marc C. "Help Stop Crippling Budget Cuts." *Blogspot.com*. 14 Feb. 2012. Web. <http://insignificantwrangler.blogspot.com/2012/02/help-stop-crippling-budget-cuts.html>.

———. "Uncrossing God: How Levinas's Ethics Might Contribute to Latour's Politics." Forthcoming.

Scharrer, Gary. "Conservative-Backed Curriculum OK'd for History Classes." *Houston Chronicle*. 12 Mar. 2010. Web. 9 Apr. 2013.

Seligman, Lara. "Did Texas Just Discover the Cure for Sky-High Tuition?" *Atlantic*. 26 Nov. 2012. Web. 9 Apr. 2013.

Strauss, Valerie. "Texas GOP Rejects Critical Thinking Skills. Really." *Washington Post*. 9 Jul. 2012. Web. 9 Apr. 2013.

Stutz, Terrence. "Texas Education Board Rejects In-depth Study of First Amendment." *Dallas Morning News*. 12 Mar. 2012. Web. 9 Apr. 2013.

Texas Education Agency. "SBOE Members." *Texas Education Agency*. 4 Jan. 2012. Web. 9 April 2013.

"The Texas Science Scholar Program." *University of Texas of the Permian Basin*. 2012. Web. 9 Apr. 2013. <http://www.utpb.edu/audience/future-students/the-texas-science-scholar-program>.

"Texas Textbook Massacre: 'Ultraconservatives' Approve Radical Changes to State Education Curriculum." *Huffington Post Politics*. 13 May 2013. Web. 9 Apr. 2013.

Travis, Scott. "College Tuition Should Vary by Degree, Florida State Task Force Says." *Sun Sentinel*. 25 Oct. 2012. Web. 9 Apr. 2013.

2012 Republican Party of Texas Report of Platform Committee. *Republican Party of Texas*. 2012. Web. 9 Apr. 2013.

# Part Two. **Conceiving Assemblages**

# 5. Rhetoric's Nonmodern Constitution: *Techne*, *Phusis*, and the Production of Hybrids

Scot Barnett, *Indiana University Bloomington*

> In following the pump, do we have to pretend that everything is rhetorical, or that everything is natural, or that everything is socially constructed, or that everything is stamped and stocked? Do we have to suppose that the same pump is in its essence sometimes an object, sometimes a social bond, and sometimes discourse? Or that it is a bit of each?
>
> —Bruno Latour, *We Have Never Been Modern*

Despite his suggestive nods to both "rhetoric" and "composition," Bruno Latour can seem an odd ally for a field beginning to consider the place of nonhumans in its histories and theories of rhetoric. As his account of Boyle's air pump reveals, Latour frequently aligns rhetoric with discourse and postmodern theories of language that privilege human symbolic action in the construction of social realities. While we may and, indeed, should challenge Latour on this narrow understanding of rhetoric, I, nevertheless, want to suggest that we take the spirit of his concerns seriously, particularly at this pivotal moment in our field's history in which we're debating what it could mean—and what it might look like—to involve nonhumans in our thinking about rhetoric. For all of our differences with Latour, we increasingly find ourselves having to answer the same question Latour puts to rhetoric—to what extent can a field that has historically defined itself in terms of human language and expression adequately account for the persuasive contributions of nonhuman agents?

While there are many ways to answer this question, there is growing consensus that nonhumans challenge traditional discursive understandings of rhetoric and, thus, call for new ways of thinking about rhetoric. As Debra Hawhee suggests in a forum on animal rhetorics,

> nonhuman animals invite those of us (human ones) interested in questions of rhetoric and communication to suspend the habituated emphasis on verbal language and consciousness. Animals instead offer models of rhetorical behavior and interaction that are physical, even instinctual, but perhaps no less artful. (83)

For theorists working in the areas of animal and posthuman rhetorics, new materialist rhetorics, and object-oriented rhetorics, the emergence of the nonhuman as a contemporary thematic seems to herald something of a historical crisis for rhetoric. Where in the past we have understood rhetoric as human symbolic action, now, with the arrival of these missing masses of nonhumans, we must think differently about rhetoric going forward. While it is not my intention to spurn such efforts, following Latour I want to explore—and encourage fellow rhetoricians to explore—other methods of accounting for nonhumans *from within the structures of rhetoric's history itself.* Modeled after Latour's historical investigations of scientific artifacts and knowledge, the method I propose does not presume a modern understanding of time that "passes as if it were really abolishing the past behind it" (*Modern* 68). Instead, it approaches the history of rhetoric as a series of nonlinear, "counterrevolutionary" practices that have collected and sorted all relevant actors irrespective of the modern tendency to divide the world up categorically between nature and culture, human and nonhuman, subject and object, and so on.

To demonstrate what a counterrevolutionary analysis of rhetoric stands to offer, I focus on a single moment in rhetoric's history—Aristotle's discussions of *techne* and *phusis*—in which the issue of rhetoric's place in a world of human and nonhuman beings arises as an implicit but, nonetheless, significant point of consideration. Rhetorical theorists have long noted the complex and sometimes contradictory ways in which Aristotle discusses rhetoric and situates it alongside other kinds of knowledge. As I argue in what follows, this "official view" of Aristotelian rhetoric has tended to overemphasize Aristotle's contributions to discursive theories of rhetoric while ignoring the degree to which Aristotle employs techne as a way to flesh out his metaphysical understanding of nature. What we have missed by tending so closely to the social and discursive aspects of classical rhetoric, in other words, is how many ancients and Aristotle, in particular, manage to situate rhetoric within the complex worldview of their time, a worldview that does not always distinguish art from the natural scheme of things. The picture that emerges when we bring Latour's nonmodern view of history to Aristotle's discussions of techne and phusis, then, is one of a highly speculative thinker puzzling over rhetoric's place in a larger universe of natural and artificial things whose actions and interactions make it increasingly difficult to distinguish one kind of being from another. Rather than proceed under the assumption that nonhumans constitute a limit case for rhetoric, I want to encourage us instead to follow Aristotle's and Latour's leads in affirming the nonmodern possibilities that are already at play in our histories and theories of rhetoric, those moments in rhetoric's history where natures and cultures, humans and nonhumans have intertwined in potentially generative ways.

## Modern Time and the Copernican Counterrevolution

For Latour, the modern conception of time is characterized by a series of ruptures and revolutions occurring within an otherwise progressive temporal trajectory. This view of history presupposes a movement away from "primitive" understandings of the world, which often confuse what is natural with what is cultural, toward more "mature" worldviews in which nature and culture are finally distinguishable from one another. "The adjective 'modern' designates a new regime, an acceleration, a rupture, a revolution in time," Latour says (*Modern* 10). This new historical regime makes possible what he calls "the Modern Constitution," a paradoxical logic that enables moderns to distribute power selectively but no less definitively among two distinct ontological zones: Nature and Society. The ability to divide the world in such ways empowers moderns to mobilize Nature and Society in whatever ways they see fit, even if the results are contradictory. Thus, Latour shows, moderns can argue that "Nature is transcendent and surpasses us infinitely" and Society is "our free construction" while claiming that Nature is "our artificial construction in the laboratory" and Society "is transcendent" (32). As long as this "work of purification" remains distinct from the "work of mediation" that produces hybrids (quasi-objects that are neither fully social nor fully natural but some mixture thereof), moderns can go on believing they are unique because of their abilities to keep Nature and Society separate and at arm's length.

Latour's thesis in *We Have Never Been Modern* and in many of the works that follow is that this work of purification is no longer sufficient to hide the hybrids produced by the very constitution that denies their existence. As a result of global environmental, political, scientific, and economic crises, which force us to confront and deal with myriad hybrid actors that are not easily reducible to the modern axes of Nature/Society and Transcendence/ Immanence, the previously distinct works of purification and mediation are becoming increasingly confused. As soon as this happens, as soon as "we direct our attention simultaneously to the work of purification and the work of hybridization, we immediately stop being wholly modern" (11). As a consequence, our past and future begin to change as well: "we become retrospectively aware that the two sets of practices have always already been at work in the historical period that is ending" (11). Once the proliferation of hybrids becomes visible to us, in other words, and once we begin to study in detail how moderns have historically managed to produce hybrids all the while eliminating them from their constitution, we find, in Latour's famous thesis, that *we have never been modern*. No one, in fact, has ever been modern. "Modernity has never begun. There has never been a modern world" (47).

For Latour, the realization that we have never been modern follows both from his observations of current states of affairs and his enduring interest in the history of science. According to Latour, the modern understanding of science is rooted in a particular conception of time and history, one that "suppresses the ins and outs of Nature's objects and presents their sudden emergence as if it were miraculous" (*Modern* 70). From the Enlightenment view of scientific progress to popular notions of science as building on and revising past theories and assumptions, moderns tend to imagine science as a steady progression from "self-imposed immaturity" to the free public use of reason, as Kant put it centuries ago. In his analysis of Boyle's air pump, for example, Latour illustrates how this exemplar of modern scientific thought, in fact, relied upon and produced a number of hybrids, from scientists who constructed knowledge in the laboratory but also "declare[d] that they themselves are not speaking; rather, facts speak for themselves" to Nature itself, which became both constructed and transcendent as a result of Boyle's experiments (29). If the pump constituted a revolution, then, it was a revolution in our ability to "mobilize Nature, objectify the social, and feel the spiritual presence of God, even while firmly maintaining that Nature escapes us, that Society is our own work, and that God no longer intervenes" (34). As we have seen, however, such revolutionary conceptions of history have the tendency to render "the work of mediation that assembles hybrids invisible, unthinkable, unrepresentable" (34). As Latour suggests of Boyle's invention, its apparent "cohesiveness" "is not sufficient to allow a clean break with the past. A whole supplementary work of sorting out, cleaning up and dividing up is required to obtain the impression of a modernization that goes in step with time" (72). Revolutions, those dramatic ruptures within the progressive march of historical time, are, thus, the "rather neat" solution "moderns have imagined to explain the emergence of the hybrids that their Constitution simultaneously forbids and allows, and in order to avoid another monster: the notion that things themselves have a history" (70).

The history of rhetoric has its own celebrated revolutions, of course, from the flourishing of rhetoric in antiquity, which brought into being more complex ways of producing and theorizing language, to the modern revival of the classical canon of invention following its separation from rhetoric in the wake of Ramist and Enlightenment emphases on logic and perspicuity. Indeed, as anyone who has taught a "history of rhetoric" seminar knows, it's quite easy—and quite tempting, I must admit—to tell rhetoric's history as a story of progress, even if progress has meant, at times, that we have had to go two steps backward into order to eventually (and inevitably) push ahead into maturity. But as Latour would argue, this is a particularly modern fable rooted in an asymmetry not only between Nature and Society but between past and future as well: "*The past was the confusion of things and men; the future is what will no longer confuse them*" (*Modern* 71; original emphasis).

Ironically, the modern historical progression from confusion/immaturity to enlightenment has not constrained our ability to imagine the possibility of nonhuman rhetorics. If anything, this notion of history actually makes the case for the inclusion of nonhumans that much easier since all the modern rhetorical theorist needs to demonstrate is that the prospect of nonhuman rhetorics constitutes a revolutionary moment in rhetoric's history that will, if properly understood, move the field further along its current path. In this vein, nonhumans simply constitute the next epoch in rhetoric's long story of progress, one that promises to destroy the past behind while charting a future in which we no longer distinguish the symbolic realm of human affairs with the agencies of nonhuman others. While the ends of such efforts may be laudable, the means by which we arrive at this conclusion leaves intact the very logics that were under suspicion in the first place. Thus, Latour's preferred way of challenging the modern constitution and its conception of history is not to argue for one more revolution but instead to undertake the more complicated task of reading historical events differently. "We have never moved either forward or backward," he concludes. All we have ever done is sort elements and actors belonging to different times. Thus, Latour says, "*It is the sorting [of these actors] that makes the times, not the times that make the sorting*" (*Modern* 76; original emphasis). In contrast to Kant's Copernican Revolution, which perfected the model "for modernizing explanations" by making the object revolve around and conform to the subject, Latour calls for "a Copernican counter-revolution" in which "[t]he explanations we seek will indeed obtain Nature and Society, but only as a final outcome, not as a beginning" (79). Nature and Society do revolve but not around one another. Instead, they revolve around "the collective out of which people and things are generated" (79). The historian's task, therefore, becomes one of sorting and collecting rather than breaking and restarting.

## Techne and Phusis: The Official Version

How might these processes of sorting and collecting enable work in rhetorical studies, particularly in histories and theories of rhetoric, which sometimes proceed as if the appearance of the nonhuman marks a decisive historical break within rhetoric itself? Though I believe a Latourian approach to history has much to teach us about the roles nonhumans and hybrids have played throughout rhetoric's long history in the West, for the sake of specificity I focus for the remainder of this chapter on a single moment in the history of rhetoric, Aristotle's conception of techne and its relationship to nature, or phusis. Following Latour's lead, I argue that a close and perhaps speculative reading of Aristotle's understandings of art and nature helps reveal, first, the extent to which the modern way of thinking about rhetoric and history persists today, and, second, how, regardless of our tendency to emphasize the social and discursive innovations within the history of rhetoric, nonhumans and hybrids have been with us from the beginning, informing our efforts to understand this thing we call rhetoric.

Let's begin on the top half of rhetoric's modern constitution, with the work of purification. In *Back to the Rough Ground*, Joseph Dunne identifies two versions of techne available to modern readers of Aristotle's works. The first "official" version can be found in such places as *Nicomachean Ethics* 6.4 and *Metaphysics* 1.1, where Aristotle most clearly attempts to define techne in contrast to other forms of knowledge and domains of being. According to Dunne, these versions of techne represent the categorized and instrumental view that Aristotle inherited from Plato and that has more or less dominated understandings of techne from classical to contemporary times. The alternative or "unofficial" version of techne, on the other hand, paints a much-different picture of techne and its place in Aristotelian metaphysics. Assembled from various references to techne scattered across the corpus, Dunne's unofficial version suggests that for Aristotle, techne was not only a mode of knowledge enabling one to have mastery over nature and artificial materials. It was also an ontological condition of possibility in its own right, one so intertwined with the movements and becomings of phusis that it led Aristotle in several places to propose techne as the means by which phusis comes into presence and into meaning as such.

Before turning to some of these unofficial accounts of techne, however, I first want to examine the official version in more detail, particularly with an eye toward how it has informed readings of techne in Aristotle's thought. As noted above, several of Aristotle's best-known discussions of techne situate it in opposition to other forms of knowing and domains of being. Janet M. Atwill notes that for ancients such as Aristotle techne "is frequently defined against *physis* (nature), *automaton* (spontaneity), and *tyche* (chance)" (70–71). Whereas techne suggests a form of invention concerned with "situations that yield indeterminacies," physis, automaton, and tyche represent absolute externalized forces that enable and constrain invention (70–71). Though there is ample evidence to suggest a more complicated relationship between techne and phusis, as I discuss below, it is, nevertheless, clear in places such as book 6 of the *Nicomachean Ethics* that Aristotle intends to differentiate the two on the basis of their distinct origins. Though techne constitutes one of five intellectual virtues, its *arche* distinguishes it from other kinds of knowledge, such as science (*episteme*), philosophy (*sophia*), intelligence (*nous*), and practical reasoning (*phronesis*). The result of this initial differentiation is an axis that separates intellectual reasoning into two distinct capacities that are differently attuned to the ways certain kinds of beings come into existence as such. On the side of those (natural) beings that are "invariable" and, thus, always the same in their being, Aristotle places episteme, sophia, and nous. And on the other side, with those (human) beings that are variable and, thus, have the potential to be other than they are, Aristotle places techne and phronesis. Thus, for Aristotle the *epistemonikon-logistikon* axis works from the beginning to classify things ontologically so that we can know "the best state of each of these two parts" and respond to each thing in kind.

Insofar as arche implies cause, Aristotle's axis suggests a further distinction among things on the basis of their relation to agency and human agents, in particular. Whereas some things *are* whether human beings act upon them or not, other things come into being as a direct result of human action in the world. Whereas episteme deals with natural "things that are eternal [i.e.]

ungenerated and imperishable (Aristotle, *Nicomachean Ethics* 1139b), techne applies to things whose cause or origin exists outside of itself—in the human maker or craftsperson. Thus, it is techne's immersion in the contingent realm of human affairs that distinguishes it from episteme and sophia (Warnick 304). Unlike *phronesis*, which enables practitioners to "act" responsibly "with regard to the things that are good or bad for man" (*Nicomachean Ethics*1140b), techne refers to a producer's "know-how" to "make" or bring a thing into being. In terms of rhetoric, this means having the knowledge to observe the available means of persuasion and determine how best to deploy those means for a given audience and with a specific end in mind. As with other *technai*, such as shipbuilding and medicine, an effective rhetor must be able to anticipate the desired end of her efforts (a seaworthy ship or a patient's good health, for example) and work methodically toward that end. Technai, thus, require producers to have knowledge of both the general and the particular, of the form a thing must take and the particular actions required in situ to produce that form. The point of emphasis for techne, therefore, is on "the maker" and her reasoned capacity to produce rather than on the thing made (*Nicomachean Ethics* 1140a). And since the affairs of human life are never fixed or eternal, technai such as rhetoric enable human beings to deliberate and take action on uncertain matters because, as Aristotle puts in the *Rhetoric*, "we debate about things that seem capable of admitting two possibilities; for no one debates things incapable of being different either in part or future or present" (1357a).

The division of faculties Aristotle presents in the *Ethics* thus breaks down along two related fronts. On the one hand, Aristotle draws distinctions between the modes of thought based on the specific kinds of beings each reveals, with episteme, sophia, and nous dealing with things that are necessary and invariable and techne and phronesis with those that might be other than they are. At the same time, Aristotle introduces another, though related, distinction based on the agent responsible for each being's existence. In the case of episteme and sophia, which deal primarily with the objects and forces of nature, the arche of a thing lies in the thing itself. An acorn, for example, contains within itself the potential to become a mighty oak tree. This potential, however, does not require an external agent to ensure its actuality; it simply requires the proper conditions and time to be what it is already becoming. A chalice or persuasive speech, on the other hand, *does* require the force of an external agent (e.g., an artist or rhetor) in order to come into being. The boundaries between phusis and techne appear then to be set. For Aristotle, phusis is "a source or cause of being moved and of being at rest in that to which it belongs primarily, in virtue of itself and not in virtue of a concomitant attribute" (*Physics* 192b21–22). In contrast, techne deals exclusively with the artificial object that *does not* have "in itself the source of its own production" (192b28–29; see also Atwill 85). The "official view" thus positions techne in opposition to other domains of being under the assumption that techne is relevant only to those things whose existence can be traced directly back to the invention and intervention of human beings. It is when we align rhetoric with this official view of Aristotelian techne, then, that we arrive at this moment of historical crisis, where rhetoric means primarily a social and discursive power, one that positions the human at the epicenter of rhetorical production and that, out of necessity, leaves nonhumans—those beings that are "indifferent to our quarrels, our ignorances, and the limits of our representations"—on the outside looking in (Latour, *Politics* 14).

## Techne and Phusis: The Production of Hybrids

To be clear, these "official" readings of Aristotle are not in themselves inaccurate or unconvincing. In fact, their problem may be that they have been entirely too convincing, allowing us to accept the idea that Aristotle never cared to involve rhetoric in the metaphysical system he was inventing. My point here is this: if we take Aristotle at his word, that techne is fundamentally opposed to nature, then we are, indeed, modern in Latour's sense of the word. If, however, we begin with a different goal in mind, that is, sorting and collecting the various and contradictory ways Aristotle re/assembles techne and phusis, then we find something else entirely: that we (rhetoricians) have never been modern and that the history of rhetoric has always been about "the multiplication of exceptions that nobody could situate in the regular flow of time" (Latour, *Modern* 73).

If not from the modern work of purification, where, then, should we begin? For starters, we will need to focus on the texts themselves—not just the *Rhetoric* but all of the works in the corpus that discuss, mention, or allude to techne and phusis (see Gross). But we must also go further than the texts to trace the networks of quasi-objects that collectively produced the historical assemblages known as Aristotelian rhetoric and metaphysics. Though Latour sometimes faults him for perpetuating the modern view of history (see, for instance, *Modern* 65–67), Martin Heidegger can help us open a way toward such a nonmodern view of Aristotelian metaphysics. In his essay "On the Essence and Concept of *Phusis* in Aristotle's *Physics B*, I," Heidegger argues that in the Western metaphysical worldview that emerged after the Greeks, the word "nature" (from the Latin *natura*) came to designate a discrete realm lying apart from or in opposition to other, more human pursuits, such as art, history, and spirit (183). While this opposition is not necessarily foreign to the Greeks, Heidegger observes that for modern readers especially there is a temptation to project this notion of nature back into Aristotle's works, as though phusis and "nature" are indeed the same thing for Aristotle. As Heidegger's careful reading of the *Physics* demonstrates, however, for Aristotle, phusis is anything but a place or a specific entity. In fact, it's precisely this confusion about nature—that phusis designates a singular being or substance—that Aristotle calls into question.

So what does Aristotle mean by phusis and techne? According to the official view discussed above, phusis and techne refer to different things or beings that have (or whose existence is owed to) different arche, one human and the other natural. As Heidegger, Dunne, and others note, however, the official view represents only one aspect of Aristotle's thinking about phusis and techne. For all of his attempts to distinguish phusis and techne, there are nearly as many passages where Aristotle rejects these distinctions in order explore alternative ways of thinking about phusis and techne. The results of these speculations suggest that for Aristotle techne and phusis are not distinct at all but are rather intertwined with one another around the larger question that is ultimately at the heart of Aristotle's writings on metaphysics: *what is being, and why are there beings at all instead of nothing* (*Metaphysics* 1028b3–5)?

As Heidegger is at pains to demonstrate, for Aristotle, being (*ousia*) does not refer to any particular being per se but, rather, indicates *the ways in which* beings lie forth and endure *as beings*, the ways beings have for presencing and holding themselves together in presence (Brogan 34). At the heart of Aristotle's understanding of being, therefore, is presencing and movement—the kind of being beings have to change and endure as changeable things. When Aristotle turns his attention to phusis and techne in the *Physics* and the *Metaphysics*, he does so with this understanding of being in mind. Rather than accept the categorical views of art and nature he inherited from Plato, Aristotle, instead, works ontologically from the reality of particular beings in order to understand the horizons that give rise to their beingness as such. As he says in the *Physics*, phusis is being itself, "a lying forth from out of itself" (192b33–39). As we saw above, unlike artifacts whose movedness (*kinesis*) originates from something else, natural beings have "the *archê* of their movedness *not* in another being but in the beings that they themselves are (to the degree that they are these beings)" (Heidegger 193; original emphasis). In Aristotle's metaphysics, then, phusis (and techne as well, as we'll soon see) refers to the presencing of beings through the kinesis that belongs to their nature as beings and not, as is often assumed, to any specific beings or places that happen today to bear the name "nature." "Everything that possesses this kind of origin and ordering 'has' phusis. And all these things *are* (have being) of the type called beingness" (*Phys.* 192b32–93a2; Heidegger, 198). Beings, in other words, *are not* phusis but are rather "from *phusis*" or "in accordance with *phusis*" (see Brogan 49–50), and it's this dynamic that Aristotle is seeking to understand.

In the same way that natural beings are in accordance with phusis, so, too, are artifacts in accordance with techne. This is perhaps a more difficult idea to grasp since in our everyday dealings with things, we tend the focus more on the properties of artifacts—the sturdiness of a wooden bedstead, for instance—rather than on the *way* artifacts *are* in their being, that is, what constitutes their movedness, presencing, and enduring as beings in the world. Early in the second book of the *Physics*, for example, Aristotle offers what on surface seems like a relatively clear rehearsal of the differences between techne and phusis.

> All [natural] things mentioned present a feature in which they differ from things which are *not* constituted by nature. Each of them has *within itself* a principle of motion and of stationariness (in respect of place or of growth and decrease, or by way of alteration). On the other hand, a bed and a coat and anything else of that sort, *qua* receiving these designations—i.e. in so far as they are products of art—have no innate impulse to change. But in so far as they happen to be composed of stone or of earth or of a mixture of the two, they *do* have such an impulse, and just to that extent—which seems to indicate that *nature is a source or cause of being moved and of being at rest in what to which it belongs primarily*, in virtue of itself and not in virtue of a concomitant attribute. (192b12–25; original emphasis)

Here we find the same distinction made elsewhere in the *Physics*, *Metaphysics*, and *Ethics*. A closer look at the passage, however, reveals that Aristotle is attempting at the same time to understand techne and phusis with respect to their comparable ways of movedness and rest. In his reading of this passage, Heidegger notes that the claim made here that artifacts "have no innate impulse to change" contradicts Aristotle's previous accounts of change and rest. According to Aristotle, there is no such thing as "rest" in the sense of not-moving or not-having-been-moved. For Aristotle, all things move and undergo change in some fundamental ways—this is what it means "to be," after all. Thus, Heidegger is left to wonder,

> Are bedsteads and garments, shields and houses moving things? Indeed they are, but usually we encounter them in the kind of movement that typifies things at rest and therefore is hard to perceive. Their "rest" has the character of having-been completed, having-been produced, and, on the basis of *these* determinations, as standing "there" and lying present before us. (192)

We tend to overlook this kind of rest because in our modern way of thinking about being.

> We are addicted to thinking of beings as *objects* and allowing the being of beings to be exhausted in the objectivity of the object. But for Aristotle, the issue here is to show that artifacts *are what* they are and *how* they are precisely in the movedness of production and thus in the rest of having-been produced. (192; original emphasis)

Unlike the inert objects that dominate our modern thinking about things, artificial things in Aristotelian metaphysics *move*—they have their way of being in movedness and rest—to no less a degree than natural beings.

That techne and phusis intertwine with another and, indeed, constitute two of the primary ways we have for understanding being as enduring presence, explains why Aristotle only rarely discusses techne in and of itself. As Dunne observes, individual treatments of techne are rare in Aristotle's writings, appearing mainly in *Nicomachean Ethics* 6.4 and *Metaphysics* 1.1. By far, Aristotle's preferred way of discussing techne is in relation to other topics, such as phusis, change (*genesis*), and life or soul (*psuche*) (Dunne 251). With respect to phusis, Aristotle draws frequently on the more accessible realm of techne to understand the beingness of phusis (Brogan 31; Dunne 336). In book 2 of the *Physics*, for example, where Aristotle raises the topic of potentiality (*dunamis*), we find a more complicated relationship between techne and phusis, one that does not necessarily indicate an equivalence (Aristotle, like Heidegger after him, will never go this far) but rather a shared connection to dunamis, to the capacity of things to be other than they are and work similarly toward some end (*telos*).

> Now intelligent action is for the sake of an end; therefore the nature of things also is so. Thus if a house, e.g., had been a thing made by nature, it would have been made in the same way as it is now by art; and if things made by nature were made also by art, they would come to be in the same way as by nature. Each step then in the series is for the sake of the next; and generally art partly completes what nature cannot bring to a finish,

> and partly imitates her. If, therefore, artificial products are for the sake of an end, so clearly also are natural products. The relation of the later to the earlier terms of the series is the same in both. (199a11–19)

Later in the same chapter, Aristotle offers a second analogy between techne and phusis.

> It is absurd to suppose that purpose is not present because we do not observe the agent deliberating. Art does not deliberate. If the ship-building art were in the wood, it would produce the same result *by nature*. If, therefore, purpose is present in art, it is present also in nature. The best illustration is a doctor doctoring himself: nature is like that. (199b26–30; original emphasis)

The logic of the analogies developed here is quite complex. As Dunne suggests, "there seems to be as much encouragement [in these two passages] to think of technê as naturelike as to think of nature as technical" (337; see also Pender 129). While the two analogies seem intended to clarify distinctions already made between techne and phusis, they actually serve to complicate the relationship to such an extent that it becomes increasingly unclear where techne begins and phusis ends. The first passage begins with Aristotle wondering what might happen if nature itself built a house. At this point, Aristotle seems well on track to keeping the analysis grounded in phusis, specifically in understanding how nature produces beings and toward what ends. By the time he arrives at the passage's concluding syllogism, however, which inverts the direction of imitation so that nature is finally understood in terms of the "for-sake-of-which" characteristic of artificial products, Aristotle has long since lost the focus of the initial proposition, leaving the analogy teetering to the point that it begins to fold back on itself. The resulting chiasmus reaches its highest point in the second analogy, which moves from a relatively clear point about the differing origins of artifacts and natural beings to a conclusion that locates purpose and movement in both phusis and techne.

Furthermore, while the image of a doctor "doctoring himself" works well to illustrate phusis and techne's comparable ways of kinesis, the decision to link a *technites*, such as a doctor to nature, further raises the possibility of techne having within itself its own source of movedness and change. A doctor, after all, can be the source and receiver of his own medical know-how. The analogy, then, suggests two notable turns in Aristotle's thinking about techne. First, it significantly complicates the understanding of techne put forward earlier in the *Physics*. There, Aristotle suggests as well that "a man who is a doctor might cure himself" (192b24). Even as he grants this possibility, however, Aristotle is quick to point out in this earlier passage that the doctor's ability to serve as both patient and doctor shares little in common with nature's ways of movedness and rest, since these capacities "belong" to natural beings "primarily" and "in virtue" of themselves whereas the doctor's techne is only enacted "in virtue of a concomitant attribute" (*Physics* 192b22–23). In other words, the art of medicine may cause a change, whether in the doctor himself or in another person, but it does so only because medical knowledge is an attribute acquired after or in excess of what nature otherwise produces in virtue of itself (*Physics* 192b30–32). When we arrive at the "doctor doctoring himself" analogy later in the same book, however, this distinction between essence and attribute all but disappears. In its place we find the possibility that phusis and techne may, in fact, possess similar sources of kinesis and change and that techne as a result may not be as indebted to the agency of the individual craftsperson as we sometimes think. For Dunne, the implications of Aristotle's analogies are clear: "they encourage us not to be so impressed by the intervention of the *technites* as to suppose that it inaugurates a new realm that is entirely different from *phusis*" (338). By suggesting that a house can be made in the same way as by nature or that a being's purpose is present equally in techne and in phusis, Aristotle seems eager to leave the question of techne and phusis undecided or at least open to further investigation.

## Rhetoric's Nonmodern Constitution

Regardless of Aristotle's intentions, what is apparent to us when we trace terms such as "techne" and "phusis" across the corpus is that "art" and "nature" are not a priori concepts for him. The goal for Aristotle is not to impose existing understandings of techne and phusis onto his metaphysics but, rather, to trace the ways artificial and natural things come into being and endure as beings in the world. Though Aristotle is clearly committed to the work of purification, he is also doing a great deal more—perhaps not "inventing our modern world" but, nonetheless, engaging simultaneously in the work of translation, that is, creating "mixtures between entirely new types of beings, hybrids of nature and culture" (Latour, *Modern* 10). And it is these hybrids, these quasi-objects that emerge out of Aristotle's ability to sort and collect the world around him, that constitute Aristotelian rhetoric, not the other way around. The history of Aristotelian rhetoric (or the history of anything rhetorical, for that matter) is, therefore, not about temporality at all. Rather, "it is a means of connecting entities and filing them away" (75). The history of rhetoric, then, is not as an irreversible advance toward progress marked by a handful of crises and revolutions but a series of events in which beings get sorted and collected. To study histories and theories of rhetoric is, thus, to study the ways rhetoricians have constituted, managed, and negotiated distinctions between humans and nonhumans. When we learn to approach events in these terms, we find that the history of rhetoric is no longer simply the history of human speakers and writers. It is the history of natural and artificial things as well (82).

The alternative historical methodology sketched in this chapter offers another approach to the question of the nonhuman and its place in the rhetorical scheme of things. Rather than conceive the nonhuman as a thematic rupture within rhetoric's emphases on language and symbolic expression, a counterrevolutionary historiography enables us to bring rhetoric's nonhumans to light while revealing *what it is we have always done*, that is, sorting and producing hybrids that are both natural and cultural, human and nonhuman, political and scientific, and so on. As John Muckelbauer suggests in terms of animal rhetorics, such an approach "involve[s] nothing short of a fundamental reorientation of the intellectual lineage associated with rhetoric—*not an abdication of this lineage but a reorientation*" (99; emphasis added). Not another revolution, in other words, just another way of understanding what it is we have always been. Rhetoric's nonmodern constitution is already here. It just needs to be ratified.

## Works Cited

Aristotle. *Metaphysics*. Trans. W. D. Ross. *The Basic Works of Aristotle*. Ed. Richard McKeon. New York: Random, 2001. Print.

———. *Nicomachean Ethics*. Trans. David Ross. New York: Oxford UP, 1998. Print.

———. *On Rhetoric: A Theory of Civic Discourse*. Trans. George A. Kennedy. New York: Oxford UP, 1991. Print.

———. *Physics*. Trans. R. P. Hardie and R. K. Gaye. *The Basic Works of Aristotle*. Ed. Richard McKeon. New York: Random, 2001. Print.

Atwill, Janet, M. *Rhetoric Reclaimed: Aristotle and the Liberal Arts Tradition*. Ithaca: Cornell UP, 1998. Print.

Brogan, Walter A. *Heidegger and Aristotle: The Twofoldness of Being*. Albany: State U of New York P, 2005. Print.

Davis, Diane. "Creaturely Rhetorics." *Philosophy and Rhetoric* 44.1 (2011): 88–94. Print.

Dunne, Joseph. *Back to the Rough Ground: Practical Judgment and the Lure of Technique*. Notre Dame: Notre Dame UP, 1993. Print.

Gross, Alan G. "What Aristotle Meant by Rhetoric." *Rereading Aristotle's* Rhetoric. Ed. Gross and Arthur Walzer. Carbondale: Southern Illinois UP, 2000. 24–37. Print.

Hawhee, Debra. "Toward a Bestial Rhetoric." *Philosophy and Rhetoric* 44.1 (2011): 81–87. Print.

Heidegger, Martin. "On the Essence and Concept of *Phusis* in Aristotle's *Physics B*, I." Trans. Thomas Sheehan. *Pathmarks*. Cambridge: Cambridge UP, 1998. 183–230. Print.

Latour, Bruno. *Politics of Nature: How to Bring the Sciences into Democracy*. Cambridge: Harvard UP, 2004. Print.

———. *We Have Never Been Modern*. Trans. Catherine Porter. Cambridge: Harvard UP, 1993. Print.

Muckelbauer, John. "Domesticating Animal Theory." *Philosophy and Rhetoric* 44.1 (2011): 95–100. Print.

Pender, Kelly. *Techne: From Neoclassicism to Postmodernism*. Anderson: Parlor, 2011. Print.

Warnick, Barbara. "Judgment, Probability, and Aristotle's Rhetoric." *Quarterly Journal of Speech* 75 (1989): 299–311. Print.

# 6. Bruno Latour Is a Rhetorician of Inartistic Proofs

Joshua Prenosil, *Creighton University*

> Rhetoric cannot account for the force of a sequence of sentences because, if it is called "rhetoric," then it is weak and has already lost.
> —Bruno Latour, *The Pasteurization of France*

Transatlantic relations between rhetoricians and Bruno Latour are complicated. In many respects, Latour and rhetoricians share many of the same concerns and goals. Both investigate the political behavior of publics, broadly conceived: the means for acting and deciding, outcomes and consequences. Both explore human-technological interaction, the recursive way that technologies shape human thought and behavior and the human-technological mediation of creative processes. Both have an interest in unearthing historically underappreciated forms of intellection, disciplines concerned with middle ground, the places where people and things, (in)dividuals, and groups convene, collaborate, and contest. Latour has provided space for rhetoric in his politics, naming rhetoric as the discipline that studies contingent deliberation ("Dingpolitik" 9). In turn, rhetoricians working in public rhetorics, pedagogy, computers and writing, and rhetorical theory have joined scholars in technical communication and the rhetoric of science who have long had an interest in Latour's work.

Nonetheless, despite mutual affinities, Latour struggles to fully engage rhetoric in all of its present, disciplinary complexity. Periodically, Latour uses the term "rhetoric" to signify an impoverished caricature of the field. He refers to rhetoric as a stylistic addition that might persuade a public given a series of stable conditions across social strata (*PF* 183–84), a middling exercise of power between serendipity and brute force (*PF* 183), a formalized, prescriptive rubric for interpreting legal forms (*ML* 128), the study of how texts create reality (*SA* 30), invective against scholars unconcerned with technical content ("New Method" 25), and a clever way to manipulate an audience and lie (*ML* 8–9; *SA* 61). As a scholar, Latour enacts a rhetorical enterprise, assuming a rhetorical stance while naming his venture as philosophy, sociology, or anthropology. Consequently, in much of Latour's work, the study of persuasion is distributed among philosophy and the social sciences.

Latour's corpus is worthwhile, and it demands a reckoning with rhetoric. As Paul Lynch notes, rhetoric and composition seems poised for a Latourian moment (459). A growing number of rhetoricians seek a conceptual vocabulary for explaining how materiality persuades and how this persuasion bears on research, teaching, and service. Latour's main contribution to the humanities and social sciences, actor-network-theory (ANT), promises an avenue for advancing rhetorical research beyond social construction and semiotics: it offers a means to account for the way that objects and people coshape decisions, judgments, and actions. Consequently, Latour's works should be unpacked through a detailed analysis of ANT and rhetoric's assumptions and goals. In this chapter, I hope to show how such an analysis articulates ANT as a theory of rhetoric. Latour's ANT is a theory and methodology specially geared for studying the available means for establishing temporally specific coagency. Accordingly, I argue that ANT is a rhetoric of inartistic proofs, connected to composition via Aristotle's *On Rhetoric*, keenly interested in the way that power is remediated in contemporary practice. Further, I contend that Latour's concept of nonmodernism, his obliteration of the subject-object split, can inform rhetoricians' understanding of inartistic rhetoric and open new avenues for rhetorical scholarship.

To recast Latour's ANT as a theory of inartistic proofs, I briefly review a few key concepts in the Latourian corpus: modernism, hybrid, quasi-object, and articulation. The chapter then discusses the history of inartistic proofs to uncover an ancient point of connection between rhetoric and ANT, demonstrating how inartistic rhetoric and actor-network-theory can be mutually edifying. Finally, I draw out some of the implications of a thoroughly rhetorical ANT in order to compose means for accommodating ANT and other power-centric theories within the rhetorical corpus. But first I begin with a summary of Latour's critique of modernism, which finds its characteristic expression through Latour's account of Immanuel Kant's philosophy.

## Latour and Modernism

For Latour, the modern impoverishment of Western thought arrives via the Cartesian split and its radicalization through Kant's transcendental subjectivity. Latour's Kant neatly divides intellectual activity into the objective sciences, which study unmediated forms of reality (*Modern* 37), and subjective philosophies, which study consciousness or the nonmaterial mediation of consciousness (*PH* 5–6). In Kant's system, Latour argues, universality is derived from scientific practice, and a system of morality is abstracted from categories inside the human mind (*PH* 6). With Kant's transcendental ego, the world of human subjectivity produces validity through verification of its own means, or the universally consistent, nonmaterial means upon which one might perceive reality (*PH* 5; *Modern* 56). Kant creates a system of epistemology to end metaphysics (11–13), privileging the human subject and its universally structured consciousness at the expense of the external world and the objects that populate it.

Kant raises Latour's hackles in a special way (Harman 71). The problem with Kant's philosophy, according to Latour, is that despite its quest for certainty, Kant's system provides no clear means for ending the systematic doubt of the external world and the material actors that shape its contours. Centering reality in epistemology rather than ontology or metaphysics creates a philosophical situation where the critique of being beyond consciousness might never find its terminus (*PH* 6–7). Kant creates the possibility of an internally derived reality that has a weak connection to the body or external objects. The connection worn thin, subsequent humanities scholars finish Kant's work, severing consciousness from its material roots, leaving meaning to study: modes of consciousness, symbol systems, frames, metaphors, and discourse, all of which circulate among nonmaterial subjects through "society" (*Modern* 62; *PH* 7). Because meaning cannot be anchored in material reality, questions of epistemology and knowledge production become questions about the possibility of knowledge, which, Latour argues, culminate with the postmodern repudiation of the possibility of knowledge and reality (*Modern* 62; *PH* 8). The modern division between subjects and objects prompts the rise of postmodernism because the division institutes a problem of relation without mediation, a paradox that can only be solved through naive dogmatism or the logical but uncomfortable conclusion that no set of knowledge might be conditionally more valid than another (*MC* 15, 29). Hence, according to Latour, postmodernism is a symptom of modernism because it is an extension of the modern separation of human culture and nonhuman nature (*Modern* 74).

In response to modernism's stable division between subjects and objects, Latour argues in *We Have Never Been Modern* that the separation of nature and culture is a practical fiction that has continued to produce, despite its dualistic foci, "hybrids" (what he would later call networks), inextricable subject-object combinations (10). Anything might be a hybrid: a religious controversy about cloning, public concern about the state of education, environmentalist protests over an oil pipeline, or the recall of a toy containing lead-based paint. Hybrids are configurations of humans and nonhumans as they dwell together: the mutually affective relationships between us and our technologies, infrastructures, and discourses. Hybrids crisscross the subject-object divide without regard for contemporary epistemological arrangements, imbricating humans, technologies, ecologies, media, and all the means of mediation among human and nonhuman actors (*Modern* 11; "Critique" 231, 237).

Latour uses the terms "quasi-subject" and, more frequently, "quasi-object" to refer on a smaller scale to the meaning-matter constitution of people and things (*Modern* 51–52, 55). Latour's neologisms seek to provide an ontologically accurate description of being, and much like Martin Heidegger's terminology, they facilitate investigation into the mutually affective relationship we share with the things around us. An example from Latour's 1999 essay collection, *Pandora's Hope*, illustrates the character of Latourian agency and ontology. In the book's second chapter, Latour follows a team of geologists, biologists, and pedologists as they attempt to answer a question about the behavior of the Brazilian *selva*, whether it is advancing or retreating—and how it might be doing so. Upon arriving in the jungle, Latour narrates, the team sets up a stake-and-twine grid on the jungle floor and a corresponding, compartmentalized box for soil samples, a pedocomparator, which the scientists must hand fill with dirt. Latour describes the work of one pedologist, René, as he plots the jungle floor.

> Consider this lump of earth. Grasped by René's right hand, it retains all the materiality of soil. . . . Yet as it is placed inside the cardboard cube in René's left hand, the earth becomes a sign, takes on a geometrical form, becomes the carrier of a numbered code, and will soon be defined by a color. In the philosophy of science, which studies only the resulting abstraction, the left hand does not know what the right hand is doing! In [ANT], we are ambidextrous: we focus the reader's attention on this

> hybrid, this moment of substitution, the very instant when the future sign is abstracted from the soil. We should never take our eyes off the material weight of this action. . . . We are not jumping from soil to the Idea of soil, but from continuous and multiple clumps of earth to a discrete color in a geometric cube coded in x- and y-coordinates. And yet René does not *impose* predetermined categories on a shapeless horizon; he *loads* his pedocomparator with the meaning of the piece of earth . . . he articulates it. (49–51; original emphasis)

The term "articulation" here is key. According to Latour, as René loads the pedocomparator, he works within the constraints and affordances of the jungle in order to create a quasi-object for use in a geological-pedological network, one with stringent standards for quasi-object production (51). For Latour, René does not just manipulate dumb artifacts: "According to René, 'It is the pedocomparator that *tells us* if we have finished a transect'" (51; original emphasis). In the modern arrangement, subjects, the scientists, would exert their agency over jungle objects while the jungle objects provide a radically stable background of reality upon which subjects act. According to actor-network-theory, the hybrid—or network—produced by scientists' activity in the jungle is always one of mutual effect: actionable entities interact, coshaping new, concrete networks that have real effects against, with, and in other networks.

## Material-Semiotic Knowledge

In response to modern and postmodern epistemologies, Latour contends that knowledge is always deeply material: it is not different in kind from a dinner plate, a barbell, a teakettle, or an automobile in that it is not allowed to escape into the subjective or intersubjective recesses of epistemology (*PH* 14). If knowledge is real and legitimate, if a particular set of knowledge counts, it must be mediated through stages of physical production (*PF* 5, 58). Further, as all real things in Latour's system, it must be capable of resistance (Harman 26). In other words, the objects of knowledge production must be capable of exerting power with and against other objects.

Latour proposes a thought experiment to demonstrate this resistance in action. He constructs a fictional scientist, "'the Dissenter,' a contrarian cynic who challenges every least detail he observes in a laboratory" (*SA* 39). Latour sets the Dissenter in a neurology lab where he disputes a progressive series of actors that produce scientific knowledge: a text, a printout, measurement equipment, syringes filled with opiates, guinea-pig guts, log books, and scientific theory encoded in tomes dating back to Isaac Newton. The Dissenter begins by asking his host for graphical evidence summarized in a scientific article on endorphin function (*SA* 39). The scientist provides the graph and then shows his guest the machine that injects guinea-pig gut with the chemical that causes undulations in the measurement apparatus and thus the graphical printout (39). Things get grisly. For good measure, the scientist orders the ritualistic slaying of a second guinea pig and performs the experiment again.

> A guinea pig is placed on a table, under surgical floodlights, then anaesthetized, crucified and sliced open. The gut is located, a tiny section is extracted, useless tissue peeled away, and the precious fragment is delicately hooked between two electrodes and immersed in a nutrient fluid so as to be maintained alive. . . . We are now in a puddle of blood and viscera, slightly nauseated by the extraction of the ileum from this little furry creature. (*SA* 66)

The dramatic action of Latour's uneasy narrative continues to build: "Faced with the thing itself that the technical paper was alluding to, the [Dissenter] now [has] a choice between either accepting the fact or doubting his own sanity—the latter is much more painful" (*SA* 70). The Dissenter is now in a precarious position. If he continues to question knowledge in the laboratory and the objects of knowledge production, he risks rousing a much-larger and more powerful enemy: all of the people and things that rely upon the scientific equipment and the theory that undergird laboratory practice (Harman 40, 42–43). Further contestation means risking reputation and livelihood (Harman 42–43).

Graham Harman, a Heideggerian-turned-Latourian, pushes Latour's Dissenter in this precarious direction, and the Dissenter begins contesting other quasi-objects in the laboratory, lab procedures and record keeping, both of which are beyond reproach, and, finally, Newton's treatise on optics (Harman 42, 44). Questioning Newton, the Dissenter becomes the laughing stock of his profession, and knowledge in the neurology lab is handily maintained (44). Harman offers Latour's Dissenter redemption years later, however, upon his invention of a scientific theory that shakes the foundation of Newtonian optics (44). Via Harman, the Dissenter is vindicated through personal and professional trials that demonstrate the strength of his new knowledge. His banishment from accepted scientific networks now seems like a tactical retreat. Former adversaries are converted into allies or are publicly shamed for their arcane beliefs (44).

Harman's and Latour's point is that knowledge never transcends the material circumstances of its development: knowledge is what can withstand, at any point in time, contestation from other knowledge networks, which are also always natural-cultural hybrids. In Latour's estimation, the separation of nature and culture leads to reductive knowledge because it diminishes a consideration of unique material agency. In the modern split, objective scientific laws or subjectivity or the conditions for subjectivity animate the world around us. In both cases, the agency of the many is reduced to the agency of a few overarching machinations. As a consequence, the ability to understand how power operates in specific situations, constituted by many unique agencies, is debased. According to Latour, reductive considerations of agency are on display in the humanities and social sciences whenever scholars claim that

> they are able to extend themselves potentially or "in theory" beyond the networks within which they practice. The butcher would never entertain the idea of reducing theoretical physics to the art of butchery, but the psychoanalyst claims to be able to reduce butchery to the murder of the father, and epistemologists happily talk of the "foundations of physics." (*PF* 187)

Too often, so Latour argues, humanities scholars apply theoretical frames at the expense of local accounts, to predictable effect. During such applications, terministic screens set conclusions and key actors, usually who or whatever is deemed less than human, are discounted from scholarly assessments.

## Latour and Power

An additional problem with such scholarly assessments, as Latour's butchery example suggests, is that they frequently fail to exert power outside the circles of influence where they are conceived and deployed. Philosophers, for example, work in relatively small circles where discipline shapes language use. Language tools (papers, books, and journal articles) developed by philosophers are very powerful within the circumscribed space of the academe. They are also formidable in the midst of other actors' language, particularly when that language (from butchers, bakers, or candlestick makers) finds itself inside academic bulwarks. In scholarly citadels, scholarly tools can easily dissect nonacademic language for knowledge production. The results of such dissection, valid as knowledge inside the academe, may be unrecognizable to nonacademic publics. Further, in the midst of such publics and cut off from its cohorts (library books, academic journals, scholars in adjoining offices, graduate students, Listservs), that knowledge (in whatever medium) can easily be overpowered: torn up, thrown away, deleted, burned, or dismissed.

Latour assumes the power of physical cohorts, networks, as a condition of knowledge production (*PF* 262). Recall the example of the guinea pig above: the guinea pig is "crucified" so that material meaning, the ileum, can be extracted from it for successive transformations via scientific practice. Once that gruesome exercise is complete, the ileum is converted into an ally in a network of scientific people and instruments. Once converted, the ileum and its network can enact knowledge/power against a marauding Dissenter, whose invasive tour of the laboratory is relatively gentler but no less an exercise of power and knowledge.

For Latour, brute physical force does not equal the creation of knowledge, but power, mediated through the tactics of research, connects scholarly practice to base Machiavellianism. According to Latour, scientific knowledge and force are intertwined, both in practice and historically. For example, in *The Making of Law*, Latour says, "In order to understand the very special mode of enunciation that one finds in the core of the laboratory, one has to look to *torture*, to the *history of interrogation* or the *subtle arts of the Inquisition*" (207; emphasis added). In Latour's ANT, making scientific knowledge (or literary knowledge, cement trucks, doctoral dissertations, or wine casks) requires physical struggle. For Latour, the struggle of knowledge production is a kind of contemporary remediation of brutal force, where a corpus is worked over by entities seeking to mold, extract from, or decimate it. As a case in point, references to contemporary knowledge production as torture litter Latour's work. Consider Latour's description of experimentation.

> An experiment is a story, to be sure—and studiable as such—but a story *tied* to a situation in which new actants undergo terrible trials plotted by an ingenious stage manager; and then the stage manager, in turn, undergoes terrible trials at the hands of his colleagues, who test what sort of *ties* there are between the first story and the second situation, later tested by others to decide whether or not it is simply a text. If the final trial is successful, then it is not just a text, there is indeed a real situation *behind* it, and both the actor and its authors are endowed with a new competence. (*PF* 123–24; original emphasis)

To be sure, Latour does not draw a simple equation between the exercise of physical power and the nuances of experimental procedure but, rather, points out, much like Michel Foucault, that power is recast in contemporary practices: new ways of doing things change the rules of power games but remain part of a power game, nonetheless.

For Latour and unlike Foucault, power is always materially imminent. At every turn, it is self-same with the behavior of actors. Further, forms of discipline and forms of remediated brute power apply as much to humans as to nonhumans. Discipline is a two-way affair. In "Mixing Humans and Non-humans Together: Sociology of a Door Closer," Latour provides a much more pedestrian example: a university administration must decide how to keep the door of a university building closed during the winter so cold air does not rush in. In Latour's scenario, the door is habitually left ajar, and a sign on the door has not changed visitors' behavior (300). Consequently, addressing the reader-as-administrator, Latour contends,

> It is at this point that you have this relatively new choice: either to *discipline* the people or to substitute for the unreliable humans a delegated nonhuman character whose only function is to open and close the door. This is called a door-closer or a "groom." The advantage is that you now have to *discipline* only one nonhuman and may safely leave the others . . . [those who leave the door open] to their erratic behavior. (301; emphasis added)

In ANT, nonhumans also discipline humans and other nonhumans. As a previous section shows, in *Pandora's Hope*, the scientific instruments of the pedologists exercise agency in scientific networks. René's pedocomparator "tells" him when he has "finished a transect" (*PH* 51). Further, the pedocomparator, a grid for organizing dirt, disciplines and orders dirt in roughly the same way that Foucault's disciplinary structures order people.

## Inartistic Proofs

Latour's obsession with the exercise of power—and his specific conception of knowledge production as a remediated form of brute force—connects him to a neglected branch of rhetorical theory. In his *Rhetoric*, Aristotle makes a basic distinction between artistic proofs and inartistic proofs. Artistic proofs, according to Aristotle, are proofs that involve rhetorical invention: audiences, enthymemes, examples, and appeals (1356a–b). Inartistic proofs are proofs "that are not provided by 'us' [i.e., the potential speaker] but are preexisting: for example, witnesses, testimony of slaves taken under torture,[1] contracts, and such like" (1355a). According to Aristotle, "one must *use*" inartistic proofs "and *invent*" artistic proofs (1355a; emphasis added). Whereas artistic proofs employ wit, facility with language, and knowledge of an audience to persuade, inartistic proofs are persuasive artifacts that generate through a previous exercise of power; inartistic proofs arrive in a court of law ready to be used by a rhetor arguing for a particular judicial outcome (1355a). Unlike artistic proofs, inartistic proofs are not created through a correspondence between the values and knowledge of an audience and the knowledge and persuasive skill of a rhetor.

Inartistic proofs generate relatively little interest in the history of rhetoric and Western intellection. Aristotle, for example, spends almost all of his *Rhetoric* discussing artistic proofs, providing an extensive typology of appeals and audience dispositions. Inartistic proofs are briefly mentioned or praised by a number of other ancient thinkers, Anaximenes, Isocrates, Julius Victor, Fortunatianus, Cicero, and Quintilian. In twentieth-century scholarship, philologists and classicists have paid attention to inartistic proofs because of the *basanos*, or Greek tradition of torturing a slave during testimony. These scholars have debated whether slaves were actually tortured for their specific knowledge of a case, the kinds of questions they were asked, admissibility in adjudication of their testimony, and the weight of that testimony in court. Philologists have analyzed the appearance of inartistic proofs on papyrus fragments of anonymous origin.[2] Finally, the basanos has generated interest from scholars who historicize and critique sovereign exercises of power.[3]

Contemporary rhetoricians, however, rarely mention inartistic proofs. Eugene Garver claims that inartistic proofs are not part of rhetoric, describing them as a form of evidence that requires little or no persuasive work on the part of a rhetor (387, 391). Wilbur Samuel Howell briefly discusses inartistic proofs as the classical base for the rhetorical separation of discourse and science (302–3).[4] These two perspectives are combined in Carolyn R. Miller's 1979 article, "A Humanistic Rationale for Technical Writing." In her article, Miller responds to a departmental proposal at North Carolina State University that excluded technical writing from fulfilling a humanities requirement in the English department (610). The proposal framed rhetoric and technical writing as plain-style adjuncts of science and engineering classes (610). Miller replies that technical writing should fulfill a humanities requirement because it is a deeply humanistic enterprise related to scientific discourse communities (615). To make this argument, Miller hangs the separation of the humanities and sciences on the subject-object split.

> Rhetoric relies upon "artistic proofs," those which are created by the art of the speaker or writer. Science has to do with what Aristotle called "inartistic proofs," facts or artifacts which exist independently of human intentions and emotions and about which deliberation is necessary. Inartistic proofs are those which have only to be found; they are just *there*—self-evident and real and objective. (613; original emphasis)

For Miller, artistic proofs are cultural, whereas inartistic proofs are natural. She contends that contrary to widespread public conceptions of science, science is also cultural, so it is also the province of artistic proofs: "Science . . . is not concerned with material things, but with . . . human constructions, with symbols and arguments" (616). Technical writing, Miller posits, is a discipline that studies the way scientists make meaning in groups. In Miller's program, technical writing—and rhetoric, generally—is a study of the meaning-making capacity of human subjects that work in symbol systems to produce assent and gain knowledge (617). By implication, Miller suggests that inartistic proofs are an empty fiction on which rhetoric, an exclusively artistic discipline, has nothing to say.

From a disciplinary perspective, the problem with Miller's conception of Aristotelian proof is that it disowns one entire, albeit neglected, side of rhetoric completely. Historically, such a move is understandable. In 1979, Miller was waging a successful campaign on behalf of technical communication in a specific institutional space. She was an instructor, not a professor, in technical communication, which was about to be axed from the humanities curriculum. Social construction was a newly valid humanities doctrine (Latour was a social constructionist then[5]). Rhetoric programs had just gained a foothold in the academe. Using the terms of social construction to justify technical communication in English was innovative argumentation.

Nonetheless, in executing her argument, Miller misreads Aristotle's description of inartistic proofs. Aristotle describes inartistic proofs as artifacts for "use," not "independent" objects that exist beyond the realm of human activity. Indeed, the most philologically notable of the inartistic proofs, the basanos is a profoundly human proof in the worst way: torture, it would seem, is specific to humans as a species (Peterson and Goodall 84). Aristotle's inartistic proofs are not proofs of objective and "independent" facts but are rather proofs concerned with temporally specific exercises of power. Under Aristotle's arrangement, torture-driven testimony and contracts do not require as much "artistic" invention because binding exercises of power have occurred upstream of public display. Torture in ancient Athens, if and when it happened, took place outside the court of law (Mirhady, "Torture" 119). The use of contracts as legal evidence, then as now, require the prior assent of relevant parties. Contracts, testimonies under torture, and witnesses must have been secured and tested prior to their deployment in adjudication. Consequently, inartistic proof might be understood as a form of persuasion that relies upon the prior securing of assent and congruity for codeployment in novel environments.[6] Testimony under torture and contracts, like witnesses, must be produced and scrutinized prior to their admission in a new setting.

What Miller frames as "objective," "independent" "artifacts" were—or are—connected and well-secured proofs that require coercion and assent prior to their "use" in new arenas. Inartistic proofs are not asymbolic exercises of power but are rather exercises of power that require advanced connectivity. Inartistic proof requires actors to secure coagency through the manipulation and fortification of other actors. To create an inartistic proof in the Aristotelian sense, assent or coagency must be achieved so that knowledge claims might be advanced in agonistic contexts. In the case of torture, an agential network is established in a most brutal and detestable way.

## Instantiations of Modernism

The modernist division between objects and subjects, nature and culture, dictates Miller's social constructionism and her conception of proofs, as it does for many of us. Under the modern arrangement for rhetoricians, "invent" and "use," the operative verbs for artistic and inartistic proofs, respectively, imply their own grammatical objects. We "use" objects—things—while we "invent" language. So Latour would argue, this reinstantiation places rhetors at the point of modernist reduction. Such instantiations are, as he points out, unnecessary. Language always arrives in media; we never encounter pure meaning without materiality. The simplest objects embed polysemies (*PF* 187). Both things bearing letters and things bearing litter are invented and used.

From an Aristotelian perspective, artistic and inartistic rhetoric study different aspects of the same political endeavor. As a largely enthymematic pursuit, artistic rhetoric studies the correspondence between interiorities, the way that internalities change through chains of mediation (Prenosil 287–88). From the metaperspective of Aristotle's definition of rhetoric, inartistic proofs might be defined as the study of the available means of establishing mediation and coagency, a study of the power and work that allows a network to be established, sustained, changed, or defeated. Not beholden to the term "network," inartistic rhetoric is the analysis of conferences of power, their historical manifestations, their tactics, and their effects.

Under the basic assumptions of the modern arrangement, this definition of inartistic rhetoric once again places us in peril of dividing subjects from objects. If power, work, and "use" are ultimately conceived as the province of human subjects, a basic division of labor remains at the level of action. People act, while things are acted upon. From an actor-network perspective, however, such a division of labor is meaningless. As seen in ANT, door closers can be disciplined by humans, humans can be disciplined by pedocomparators, and pedocomparators can discipline soil. "Use" in Latourian ontology is always a messy, multidirectional verb. Latour provides an illustrative example: a puppet is a dramaturgical object and well-established metaphor for people and governments lacking agency. Puppeteers use puppets, but even in this relationship, the user's full leverage is doubtful (*RS* 214). Latour says,

> [The puppeteer] will tell you, as will everyone else—as will any creator and manipulator—that her marionettes dictate their behavior to her: that they make her act; that they express themselves through her; that she could never manipulate them or mechanize them. And yet she holds them, dominates and masters them. She will straight-forwardly admit that she is slightly outstripped by what she controls. (*MC* 62)

From an actor-network perspective, control or power is always a tenuous thing; the available means of establishing agency can easily slide sideways on a purportedly potent actor or collective. Change in networks is standard, while stability is peculiar. From the perspective of distributed agency, discussing "use" as a human and nonhuman activity allows scholars of power to investigate both change and stability, the mutually affective, agential relationships that pervade the contemporary world.

Ultimately, Latour is a rhetorician of inartistic proofs because he studies the available means of establishing coagency, power that is always achieved through imminent material-semiotic actors in a network. Like Foucault, Latour is interested in describing the way that the mediation of power changes over time. Indeed, for Latour, material-semiotic power mediates all things, including time. Unlike Aristotle and much like Heidegger, for Latour, time is always measured and generated by the change in actors at local sites. The humans and nonhumans that populate the world compose time through their interconnected deployment of agency, and temporal coherence is only achieved through a coordinated and pervasive exercise of power that disciplines humans and nonhumans to march in Gregorian step (*MC* 72–74).

In making the argument that Latour is a rhetorician of inartistic proofs, my goal is not to force Latour—or Latourians, actor-network theorists, or the hordes of Foucauldians—to recast themselves as rhetoricians but, rather, to demonstrate that rhetoricians and compositionists can use ANT to study materiality and power *as rhetoricians and compositionists*. As a rhetoric of inartistic proofs, ANT is a theory par excellence for explaining how people and things work together to effect change because it allows for a whole range of actors, social media, TV cameras, cell phones, maps, bullhorns, organizational charts, e-mail lists, and informational websites, along with human actors, to exercise political power. ANT is an ideal theory for moving forward with rhetorical research into power because it does not reduce the agency of any actor to any other unless one actor has fully leveraged another, and even here, as we have seen, ANT is dubious as to whether or not a complete reduction is possible. It is especially useful for tracing the subtle and not-so-subtle acts of power among humans and nonhumans that produce political effects, broadly conceived.

By way of inartistic proofs, rhetoricians have license to use ANT in order to advance rhetorical scholarship. Further, the argument in this essay might be extended to a number of other theories and theorists. I have implied that the later work of Michel Foucault is an inartistic rhetoric alongside Latour's work. Indeed, as John Muckelbauer points out, Foucault's philosophy is precisely a philosophy of resistance, a theory of co- and counter-agency (73, 80). It might easily be classed as a rhetoric of inartistic proofs.[7] The same applies to Gilles Deleuze's refiguring of Foucauldian disciplinary structures in his analysis of control societies (4). The same could apply, too, to any number of theorists working in the humanities and social sciences: Donna Haraway, Elaine Scarry, Avital Ronell, Nicolas Rose, and Manuel Castells, among many others.

Rhetoricians should explore the range of inartistic proofs. They should also be careful not to see this line of argument as a means to grab disciplinary power but rather as a means to move, as Nathaniel Rivers suggests, nimbly among disciplines, using other disciplines' frames and methods *as rhetoricians* (159). The argument here reinforces the capacity of rhetoricians to do what they have already done, borrow from diverse fields in order to compose a "dappled" scholarly force with an extensive body of skills and knowledge and a growing capacity to publicly evince rhetoric's value as a mobile and adaptable form of intellection.

## Notes

1. Aristotle, writing in a society with a legitimate judicial space for torture-driven testimony, admits,

> It is necessary to say that torture is not reliable; for many slow-witted and thick-skinned persons and those strong in soul nobly hold out under force, while cowards and those who are cautious will denounce someone before seeing the instruments of torture, so that there is nothing credible in tortures. (1377a)

One wonders what he would think of torture in contemporary Western societies, where torture undermines political and judicial legitimacy.

2. See Dorjahn, "On Slave Evidence in Greek Law"; Gagarin, "Torture of Slaves in Athenian Law"; Gaines, "On the Rhetorical Significance of P. Hamb"; Mirhady, "Oath Challenge in Athens," "Non-technical Pisteis in Aristotle and Anaximenes," and "Torture and Rhetoric in Athens"; Thompson and Headlam, "Slave Torture in Athens"; and Thür, "Reply to D. C. Mirhady."

3. See Peters, *Torture*, and Ronnell, *Test Drive*. See also Foucault, *Discipline and Punish*, and Scarry, *Body in Pain*, though they do not use the term "basanos" directly.

4. Howell admits that the "external realities" of inartistic proofs are now of interest to rhetoricians who, presumably, work in a tradition of artistic proofs (303).

5. In 1979, Latour and Steve Woolgar published *Laboratory Life*, a social constructionist account of scientific practice at the Jonas Salk Institute.

6. This is not to say that deployment always works out in expected ways. See Latour, *Making of Law*, 144–51.

7. Such a recasting of Foucault's work would further explain rhetoricians' obsession with his work since the publication of *Discipline and Punish*. For a productive critique of that obsession, see Schilb, "Turning Composition toward Sovereignty."

## Works Cited

Aristotle. *On Rhetoric*. Trans. George A. Kennedy. New York: Oxford UP, 1991. Print.

Crawford, Hugh. "Interview with Bruno Latour." *Configurations* 1.2 (1993): 247–268. Print.

Deleuze, Gilles. “Postscript on the Societies of Control.” *October* 59 (Winter 1992): 3–7. Print.

Dorjahn, Alfred P. “On Slave Evidence in Greek Law.” *Classical Journal* 47.1 (1952): 88. Print.

Foucault, Michel. *Discipline and Punish: The Birth of the Prison*. Trans. Alan Sheridan. 2nd ed. New York: Vintage, 1995. Print.

Gagarin, Michael. “The Torture of Slaves in Athenian Law.” *Classical Philology* 91.1 (1996): 1–18. Print.

Gaines, Robert N. “On the Rhetorical Significance of P. Hamb. 131.” *Rhetorica: A Journal of the History of Rhetoric* 7.4 (1989): 329–340. Print.

Garver, Eugene. “Aristotle’s ‘Rhetoric’ on Unintentionally Hitting the Principles of the Sciences.” *Rhetorica: A Journal of the History of Rhetoric* 6.4 (1988): 381–393. Print.

Harman, Graham. *Prince of Networks: Bruno Latour and Metaphysics*. Victoria: Re.press, 2009. Print.

Howell, Wilbur Samuel. “Renaissance Rhetoric and Modern Rhetoric: A Study in Change.” *The Province of Rhetoric*. Ed. Joseph Schwartz and John A. Rycenga. New York: Ronald, 1965. 292–308. Print.

Kant, Immanuel. *The Critique of Pure Reason*. Trans. J. M. D. Meiklejohn. Charleston: Forgotten, 2008. Google Books. Web. 1 May 2012.

Latour, Bruno. “From Realpolitik to Dingpolitik or How to Make Things Public.” *Making Things Public: Atmospheres of Democracy*. Ed. Latour and Peter Weibel. Cambridge: MIT P, 2005. 4–31. Print.

———. *The Making of Law: An Ethnography of the Conseil d’État*. Trans. Barina Brilman and Alain Pottage. Cambridge: Polity, 2010. Print.

———. “Mixing Humans and Nonhumans Together: Sociology of a Door Closer.” *Social Problems* 35.3 (1988): 298–310. Print.

———. “A New Method to Trace the Path of Innovations: The Sociotechnical Graph.” Trans. Gabrielle Hecht. *bruno-latour.fr*. Bruno Latour, n.d., 1–38. Web. 1 May 2012.

———. *On the Modern Cult of Factish Gods*. Trans. Catherine Porter and Heather MacLean. Durham: Duke UP, 2010. Print.

———. *Pandora’s Hope: Essays on the Reality of Science Studies*. Cambridge: Harvard UP, 1999. Print.

———. *The Pasteurization of France*. Trans. Alan Sheridan and John Law. Cambridge: Harvard UP, 1988. Print.

———. *Politics of Nature*. Trans. Catherine Porter. Cambridge: Harvard UP, 2004. Print.

———. "The Powers of Association." *Power, Action, and Belief: A New Sociology of Knowledge?* Ed. John Law. Boston: Routledge, 1986. 264–280. Print.

———. *Reassembling the Social: An Introduction to Actor-Network-Theory.* London: Oxford UP, 2005. Print.

———. *Science in Action: How to Follow Scientists and Engineers through Society.* Cambridge: Harvard UP, 1987. Print.

———. "Visualization and Cognition: Drawing Things Together." *Article de Bruno Latour* 21 (1985): 1–32. Web. 5 March 2012.

———. *We Have Never Been Modern.* Trans. Catherine Porter. Cambridge: Harvard UP, 1993. Print.

———. "Why Has Critique Run Out of Steam? From Matters of Fact to Matters of Concern." *Critical Inquiry* 30.2 (2004): 225–248. Print.

Lynch, Paul. "Composition's New Thing: Bruno Latour and the Apocalyptic Turn." *College English* 74.5 (2012): 458–476. Print.

Miller, Carolyn R. "A Humanistic Rationale for Technical Writing." *College English* 40.6 (1979): 610–617. Print.

Mirhady, David. "Non-Technical Pisteis in Aristotle and Anaximenes." *American Journal of Philology* 112.1 (1991): 5–28. Print.

———. "The Oath-Challenge in Athens." *Classical Quarterly* 41.1 (1991): 78–83. Print.

———. "Torture and Rhetoric in Athens." *Journal of Hellenic Studies* 116 (1996): 119–131. Print.

Muckelbauer, John. "On Reading Differently: Through Foucault's Resistance." *College English* 63.1 (2000): 71–94. Print.

Peters, Edward. *Torture.* Expanded ed. Philadelphia: U of Pennsylvania P, 1999. Print.

Peterson, Dale, and Jane Goodall. *Visions of Caliban: On Chimpanzees and People.* Athens: U of Georgia P, 2000. Print.

Prenosil, Joshua D. "The Embodied Enthymeme: A Hybrid Theory of Protest." *JAC* 31.1–2 (2012): 279–303. Print.

Rejali, Darius. *Torture and Democracy.* 4th ed. Princeton: Princeton UP, 2009. Print.

Rivers, Nathaniel. *Cultivating Rhetorics: Exploring and Exploiting the Emergent Boundaries of Nature and Culture.* Diss. Purdue University, 2009. Print.

Ronnell, Avital. *The Test Drive.* Champaign: U of Illinois P, 2005. Print.

Scarry, Elaine. *The Body in Pain: The Making and Unmaking of the World.* New York: Oxford UP, 1985. Print.

Schilb, John. "Turning Composition toward Sovereignty." *Present Tense: A Journal of Rhetoric in Society* 1.1 (2010): N. pag. Web. 5 Mar. 2012.

Thompson, C. V., and J. W. Headlam. "Slave Torture in Athens." *Classical Review* 8.4 (1894): 136–137. Print.

Thür, Gerard. "Reply to D. C. Mirhady: Torture and Rhetoric in Athens." *Journal of Hellenistic Studies* 116 (1996): 132–134. Print.

# 7. Is No One at the Wheel? Nonhuman Agency and Agentive Movement

Ehren Helmut Pflugfelder, *Oregon State University*

When driving a car, I often find myself thinking about Norbert Wiener, the so-called father of cybernetics. Two things bring him to mind: his conflation of the kinesthetic sense of people and machines, and his equation of human perception and communication with information. While Wiener wrote about computing technology in the 1950s, and I drive a Subaru in the 2010s, there is something about the experience of moving through the world by means of automobile that seems to trigger the most confusing sensations of agency.[1] After all, while looking for my car keys and walking to the garage, I am confident that I am about to drive my car, but later, when driving it, I am never certain where agency lies in this strange entanglement of human-vehicle interaction. Wiener gave more agency to the driver, but architect Lars Spuybroek is less certain. He argues that when in a car, a human body takes on the prosthesis of the vehicle, because "[t]he body's inner phantom has an irrepressible tendency to expand, to integrate every sufficiently responsive prosthesis into its motor system, its repertoire of movements, and make it run smoothly" (33). For Spuybroek, "a car is not an instrument or piece of equipment that you simply sit in, but something you merge with" (33). That such arguments need to be made at all suggests the surprising ease in which we understand agency as a *human* capability.

In this essay, I make some different claims about the nature of movement and employ Bruno Latour's conception of actors and actor-network-theory (ANT) to complicate more traditional conceptions of agency within rhetoric studies. Specifically, I illustrate how agency is often theorized as only being able to take root in or through human subjectivity, even though the human subject is understood to be a fragmented, unstable positioning, heavily informed by semiotic, social, material, and spatial factors. Latour's work on distributed, non-human agency puts these human-centric claims into perspective and muddies many postmodern accounts of agency. Following Carolyn R. Miller's work on the usefulness of kinetic energy in questions of agency and automation, I suggest that attending to *kinesis* forms of movement provides new insight into the shared agency of complex constellations of humans and nonhumans, before focusing on a specific example of agency within a driver-vehicle environment.

## Rhetorical Agency

The nature and power of agency and the status and positioning of agents have long been disputed facets of rhetorical theory, from Gorgias's concern over the power of language in his *Encomium of Helen*, where human agents can be at the mercy of an almost magical rhetoric, to Plato's allegory of the charioteer in the dialogue *Phaedrus*. Thus, the nature and extent of what has been traditionally understood as human agency in rhetorical situations have played a large role in grounding theories and pedagogies of rhetoric. The underpinnings of rhetoric and composition, as a field, are, likewise, built upon such foundational claims. For many, the modern argument emerges from Lloyd F. Bitzer's "Rhetorical Situation" and Richard E. Vatz's counterargument in "The Myth of the Rhetorical Situation." For Bitzer, material conditions and contexts invite rhetorical response that comes into existence "for the sake of something beyond itself" (3–4). In this model, once an "appropriate" rhetorical response is identified, it can effect real change within a given situation. Vatz, on the other hand, focuses on seeing situations *as rhetorical*, where they "obtain their character from the rhetoric which surrounds them or creates them" (159). This contrast opened up further discussion of agency in rhetoric as either emergent from the material or social situation or as part of representational symbol systems. It is certainly not radical to claim that much rhetoric and composition scholarship in the latter half of the twentieth century has been derived from Vatz's conception of agency.

To some degree, Vatz's claims about agency have rooted themselves in rhetorical study because his positioning of agency as rhetorical and situationally emergent aligns with the general postmodern conception of subjectivity and power. Carl G. Herndl and Adela C. Licona's own articulation of postmodern agency emerges through their identification of the "agent function," which is correlative to Michel Foucault's "author function" (136). They, too, recognize, "Despite the powerful and widely accepted poststructural critique of the individual, [. . .] theories of agency remain haunted by a hangover from romantic voluntarism," the idea that agency can be "possessed" by individuals

(139). In order to avoid falling into a notion of the solitary (genius) author or isolated rhetor, they identify the position of the agent as a subjectivity that can be taken up when "material, (con)textual, and ideological conditions and practices" are opportune (146). This shifting agent-position acts as a node within a network of power, much like Karlyn Kohrs Campbell's description of agency as a "point of articulation" for "the capacity to act, that is, to have the competence to speak or write in a way that will be recognized or heeded by others in one's community" (2–3).[2] Such versions of rhetorical agency avoid locating it as derived entirely from the rhetorical situation or able to be possessed by agents in a stable, consistent fashion, though they do identify agents as human and describe agency only within the context of human availability. That is, even though agency is explained as rather amorphous and existing at the intersection of a network of symbolic, material, social, and affective forces, the agent function and the agent as a point of articulation are rendered salient through human actions. To identify this as a point of contention might seem odd. However, Latour's long-standing claims about humans and nonhumans call this assumption into question.

Latour's project of identifying agency within ANT is surprisingly direct, yet rather controversial for the rhetoric community to accept. One of his most fundamental assertions is that both humans and nonhumans have agency within networks of distributed power. Nonhumans can be objects and things, sure, though also animals, weather, political structures, institutions, ideological instantiations, laws, and other hybrid formations that exist in the "parliament of things" (*Modern* 142–45). In such a parliament, things, including humans, never speak on their own but are rendered through a network of translations, including human explanation and classification, that modernity has imposed, though rarely acknowledges. Specifically, Latour critiques science done in the name of objective empiricism as fostering a taxonomy that ignores the translation work of human and nonhuman actors. In the past, scholars of the rhetoric of science have argued for comparable, though varied, rhetorical readings of scientific discourse and meaning making.[3] Further, this "parliament of things" is democratic insofar as there are no ingrained or preternatural hierarchies of importance for things. As Latour argues, once we assume that a parliament of things can exist, we agree "[t]here are no more naked truths, but there are no more naked citizens, either. The mediators have the whole space to themselves" (*Modern* 144). Key here is that humans are no longer trusted as the central translators of all meaning, even when we observe the scientific method or pursue research supposedly free of ideology. Empirical research performed in the name of objectivity often only replicates biases inherent in the conditions of empirical study. Or, to put it another way, in attempting to defend the rights of humans as a special category of translator, one does "*not establish democracy; one makes it increasingly more impracticable every day*" (*PN* 69; original emphasis). Adopting such a position is also an important value in avoiding human-centric conception of agency, a stance many rhetoricians hold.

## Techne and Agency

Agency, understood as human capacity and response-ability for action emergent from human perception, is founded upon the belief that linguistic symbol systems are largely constitutive of knowledge and meaning. In part, this humanism underscores many pedagogical assumptions where agency is a necessary fiction and where language is assumed to identify and construct both subject positions and their attendant agencies. Levi R. Bryant, in *The Democracy of Objects*, argues that this humanism has come about because of the hegemony of epistemology in philosophy. For him, it holds philosophy (and rhetoric as well) to "a thoroughly anthropocentric reference. Because the ontological question of substance is elided into the epistemological question of our knowledge of substance, all discussions of substance necessarily contain a human reference" (19). Bryant finds that many poststructural and postmodern accounts of knowledge that place subjectivity within the context of linguistic symbol systems implicitly remain in the domain of language-using animals. These suppositions guide many rhetoricians' approaches to agency as the general domain of human perspective that governs what counts as evidence for knowledge claims. Such a perspective harkens back to Aristotle's definition of *techne*, the larger category of making and using arts that contains the art of rhetoric.

Aristotle argues that techne is "craft knowledge" that is "concerned with coming to be," although techne is "not concerned with things that are or come to be by necessity; or with things that are by nature, since these have their origin in themselves" (1140a12–15). In most cases, techne is understood as relevant to human-generated arts. Further, for Aristotle, techne comes from humans' ability to reason—without such a capacity, we would be rendered incapable of acting upon things in the world in a systematic way. That so-called natural things are not created (nor developed nor moved) through reason is essentially the Aristotelian distinction between art and nature but also central to his definition of *physis*. For example, Aristotle claims that a bed has no "innate impulse to change" into a bed by itself—we make it into what it is. Any impulse for change or movement it has is from its constitutive material construction, which, Aristotle argues, "seems to indicate that nature is a principle or cause of being moved and of being at rest in that to which it belongs primarily, in virtue of itself and not accidentally" (192b22–23). This differentiation is important, because Aristotle distinguishes where techne is applicable in order to ground what kind of reasoning a techne can be. Since techne concerns the art of making artificial things, where "none of them has in itself the principles of its own production," techne becomes understood as aligned with productive thinking and productive making arts applied to inert things (192b28–29).

In Aristotle's definition, the scope of rhetoric ends at the limits of human perception and performance. Rhetoric is still broadly understood as a techne, the confines of which are explained as the limits of human interaction upon that which cannot come into existence by itself. I believe it is fair to claim that rhetoricians, in general, have cared not to investigate material worlds that supposedly exist beyond human sensitivity or perception. Certainly, our assumption that agency is tied to human subjectivity (whatever permutation of subjectivity that we value) mirrors this long-standing belief of the role and position of rhetoric. However, a return to a more recent discussion among Cheryl Geisler, Christian Lundberg, and Joshua Gunn over the role and nature of agency in rhetorical studies offers us a somewhat clearer perspective on how rhetoricians could employ a conception of distributed and nonhuman agency.

## Distributed and Nonhuman Agency

The dialogue over agency at the 2003 Alliance of Rhetoric Societies, and the subsequent debate over the general consensus about agency in the pages of *Rhetoric Society Quarterly* brought additional issues of subjectivity and the role of agent positions to light. Geisler attempted to summarize the collective wisdom of the conference and express some of the dominant positions about agency discussed there. She felt that the most important discussions concerned the rhetor's ability to act; most conference-goers, she claimed, gave the agent some level of efficacy for action (12). If agency is a theoretical illusion, as some suggested, then it was a necessary illusion because the danger in recognizing agency as a complete illusion would possibly render the field of rhetoric irrelevant (Geisler 16). Lundberg and Gunn's counterargument came in the form of a critique of Geisler's basic assumptions and seemingly casual dismissal of Gunn's claims. They argue that Geisler confuses agent and agency while conflating posthumanism and postmodernism—and that such a conflation suggests agency is *mere* illusion (86). Most damning of their three counterpoints addresses Geisler's reduction of agency and agent to the same concept. Through the work of Jacques Derrida, Jacques Lacan, and Michel Foucault, Lundberg and Gunn call into question the distinction between agency, "the production of effect or action," and agent, "the presumed origin of effect or action" (88). While Geisler claims situations may be socially and rhetorically constructed (see Vatz), her articulation of agent is not constructed in the same way, or at least to the same degree, which allows for the "possession" of some *thing* called agency. Disagreeing with Geisler, Lundberg and Gunn find that agency should be considered akin to a possessing spirit—something that, depending on a range of conditions, can be hosted in various possible agents. Lundberg and Gunn's argument opens up the potential for agency to be freed of humanist confines and at least offers the prospective for nonhuman agents. If we find that agency is, indeed, like a kind of floating specter than can inhabit various agent positions, then we are more likely to (self-consciously) bump into a range of agent-positions-as-things-in-the-world as we go about our daily lives. Frustratingly, however, most examples of agency are offered as human rhetors finding and articulating agency or otherwise emerging in/as the agent. There is very little discussion of nonhuman agents as rhetors, aside from indirect discussions on the sometimes powerful positions occupied by various technologies that affect our thoughts and actions. To be clear, I am not counting Lundberg and Gunn, Herndl and Licona, or Campbell as thinkers who ignore all forms of nonhuman agency, but I do want to complicate the dominant assumptions of humans-as-agents within rhetoric studies, and Latour's work on hybrid objects aids in this complication.

The ANT Latour has spent much of his career articulating includes, as a fundamental assertion, that we cannot divide cognition from material-biological form nor culture from technology. Latour finds that the term "collective" better represents interactions between humans and nonhumans, both of which are granted agency to act. Collectives assume that human and nonhuman "actants"/agents exist on an ontologically level playing field, each impacting the other in a network of forces. When movements are performed in these networks, we do not recognize them as only originating from humans but from "*an association of actants*" (*PH* 182). While it may seem as if humans are irrelevant in this formulation, because ecologies of things would go on taking up agent positions regardless of whether or not we enter into the picture, that is not the case. Though humans and nonhumans are on a level playing field to begin with, a flat ontology does not necessarily mean that all things are *perpetually equal* but that they have no innate inequality. As Ian Bogost neatly explains, "*all things equally exist, yet they do not exist equally*" (11; original emphasis). Humans can and do rise to exert more power and host a greater share of agency in a network of actants, even though the work of humans (and nonhumans) in these collectives is often that of translation, delegation, mediation, and sorting, among other actions (*Modern* 137–38).

Significant, because humans are always immersed within constellations of actants, what is human or nonhuman cannot be clearly rendered. We have no specific access to pure subjects or pure objects. Instead, Latour claims, we have quasi-subjects and quasi-objects (*Modern* 53). These quasi-formations highlight things' tendencies toward subject-ness or object-ness but refuse to cleave them apart and place then into neat categories. Instead of a humanist subject or a postmodern, fragmented, socially constructed subject, the quasi-subject is a hybrid of various discourses, material effects, semiotic codes, and affective fields. Latour identifies such hybrid-formation quasi-subjects as "imbroglios of science, politics, economy, law, religion, technology, [and] fiction" (*Modern* 3). This conception of hybrids develops in part from Donna Haraway's articulation of "monsters" as lived fictions of created natural objects. Haraway certainly influenced Latour, as his definition of a hybrid comprises an array of these same practices and forms (scientific, sociological, and rhetorical). In order to illustrate these quasi-subject hybrids, Latour famously rereads the bumper-sticker phrase "Guns don't kill people, people kill people." In his eyes, a person with a gun is a fundamentally different kind of subject than without. Either a gun-citizen or a citizen-gun, when someone holds a gun, that person exists as another subject and the gun as another kind of object: "The gun is no longer the gun-in-the-armory or the gun-in-the-drawer or the gun-in-the pocket, but the gun-in-your-hand, aimed at someone who is screaming" (*Modern* 179–80). These imbroglios alter our agent positions in such a fundamental way *because* rhetorical agency is fundamentally altered in the constellation of actants with which we have formed close agentive partnerships. As such, agency for rhetorical power is distributed within and among these quasi-forms.

## Agentive Movement

Latour's description of these quasi-subjects is not indicative of a "special case" where only certain technologies or specific situations guide the formation of (even mostly human) agent positions. Agency inhabits human/nonhuman hybrids in many and varied forms (and always more than one agent position at a time). Simply because we recognize couches, tea kettles, flatworms, and flying fish as separate objects does not mean they are not constantly immersed in constellations of power in much the same way we feel as though we are. I can think of no better deep exploration of nonhuman agency than that described in Latour's *Aramis, or the Love of Technology*. In this larger work, Latour employs a version of ANT to explore why a large-scale, innovative transportation project was cancelled after many years of investment, research, and production. From 1969 to 1987, thousands of engineers, designers, officials, and managers worked to complete Aramis, which was to replace the Paris metro. Latour explores reasons why Aramis was not implemented through the fictional interaction of a sociology professor who has been tasked with writing a report as to why Aramis "failed" and a young engineer, as well as a surprising third character, Aramis itself. In showcasing his methodology to "follow the actors," Latour "channels" Aramis's agency and represents it as another voice in the text, one that exists in print in dialogue with the human agents, interview transcripts, and the technical and legal documents from the project (10).

That Latour showcases this form of agency so dramatically through a large-scale *transportation* project, specifically, is fitting for his claims concerning agency. After all, there are few positions we encounter on a daily basis where we share agency with such an immersive, powerful, and complex coordination of things as in our daily experience of transportation. Further, the driver-car assemblage stands as one of the most virulent forms of this hybrid agent position. In the car, we are "geared" to the world, perceiving the technology of mobility with our senses in order to navigate space (Dant 71). As I have argued previously in "Something Less Than a Driver," the driver-car assemblage in which we understand and judge our immediate sensory field focuses on things like speed, distance, road surface, texture, wind, sign systems, other drivers, and so on. Mobilities scholar John Urry offers a more complete definition of this "automobility" as a "double resonance" "of the way in which the car-driver is a 'hybrid' assemblage, not simply of autonomous humans but simultaneously of machines, roads, buildings, signs and entire cultures of mobility" (18). As Latour expresses in *Aramis*, these same automobility technologies are particularly good locations (and events) through which we are able to understand the distributed power of rhetorical agency between and among human and nonhumans. Mobility technologies are desirable examples for analysis because they showcase the kinds of rhetorical movement that take place—a literal movement, a kinetic energy that evinces distributed agency.

## Kinetics

Few scholars take on the assumptions about rhetorical agency that keep us from recognizing shared agent positions better than Carolyn Miller. Miller surveyed teachers of composition and public speaking as to their opinions on a fictional product called AutoSpeech-Easy, software that when paired with a camera and microphone, offers autonomous, accurate assessments of students' speeches. Unsurprising, she finds that automated assessment technologies (sometimes considered "robo-grading" systems) "cut to the heart of the theoretical and ideological concerns about agency" and ask whether posthumanist theory can "disperse agency to a machine" (145). She explains that most rhetoricians restrict the attribution of agency to humans because speech (the quintessential rhetorical performance) "tempts us to focus" heavily on bodily performance, motion, and presence while recognizing agency as something that humans possess prior to a rhetorical act (147). The problem we have with performing for an automated assessment system "is not that it is inscrutable—audience is always inscrutable to at least some degree—but that we are unwilling to grant it such [agentive] presence and therefore cannot, in an important sense, perform" (149). In order to combat these notions, Miller argues that we should focus on agency as the *kinetic energy* of rhetorical performance. If we see agency as a shared performance between rhetor and audience but do not recognize nonhumans as able to "have" agency in the first place, we also fail to see nonhumans *as part of that audience*. Miller is right that kinetic energy is created during rhetorical performance; however, I also argue that we create the kinetic energy of rhetorical performance even when we are much less consciously aware of that performance.

We often assume that rhetorical performance involves "forethought," and for performances, such as premeditated speeches, directed toward assessment software or live audiences of people, this is certainly accurate. However, there are countless instances in everyday life when we are unconscious of our rhetorical acts, yet perform them, nonetheless. If we consider rhetorical performance as also existing in mundane, everyday activities, our conceptions of agency must change as well. When agency is only recognized as "potential agency," Miller contends, "it will be thought of as a possession or property of an agent (like a stationary stone), but if agency is a kinetic energy, it must be a property of the rhetorical event or performance itself" (147). Such everyday rhetorical performance involves shared agency, which can be observed through movement itself. Following from the work of Latour, I claim that it is possible to understand the observation and theorization of kinetic energy, or *kinesis* forms of motion, as a method for recognizing distributed rhetorical agency in constellations of humans and nonhumans.

The term "kinetic energy" is derived from the Greek *kinesis*, which Aristotle claimed was imperfect movement, that is, movement with limits, such as (in Aristotle's examples) learning, being cured, walking, thinking, and house building. In some respects, kinesis is Aristotle's more general word for change, including movement, and Miller's characterization of kinetic energy as performed movement is certainly appropriate. Additionally, Aristotle argues that kinesis motions cannot be said to have happened until they are complete. For example, one cannot be said to have built a house until the action of building a house is over—in other words, kinesis motions are generally defined through their involvement with physical objects or movement among things in the world. Unlike *energeia* forms of movement, kinesis movements cannot be constant and always ongoing. J. L. Ackrill, likewise, describes kinesis as "an *energeia* in the wide sense, an actuality as opposed to a potentiality" (142). For example, a kinesis movement like "building a house" is not complete until the house is built. I prefer to think of kinesis as movements in the world that accompany states of being—ones that have determinate steps or sequences of subaction that establish the focus, length, and completeness of the entire movement. For Aristotle, the identification of kinesis does not lie in the specific kinds of movement used as examples above but in the essence of the movements themselves. The determining concern is not whether movement takes place among or with material forms or is performed by humans but whether movement has, as part of its own coherence, a limit (Ackrill 146).

Kinesis movements happen all of the time, too, regardless of whether we contemplate the agentive capacities of our audiences or consider agency as only emergent within or between humans. Certainly, we may balk at the ability of a nonhuman conversation partner to assess the rhetorical quality of our speeches, but do we feel the same toward the myriad nonhumans involved with the rhetoric performance of driving a car? Such "covert" performances are, likewise, expressed through kinetic forms of movement, yet because they exist in quotidian, everyday performances, we evince far less concern over nonhuman agency as it emerges through interaction. Understandably so, because our automobiles do not threaten us with failing grades if our performance is inadequate. However, automobiles do crash, and when they do, they belie the shared agency of our movements. Though we may see ourselves as having complete control of our vehicles (and claim to feel it, too), where the agency of the automobile ends and where our agency begins is indeterminable. While lawsuit verdicts and insurance investigations may render the two distinct, the actual rhetorical performance blends the humans and nonhumans of vehicular transportation so completely that at very few points within automobile operation are we able to state who is driving whom or if any "one" agent is in control.

Kinesis may seem like a convenient concept for complicating agency—after all, if we identify agency through kinetic movements, then we give up any claims to the "ownership" or "possession" of agency—yet, it also performs an ontological function as well. Kinesis forms of motion are more than just the movements we can observe and, therefore, use to complicate agency but operate as manifestations of being in the world. For Martin Heidegger, kinesis is not simply a kind of moving about, not "merely one state among others, but [. . .] an *essential determination* [where] *motion as a mode of Being is fundamental*" (142; original emphasis). Being is comprised essentially as/through motion and essentially; motion always *is*. There is always something moving, that is, there is no state that does not include motion, because things can only *be* if there also exists some variety of kinesis present (147). Ontologically speaking, the very nature of existence requires some kind of physical manifestation of motion. Kinesis happens in movement but in rest, too, as Heidegger argues: "There is also *kinesis* even if all there is is something at rest" (147). Kinesis occurs when one is making a speech, driving a car, or building a boat, as the movements required to perform the incomplete (time-limited) motions of any of these performances (speaking and gesturing, steering and braking, hammering and chiseling). If we understand agency as distributed between humans and nonhumans, emergent in performance, and observable through kinetic energy, what results is a representation of agency as an ontological condition. That we can see automobility as a way of being in the world (a performance that allows the world to show up for us in unique ways) underscores the deep and complex relationship of agency to being.

## Colorless Green Leaves Spin Agency

An example of how we can recognize the shared agency in performance through the observation of kinesis occurs in the persuasive space between a driver and an automobile dashboard. All vehicular interfaces offer up instances of how a technology can function in a constellation with the user so as to shape movement in the world. Further, we can read these dashboards for how they enable and compel forms of rhetorical movement that blur distinctions between human and nonhuman agency. For example, the much-lauded Chevrolet Volt electric car sports several features on its dashboard interface that function with and persuade the driver to make the most efficient use of the fuel-saving drivetrain. Specifically, the Configurable Cluster Display, when in Enhanced Mode, shows a rotating green sphere of leaves sitting in the center of a vertical gauge. The Volt's promotional materials suggest that when in motion, the driver-car should attempt to

> keep the sphere balanced in the middle. If the ball turns yellow and travels above the center of the gauge, the vehicle is accelerating too aggressively to achieve maximum efficiency. If it travels below the center of the gauge, you're braking too aggressively to capture energy from regenerative braking. (Chevrolet)

The metaphor that the rotating green-leaf ball serves to enable is something like "balanced, green leaves equal more efficient driving." Aside from sounding like a Chomskian nonsensical, the interactive leaf ball traffics on the assumption that both the color green and images of plant life are enthymematic for environmental responsibility. Though we know that spinning green-leaf balls and ecological driving habits are not the same thing, the metaphor often carries through.

The kinesis movements that result from this constellation of humans and nonhumans are wide-ranging and complex. If the metaphor is successful in providing a compelling interaction, the driver may try to keep the ball of leaves centered and green by using a light touch on the accelerator, cruise control, or attempts at long, slow braking zones (which recover more kinetic energy in vehicles equipped with regenerative braking). Although it would take a long-term observation of the driver-vehicle environment or perhaps a Chevrolet engineer to examine the Volt's "black box" to determine whether these movements did occur, it *would* be possible. Further, this observation of movement would not be limited to those of the human driver but would include those of nonhuman agents as well. We could also count the spinning of a flywheel, the discharge of a battery, the pressure in a brake line, the surface of the road, or the persuasive shape of the Volt itself. In order to fully account for all of the agents, we might be tempted to create a large table of their varying relations and powers and chart all of the movements they perform or enable to be performed (together and separately) in a situation. Thankfully, such a task would be both maddening and unnecessary, not only because no one would be interested in doing the work but also because even a complete table of agential movements would not "account" for agency. Examining kinetic movements could aid in the identification of actors, though *no list of actors and the movements they perform will fully account for agency.* For that, we would also want a rich description of how the most influential actors interact, which, in this example, would likely be the spinning green leaves of the Volt's Enhanced Mode, the movements and stated intentions of the driver, the electric engine, and the particular manifestations of the roadway. Rich descriptions of these exchanges could illustrate the flow of agency among these actors as well as the movements they perform. And, since agency cannot be possessed but embodied and performed, researchers utilizing these concepts could map actors' roles so that they form a conversation representative of agency, much as Latour does, albeit with alternate methodological assumptions, throughout *Aramis.*

In *Aramis*, Latour employs his ontosociology and identifies the actors and the forces that make up any given sociotechnical situation. Instead of a "context," a concept Latour sees as inadequate, he focuses on the *network of actors*, and his methodology is sometimes expressed as a drive to scrutinize those in the network of forces that impact a particular question of agency. He follows both humans and nonhumans because, as he argues elsewhere, "No observer of human collectives, for at least the past two million years, has ever been faced with pure social relation, and none of course, *especially* in high-tech modern settings has ever been faced with a pure technique" ("Ethnography" 380). In order to identify all of the translations at work within a network, Latour moves slowly, pausing to listen to every *thing*, because his guiding focus is to avoid discriminating between humans and nonhuman agents. Thus, one of his primary maxims is to consider all sources and "keep everything flat" (*RS* 190). Latour's methodology in *Aramis* could provide rhetoric scholars with a surprisingly helpful template for exploring complex, situated realms of agency, especially if rhetoricians are interested in tracking agency between humans and nonhumans and identifying how all things in the world perform the work of translation. The advantages to attempting such a Latourian study while attending to kinetic movement, in particular, are threefold: we are made aware of the differences between agent and agency, we are more attune to all actors' function as translators, and we avoid locking nonhumans out of agentive roles—the roles they so obviously play in everyday life.

Agency is not "tabulated" so much as experienced, and observing kinetic movement is beneficial primarily in that it helps complicate a simplistic understanding of agency as a possession that humans can wield. Here, I have attempted to show one method for identifying agency through understanding what moves and how that movement occurs. Though the limits of this essay do not allow me to provide a lengthy, thick description of such a driver-vehicle interface, I am interested in the potential of such empirical observation and rhetorical and ontological analysis for understanding complex hybrid agencies. Latour's methodology for identifying agency and my own articulation of a movement-based focus for such inquiries allow rhetoricians the freedom to consider a wider range of observable forces in their studies. While we would never want to be confined to mechanistic views of human agency, derived solely from physical movement, neither would we want to stop theorizing agency where human intentionality ends. Such theorizing is necessarily going to become more important, too, as autonomous technologies, such as parallel-park assist, lane-departure corrections, automatic accident-avoidance brake systems, and, of course, Google's self-driving car, begin to find their way into our everyday lives. Attending to the broad range of kinetic movements along with more traditional rhetorical methods may promote a flatter rhetoric—one more attentive to the influences and interactions between humans and nonhumans.

In *Rhetoric and Philosophy in Conflict*, Samuel Ijsseling asks, "Who is actually speaking whenever something is said?" and answers, somewhat cagily, that "speaking is always speaking *before another* and writing is always writing *for another*" (134). Individual language acts are never actually that—never alone in the world of influences from other people, cultures, materials, places, and discourse itself. Though Ijsseling addresses intersubjective and intertextual webs of meanings in order to understand how communication is compelled and impelled, an attention to kinetic energy may allow us to seek out such questions in the realm of the human and nonhuman parliament of things. In the example pursued here, I asked, "Who is actually driving when something is being driven?" In some ways, the answer comes back as, "no one." No *one* is ever at the wheel.

## Notes

1. Wiener is sometimes brought into conversations about posthuman agency explicitly because he equated the human with the technological, to some degree understanding human affect, motion, and cognition as the information we receive from and impart to our environment.

2. Jennifer Daryl Slack, David James Miller, and Jeffrey Doak in "Technical Communicator" provide a clear explication of authorial and agentive positions at work in twentieth-century technical communication. Their stance on "articulation" within technical communication sees it as more amenable because it offers technical communicators relational agency within complex networks of agents, some of which are understood as material.

3. The discourse that comprises the "rhetoric of science" is certainly nuanced, and while I do not want to oversimplify the differences among these authors' positions, together they provide a useful overview of the field. Several especially informative texts include Charles Bazerman, *Shaping Written Knowledge*; Alan Gross, *Rhetoric of Science*; Dilip Parameshwar Goankar, "Idea of Rhetoric in the Rhetoric of Science"; and Randy Allen Harris, "Knowing, Rhetoric, Science."

## Works Cited


Ackrill, J. L. *Essays on Plato and Aristotle*. Oxford: Oxford UP, 1997. Print.

Aristotle. *Physics. The Complete Works of Aristotle*. Ed. Jonathan Barnes. Oxford: Oxford UP, 1984. Print.

Bazerman, Charles. *Shaping Written Knowledge: The Genre and Activity of the Experimental Article in Science*. Madison: U of Wisconsin P, 1988. Print.

Bitzer, Lloyd F. "The Rhetorical Situation." *Philosophy and Rhetoric* 1.1 (1968): 1–14. Print.

Bogost, Ian. *Alien Phenomenology, or, What It's Like to Be a* Thing. Minneapolis: U of Minnesota P, 2012. Print.

Bryant, Levi R. *The Democracy of Objects*. Ann Arbor: Open Humanities, 2011. Print.

Campbell, Karlyn Kohrs. "Agency: Promiscuous and Protean." *Communication and Critical/Cultural Studies* 2.1 (2005): 1–19. Print.

Chevrolet. "2011 Chevy Volt—Dashboard | Instrument Cluster Display | Electric Car." *YouTube*. 28 Sept. 2010. Web. 20 Jan. 2013. <http://www.youtube.com/watch?v=xtMACEqCgDg>.

Dant, Tim. "The Driver-Car." *Theory, Culture & Society* 21.4–5 (2004): 61–79. Print.

Geisler, Cheryl. "How Ought We to Understand the Concept of Rhetorical Agency? Report from the ARS." *Rhetoric Society Quarterly* 34.3 (2004): 9–17. Print.

Goankar, Dilip Parameshwar. "The Idea of Rhetoric in the Rhetoric of Science." *Southern Communication Journal* 58.4 (1993): 258–295. Print.

Gross, Alan G. *The Rhetoric of Science*. Cambridge: Harvard UP, 1990. Print.

Harris, Randy Allen. "Knowing, Rhetoric, Science." *Visions and Revisions: Continuity and Change in Rhetoric and Composition*. Ed. James D. Williams. Carbondale: Southern Illinois UP, 2002. Print.

Heidegger, Martin. *Basic Concepts in Ancient Philosophy*. Trans. Richard Rojcewicz. Bloomington: Indiana UP, 2007. Print.

Herndl, Carl G., and Adela C. Licona. "Shifting Agency: Agency, Kairos, and the Possibilities of Social Action." *Communicative Practices in Workplaces and the Professions: Cultural Perspectives on the Regulation of Discourse and Organizations*. Ed. Mark Zachry and Charlotte Thralls. Amityville: Baywood, 2007. 133–153. Print.

Ijsseling, Samuel. *Rhetoric and Philosophy in Conflict*. The Hague: Nijhoff, 1976. Print.

Latour, Bruno. *Aramis, or the Love of Technology*. Trans. Catherine Porter. Cambridge: Harvard UP, 1996. Print.

———. "Ethnography of a High Tech Case: About Aramis." *Technological Choices: Transformations in Material Cultures since the Neolithic*. Ed. P. Lemonnier. London: Routledge, 1993. 372–398. Print.

———. *Pandora's Hope: Essays on the Reality of Science Studies*. Cambridge: Harvard UP, 1999. Print.

———. *Politics of Nature: How to Bring the Sciences into Democracy*. Trans. Catherine Porter. Cambridge: Harvard UP, 2004. Print.

———. *Reassembling the Social: An Introduction to Actor-Network-Theory*. Oxford: Oxford UP, 2007. Print.

———. *We Have Never Been Modern*. Trans. Catherine Porter. Cambridge: Harvard UP, 1993. Print.

Lundberg, Christian, and Joshua Gunn. "'Ouija Board, Are There Any Communications?': Agency, Ontotheology, and the Death of the Humanistic Subject, or, Continuing the ARS Conversation." *Rhetoric Society Quarterly* 35.4 (2005): 83–105. Print.

Miller, Carolyn R. "What Can Automation Tell Us about Agency?" *Rhetoric Society Quarterly* 37.2 (2007): 137–157. Print.

Pflugfelder, Ehren Helmut. "Something Less Than a Driver: Toward an Understanding of Gendered Bodies in Motorsport." *Journal of Sport and Social Issues* 33.4 (2009): 411–426. Print.

Slack, Jennifer Daryl, David James Miller, and Jeffrey Doak. "The Technical Communicator as Author: Meaning, Power and Authority." *Journal of Business and Technical Communication* 7.1 (1993): 12–36. Print.

Spuybroek, Lars. *The Architecture of Continuity: Essays and Conversations*. Rotterdam: NAi, 2009. Print.

Urry, John. "Inhabiting the Car." *Against Automobility*. Ed. Steffen Böhm, Campbell Jones, Chris Land, and Matthew Paterson. Oxford: Wiley-Blackwell, 2006. Print.

Vatz, Richard E. "The Myth of the Rhetorical Situation." *Philosophy and Rhetoric* 6.3 (1973): 154–161. Print.

# Part Three. **Convening Assemblages**

# 8. The Whole of the Moon: Latour, Context, and the Problem of Holism

Thomas Rickert, *Purdue University*

Recent scientific studies on wine tasting show most people to be, in a word, gullible. Experiments have demonstrated that one's sense of the taste and quality of a wine is rarely determined by what is actually in the glass. Rather, contextual factors, such as a vintner's name, a wine's reputation, or the price—especially the price—determine a drinker's experience. In blind taste testings, wine drinkers generally prefer the wines labeled as expensive, even if it is actually cheap plonk in the glass (albeit, presumably competently made plonk). Brain scans demonstrate that the drinkers are not dissembling, either: brain activity corresponding to heightened pleasure tends to accompany wines perceived as expensive and are lacking in ones that are not.[1] The evidence is clear. The wine itself contributes little to our experience of its pleasure and quality, suggesting that we might as well drink cheap. Training in wine tasting allows for slightly more discrimination between fine and cheap wine but not exceptionally so. Thus, taste, setting, and pleasure come to rest on factors such as vintner, marketing, pricing, and wine-critic wizardry. The result is an elevation of context over the object.

This is an apt beginning point in an essay on Bruno Latour, not least because Latour himself is a member of a famous wine-producing family (they produce Louis Latour wines) in Beaune, a region within Burgundy, France. But there is further aptness, since Latour has made a number of critical remarks about context, preferring the labor of detailing the particularities—the things and objects—that make up an assembled entity. This essay explores these critiques of context and their link to scientific work and politics. The import of these wine studies is that they demonstrate that the question of context will not leave us alone, being yet another permutation of the realist/idealist debate: to what extent is the taste of wine objective, really there in the glass, and to what extent is it subjective, the result of situational, social, or symbolic practices? In all his work, Latour has been very compelling on the necessity of overcoming subject/object, nature/culture dichotomies, but that alone does not settle the issue here. To what extent does context determine the active variables, in this case the taste of wine, and to what extent does context emerge as an assemblage of complexly interactive variables (or actants)? I argue that context is irrepressible and that it is a variety of hybrid actant, which an intensification of Latour's own theories can demonstrate.

## Contextualizing Latour

While Latour has made his name in science studies, he has consistently developed a rhetorically suffused politics alongside his scientific interests. This makes sense: if science entails more than simple fact-finding and truth delivery, then considering its techniques, artifacts, and procedures necessitates exploration of its social, political, and material emplacement. A prominent example of Latour's new materialist politics is his notion of *dingpolitik*—a politics of things. In "From Realpolitik to Dingpolitik," Latour notes that politics is rhetorical; it involves assembly and persuasion. Each necessitates the other: persuasion is achieved through an assembly of actants, and an assembly of actants is achieved through forms of persuasion. These assemblies are not confined to the social—that is, human actants—but, rather, include nonhumans. The social is inseparable from its material infrastructure. A Latourian public is composed of collectives of human and nonhuman actants, making it a sociomaterial stitch work constantly reweaving itself into new collective forms (*PN* 161–63, 174–75).

It is not just that Latour upholds the necessity of persuasion in the face of what science—among other entities—wants to call "facts" about objective matter. Rather, it is that he also takes the objects that surround us and conjoins them with the urgencies of our concerns. Objects become rhetorical because they are inseparable from what engages us and, thereby, assemble us as a public. This is dingpolitik: a new gathering of elements and, of course, people but also the things that populate the world and matter to us. As Latour puts it, "objects—taken as so many issues—bind us all in ways that map out a public space profoundly different from what is usually recognized under the label of 'the political'" ("Dingpolitik" 5). A dingpolitik thematizes a goal Latour had long been working toward, summarily stated in *Pandora's Hope*, that "political representation of nonhumans seems not only plausible now but necessary"

(202). The import for Latour is that science and dingpolitiks can commingle, thereby giving greater place and value to nonhuman elements.

Latour provides many advances, but there are also some problems, as indicated in my opening wine example. To what extent can we adhere to Latour's Husserlian-derived dictum to follow the things themselves? That question opens up a tension between two organizing ideas. First, we have *assemblage*, in which persuasion becomes a matter of conjoining allies and relevant parties, material and otherwise, with the resultant analytical and rhetorical work conceived as following the particular trajectories of these parties. This is opposed to a second organizing idea, *context*, particularly a holistic notion of the "as a whole." Latour often derides context as a wrong move, a crutch; indeed, he arguably never gets more explicit on this point than when he claims, quoting Rem Koolhaas, that "context stinks!" (*RS* 148). Context misleads insofar as it substitutes a background explanation for the rich and hard work of concrete description (*RS* 143–44). That is, context posits an overarching narrative to explain what should really emerge from the description of the complex and specific variables making up an assemblage.

This argument could be seen as troubling for rhetorical theory, which, like many disciplines, relies heavily on notions of context, particularly when conceived as some form of periodization or categorization. Context underpins or otherwise organizes the most common rhetorical concepts. For instance, the communications triangle (commonly understood to involve a sender, message, receiver, and discourse, but there are other versions) functions as context, and it is in fact derived from Aristotle and his map of rhetorical appeals—*ethos*, *pathos*, and *logos*.[2] Lloyd F. Bitzer's conception of the rhetorical situation is another form of context, in this case invoking "persons, events, objects, relations, and an exigence which strongly invites utterance" (5). While Bitzer's conception has been critiqued, the basic point remains: rhetoric emerges in situations, or contexts, which give place and bearing to what transpires. Indeed, it is with a background such as Bitzer's that we see how important a role context plays in other rhetorical concepts, particularly where we derive notions of appropriateness or fittingness within a larger sphere—*kairos* and *doxa* come to mind here. What I seek to do in this essay is take Latour's critique seriously but at the same time use it to rejuvenate a notion of holism as essential for rhetorical theory and, I hope, gain a new perspective on what context is and how we understand its rhetorical work. Put reductively, I am arguing that context retains its holistic dimension but that this scope is neither stable nor the sole result of human doing.

## Dingpolitik: From *Vir Bonus* to *Res Bona*

Latour's dingpolitik aims at putting *things* back into political work, which mirrors Latour's understanding of how scientific work proceeds. To theorize how this politics must be different, Latour picks up Martin Heidegger's etymology of the word "thing," showing that it (and its cognates *ding*, *ting*, *althing*, etc.) has long designated not just a mundane object but an assembly of people gathered together to discuss matters of concern ("Dingpolitik" 22–23). Latour is not nostalgic here; he simply seeks to show that our customary distinction between the realms of matter and sociality runs counter to the word's inherent meanings. In a Latourian idiom, the word "thing" comes to designate a hybrid actor (i.e., a composite of materiality and meaning) that, in turn, helps to gather allies for envisioning and enacting a new politics, a dingpolitik. This amounts to what he calls a "new eloquence" ("Dingpolitik" 20). To return to my opening example, we might note that the wine industry, while not being directly political, might better exemplify Latour's point about the "thing," since viticulture is fundamentally oriented toward and galvanized by a valuation of the nonhuman (ground, vines, grapes, weather, etc.). So, perhaps we can think of dingpolitiks as an attempt to bring to politics and political rhetoric a sensibility to the nonhuman already practiced in other arenas.

There are two movements to dingpolitik's enactment: finding the relevant elements and marshaling proofs to spur action. First, we must detect the relevant parties that need to be included, which necessarily also requires the work of demonstrating influence and connection. This is relationality, strongly construed. The networks in actor-network-theory (ANT) are on this account not preestablished, so that we simply observe, diagram, describe, and explain; rather, we do the work of establishing that connective networks are there, in howsoever form they exist. Not *network*, says Latour, but *worknet*—one does the work to establish what the network will have been (*RS* 143). As Latour puts it in *Politics of Nature*, what becomes knowable does so insofar as "it has been formed through networks of instruments; it is defined through the interventions of professions, disciplines, and protocols; it is distributed via databases; it is provided with arguments through the intermediary of learned societies" (4). In this sense, detecting the relevant parties cannot simply be identifying things of concern; it has to be demonstrated how things become concernful within larger assemblages, and this demonstration is itself a "worknetting" of larger assemblages.

After detecting the relevant parties, the next step is to marshal proofs so that political deliberations can lead to wise and informed decisions. Latour notes that this step has many old names, including eloquence, rhetoric, and sophistry, and he comments that we might need to rescue them from the "dustbin of history" ("Dingpolitik" 18–19). While rhetoric is, perhaps, less in need of rescue than Latour's hyperbole suggests, still, fresh understandings of rhetorical work remain useful if not galvanizing. For Latour, rhetoric's rejoinder to science is that, first, science is inevitably connected to the political, and, second, that there can be no simple wielding of knowledge and fact, as if these things are transparently given and directly potent. Rather, they require the connective work of rhetorical appeal.

One of Latour's examples is Colin Powell's argument to the United Nations Security Council that weapons of mass destruction (WMDs) existed in Iraq. Powell's presentation of the evidence for WMDs needed an accompanying examination of the procedures substantiating the "facts"—lacking that, the facts are poorly assembled. This gets us to the heart of Latour's understanding of political representation. Facts are not simply achieved and presented. To present them as such is a misrepresentation, since it denies to representation "any *re*-presentation . . . any opaque layers of translations, transmissions, betrayals . . . any complicated machinery of assembly, delegation, proof, argumentation, negotiation, and conclusion" ("Dingpolitik" 26). The advance of Latour is, thus, to extend the range of the political and, thereby, also stretch rhetoric to include elements it has customarily excluded. Everything is assembled, and the best politics stems from and looks to what is well assembled—and, thus, to what traces the best eloquence as well. We move from the *vir bonus* to the *res bona*—from "the good man speaking well," the customary translation of Quintilian's "*vir bonus dicendi peritus*" in the *Institutes* 12.1.1 to "the good thing assembled well" (*bonum arte convenit*, perhaps, or *res bona convenerunt bene*).

## The Bling in Assembling/Disassembling

Despite Latour's advances, in other ways he is more traditional. Certainly, he maintains a commonplace understanding of persuasion as intended influence. Influence may well be achieved through assembly, but it is still a matter of inducing assemblages of humans to agree on what is to be done and how it is to be pursued. Thus, Latour frequently defines rhetorical power as alliance, so that the strength of a position depends on the connections created. The rhetorical power of a team of scientists, for instance, can be augmented politically by forging alliances with, say, certain religious groups, who together work toward shaping a new, common policy. The creation of alliances is itself rhetorical, of course; as Latour claims in *Pandora's Hope*, alliances are a matter of the "labor of making people interested" (104). Thus, some forms of science cannot proceed without very particular forms of rhetorical work in garnering the interests of, as Latour describes it, the "rich and well endowed" (104). Money and status, in other words, are here acknowledged as integral to the pursuit of rhetorical power since they result from and further pursue rhetorical power. Other such examples abound in Latour.[3]

Rhetorical power as accumulation is a special kind of addition that transforms what the elements are and how they work together. This is what makes the res bona a hybrid: to use one of his more famous examples, it is not citizen + gun, meaning two different actants with different ontological statuses but a hybrid actant with different affordances than previously, "a citizen-gun, a gun-citizen" (*PH* 179).[4] And, to recap, this was the key to Latour's conception of dingpolitiks: the introduction of new objects is not just an addition of nonhumans into a traditionally human process but an addition that transforms how representation takes place. The emphasis on the "re" in representation, in turn, asks how an assemblage is assembled. The genuine Latourian counterpart to assembly is, therefore, disassembly, since that it is how we determine if what has been constructed is, in fact, a res bona, a good thing assembled well.

Let us return to Latour's claim in *Reassembling the Social* that for ANT, contexts or frameworks are problematic and best avoided. In the guise of a professor advising a student, Latour states, "I've never understood what context meant, no. . . . it doesn't add anything to the picture. . . . [T]he context . . . is precisely the sum of factors that make no difference to the data, what is common knowledge about it" (*RS* 144). Latour advises the student to avoid all frameworks and contexts and just describe, since objects are made of multiple layers, and, therefore, "[i]t's the object itself that adds multiplicity, or rather the thing, the 'gathering'" (*RS* 144). Latour's argument certainly puts the bling back in reassembling—and disassembling ("Dingpolitik" 34–35). This is so equally for science as politics or any forum where research is required. Indeed, we see here why Latour emphasizes writing and description as the essence of scientific work. Knowledge emerges from following where the objects lead. Latour confesses, "That's why I am teaching nothing but writing nowadays. I keep repeating the same mantra: 'describe, write, describe, write'" (*RS* 149).

It is easy to agree with much of Latour's animus toward contextual explanation. Explaining the desire for academic jobs as the result of "market pressure"—one of Latour's sarcastic list of suspect contextual moves—is not an explanation but a resting on received doxa (*RS* 147). Such explanations function as trivial epideictic to the power of opinion, substituting for knowledge an overarching narrative, itself difficult if not impossible to prove, as the frame that determines all the other elements. Instead, one must attend to everyday micropractices and eschew overarching narratives of context.[5] Context is, thereby, fractured into potentially infinite manifold, which dissolves its explanatory power. However, as suggested in my opening wine example, context has a way of remanifesting itself.

## Boundaries of Context

Here we come to the crux of the matter: on the one hand, Latour compellingly argues that context blocks richer explanations necessary for successful scientific and political work; on the other, I am suspicious of Latour's dismissal of context, in howsoever nuanced a fashion, as if the object in an assemblage itself suffices as guide to knowledge. Latour's remarks about context indicate that he thinks of it as a humanly produced narrative and, hence, subjective and deficient. However, can we augment Latour on this issue and theorize context as a quasi-element that simultaneously functions within and frames a scenario? Being simultaneously a boundary and an element, we must then ask if context can be also be understood beyond the nature/culture, subject/object divides, which is to say that in the end context and framework are, like the thing of dingpolitik, not solely of human devise.

The opening wine example asks about this very dimension of context, for it implies that even so "subjective" a notion as taste is indissoluble from other contextual f/actors, both human and nonhuman, and hence has an "objective" component. Taste is not an isolatable and exclusively personal phenomenon; it is fundamentally interwoven with contextual. As the wine experiments show, defining experience exclusively as subjective produces skewed results, implying that people are malleable dupes in the face of solid objectivity. What we equally see is that the subjective presuppositions built into the experiment directly bind the results to subjectivism—the conceptual boundary of the experiment is translated into a boundary for what constitutes human being. It is clear that this is inadequate and unscientific since it assumes something that should itself be subject to proof. To do this, we might reenvision context as having a dual role: a framing narrative that must, in turn, be concretely brought back into the scenario it helps contour. Just as in other aspects of Latour, the solution is to see that context is not a human projection overlaying and distorting factual reality but itself a hybrid actant.

Perhaps, it is again a matter of pushing Latour harder on his basic premises. Context, then, like Latour's hybrid actants, would traverse the divides between nature/culture, mind/body, and body/world. Further, context is always buoyed up by and derived from an "as a whole" that has (at least) two dimensions. The first is the holistic, material ecology within which things find their roles and actions. This can include what we call "subjective" experience—indeed, it requires it as at least one vector in the contextual fabric. The second, which can be harder to attune ourselves to, might be described as the "relation of relations"—the undergirding logos from which things and language emerge in their meaning and bearing. The mention of language is important here; it is often assigned to human being, but in the sense I am using it here, it both involves and transcends human being.[6] Both these dimensions of the "as a whole," or the chorographic background, are involved with the assemblages Latour presents, but they also transcend and inflect them.

The first dimension, the holistic, material ecology, has the more obvious resonance with Latour's understanding of assemblage. Karen Barad's marvelous book *Meeting the Universe Halfway* provides an illuminating example. In 1922 Otto Stern and Walther Gerlach set out to conduct an experiment proving the reality of space quantization and, thereby, provide support for quantum theory against classical physics (Barad 162–63). Due to space constraints, I will skip the specific details of the experiment and, instead, note two important points. First, the experiment did not, in fact, succeed, although it did lead to some key fine-tuning that resulted in a later, successful experiment. However, the fine-tuning was itself only made possible by the fact that one of the experimenters, Stern, a male assistant professor with a low salary, smoked cheap cigars. The cheap cigar produced sulfurous smoke, which proved crucial in generating the experiment's results. However, following the cigar's affects led to further the further realization that the experiment did not, in fact, prove the reality of space quantization but rather electron spin (Barad 166–67). Now at first glance, we might claim that this simply follows Latour's claim that if we attend to objects, they will themselves add multiplicity. In this case, we can detect the smoke, and soon enough, through description and writing, we will find the fire, which, in this case, is the smoke's impact on the experiment, and, thereby, redescribe the experiment's actants, horizons, and results.

But if we look again, things get tricky, since the construction of an experiment explicitly and implicitly draws boundaries. These boundaries are inseparable from an awareness of context, since context contours how the various elements show up for us. Barad's Stern and Gerlach example indicates that an assemblage needs more to be understood than the incorporation of added elements that make a difference. Rather, incorporating a new element, in this case, cheap cigar smoke, transforms the very framework for understanding what an experiment is—and what it can ultimately prove. There are both resonance and dissonance with Latour on this point. With Latour, Barad will agree that the experiment—that is, everything the experiment entails and requires to be performed—is not solely a matter of human doing since it is an ensemble of interacting human and nonhuman actants. But what Barad adds that Latour is less successful at articulating is the background out of which experimentation itself proceeds; indeed, the problem of the cigar smoke is precisely an issue of that kind of overarching framing. At what point does it become understood as integral to the experiment, even if it was an aleatory element uncontrolled for in the original conception? What allows for the emergence of that judgment?

## Context as Plasma or Holistic Background?

Latour, I think, is himself aware that some other modality of context remains necessary, some hollow that grants place and bearing to the present world. Indeed, it is this problem that inspires Latour's recourse to what he calls *plasma*. The networks/worknets do not hook *everything* together, nor can any understanding of the social not include what is, as Latour terms it, "unformatted phenomena" (*RS* 234–44). This background is not hidden, just unknown, "providing the resources for every single course of action to be fulfilled" (244). In other words, no actant, human or nonhuman, is sufficient to reveal all that takes place in the world to explain an action. Hermeneutics is not solely a human domain but "a property of the world itself" (245). These "missing masses" are much larger than the revealed world; if one were to equate the known world with London's subway, the rest would encompass all else in London (244, 245).[7]

In the Stern and Gerlach experiment, Latour would likely consider the cigar smoke to be plasma prior to its recognition as an actant. Initially, the experiment excluded it; only after further research and insight did it become significant. In this way, a small amount of plasma was reclaimed for and, thereby, extended the (human) known world. Plasma, then, functions akin to but differently than context since it becomes a materialist backdrop for action. As a concept, plasma gives a particular reality to what we do not know, and it further underscores that *human* knowledge is only one small portion of what might be reclaimed from plasma, since all other actants, human and nonhuman, have their specific means of hermeneutic encounter that bring plasma into the "known," or, perhaps, better put in a less anthropocentric Heideggerian idiom, brings plasma to presence. Plasma remains different from context because it does not substitute explanatory narratives to account for what we do not know—"market pressures," "neoconservative ideology," and so on. Latour's plasma trumps context because it preserves the (Husserlian) dictum to follow the things themselves; thus, "describing, writing, describing, writing" is what brings some measure of unknown plasma into understanding and knowledge.

The second dimension of context, one that is overarching and encompassing, will be the more difficult claim to make. In arguing for a chorographic background from which and within which things derive their meaning and value, I am also placing rhetoricity in the "as a whole" that transcends human doing. In other words, objects and events come to lay claims upon us in ways Latour cannot well account for. For Latour, political progress is a matter of bringing in what has been excluded—things of concern—by means of alliance and representation. Whether that is the work of politics or science, it proceeds by reclamation of the vast background of plasma. But we need another dimension in order to account for our initial sense of the "howness" of things. How is it that we perceive them, not *that* they are, but *how* they are? What is not said here, and what I think we need, is a nonsubjective understanding of value, loosely understood, that springs from a fundamental rhetoricity conceived beyond the subject/object, nature/culture, and so on divides.[8]

Rhetoric, as affectability, is not flat, not solely accumulative; in order to affect, to galvanize, it needs an orientation or situation from which it derives its trajectory. For instance, it is one thing to assert that nonhumans must be included in the parliament of things. But it is another thing to assert, as Barad does, that we must attend to differential constitutions, that is, differences in how things come to constitute themselves in our engagements with them (59). Where comes the sensibility that we should include nonhumans (or humans who have been differentiated and ignored, for that matter) in the parliament? How do we move from subjective *exhortation*, with Latour urging us to include nonhumans, to a transsubjective *call* (or attunement), whereby nonhumans are already understood as making claims for inclusion? How, that is, does our context, or interpretative horizon, shift sufficiently so that context itself ceases to be an exclusively human domain and itself opens up to the claims of nonhuman others?

Two ideas are central here. First, context is not solely a matter of human projection, a point with which Latour might agree, but, second, context invokes a holistic gathering as well, a point to which Latour objects. And, yet, its necessity remains. Here let us turn to Heidegger's example of a badly positioned blackboard in *The Fundamental Concepts of Metaphysics*. Heidegger notes that it is poorly positioned both for the teacher, who must continuously walk over to it, and for the students, who have a hard time seeing it (344). On first impression, this may appear to be a simple matter of subjective judgment, which hardly seems an advance. However, Heidegger claims the opposite, that the poor position of the board is *objective*—even more so, he notes, than its black color (344). The blackness of the blackboard would exemplify the first dimension of context, since the color black stems from minimalized light reflection. We could consider this material example an instance of Latour's plasma, the "missing masses" bearing up the known and the visible. To get at the second dimension of context, however, we need a shift, since adding more variables—such as the lectern, the windows, the teacher's ridiculous bowtie, the play of light, and so on—only extends our reach into plasma. This is an improvement, but it still remains at the level of assemblage. Nor does it suffice to render the board as poorly placed. We need the second dimension of context to get at the sensibility we call placement. Heidegger explains that "it is out of the lecture theatre that we experience the bad position of the board in the first place"; we do not get a sense of the lecture theater from the poorly placed board; rather, the manifestness of the lecture hall comes first, and, therefore, it is the "*condition of possibility* of the board in general being something we can make judgments about" (345; original emphasis). As in Barad, a contextual shift is necessary above and beyond following the actants themselves that renders them meaningful in a newly significant way. It is not a matter of there being lots of things that add up to a context. Instead, there is already something that is a whole, within which and from which we then proceed.[9] Thus, context is transsubjective in how it exceeds and contours the assemblages within which it emerges.

## Concluding Wine-Filled Postscript

This chapter has so far discussed how Latour's dingpolitiks opens up politics for humans and nonhumans, forces and technologies, in ways that allow for superior deliberation and decisioning. However, context on Latour's read becomes an artificial framework that substitutes for the hard work of describing objects in their complexifications, alliances, and pulsions. Certainly, we cannot simply discount Latour on this point; the artificial importation of a framework can divert and distort from what the object offers. Yet, context remains irrepressible. Indeed, our sense of what an assemblage might be is itself already spoken (preassembled) within this background. If Latour's dingpolitik is to have real political grip, then we must wrestle with the "as a whole" from out of which the possibility of value and inclusion already speak. Rhetorical power works beyond the levels of force, induction, and alliance. The presence of objects in political forums is not solely a matter of, say, rainforests gaining powerful allies who will come to represent them. Rather, there has to be a transformation in the "as a whole" out of which the place, bearing, and value of rainforests can be understood. There needs to be a change in *attunement*, with attunement understood here as nothing subjective. The opening wine example illuminates what dingpolitiks lacks, since there is no exhortation to include earth, grapes, sun, weather, and land as part of the fabric of viticulture and enology—such practices, rather, bring these things forward as already hearkened to and valued. Indeed, as words such as *terroir* indicate, they are just as integral to the taste and enjoyment of wine.

One might protest, however, that practices of growing and making are sufficiently different from politics that the analogy goes awry. So let us delve more directly into the question of the assumed subjectiveness of taste and judgment, since these are just as fundamental to politics. The conundrum was to what extent the "real" taste of wine is in the fluid or in the contextual factors—price, the critic's ratings and descriptions, the vintner's techniques, the glass one drinks from, the setting, food, and companionship, and so on. I have argued that the way the question is asked already creates the problem, since the experiments operate as if taste is an objective, measurable quality residing exclusively in the wine. Human taste is imperfect compared to lab equipment and statistical analysis. Thus, they prove what they assume: contextual factors are misleading epiphenomena clouding the objective wine quality. That such factors measurably transform brain activity, interesting, does nothing to suggest that the body/world dichotomy may be less certain than assumed. They do not even pair wine with food![10] The experimenters' assumption of this split becomes essential to the experiment (a question of boundary, as I have argued) and leads to the conclusion that we are simply and easily fooled.

Latour's big advantage is to demonstrate that a glass of wine is not an isolatable object but rather an assemblage, one that includes the growth of the grapes in the vineyard, their production into wine, and the arrival of the wine in the glass. It also includes the wine's alliances: the bottle and glass, the discourses surrounding it, the setting, one's companions, the accompanying food, and so on. We could follow, describing and writing, all these variables and learn much. The taste of the wine would be a symphony of these elements, and the ultimate pleasure (or displeasure, perhaps) that results even evokes plasma, the unknowns that, nevertheless, remain as the material conditions for the wine's being there in all its gladsome promise.

This certainly gives us a fair and richer accounting of wine, but it still stops short of rendering the how of the wine or an understanding of our judgment. It is only within a larger, holistic context that we pull out why we are drinking the wine, how it fits into our situation, and how its specific blend of flavors and scents affects us within that situation. Note that in line with Latour and contrary to the wine-tasting experiments, the wine and other nonhuman variables are considered part of what makes context (it is not person + wine but a person-wine hybrid actant connected up to a larger assemblage). However, our sense of taste is not solely circumscribed by the immediate interaction of fluid on the tongue—taste is itself transhuman. A consideration of wine's profound role in mood modulation, sociality, work, community, ritual, and the sacred makes this realization concrete. Wine is fully integrated into all aspects of the lifeworld. This holistic dimension, however, is so profound precisely because wine, as a special kind of nonhuman thing, already lays claims on us. What makes wine special in its nonhumanness is precisely its laying claims on us, a power few nonhuman things have within contemporary, Western-styled existence. Human valuation of wine is so vital because the wine takes part in its own valuation.

Wine claims its value within a larger whole that emerges via logos and *praxis*—and this can include something as seemingly ephemeral as taste. Taste, in other words, is not a singular datum but a context-derived judgment, with context understood not simply as an agglomeration of variables but as a chorographic background. This is why wine can never be reduced to taste alone, except perhaps in science experiments and the American predilection for numerical wine scores. Wine is social, accompanying meals and gatherings. Wine is ritualistic, accompanying celebrations and mournings. Wine is sacred, accompanying festivals and worship. Borne up within a whole that includes humans and nonhumans (including the gods), wine becomes an actant not only because we grant it powers or because it garners allies but also because it has come to make claims on us, in what we might consider a very subtle rhetoric.[11] And this rhetoric is itself neither human nor nonhuman but their hybrid coachievement, derived from a whole that is neither static nor deterministic but continually manifested through deed and word.

Finally, then, we might say that wine readily exemplifies in our everyday practices what Latour exhorts us to achieve with the parliament of things. We can only see this when we move beyond the first dimension of context to the second. This, I believe, gives us much to build on for bringing forth an essential rhetoricity in the world, including modalities of valuation and judgment that cannot be understood solely in terms of accumulation and force. Further, such rhetoricities take on elements of the human and nonhuman and, in this way, bring forth great potential for a more attuned dingpolitik, one made perhaps more realizable on the recognition that we have in small fashion already achieved it.

## Notes

1. See studies by Plassmann et al. and Goldstein et al. Intriguing rhetorical anecdote: lead author Robin Goldstein's published e-mail is from fearlesscritic.com.

2. James L. Kinneavy's *Theory of Discourse* is important for distilling the rhetorical triangle from communication theory and Aristotle. The triangle shows up in numerous disciplines beyond rhetorical studies, including sociology, political science, and more.

3. See, for instance, his famous example of the speed bump, whereby the desire to slow automobile drivers down is "translated" by road engineers into a hump of pavement, which induces drivers to slow down less they damage their vehicle or injure themselves (*PH* 186). Another famous example would be the Berlin key, which induces its user to lock the door at certain times of the day ("Berlin"). In these and other cases, persuasion is direct, intended influence.

4. In her essay-in-progress, "Mattering Gender: Technical Communication and Human Materiality," Jennifer Bay points out that the citizen-gun is a particularly loaded example, fraught with implications Latour seems uninterested in pursuing. For instance, the citizen-gun is stereotypically male.

5. I do not have space to explore this here, but Latour's critique of context resonates strongly with two other French thinkers, Jacques Derrida and Michel de Certeau. Derrida's "Signature Event Context" argues that no context is absolutely determinable for stabilizing the meaning of anything (310). De Certeau argues that it is problematic to assume that overarching narratives actually give an accounting for everyday practices. At some point one has to attend to what people actually do and how they do it.

6. Heidegger has famously claimed that language speaks; among several examples, see *Principle*, 96.

7. Latour rather evocatively evokes plasma in the little known, occasional piece *Paris: Invisible City*; it is curious that many of Latour's primary metaphors and descriptors for plasma involve cities.

8. Particularly important here is Diane Davis's argument in *Inessential Solidarity* for an originary affectability that comes prior to the social and, therefore, simultaneously founds and circulates within it.

9. Rhetorical concepts, such as kairos and doxa, require both the first and second dimensions of context to gain their vitality. They are not simply accumulative; both manifest a holistic context within which their affective trajectories derive.

10. Note that food could easily be included in the experiments so that taste was evaluated across different foods. It is in keeping with the scientist's assumptions of taste's subjectivism that it is not.

11. Carolyn Miller argues for the role of human attribution (the Eliza effect) in nonhuman agency.

## Works Cited

Barad, Karen. *Meeting the Universe Halfway: Quantum Physics and the Entanglement of Matter and Meaning*. Durham: Duke UP, 2007. Print.

Bay, Jennifer. "Mattering Gender: Technical Communication and Human Materiality." *Feminist Rhetorical Science Studies*. Ed. Julie Jung and Amanda Booher. TS.

Bitzer, Lloyd F. "The Rhetorical Situation." *Philosophy and Rhetoric* 1.1 (1968): 1–14. Print.

Davis, Diane. *Inessential Solidarity*. Pittsburgh: U of Pittsburgh P, 2010. Print.

de Certeau, Michel. *The Practice of Everyday Life*. Trans. Steven Rendall. Berkeley: U of California P, 1984. Print.

Derrida, Jacques. "Signature Event Context." *Margins of Philosophy*. Trans. Alan Bass. Chicago: U of Chicago P, 1982. 307–330. Print.

Goldstein, Robin, Johan Almenberg, Anna Dreber, John W. Emerson, Alexis Herschkowitsch, and Jacob Katz. "Do More Expensive Wines Taste Better? Evidence from a Large Sample of Blind Tastings." American Association of Wine Economists. *AAWE Working Paper* 16 (April 2008): 1–14. Print.

Heidegger, Martin. *The Fundamental Concepts of Metaphysics: World, Finitude, Solitude*. Trans. William McNeill and Nicholas Walker. Bloomington: Indiana UP, 1995. Print.

———. *The Principle of Reason*. Trans. Reginald Lilly. Bloomington: Indiana UP, 1996. Print.

Kinneavy, James L. *A Theory of Discourse*. New York: Norton, 1971. Print.

Latour, Bruno. "The Berlin Key, or, How to Do Things with Words." *Matter, Materiality and Modern Culture*. Ed. Paul Graves-Brown. New York: Routledge, 2000. 10–21. Print.

———. "From Realpolitik to Dingpolitik." Ed. Latour and Peter Weibel. *Making Things Public: Atmospheres of Democracy*. Cambridge: MIT P, 2005. 1–31. Print.

———. *Pandora's Hope: Essays on the Reality of Science Studies*. Cambridge: Harvard UP, 1999. Print.

———. *Politics of Nature*. Cambridge: Harvard UP, 2004. Print.

———. *Reassembling the Social: An Introduction to Actor-Network-Theory*. New York: Oxford UP, 2005. Print.

Latour, Bruno, and Emilie Hermant. *Paris ville invisible*. Paris: LaDécouverte–Les Empêcheurs depenser en rond, 1998. Trans. Liz Carey-Libbrecht. *Bruno Latour*, Feb. 2006, 1–103. Web. 9 Feb. 2013. <http://www.bruno-latour.fr/sites/default/files/downloads/viii_paris-city-gb.pdf>.

Miller, Carolyn R. "What Can Automation Tell Us about Agency?" *Rhetoric Society Quarterly* 37.2 (2007): 137–157. Print.

Plassmann, Hilke, John O'Doherty, Baba Shiv, and Antonio Rangel. "Marketing Actions Can Modulate Neural Representations of Experienced Pleasantness." *Proceedings of the National Academy of Sciences* 105.3 (2008): 1050–1054. Print.

# 9. Bruno Latour's Posthuman Rhetoric of Assent

Collin Gifford Brooke, *Syracuse University*

Wayne C. Booth is not a name that most rhetoric scholars would identify with postmodernism. And yet, in the introduction to *Modern Dogma and the Rhetoric of Assent*, Booth explains that the lectures upon which that book is based "are intended as an introduction to one of many possible directions in which postmodernist rhetoric about values can earn its legitimacy" (xi). If we think about Booth's as one of the first attempts to articulate a postmodern rhetoric, Bruno Latour occupies the other end of the spectrum. In *We Have Never Been Modern*, published some twenty years later, Latour attempts to sound the death knell for postmodernism, seeing it not as the radical break promised by its advocates but, rather, as a continuation of modernism's deeply flawed assumptions. Operating in different times and intellectual milieus and working with largely distinct disciplinary traditions, Booth and Latour make for an unlikely pair, at best. This chapter argues that there is something to be gained by the juxtaposition of certain of their works.[1] On the one hand, Booth's work on what he calls a "rhetoric of assent" gives us a perspective from which to consider Latour's relationship to rhetorical studies; on the other, Latour's current popularity might serve to breathe new life into what is admittedly a minor work of rhetorical theory, or at least revitalize certain of its concepts.[2] Relevance, as Latour himself reminds us in *Reassembling the Social*, is the consequence of particular kinds of textual accounts, and, thus, my goal in this chapter is to stage an encounter among these texts, alert to the various resonances that may emerge.

Curiously enough, there are parallels at the very outset of *Modern Dogma* and *We Have Never Been Modern*. Booth begins his lectures by describing an encounter with a "curiously anonymous Chicago magazine" called *Seed*, where he finds "Letter from Tim Leary" and two readers' comments attesting to the letter's veracity or lack thereof. For Booth, *Seed* typifies the current rhetorical "crisis" that is the topic of his book, the devolution of discourse and rhetoric into manifesto. *Modern Dogma* begins with Booth's puzzlement over the inability of political protesters to make their cases heard, but as he investigates, he finds that on every side, "passionate commitment has lost its connection with the provision of good reasons" (xi). Even the suggestion that we should have time for reflection and discussion of "good reasons," Booth explains, is rejected, for it means that he does not agree and has "taken sides." In this atmosphere, rhetoric is reduced to the "art of winning." Although the crisis that Latour identifies seems far removed from American campus politics of the late 1960s and 1970s, he, too, begins his book with reference to a periodical. *We Have Never Been Modern* starts on the pages of Latour's "daily newspaper," where hybrids of "all of culture and all of nature get churned up again every day" (2). While there are certain segments of the paper—"soothing features"—that focus exclusively on politics or literature, most of them collapse those boundaries in their pursuit of these hybrids. For Booth, the problem is that "we have lost our faith in the very possibility of finding a rational path through any thicket that includes what we call value judgments" (7). Interesting, this is not so far away from the crisis that Latour identifies.

> Either the networks my colleagues in science studies and I have traced do not really exist, and the critics are quite right to marginalize them or segment them into three distinct sets: facts, power and discourse; or the networks are as we have described them, and they do cross the borders of the great fiefdoms of criticism. . . . Either we have to disappear, we bearers of bad news, or criticism itself has to face a crisis because of these networks it cannot swallow. (6)

To see the parallel here requires us to bracket off a very important distinction, of course. Where Booth's emphasis above is on finding that "rational path," Latour's is very clearly on recognizing the "thicket," and that distinction is crucial for understanding how these projects differ from one another. This is a distinction that we will return to later; for the moment, it is worth reflecting on the parallels between the exigences that Booth and Latour articulate.

Latour is explicit about the dangers that the rational path of disciplinarity poses for the kind of work he does. He goes so far as to identify E. O. Wilson, Pierre Bourdieu, and Jacques Derrida as representatives of the "three distinct sets" cited above and argues that a "patchwork" of scholarship that tried to incorporate the positions of all three would be "grotesque." So long as these three camps maintain some minimal distance from each other, "our intellectual life remains recognizable," he explains (6). The question of recognizability is raised early in Booth's text as well; in his introduction, he comments, "I would expect some readers to be puzzled about where in the intellectual landscape such rhetorical study lies" (xii). Booth's tone is perhaps more sanguine than Latour's, however. Booth recounts discussions he has with members of various disciplines, each of whom suggests that while Booth's topic is germane, he is going about it "without proper professional terminology." Much like the science studies that Latour champions in *We Have Never Been Modern*, Booth's exploration of rhetoric would have been far less recognizable to his audience at the time.[3] It is no accident that he closes his book with both an appendix of relevant sources from other fields and a preface to his bibliography that lists a number of scholars working explicitly in the rhetorical tradition. Booth provides a great deal of context not only for his argument but also for the nascent disciplinary field that his work occupies.

While their disciplinary affiliations might not be readily identifiable, both Latour and Booth offer fairly elaborate models to identify the forces that are the respective targets of their work. Booth identifies five kinds of modern dogma, each of which flows from "the modernist way of splitting up both the world as it is and the world as it is inquired into"; he draws explicitly on both Kenneth Burke's pentad and Aristotle's four causes.

> In practice the dogmas we turn to now tend to together, reinforcing each other to constitute the almost overwhelmingly persuasive travel worldview of modernism. But it will be useful to think of them as falling into five kinds. There are dogmas about (a) the *methods* or means for producing change; (b) the *nature* of the thing changed—the mind or soul or self or person or organism (though I have talked only of "changing minds," I intend the word mind in the broadest possible sense); (c) the *scene* of change—the world in which that thing changed, the "mind," finds itself; (d) the *principles* or basic *assumptions* about truth and its testing—the ground and nature of change; and (e) the *purpose* of change. (22)

Booth's five dogmas represent questions that are answered differently depending upon one's allegiances; he outlines how "scientismist" and "irrationalist" thinkers each take them up or, in the case of Bertrand Russell, how one thinker might occupy several irreconcilable positions. In *We Have Never Been Modern*, each of the three disciplinary "sets"—nature, power, and discourse—provides one of the "misunderstandings" that Latour seeks to redress, but *Reassembling the Social* both expands upon that number and shifts its focus. Latour's more recent book describes five "uncertainties" for which a "sociology of the social" has produced increasingly unsatisfying answers: the nature of groups, the nature of actions, the nature of objects, the nature of facts, and the type of studies conducted by social scientists (22). Put thus, the overlaps between Latour's "pentad" and Booth's seem faint, indeed. But the task of sociology for Latour is "to deploy actors as networks of mediators" (136), and that task gathers these uncertainties in a particular fashion.

> This is exactly what the five uncertainties added together might help to reveal: What is the social made up of? What is acting when we are acting? What sort of grouping do we pertain to? What do we want? What sort of world are we ready to share? All those questions are raised not only by scholars, but also by those they study. (138)

The particulars of these schemes may differ, but both Latour and Booth refuse the distinction between academic and general practice of their respective methods. Just as Booth finds the modern dogmas at play in the anonymous articles of *Seed*, Latour finds hybrid collectives of associations in the pages of his daily paper. It would be possible to continue in this vein for the remainder of this chapter, isolating elements from the works of Booth and Latour, highlighting certain connections and casuistically stretching others, perhaps. But there are broader themes that both unite their work and provide some grounds for considering how their projects diverge, and it is worth turning to those themes at this point.

## Incommensurability

> They raise what had been only a distinction, then a separation, then a contradiction, then an insurmountable tension, to the level of an incommensurability.
>
> —Bruno Latour, *We Have Never Been Modern*

Both Booth and Latour address their respective projects to the epistemological incommensurability of nature and culture (or fact and value, as Booth expresses it). Whether this incommensurability is precisely the same for each writer is difficult to discern; they come at it from different directions and offer different terms for it, and their projects are sufficiently distinct to raise the question, at least. Latour spends the first part of *We Have Never Been Modern* historicizing the gap, tracing it back to the work of Robert Boyle and Thomas Hobbes and then forward to the postmoderns, who, far from overcoming it, exacerbate it to the point that Latour lacks the terms "ugly enough to designate this intellectual movement" (61). For Latour, the answer is ontological; it is not that hybrid quasi-objects are new but that understanding them through the lens of an artificial nature/culture dichotomy was a mistake that was compounded and reinforced for hundreds of years.

Compared to Latour's historicization and careful deployment of specialized terminology, Booth's fact-value split runs the risk of appearing facile. He covers some of the same historical ground as Latour but does so in the space of a couple of paragraphs (14–15). And, yet, some allowance must be made for both the separation in time, space, and genre between the two. Booth's book collects a set of lectures offered to a general, albeit educated, audience, one unlikely to have either the familiarity or the patience to listen to the kind of terminological intricacy that Latour's book offers. Booth admits as much: "I cannot trace here the story of the rise and fall of the disjunction, and of various conclusions thought to follow from it" (15). While Latour's focus is ontological, Booth's is more pragmatic and/or communicative. The fact-value split deploys itself for Booth in our inability to engage in discourse with those with whom we disagree. We might argue that Booth attends to the consequences of incommensurability while Latour turns to its root causes. I want to avoid this characterization, however; it runs the risk of treating epistemology as a mere symptom and rhetoric as doubly symptomatic.[4] This critical stance has its roots in Plato's various dismissals of rhetoric, denying any sort of generative or constructive capacity to it.

And, in fact, both writers resist these kinds of symptomatic formulations explicitly. For Booth, motivism is one of the dogmas that the fact-value split deploys, and he spends much of his first lecture discussing it. He offers several examples of thinkers who refuse to consider the language and reasons of others, because "mere rhetoric" can only be a rationalization for the "true" motives lurking behind it. It is not that such inquiry cannot itself produce important insights; Booth acknowledges the "impressive chain of intellectual successes" that have come from treating rhetoric symptomatically. But he also rejects the notion that such "suspicion" should become our default mode of inquiry. There are echoes of this rejection in Latour's delineation of a "sociology of the social" and his own "as-sociology," the discussion that opens *Reassembling the Social.*

> This version of social theory has become the default position of our mental software that takes into consideration the following: there exists a social "context" in which non-social activities take place; it is a specific

> domain of reality; it can be used as a specific type of causality to account for the residual aspects that other domains cannot completely deal with. . . . [S]ince ordinary agents are always "inside" a social world that encompasses them, they can at best be "informants" about this world, and, at worst, be blinded to its existence, whose full effect is only visible to the social scientist's more disciplined eyes. (3–4)

It is worth comparing Latour's remarks to the anecdote that Booth offers about the University of Chicago historian tasked with understanding faculty reactions to student protests: "The only subject of interest was the *true* class motives *underlying* their surface rationalizations" (34–35). Both Latour and Booth explicitly reject the default of suspicion that necessarily accompanies treating rhetoric as symptomatic.

This is not to suggest that is no difference between Booth and Latour here but, rather, that we might read them as complementary in ways that might not be immediately apparent. The incommensurability that Latour decries is not as stable as its long history might suggest. By tracing its history back to the point where it emerges as a distinction that responds to particular networks of circumstances, Latour treats the nature/culture divide as historical rather than inevitable. Nor does Booth assume that the fact-value split is simply a given. Instead, he demonstrates how it accomplishes certain rhetorical purposes to the exclusion of others and, more important perhaps, how those writers who deploy this dichotomy reinforce its popularity as a strategy. Much as Latour identifies those three disciplinary sets, each of which operates by relying on a false distinction from the others, Booth describes scientism and irrationalism as opposed perspectives that leave the underlying structure of their difference intact. Booth and Latour do not see this incommensurability in quite the same terms, but both see it as a deeply rooted problem, albeit, one that is both constructed and eventually mutable.

## Rhetorics of Assent

> Rejecting the dogmas of modernism can in itself settle no questions; indeed, for a true believer it can be positively unsettling.
>
> —Wayne Booth, *Modern Dogma and the Rhetoric of Assent*

If we see Booth's and Latour's projects as complementary when it comes to the divide that provokes their respective responses, then it makes sense to investigate the responses themselves. Booth is explicitly interested in advancing a "rhetoric of assent."

> In view of these troubles with systematic doubt, it scarcely seems unreasonable to try out other ways of looking at what we know. Instead of making doubt primary, let us see what happens if we know whatever we can agree together that we have no good reason to doubt, whether or not we can apply other more formal tests of doubt. In this view, assent becomes the prior act of knowing. (106)

There are some obvious objections—such as whether this obligates us to assent to anything whatsoever—that Booth settles quickly through recourse to intersubjectivity. He raises a number of more principled arguments as well,[5] but his position remains throughout that "from birth our primary movement is toward the world, to grasp it, assenting to and taking in other selves, new truths, the whole world. Our withdrawals and rejections come always in the light of some affirmation that been denied or that is being threatened" (194). Assent for Booth is not the necessary outcome of rhetoric nor even necessarily probable; rather, it is rhetoric's prerequisite.

The centerpiece of *Modern Dogma* is a careful step-by-step progression through Booth's articulation of a rhetoric of assent. He begins from the premise that we are fundamentally symbol users capable of understanding each other through symbolic activity. That activity and understanding is how we construct ourselves as selves, and we specifically *intend* to construct and/or change others through symbols. Booth pauses at the next step of his argument to focus more intently on the idea that we are capable of inferring each other's intentions. We rely upon our own convictions, the degree to which those convictions match with others', the degree to which they cohere with prior knowledge, and our ability to demonstrate or communicate our knowledge to others. We know each other's intentions "under the aspect of values," and despite the many shared values we hold, our intentions and value will inevitably conflict (112–25). For Booth, transformation is a crucial value, a process that is ongoing. Shortly after he lays out his assumptions, he turns to his statement regarding the purposes of such rhetoric.

> The supreme purpose of persuasion in this view could not be to talk someone else into a preconceived view; rather, it must be to engage in mutual inquiry or exploration. . . . The *process* of inquiry through discourse thus becomes more important than any possible conclusions,

> and whatever stultifies such discourse becomes demonstrably wrong. (137; original emphasis)

Over forty years later, it is hard to assent to the naive optimism of Booth's project. For scholars raised on critiques of Jürgen Habermas, public sphere theory, and the myriad relationships between power and discourse, *Modern Dogma*'s humanist idealism must seem as untenable to us as Bertrand Russell's conflicted modernism did for Booth.

And, yet, given Booth's commitment to transformation, perhaps it is worth offering his project a tentative assent as we consider it in light of Latour. While four of the five "sources of uncertainty" Latour outlines are ontological, the fifth, "writing down risky accounts," is explicitly rhetorical, and there are interesting resonances with Booth's project. For example, just as Booth would have us assent to others' rhetorical activity (until such time as reasons to doubt present themselves), Latour's treatment of actors is similarly respectful: "We have to resist pretending that actors have only a language while the analyst possesses the *meta*-language in which the first is 'embedded'" (*RS* 49; original emphasis).[6] The preconceived views that Booth warns against, both those that we may hold and the hidden motives we ascribe to our interlocutors, function metalinguistically to "stultify" discourse, for Booth and for Latour.

For the discipline of sociology, Latour's answer is the practice of description rather than explanation, the duty "to retrace the many different worlds actors are elaborating for one another" (49). This entails treating them as *mediators*, capable of transformation and translation, as opposed to *intermediaries*, who "transport meaning or force without transformation" (39). If rhetorical actors are simply intermediaries, symptomatically performing their hidden motives, then rhetoric itself becomes shadow play. Furthermore, the practice of writing accounts (sociological, rhetorical, or otherwise) of these actors would itself be intermediary in this formulation, a symptom of a symptom. For Latour, this could not be further from the truth, however. Treating writing this way is only possible "if the mediating constraints of writing are either ignored or denied" (128), a strategy he clearly disapproves of. For Latour's sociologist, the textual account is a laboratory, and the account itself can succeed or fail just as an experiment might. When that account "allows the writer to trace a set of relations defined as so many translations" among mediators, it is successful; by contrast, "in a bad text only a handful of actors will be designated as the causes of all the others, which will have no other function than to serve as a backdrop or relay for the flows of causal efficacy" (129, 130).

At the heart of Latour's own account is a kind of assent, to complexity of associations and to the capacity of actors for transformation, both of themselves and of others. In a talk delivered at Stanford in 2003, he asks, "What would critique do if it could be associated with *more*, not with *less*, with *multiplication*, not *subtraction*?" (248; original emphasis).[7] This is not as far as it might seem from Booth's substitution of assent for doubt as our default condition; like Booth, Latour suggests earlier in that talk that our contemporary emphasis on critique might have led to an "excessive distrust" that leaves us ill-equipped to confront matters of concern. While he draws on different terms at different times to describe his project—gathering, associations, compositionism, and so on—Latour offers us a rhetoric of assent, urging us to grant actors their full status as mediators, their capability for transformation, in much the same way that Booth asks us to approach rhetoric as a site where minds can be changed, both our own and others, and we can change them.

## Human and Posthuman Rhetorics

> Subjectivity is not a property of human souls but of the gathering itself.
>
> —Bruno Latour, *Reassembling the Social*

The most important distinction between these rhetorics of assent, however, is ontological; we have largely ignored the fact that Booth and Latour mean very different things when they speak of actors. The connections between Booth's focus on "changing minds" and Latour's emphasis on the transformative capacity of mediators are apparent if we focus on the parallel activities of persuasion and transformation. When we ask how these activities are accomplished, however, the differences between Latour and Booth become quite clear. For Booth, rhetoric is an art practiced by humans; his rhetoric of assent assumes human participants are both the subjects and objects of discourse. Rhetorical activity is the process by which humans engage in the mutual inquiry and exploration that represents Booth's ideal. Considering the time when Booth delivered his lectures, this is hardly unusual; it would not have occurred to him that he might need to defend restricting his account to human activity.

We can take this a step further: Booth's account of rhetoric is a largely unmediated one. The rhetorical situation he imagines features generic human actors conversing and granting each other the benefit of the doubt. Although he does turn to textual examples throughout the book, for the most part, such texts merely provide occasion for human discourse. For example, he discusses the first sentence of Jane Austen's *Pride and Prejudice*, not to consider what Austen might have intended so much as to consider what he and his audience might be able to agree upon with regard to its meaning (117). The model Booth offers is one that valorizes conversation; it is a sign of breakdown when the students and faculty on the University of Chicago campus stop talking to one another and begin to circulate "mimeographed sheets" denouncing the opposing side (8). More important, though, Booth's discussion does not really account for the ways that social relations, institutions, organizations, and a host of other factors mediate rhetoric.

One of the characteristic features of Latour's work is its emphasis on nonhumans; as the epigraph for this section suggests, subjectivity is for Latour the consequence of mediation rather than a quality exclusively possessed by humans. In *We Have Never Been Modern*, Latour traces what he calls an asymmetry between humans and nonhumans back to the split between nature and culture. This distinction actually instantiates mirror-image asymmetries, as the sciences work to bracket off human factors and the cultural disciplines focus on human activity to the exclusion of all else. In reversing this distinction, Latour adopts a generalized principle of symmetry, whereby we consider "the production of humans and nonhumans simultaneously" (103). Culture and nature are not opposite poles that must be treated equally; for Latour, the very idea of treating them as separate poles is itself a function of the modern constitution of knowledge. Similarly, Latour is less interested in somehow "elevating" nonhuman actors to the "level" of humans.

> Where are we to situate the human? A historical succession of quasi-objects, quasi-subjects, it is impossible to define the human by an essence, as we have known for a long time. . . . If the human does not possess a stable form, it is not formless for all that. If, instead of attaching it to one constitutional pole or the other, we move it closer to the middle, it becomes the mediator and even the intersection of the two. The human is not a constitutional pole to be opposed to that of the nonhuman. The two expressions "humans" and "nonhumans" are belated results that no longer suffice to designate the other dimension. (136–37)

It is not that humans have no place in Latour's ontology; instead, he is interested in moving past the "reduced form of humanity" that isolates it from the broad range of mediators that circulate throughout the world.

This is perhaps the sharpest distinction to be drawn between Latour's work and Booth's: the ideal model of rhetorical interaction that Booth proposes is abstracted from the empirical world that Latour asks us to engage with. And, yet, within Booth's account of rhetoric, there are some suggestive passages that may close this gap. While Booth restricts his description to human activity, those humans are not fully formed, discrete individuals; we are "in large degree what other men and women have created through symbolic exchange. Each of us 'takes in' other selves to build a self" (114). The rhetoric of assent is, for Booth, a commitment to the mutual, rhetorical construction of self.

If our selves emerge as a consequence of rhetoric, and we commit to the continued possibility of that emergence, we are not as far from Latour as it might seem. For the most part, Booth does not explore this line of reasoning, except in a single footnote. He begins by acknowledging that rhetoric as he defines it can reasonably be attributed to "higher animals," such as pets. But the distinction between higher and lower animals is quickly erased.

> There is a sense in which even the lowest animals can be said to intend meanings or to influence the rest of the world rhetorically; I would not even resist defining the universe as essentially rhetorical: it is created, as Whitehead says, in processes of interchange among its parts. Each least particle—whatever that turns out to be—just like each gross beast and "dead" star, could be defined as a steadily changing "field of influences," receiving, processing, and transmitting "information." Such a heady flight, however, takes us nowhere; we have only turned "rhetorical influence," originally a literal concept, into a foggy metaphor. (125–26n)

That Booth sets aside this idea as quickly as he does places him firmly among those modernists whose work Latour urges us to reject. Booth is more interested in establishing rhetoric as a discipline distinct from sociology, psychology, and others, in making his work intellectually "recognizable" as observed earlier. In order to do that for the audience he addresses, Booth focuses his attention on a humanistic rhetoric, even if it belies the broader sense of assent that we might attribute to Latour. When we read the two in concert, however, Latour allows us to pick up those elements of Booth's work that he sets aside, and this, in turn, provides us with a perspective from which to think about Latour's potential contributions to rhetorical studies.

A few thoughts about the notion of reading two disparate thinkers in concert, holding their work in a kind of symmetry, conclude this chapter. The first principle of symmetry, according to *We Have Never Been Modern*, "requir[es] that error and truth be treated in the same terms" (92). Rather than locating truth on the side of nature (and the sciences) and error on the side of culture (and humanities or social sciences), this first principle urges us to understand how all phenomena, from flying saucers to black holes, are hybrids whose "truth" or "error" emerges from networks that include culture and nature, humans and nonhumans. As Latour explains in *Reassembling the Social*, the question is not whether knowledge is constructed or not; all knowledge is constructed, but not all knowledge is constructed *well* (90–91). This first principle of symmetry has provided a certain amount of guidance for this chapter: rather than attempting to read Booth and Latour against each other or to see one of them as more "true" than the other, I have tried here to read them in parallel, in order to seek out those resonant ideas from each.

On the one hand, it is relatively easy to read and understand Booth's work as a product of its time. Working largely prior to any sort of disciplinary or institutionally approved conception of rhetoric, Booth makes the case both for rhetoric's relevance and for its particular discursive and ethical approach to the apparent incommensurabilities in the political conversations of the time. There is an idealism to Booth's work, a belief that "good faith" discourse can resolve our disagreements, but I argue that the rhetoric of assent runs more deeply than the humanist implications that he traces from it. Even though Booth ultimately does not pursue the idea of rhetoric as a "field of influences," he explicitly establishes the possibility for that idea in his emphasis on the capacity for rhetoric to transform others as well as ourselves. Rhetoric for Booth is a force of mediation (in Latour's sense).

If Latour allows us to separate out those elements in Booth's work that lend themselves to a more contemporary reading, Booth's account, in turn, can help us to contextualize Latour in rhetorical studies. Just as Booth refuses the distinction between fact and value, Latour urges us to assent to the associative networks of mediators that (post)modernist asymmetries render invisible. Rhetoric is not the only form of association that can connect and collect mediators into networks, but it is crucial, nonetheless. Booth's rhetoric of assent requires us to place ourselves and our ideas at "risk" of transformation; Latour reminds us that our accounts must risk failure as well if there is anything to be gained by them. Writing is one of the means we have of tracing out associations, accounting for the various mediators (human and nonhuman) that produce the social, and generating the networks themselves.

Perhaps most important, we should recall that for Latour, network is not a thing out there but, rather, "an indicator of the quality of a text about the topics at hand," and in that sense, a network is a fundamentally rhetorical achievement. Similarly, Latour's relevance to rhetorical studies can only be a consequence of our field's engagement with his work. This engagement transforms his work just as the consideration of Latour changes ours; his relevance must be an outcome of our scholarship rather than a precondition. If nothing else, the rhetorics of assent offered by both Booth and Latour suggest that it is worth our time to pursue that possibility.

## Notes

1. This chapter focuses primarily on Booth's *Modern Dogma* and Latour's *We Have Never Been Modern* and *Reassembling the Social*. I make no claim that these texts are somehow representative of the writers' much more extensive bodies of work, nor do I suggest that other combinations of texts would prove more or less productive. My approach here is abductive (in the Peircean sense) and experimental, an attempt to explore the possible connections among these three texts.

2. In "Grasping Rhetoric and Composition by Its Long Tail," Derek Mueller examines twenty-five years of citations in *College Composition and Communication*, from 1987 to 2011. During that time frame, Booth is only cited fourteen times in the pages of *CCC*, and none of those are citations of *Modern Dogma*. While this is neither conclusive nor exhaustive, it does suggest the marginal status of that book.

3. Although the journal *CCC* first appears in 1950, many scholars credit the 1966 Dartmouth Conference on the teaching of English as the origin for what would become the discipline of rhetoric and composition.

4. For example, I am considering the Gorgian trilemma and the way that it nests ontology, epistemology, and communication.

5. Booth is not urging us to assent in the face of others' bad behavior or to ignore the fact that assent to one position often entails rejecting another, for example.

6. One crucial distinction here is the breadth with which Latour defines "actors," of course. The following section considers the question of humans and nonhumans.

7. This talk was later published in *Critical Inquiry* as "Why Has Critique Run Out of Steam? From Matters of Fact to Matters of Concern."

## Works Cited

Booth, Wayne C. *Modern Dogma and the Rhetoric of Assent.* Chicago: U of Chicago P, 1974. Print.

Latour, Bruno. *Reassembling the Social: An Introduction to Actor-Network-Theory.* New York: Oxford UP, 2005. Print.

———. *We Have Never Been Modern.* Cambridge: Harvard UP, 1993. Print.

———. "Why Has Critique Run Out of Steam? From Matters of Fact to Matters of Concern." *Critical Inquiry* 30.2 (2004): 225–248. Print.

Mueller, Derek. "Grasping Rhetoric and Composition by Its Long Tail: What Graphs Can Tell Us about the Field's Changing Shape." *CCC* 64.1 (2012): 195–223. Print.

# 10. Latourian *Memoria*

Jeremy Tirrell, *University of North Carolina Wilmington*

Determining how to address digital technology in all its forms is one of the most salient challenges of modern rhetoric and composition studies, because it concerns the basal issue of what it means to know in an era of distributed knowledge and nonhuman actants. The contemporary status of memory and its role in cognition are integral to this matter, particularly, as digital networks that store and rapidly retrieve vast amounts of multimedia data become progressively insinuated into quotidian existence. This development suggests the need for a reexamination of the canon of *memoria* to determine how rhetoricians and compositionists might appropriately understand the relationship between memory and thought in a contemporary digital milieu and how to address this connection effectively.

Recent attempts to explore these matters through a posthuman framework have granted productive insights. In particular, Collin Brooke's 2000 article "Forgetting to Be (Post)Human: Media and Memory in a Kairotic Age" and the "Persistence" chapter of his 2009 book *Lingua Fracta: Towards a Rhetoric of New Media* provide some of the most fecund, sustained thought yet offered about memoria's changing nature in a digital milieu. Nevertheless, I argue that posthuman views of memory inherently adhere to a retrograde Platonism that does not account for the radical potentials of digital technology. In place of a posthuman orientation, this chapter offers a memoria framework drawn from the critical thought of Bruno Latour. Through the proffered lens, memory becomes an act of translation among irreducible human and nonhuman actors in local occasionalist networks. Such a model appropriately accommodates the burgeoning role of nonhuman actants and thoroughly sheds the Platonism that has influenced understandings of memoria since the classical era and persists in posthuman accounts of memory's function within a digital milieu.

The aspects of Platonic memory relevant to this discussion are its prosthetic treatment of nonhumans and its endorsement of durable essences. These elements are visible in Plato's fundamental distinction between authentic human knowing and inauthentic artificial reminding, which most notably appears in Socrates's well-known screed against writing in the *Phaedrus*. Jacques Derrida comments in the "Plato's Pharmacy" section of *Dissemination* that through his parable of Theuth and Thamus, Plato attacks "the substitution of the mnemonic device for live memory, of the prosthesis for the organ; the perversion that consists of replacing a limb by a thing" (108). This prosthetic division, which distinguishes internal, active memory from external, static reminder, has so dominated understandings of memoria that it has become naturalized, yet it is not the simple act of transcribing knowledge into a fixed format that Plato abhors—it is the different forms of cognition that writing enables and their corruption of what for Plato is the essential human act of thinking. Gregory L. Ulmer identifies this distinction in *Applied Grammatology*, stating that Plato condemns writing "not just as 'writing-down' but as a whole theory of the relation of memory to thought" (69). In Plato's cosmology, the human qua human becomes diminished by outsourcing some of his cognitive labor onto material memory objects, even ones that remain subservient. Plato's anxiety about writing—or rather his ambivalence, given that history knows him *because he wrote*—is linked with a shift in the relationship between memory and thought and its effects on human knowers.

I contend that a version of Plato's prosthetic essentialism persists in posthuman understandings of memoria despite an avowed rejection of them. I here turn to Brooke's reformation of memoria precisely because it is recent, thoughtful, and fertile. His work demonstrates that posthumanism inherently functions within a Platonic framework that extends intellectual traditions predicated on a separation of human from other and a temporality in which essential substances endure through a chronological medium.

Brooke explicitly attempts to reject what he calls the "Platonic attitude" toward memory, arguing that it "has left us with a legacy of considering memory in terms of absence and presence" (*Lingua Fracta* 144). Brooke sees this as a reductive spatialization of memory, limiting it to a consideration of whether information is at hand or not. In place of the binary of presence and absence, Brooke adopts the axis of pattern and randomness N. Katherine Hayles articulates in *How We Became Posthuman* to reconceive classical memoria in a digital milieu as *persistence*. His concept has clear and intentional temporal dimensions that he connects with the classical concepts of *kairos* and *chronos* in "Forgetting to Be (Post)Human." Brooke contends that spatialized memory models neglect memoria's temporal aspects and, thus, undermine its status as a practice.

Brooke concretely outlines how his model operates in the "Persistence" chapter of Lingua Fracta. It entails a two-tiered system wherein individual humans use particular technologies to augment their personal memory operations. At a broader collective level, multiple humans undertaking these practices become connected through other digital technologies that collate their activities into emergent social patterns, or what Brooke calls "cultural memory" (166). Brooke preserves memory's conventional personal storage function, stating that the existence of new memory operations does not negate previous ones (157). He specifically identifies RSS feed readers as storage augmentations: "For those users who make regular use of RSS or Atom feeds, aggregators have become, in a short time, an indispensable extension of their memory as we traditionally understand it" (161–62).[1] Brooke here explicitly casts feed readers as Platonic memory prostheses while curiously describing memory through the spatial terms he rejects at the beginning of his work; he uses similar spatial language in keeping with the distributed cognition theories he disregards through his earlier statement that "like many other technologies, my aggregator distributes my memory, freeing me of the need to remember each site individually" (160).

This prosthetic, spatialized character may be allowed because Brooke here discusses memory's conventional storage function as it has been remediated by digital technology; however, he goes on to identify new memory possibilities aligned with "persistence of cognition," which also have a similar prosthetic character (162). Brooke illustrates these new memory operations through his own practice with tag clouds, which he uses to visualize over time multiple RSS feeds that he otherwise would not track individually.[2] These visualizations present evolving snapshots of terms that occur frequently across multiple conversations. Brooke states, again in spatial terms, "Assigning 20 or 30 feeds to a tagcloud allows me to distribute the kind of scanning, feed-forward reading that I would otherwise have to do myself. The cloud 'remembers' the most important topics over the course of a week or month" (162). For Brooke, tag clouds thus serve as intellectual concierges, identifying potentially salient topics for him without need of continual guidance.

Brooke's persistence of cognition indeed seems novel and enmeshed in a digital milieu encompassing humans and nonhumans: people publish data to websites; machines then perform memory acts with each other, converting the data to RSS feeds that are automatically aggregated and visualized as tag clouds; these clouds suggest new conversations in which other humans can participate; when they do, their individual operations contribute to this reciprocal social plexus. This is precisely the "feed-forward" dimension that

Brooke identifies: practices that are not just limited to an individual using a storage prosthesis to manage his own thoughts but memory operations that filter upward, connecting humans and machines and generating relevant knowledge at a macrolevel. Brooke's model is valuable in a digital milieu because it emphasizes the cultural scale over the personal. Individual human acts are important for their own sake, but they are more valuable as the distributed elements of a larger system entangling humans and nonhumans; people become neurons in an expanded cyborg social mind. A conventional hierarchy is, thereby, inverted such that collaborative cognitive acts are more salient than individual information retention.[3]

Despite this novel memory aspect, it must be acknowledged that Brooke's model is in many ways a continuation of prosthetic and essentialist Platonism rather than a break from it. In Brooke's formulation, external machines remain subservient to human agents as the former dutifully cull data into recognizable patterns ready for human engagement. Memory remains at both the individual and social tiers a stable, iterative archive. The contents of personal and cultural memories are subject to flux precisely because they are durable entities. Change is inherently an aspect of substances that retain a coherent essence as their traits shift within a temporal medium. Brooke likely would agree with this assessment, as the title of his chapter is "Persistence," explicitly defined as "the construction (and dissolution) of patterns over time" (151).

Brooke views his attempted despatializing and retemporalizing of memory as the means to cast it as a practice rather than an object subject to the Platonic presence/absence binary. In the introduction of "Persistence," he asserts that "perhaps more than any of the other four canons, memory is the one canon whose status as *practice* is in need of rehabilitation" (144; original emphasis), and later in the work, he resolves that "a focus on temporality in the context of memory allows us to examine that canon as practice" (151). Yet, it is precisely his temporal focus that casts memory at both the personal and cultural levels as a thing rather than an event.[4] The scenario he identifies—digitally augmented humans making progressive contributions to personal archives from which coherent patterns in a larger cultural aggregate emerge—requires a view of memory as a persistent substance. Indeed, Brooke consistently articulates memory in material, spatial terms, despite his espoused resistance to doing so. As such, his rejection of distributed cognition and spatialized memory seems contradictory.

Brooke's perspective is undoubtedly valuable and appropriate to the current digital milieu, but it is not the only option. It is possible to understand memory not as the practice of routinely contributing to a persistent archive but as an event. Perhaps more than any other contemporary theorist, Latour helps us do this. In "Forgetting to Be (Post)Human," Brooke uses Latour's *We Have Never Been Modern* and Hayles's *How We Became Posthuman* "in an effort to articulate a space for posthumanism that is distinct from the modern/post-modern complex" (776). Brooke denies that posthumanism is a continuation or component of postmodernism by drawing from Latour's position that there has never been a full severance of nature from culture, a split that is required by modernism and exacerbated by postmodernism. Brooke's posthumanism is in Hayles's vein, connected with the legacies of humanism and cybernetics rather than the conflict between modernism and postmodernism. As such, Brooke's posthuman memoria, transformed into *persistence*, focuses on issues of information and embodiment; his is a cyborg memory that values the coherence of a human subject and its nonhuman complements. Brooke uses Latour to enable a posthuman memory model liberated from the baggage of both modernism and postmodernism, but were we to make Latour the cornerstone of our model instead of Hayles, we likely would not view memory as the ongoing practice of humans using machines to create persistent patterns but something quite else: a specific, unique, perishable act among equivalent actants. This would be a model without conventional temporality, leaving things no medium in which to persist, because, in Latour's words, "Everything happens only once, and at one place" (*PF* 162). This would be a model that does not distinguish between humans and nonhumans and, thus, could not privilege one over the other, because as philosopher and Latour commentator Graham Harman articulates, for Latour "atoms and molecules are actants, as are children, raindrops, bullet trains, politicians, and numerals. All entities are on exactly the same ontological footing" (14). Such a model also could not support the division into tiers of individuals and their cultures, nor could it permit a hierarchy between them. In short, by turning to Latour, we can break more completely from prosthetic, essentialist Platonic memory, embrace more fully the implications of existing in a digital milieu, and position memory more appropriately as an act instead of an archive.

Two significant aspects of Latour's thought drive its separation from Platonism, including the version embedded in Brooke's posthuman persistence: an equivalent agency afforded to all actors, be they human or other, and a kairotic temporality that denies durable essence. We will examine each of these concepts in turn, beginning with Latour's erasure of distinction between human and nonhuman entities. For Latour this is not a breach in need of repair; as articulated in *We Have Never Been Modern*, the parsing itself implicitly endorses a baseless opposition between culture and nature.[5] Brooke uses Latour's denial of this binary schism to sever posthumanism from postmodernism, but it can have more fine-grained, radical effects. Because there are no separate categories of human and other in Latour's thought, only equivalent actors, his flat ontology establishes a cosmos in which "*any thing* that does modify a state of affairs by making a difference is an actor" (*RS* 71; original emphasis). Actors are unique occurrences with equal rights as agents. There is no special privileged class, a distinction granted to humans under posthumanism (as its name implies) and preserved in Brooke's persistence. The leveling of actants is characteristic of Latour's actor-network-theory: a litmus test of which is "the precise role granted to non-humans. They have to be *actors* [. . .] and not simply the hapless bearers of symbolic projection" (*RS* 10; original emphasis). For Latour this democratic assemblage of actors is all that exists and can permit no division into different orders and hierarchies.

A corollary of this position is that there is no primary substance, force, or essence that underpins and determines actors; this is Latour's principle of irreduction, explicitly established in the "Irreductions" section of *The Pasteurization of France* through the statement, "Nothing is, by itself, either reducible or irreducible to anything else" (158). However, this does not mean that actors are impenetrable wholes nor that Latour has replaced a single atom with a plurality of them. Rather, as Latour asserts a few sentences later, "Everything may be made to be the measure of everything else" (158). In Latour's thought, actors coalesce through their associations with other actors. They are defined by these alliances, as evident in his statement that "nothing is by itself ordered or disordered, unique or multiple, homogeneous or heterogeneous, fluid or inert, human or in-human, useful or useless. Never by itself, but always with others" (*PF* 161). Thus, in Latour's cosmology, an actor is quite literally the result of its interactions with other actors.

Within this relational structure, actors are progressively more intelligible through a thorough examination of their associations. This is the sociological practice Latour outlines in *Reassembling the Social*, which does not seek to grant social forces agency as a discrete category of influences but rather to trace the associations that constitute actors (5). Latour articulates this distinction by asserting that through his proffered view "'social' is not some glue that could fix everything including what the other glues cannot fix; it is *what* is glued together by many *other* types of connections" (5; original emphasis). This language suggests that Latourian actors are not autonomous entities that make discreet connections with each other, as this would establish distinctions amongst actors, their linkages, and an undifferentiated backdrop. Only fully deployed actors exist in Latour's cosmos. There is no separate void, no "ether" across which actors connect (*PF* 162). Instead, association occurs through what Latour deems *translation* (*PF* 167). In this formulation, all actors are agential aspects of an act rather than implements subject to a driving will. Harman articulates this idea in a passage that is worth quoting at length.

> No layer of the world is a transparent intermediary, since each is a medium: or in Latour's preferred term, a *mediator*. A mediator is not some sycophantic eunuch fanning its masters with palm-leaves, but always does new work of its own to shape the translation of forces from one point of reality to the next. Here as elsewhere, Latour's guiding maxim is to grant dignity even to the least grain of reality. Nothing is mere rubble to be used up or trampled by mightier actors. Nothing is a mere intermediary. Mediators speak, and other mediators resist. (15; original emphasis)

Harman's mention of "dignity" is key here and a main distinction between Latour and prosthetic orientations, including Brooke's posthuman persistence. Latour's cosmos is one in which acts are messy, collaborative constructions among unique actors of equivalent status. We can assert that actors express varied strength within a particular act, but this imposes a retroactive teleology dependent upon a chosen outcome. There is a sort of relativity in Latour's positioning. Actors are not discretely connected but mutually constitutive, such that each is explicable as the sum of the others.

An implication of Latour's leveling of actors and their constitution through translated alliances is that the characteristic intellectual traits we associate with humans, including thought and reason, lose their purchase. Latour's position is not, as Brooke asserts of posthumanism, a development of the humanist mode. In "Irreductions," Latour reiterates that "we neither think nor reason" and "we do not think. We do not have ideas" (186, 218). Harman clarifies these counterintuitive remarks through an appeal to Latour's unification of what would, otherwise, be separated into intellectual and natural forces. Harman states that for Latour,

> There is no such thing as "thinking" as a special critical transcendence that leaps beyond the world and reflexively sees things "as" they are. Instead, the relation between my mind and the room is metaphysically no different from the relation between the computer and the desk within that room. (35)

Latour thus avoids panpsychism, or the position that all inanimate objects think and feel as humans do, by shifting this presumed hierarchy. Latour does not anthropomorphize the material world but instead materializes the anthropocentric world by rejecting thinking as a special, higher-order activity. Yet, he does not cast humanity as the mere implement of technological determinism. Latour provides a fine-grained model that productively grapples with the many ways actors, both human and other, act as material entities. He clarifies these nuances through a sustained passage in *Reassembling the Social*.

> This, of course, does not mean that these participants "determine" the action, that baskets "cause" the fetching of provisions or that hammers "impose" the hitting of the nail. Such a reversal in the direction of influence would be simply a way to transform objects into the causes whose effects would be transported through human action now limited to a trail of mere intermediaries. Rather, it means that there might exist many metaphysical shades between full causality and sheer inexistence. In addition to "determining" and serving as a "backdrop for human action," things might authorize, allow, afford, encourage, permit, suggest, influence, block, render possible, forbid, and so on. (71–72)

Clearly, these elements of Latour's critical thought have significant implications for a memoria model attuned to a digital culture. The lack of distinction between humans and nonhumans, including digital machines and networks, means that memory cannot be an anthropocentric act. The denial of thinking as a special kind of transcendent activity removes memory's conventional status as a subset of human cognition. Nonhumans of all types, including technological instantiations, such as digital machines, become full partners in memory acts and cannot be, as they are for Brooke, subservient prostheses of storage and curation. Further, Latour's translation negates discrete acts of encoding and retrieval, because there cannot be transparent passing of discrete data by autonomous entities.

A related aspect of Latour's flattened, nonessential ontology that has significant implications for memoria is its unconventional, kairotic temporality. As previously mentioned, this is the second main aspect of Latour's thought that negates Platonism as it pertains to memory and separates from Brooke's chronos-invested persistence. For Latour, there is no substance that endures through a distinct temporal medium; there is no conventional chronos, or duration. This transforms memory into an isolated act rather than a stable archive or a practice persisting through time. Latour contends that "each entity is an event," a completely individuated, unique occurrence (*Modern* 81). A consequence of this, as Harman states, is that "entities for Latour *must* be a perpetual perishing, since they cannot survive even the slightest change in their properties" (104; original emphasis). This means that acts exist only as snapshots—or what Latour calls "performances" in *Pandora's Hope*—each moment being wholly unconnected to those previous and subsequent (167). Because actors are fully deployed in each moment, there is no residue or potential to carry over. Acts are like the frames of a film. Harman contends that this formulation makes Latour an implicit "ally of the doctrine of continuous creation" (46), and he sees an unprecedented shift in Latour to a metaphysical position of "local occasionalism," wherein entities are mutually constitutive without the need of an overriding substance, such as God or the human mind (112–16).

Latour's local occasionalism leads to a temporality that may be understood to favor kairos over chronos. It cannot, as Brooke's posthuman persistence does, find room for both. Time becomes not an independent medium in which actors endure but a product of acts themselves. We see in Latour a notion wherein past and future are not discrete entities but only ever present. Actions invoke interpretations of these aspects. In *Pandora's Hope*, Latour discusses this concept, which he terms "the puzzle of backward causation," through a prolonged example addressing Louis Pasteur's discovery of microbes (168). Latour makes the counterintuitive claim that microbes did not exist before Pasteur's experiments in 1864; rather, after 1864, microbes had always existed. Latour clarifies that the past is always partially an aspect of the present moment: "there is also a portion of what happened in 1864 that is produced *after* 1864 and made retrospectively a part of the ensemble that forms, from then on, the sum of what happened in the year 1864" (*PF* 172; original emphasis). Latour here takes seriously the temporal ramifications of his local occasionalism. If there is no enduring past, then microbes could not exist before their discovery because there was no stable *dureé* previous to that action. Microbes were not there all along in the conventional sense because nothing could be there all along. The present reinterpretation does not retroactively construct the physical presence of microbes in the previous years because there is no temporal medium into which they can be inserted. Instead, we can say that in 1863 the past and present were free of microbes; after 1864, microbes had been there the whole time.

For Latour, what seem to be the same entities persisting through time and change are reinterpretations he calls "trajectories" (*Modern* 87). Like Pasteur's microbes, trajectories are assembled into coherent aspects of duration. An actor has no persistent essence, but a form of historical revisionism gives it an ersatz durability. The present moment grants the actor a trajectory that extends into a fictional past and projects forward into an equally nonexistent future. What we commonly view as stability is for Latour a useful illusion. Harman captures this sentiment: "a merely apparent essence will gradually condense from this grand drama of instantaneous points and flying trajectories; even once it crystallizes, the essence will have only a pragmatic value in helping us identify certain things as the same" (65). We can and do create duration but like the illusion of movement on a movie screen, it is composed of flickering, isolated moments.

Latour's temporality has significant implications for a contemporary memoria. Conventionally, memoria has been tightly associated with chronos; individual memories are as moments frozen within a continuing duration, and their highest function is to remain stable despite ongoing circumstantial fluctuations. The notion of an archive is predicated on a form of stability, wherein stored things remain static. Retrieved memories are verified through comparison to an objective standard of what *actually* occurred. Latour's kairotic temporality denies all of this. Memory cannot be a process of fixed storage and retrieval; it is always a new assemblage in the present moment. A Latourian memoria cannot be, as Brooke proffers, the persistent practice of incrementally augmenting a durable archive.

The character of a Latourian memoria is now clear. Within a Latourian memoria, memory is no longer the special privilege of humans but the prerogative of all actors. It is an ephemeral event rather than a durable archive or a habituated practice. It is characterized by momentary generation rather than access of stable resources, be they biological, technological, or other. It cannot permit differentiated processes of storage, retention, or retrieval. Memory is the always-new interpretation of the present moment through an assembled trajectory, which invokes a contingent alliance among actors understood as bundles of relations without need of a transcendent metasubstance. Such alliances define a memory act within a local occasionalist network as a necessarily contingent, perishable performance. A Latourian memoria is, thus, quite distinct from the more Platonic orientation of Brooke's posthuman model.

The advantages of a Latourian perspective in digital culture are evident: it provides a grammar and framework that accounts for the proliferating nonhuman agents assuming heretofore human cognitive tasks, and it permits a range of agencies and relationships, even when humans are not directly involved. All of this should be strangely comforting to Plato because it resolves his anxiety regarding technological impingement on essential humanity, if not in the way he envisioned. A Latourian memoria denies that we are being pushed out of the catbird seat because there is no such dominant position. Memory is not being colonized but multiplied through association with more and better partners. All actors are gaining increased possibilities for association. Because humanity's status, like that of any agential group that could be artificially designated, is continually new, it cannot be depreciated. This changes the narrative from one of dismal Platonic diminishment to one of expanding productive partnerships.

These benefits motivate my argument for the appropriateness of a Latourian memoria: it is better able than other models, including those grounded in posthumanism, to account for matters that are relevant *now*. Admittedly, Latour's framework, like any other, has its limitations and contestable elements. A principal example is that Latour's defining of actors through their associations leads to a circularity Harman calls an "*infinite regress of actors*" (106; original emphasis). Although we can better understand an actor by tracing its relations, we can never reach this process's end state because there is no final atom to uncover; we are always led to other actors, and the process begins anew. This is not a flaw of Latour's critical thought but a consequence of his irreduction.[6] By denying the necessity of a transcendent substance and focusing exclusively on local relations, Latour frees us from an opaque essentialism but inevitably leads us into strange outcomes, such as infinite regression. Relatedly, because Latour's cosmos consists only of instantaneous, fully deployed actors with nothing *in potentia*, it struggles to explain change.[7] Such is the result of a kairotic temporality that fundamentally isolates instances. Without chronological duration, there can be no development initiated by internal or external forces.

Additionally, some might balk at the dehumanized tenor of a Latourian memoria; however, there is always tension in the relationship between an individual and its contexts, however those concepts are defined. The civic focus of classical Greece and Rome and the political *vita activa* of Renaissance humanism arguably privileged social aspects over individual fulfillment. Many religious frameworks advocate suppressing individual life in favor of service to a greater deity or deities. Both of these examples preserve humanity's special privilege, but this is frequently denied in contemporary ecological orientations, wherein humanity becomes simply another component of a global biological or material network. A Latourian mode would share this latter perspective, although not its conventional resistance to artificial technology. For Latour all actors are equivalent, so there is nothing nobler in people, animals, or plants than there is in highways, neoconservatism, or Google.

The limitations of and objections to Latour's critical framework are no more damning than those of other perspectives; nevertheless, they evince Kenneth Burke's aphorism from *Permanence and Change* that all forms of insight are predicated on exclusion and, thus, are inherently neither true nor false but rather contextually better or worse (49). The issue is what is most productive, most appropriate for the present moment. I have provided my arguments for why a Latourian framework more fully accounts for the salient aspects of the current digital milieu. However, there is a final step to undertake. Just as Brooke uses posthumanism to transform classical memoria into contemporary *persistence*, so, too, must I articulate the form a modern memoria might assume within a Latourian orientation. I have asserted in this text that a Latourian memoria denies humans' special privilege and embraces a momentary kairotic assembly rather than a chronos-driven durable archive. Within this framework, actors' (human and nonhuman) agential role is to form strong alliances through productive but necessarily contingent and perishable associations. In this sense, Latourian memory is something of an anti-memoria. Thus, as an alternative to posthuman *persistence*, I offer a Latourian *lethe*.[8] In classical mythology, Lethe was one of the five rivers in Hades, and drinking from it caused forgetfulness. In some narratives, such as Virgil's *Aeneid*, drinking from the river and forgetting a past life were required of shades so that they might be reborn in a new form. For our purposes, lethe may be understood as the cultivated screening of superabundant information to form continually new correlations. Our Latourian memoria is not training in storage and retrieval nor the leveraging of prostheses but generative deletion. It is discovering how to forget productively.

This emphasis on forgetting's importance in memoria seems counterintuitive, but we might buttress it by acknowledging the brain's significant effort at rapidly deleting information. Recent neurological research demonstrates that forgetting is not the simple attenuation of otherwise-persistent data in the brain. The brain actively deletes material at a "surprisingly high" rate (F. Wolf). In somewhat Latourian language, neuroscientist Fred Wolf suggests that the cerebral cortex is "specifically tailored to the processing of brief snapshots of the outside world." Science writer Matthew Humphries comments that "the high rate of data loss in the brain suggests we are wired to quickly process information and act on it before moving to the next batch of data to begin processing again." This depiction upends the image of the brain as an extensible file cabinet that wrangles all new sensory data into an orderly catalog; rather, the brain exists within the momentary intersection of relational data.

Moreover, in an appropriately Latourian twist, research has suggested that forgetting's exigency is not limited to humans. The 2011 article "Using Computational Patients to Evaluate Illness Mechanisms in Schizophrenia" by Ralph E. Hoffman et al., draws connections between forgetting's function in human brains and computer networks. Researchers in this study created a computer model that was unable to remove information at a particular rate. Their findings suggest, as science writer Daniel Oppenheimer states, that computer networks encumbered with superfluous data show symptoms of "a kind of virtual schizophrenia." Oppenheimer clarifies that this study supports the "hyperlearning hypothesis," which connects schizophrenia with an inability to jettison information at a typical rate, leaving sufferers overloaded with sensory stimuli and unable to identify meaningful signals: "They start making connections that aren't real or drowning in a sea of so many connections they lose the ability to stitch together any kind of coherent story." This study underscores not only a crucial Latourian similarity between human and nonhuman actors but also the importance of memory turnover and the cumbersome, even damaging, effects of comprehensive retention. It recalls sentiments expressed about the venerable software program Xanadu, labeled by *Wired* magazine as the longest-running vaporware project in digital computing history (G. Wolf 1). In an era before the World Wide Web, Xanadu sought to do nothing less than correlate the world's information through a global hypertext platform. In a retrospective about the project, programmer Rob Jellinghaus reflects on how the idealized concept of perfect retention became both a theoretical and technical liability, noting that thought is based on selection, which makes complete remembrance similar to complete forgetfulness (G. Wolf 23). Jellinghaus's sentiments about the benefits of forgetting are shared by Viktor Mayer-Schönberger, who argues in *Delete: The Virtue of Forgetting in the Digital Age* that "through perfect memory we may lose a fundamental human capacity—to live and act firmly in the present" (12). In a Latourian memoria, the fully deployed present is all that exists. An appropriate response to it is vital.

These examples and Mayer-Schönberger's discussion of the sometimes-debilitating effects of photographic memory suggest that complete retention is not an appropriate goal for memoria (12–13). However, lethe should not be understood as its opposite: complete unmindfulness. We should not eschew a virtual schizophrenia by perusing a virtual dementia. Balance may be found in a shift of expectations and acts to encourage connection rather than rapacious collection. This move would help prevent a Latourian memoria from exhibiting the untenable Platonism evident in other frameworks. It is possible that the digital era's information glut and the mild mental perturbation that seems to characterize it are related to volume, and no amount of lifehacking or e-mail wrangling can surmount it. Of course, we are unable to delete memories selectively as is the protagonist of the film *Eternal Sunshine of the Spotless Mind*—nor likely should we endeavor to do so at this juncture.[9] However, we do have options about how to utilize memory. Building more comprehensive mental frameworks to channel the expanding flood of data will consistently lead to problems of scale; we simply cannot handle it all as individuals, nor would it be preferable for each of us to do so. If we as separate actors abandon mastery as a goal and instead function as agents of correlation, then systemic expansion becomes productive rather than overwhelming. Those anxious over the cognitive shift digital technology is fomenting might complain that this is poor thinking—that it is only treading in the shallows, to reference Nicholas Carr's eponymous jeremiad. But, of course, this is a criticism founded on a Platonic notion of what *we* are and how to demarcate the boundaries that include *us*. The rise of digital actants is making it more difficult to maintain the pleasant fiction that existence is at our prerogative. Within a Latourian memoria, the goal is not to make individual humans more perfect; the goal is to make the cosmos more generative. We as human actors have our role to play, and its character is correlation rather than storage and recall.

I return to this text's central assumption that the increasing pervasiveness of digital technology is one of the most significant trends in contemporary rhetoric and composition studies. The proliferation of digital actors is making our customary human entitlement less tenable. We must reexamine those traits and acts that we believe are indicatively ours to articulate human agency within a modern cognitive network. I assert that Latour's critical thought is a productive aspect of this exploration. What this text outlines is admittedly contestable and circumscribed, but it is put forth in the spirit of works such as Latour's "Why Has Critique Run Out of Steam? From Matters of Fact to Matters of Concern" and "An Attempt at a 'Compositionist's Manifesto.'" Such texts acknowledge that all postulations necessarily have points of contention, but, regardless, we should attempt generative assertions. As rhetoricians and compositionists, we should recognize that perspectives are inherently interested. Our task is to determine what admittedly imperfect option is most appropriate, most efficacious for the current moment.

## Notes

1. RSS feeds are short updates published by websites. RSS feed readers (or aggregators) collect these updates from multiple websites as directed by a user. This provides the user with a digest of multiple sites, obviating the need to visit each site individually.

2. Tag clouds are collections of keywords that are visually differentiated, usually by font size, based on their frequency of occurrence in a text or group of texts.

3. This may help explain the recent trend of such activities as the mass recording of live events and the sharing of food imagery through Instagram; the important experience is not the personal encounter but the contribution of a record to the social aggregate.

4. This is particularly due to Brooke's embracing of *chronos*, articulated most explicitly through his statement in "Forgetting to Be (Post)Human" that "while a postmodern rhetoric might privilege *kairos* over *chronos*, a posthuman rhetoric would find room for both" (791).

5. Latour's book aligns the attempted bifurcation and its consequents—including attempts at reunification—with modernism, but the same line of thought is visible in Plato's earlier division of natural from artificial.

6. Harman points out that what prevents infinite regression in other frameworks is the existence of some inviolable substance.

> Traditional realism usually accepts some ultimate substance, whether it be otherworldly exemplars (Plato), concrete individual things (Aristotle), God (Augustine, Spinoza), mirror-like monads (Leibniz), indestructible physical matter (Democritus, Marx), or some variant of these. But these substances are merely treated as the terminal black box—a final stratum of reality that can never be opened and examined. (72)

7. Latour grapples with this limitation near the end of *Reassembling the Social*, granting that there must be unaccounted remainders or "missing masses" in his formulation (244). He postulates a form of unarticulated being called "plasma," which he attempts to distinguish from an essential substance by arguing that it is "simply *unknown*" (244; original emphasis). This explanation is dubious and seemingly undermines his main principle of irreduction by inventing exactly the kind of opaque substance he attempts to exclude. It would be more consistent simply to accept that a Latourian framework cannot account for change in ways that other models do.

8. It is worth noting that Martin Heidegger invokes *lethe* as the counterpart of *aletheia*, or unconcealment. Also, Harald Weinrich's *Lethe: The Art and Critique of Forgetting* examines the role of forgetting in literature and philosophical history. As such, lethe already has been variously appropriated within different intellectual traditions.

9. Surprisingly, a version of this process is now available. Some neurobiological research is explicitly aimed at lessening the effects of traumatic memories by developing pharmacological means to attenuate memory reconsolidation. See Brunet et al.

## Works Cited

Brooke, Collin. "Forgetting to Be (Post)Human: Media and Memory in a Kairotic Age." *JAC* 20.4 (2000): 775–795. Print.

———. *Lingua Fracta: Towards a Rhetoric of New Media*. Cresskill: Hampton, 2009. Print.

Brunet, Alain, S. P. Orr, J. Tremblay, K. Robertson, K. Nader, and R. K. Pitman. "Effect of Post-Retrieval Propranolol on Psychophysiologic Responding during Subsequent Script-Driven Traumatic Imagery in Post-Traumatic Stress Disorder." *Journal of Psychiatric Research* 42 (2008): 503–506. Print.

Burke, Kenneth. *Permanence and Change*. Berkeley: U of California P, 1984. Print.

Carr, Nicholas. *The Shallows: What the Internet Is Doing to Our Brains*. New York: Norton, 2010. Print.

Derrida, Jacques. *Dissemination*. Trans. Barbara Johnson. Chicago: U of Chicago P, 1981. Print.

*Eternal Sunshine of the Spotless Mind*. Dir. Michel Gondry. Focus Features, 2004. Film.

Harman, Graham. *Prince of Networks: Bruno Latour and Metaphysics*. Melbourne: Re.press, 2009. Print.

Hayles, N. Katherine. *How We Became Posthuman: Virtual Bodies in Cybernetics, Literature, and Informatics*. Chicago: U of Chicago P, 1999. Print.

Hoffman, Ralph E., U. Grasemann, R. Gueorguieva, D. Quinlan, D. Lane, and R. Miikkulainen. "Using Computational Patients to Evaluate Illness Mechanisms in Schizophrenia." *Biological Psychiatry* 69 (2011): 997–1005. Print.

Humphries, Matthew. "Our Brains Forget Information at a Rate of 1 Bit per Second per Neuron." Geek.com. *Ziff Davis*, 25 Jan. 2011. Web. 8 Aug. 2012. <http://www.geek.com/geek-cetera/our-brains-forget-information-at-a-rate-of-1-bit-per-second-per-neuron-1308566/>.

Latour, Bruno. "An Attempt at a 'Compositionist Manifesto.'" *New Literary History* 41 (2010): 471–490. Print.

———. *Pandora's Hope*. Cambridge: Harvard UP, 1999. Print.

———. *The Pasteurization of France*. Trans. Alan Sheridan and John Law. Cambridge: Harvard UP, 1988. Print.

———. *Reassembling the Social: An Introduction to Actor-Network-Theory*. New York: Oxford UP, 2005. Print.

———. *We Have Never Been Modern*. Trans. Catherine Porter. Cambridge: Harvard UP, 2002. Print.

———. "Why Has Critique Run Out of Steam? From Matters of Fact to Matters of Concern." *Critical Inquiry* 30 (2004): 225–248. Print.

Mayer-Schönberger, Viktor. *Delete: The Virtue of Forgetting in the Digital Age*. Princeton: Princeton UP, 2009. Print.

Oppenheimer, Daniel. "Scientists Afflict Computers with Schizophrenia to Better Understand the Human Brain." University of Texas at Austin News. *University of Texas at Austin*, 5 May 2001. Web. 8 Aug. 2012. <http://www.utexas.edu/news/2011/05/05/schizophrenia_discern/>.

Plato. *Phaedrus*. Ed. Harvey Yunis. Cambridge: Cambridge UP, 2011. Print.

Ulmer, Gregory L. *Applied Grammatology: Post(e)-Pedagogy from Jacques Derrida to Joseph Beuys*. Baltimore: Johns Hopkins UP, 1985. Print.

Virgil. *The Aeneid*. Trans. Robert Fagles. New York: Viking, 2006. Print.

Weinrich, Harald. *Lethe: The Art and Critique of Forgetting*. Trans. Steven Rendall. Ithaca: Cornell UP, 2004. Print.

Wolf, Fred. *Out of Mind in a Matter of Seconds. Max-Planck-Gesellschaft*, 24 Jan. 2011. Web. 8 Aug. 2012. <http://www.mpg.de/1046804/brain_forgetting>.

Wolf, Gary. "The Curse of Xanadu." Wired.com. *Condé Nast Digital*, June 1995. Web. 26 Feb. 2013. <http://www.wired.com/wired/archive/3.06/xanadu.html>.

# Part Four. **Composing Assemblages**

# 11. How Bruno Latour Teaches Writing

Marilyn M. Cooper, *Michigan Technological University*

In a "somewhat Socratic" dialog at the London School of Economics (LSE), Bruno Latour tells a doctoral student, "I am teaching nothing but writing nowadays." He explains that a text is "the functional equivalent of a laboratory. It's a place for trials, experiments, and simulations" (*RS* 148). His definition reminds us of the definition of an essay as an attempt, in Latour's world an attempt at composing knowledge. In many of his works, Latour insists that his "compositionist" approach requires attunement, experience, and repeated efforts—work—and that it is not a matter of mastery but of a collaborative construction project in which humans and nonhumans participate as actors, or actants. In this essay I draw on Latour's understanding of knowledge as a mode of existence to suggest a new way to think about and teach research writing.

Latour has quite a lot to say about compositionism, which he offers as an alternative to the Scylla and Charybdis of critique and social construction. While a critic debunks, deconstructs, or decomposes in order to reveal an underlying reality, a composer makes knowledge by describing and assembling. And while a social constructivist, if not committed to what he has constructed as part of reality, risks relativism, a composer recognizes what she has made as real but never as entirely her own creation. Knowledge is always *common* but also always *provisional*; it is, as an ornithologist I read recently says, "truth-for-now" (Birkhead 141). The composing of knowledge, like the assembly of a collective that Latour examines in *Politics of Nature*, must be started over again every single day (146, 147). Nor are there for compositionists underlying forces, such as nature or society or language, determining what people or things do; there is nothing to uncover beneath words or behavior.

Instead, as Latour tells the student who comes to him for help with his thesis, what compositionists do is "describe, write, describe, write" (*RS* 149). He explains, "Depending on what happens in [your text], there is or there is not an actor and there is or there is not a network being traced. And that depends entirely on the precise ways in which it is written" (*RS* 149). The student complains that that's not what his supervisor wants, that he still needs "to put [his data] into a frame, find a typology, compare, explain, generalize" (*RS* 149). Latour says that that's what the actors the student is studying are doing, and that's what he should be describing. He asks the student, "Why would you be the one doing the intelligent stuff while they would act like a bunch of morons? What they do to expand, to relate, to compare, to organize is what you have to describe as well." And he advises, "Simply *go on with* the description" (*RS* 150; original emphasis). At a symposium at the LSE, Latour again argues that "a serial redescription which starts again . . . every morning" is a powerful method in both social sciences and in philosophy (*PW* 76). As he says, this is the essential work of the compositionist: "We accompany the task of the entities in their survival, so to speak, and their maintaining their subsistence in a very, very practical matter" (*PW* 74).

As Latour suggests in his discussion with Graham Harman in the LSE symposium, his approach to composing is heavily influenced by Alfred North Whitehead and William James. When he advises the student to describe rather than to explain or generalize, he is drawing on Whitehead's notion of actual occasions, or actual entities. As actual entities explain themselves, all a social scientist can do is describe what the actual entity is doing, thereby accompanying the entity in its subsistence, or what Latour also calls its "explanatory trajectory" (*PW* 67). And when Latour advises the student to go on with the description, he draws on James's notion that the pragmatic truth of entities relies on an established continuity of connection, a trajectory in which entities change over time yet still remain the same entity. If the student is to accompany entities in maintaining their subsistence, he, therefore, needs to engage in the parallel trajectory of the composing of knowledge—serial redescription.

Unpacking this rather-dense redescription of Latour's advice on writing requires, first of all, that I consider what Whitehead means by actual occasions/entities, and what James means by truth. Then I consider how the existence or nonexistence of the actor and network in the student's text depends on the precise ways in which he writes it and what Latour means by the composing of knowledge as a mode of existence. And finally I offer an example of how Latour's approach to writing might work out for a composition student researching and writing a paper.

Latour describes his current work as a kind of experimental or empirical metaphysics that combines sociology and philosophy. He rejects Harman's assertion that "metaphysics should be able to define the furniture of the world in a sort of coherent way," arguing that "empiricism is not about small details which could be added up by another profession [such as philosophy]. Empiricism means that the details of the actual occasions are the important theoretical features that we want to detect" (*PW* 44). For Whitehead, actual entities, which include not only beings or things but also feelings, sensations, beliefs, networks—anything that can be said to exist at a particular moment—are actual by virtue of the fact that they are absolutely unique. They resist any sort of generalization or explanation because they are what they are by virtue of the specific conditions of their becoming in a particular instance—their details. This is why Latour tells the student that instead of adding contextual explanations, he should "deploy the content with all its connections and you will have the context in addition" (*RS* 147).

Actual entities are, thus, their own reasons; as Whitehead says, "To search for a *reason* is to search for one or more actual entities" (*Process* 24). Actual entities derive from his ontological principle—"there is nothing which floats into the world from nowhere" (*Process* 244)—which Isabelle Stengers says takes up "the paradigmatic rationalist cry: 'nothing happens without a reason!'" but with a difference (261). The difference for Whitehead is that the reason for an actual entity is not found in something else; rather, it is a decision made by the actual entity, which "'decides for itself': thus, and not otherwise" (Stengers 263). Stengers says, "No explanation can lay claim to a higher instance of justification than what makes a difference for [the actual entity], what matters for it. . . . A being becomes determined by determining its reasons" (262–63). Latour protests his student's desire to provide a framework or structure to explain his actors' actions because it reduces the actors (actual entities) to realizing a potential or serving a function that comes from outside them, rather than being a decision based on what they understand as making a difference, as what matters in their situation: "An actor, if words have any meaning, is exactly what is *not* substitutable. It's a unique event, totally irreducible to any other" (*RS* 153; original emphasis). Each actor in each particular situation or moment of the process that is the network is an actual entity, and to describe their actions as they expand, relate, compare, organize is to explain them.

Stengers offers the example of a judge's decision.

> The decision must be based on multiple considerations, and yet the judge is anything but submissive, for it is the decision itself that has assembled these considerations, and presented them in a way that makes the judgment their consequence. . . . Nothing is a reason independently of the

> way in which a decision produces it *qua* the reason for this decision or this actuality. (263)

Thus, if Latour's student describes in detail what his actors are doing, he will have provided the only explanation possible for them. Stengers says, "There is no stable difference between explanation and description, but only distinctions dealing with what matters, and with the environments required by what matters" (262).

The approach Latour suggests to his student is not only empirical but also experimental. While a structuralist explanation represents actors as realizing potentialities, an experimental description represents actors as "rendering virtualities actual" (*RS* 155; Latour ascribes the language to Giles Deleuze). Such an approach requires "very specific texts" and "very specific protocols" (*RS* 155). In *Politics of Nature*, he argues,

> An experiment, as etymology attests rather well, consists in "passing through" a trial and "coming out of it" in order to draw its lessons. It thus offers an intermediary between knowledge and ignorance. It defines itself not by the knowledge that is available at the start, but by the quality of the learning curve that has made it possible to pass through a trial and to know a little more about it. (195–96)

Experiments, whether in an actual laboratory or in a written text, are a way of engaging entities in a trajectory of composing knowledge. Another reason Latour rejects Harman's version of metaphysics is that it offers no way to come to a decision based on knowledge: "if we have to begin to agree about the furniture of the world (are the objects held up by an inner kernel or connected? do we touch the object or not?) then politics is certainly finished, because there is actually no way we will settle these questions" (*PW* 46). Thus, he turns to James's pragmatic understanding of truth that establishes "the continuity of a trajectory of learning" that makes it possible to make new knowledge (*PW* 65).

In James's account, truth does not transcend experience but arises out of the process of connecting past knowledge and new experience in a way that makes a concrete difference. Pragmatic truth is "essentially bound up with the way in which one moment in our experience may lead us towards other moments which it will have been worthwhile to have been led to" (74). As "the process of being guided" by what's important, truth agrees with reality only in the sense that the "conduction from present idea to a future terminus . . . [runs] prosperously." In other words, to be true, an idea or a theory must work:

it "must mediate between all previous truths and certain new experiences. It must derange common sense as little as possible, and it must lead to some sensible terminus or other that can be verified exactly" (78). The pragmatist, more than anyone else, James says, "feels the immense pressure of objective control . . . pent in . . . between the whole body of funded truths squeezed from the past and the coercions of the world of sense about him" (84).

As Latour says, in experiments ideas pass through a trial, and we know a little more. In his dialogue with the student, he is not very specific about how a text can succeed in composing knowledge other than telling the student that his text needs to be like successful laboratories: "To become relevant you need extra work" (*RS* 155). The extra work involves verification that renders truths "funded," as James says. James discusses direct and indirect forms of verification—truth may be agreement with experience or among ideas (theories)—but he emphasizes that a verified truth is not a final terminus. It is instead always temporary, a half-truth. He explains,

> The "absolutely" true, meaning what no farther experience will ever alter, is that ideal vanishing-point towards which we imagine that all our temporary truths will some day converge. . . . Meanwhile we have to live to-day by what truth we can get to-day, and be ready to-morrow to call it falsehood. (80)

This "continuity of the trajectory of the production of proof" that Latour finds so interesting in James's writing is the basis of what he highlights as the learning curve that characterizes a good experiment (*PW* 65). Perhaps even more so than James, Latour emphasizes that trajectories lead to provisional totalities: "A good experiment is not one that offers some definite knowledge, but one that has allowed the researcher to trace the *critical path* along which it will be necessary to pass" to collect a "provisional totality" (*PN* 196, 199; original emphasis). Unlike James and like Whitehead, Latour does not see yesterday's truths as false, only as partial. Discussing "myths" such as the myth of finite facts, Whitehead argues, "None of these logical or scientific myths are wrong, in an unqualified sense of that term. . . . Its truth is limited by unexpected presuppositions; and as time goes on we discover some of these limitations" (*Modes* 11). Discovering the limitations is the project of serial redescription.

For Latour, as for Whitehead, knowledge exists in the world, not in the mind, and Latour postulates different trajectories, or modes of existence, for entities. An actual entity subsists in a trajectory of becoming, but it can also find another mode of existence when it is recruited into an experimental trajectory. This is what Latour means when he tells the student that "we accompany the task of the entities in their survival." In the LSE symposium he says that he is not interested in what objects are but rather "the question of the continuation of time of the inanimate": "Once substance has been excluded, subsistence comes to the fore, and then the big question is how many ways are there for entities to graze their subsistence in the green pastures" (*PW* 48). Addressing this question in "A Textbook Case Revisited," he distinguishes two trajectories, or modes of existence: the mode of subsistence and the mode of reference. The *mode of reference* is his new term for the learning curve that distinguishes good from bad experiments, and in this discussion he also is more explicit about the work that a good experiment necessitates and about the notion of serial redescription.

The "textbook case" Latour instances in this discussion appears in an exhibition at the American Museum of Natural History that shows classic and revised versions of horse evolution through two arrangements of fossil skeletons accompanied by "videos of scientists at work, little biographies of famous fossil-hunters at war with one another, with even different reconstructions of skeletons to prove to the public that 'we don't know for sure'—a frequent label in the show" ("Textbook" 86). One arrangement is the "textbook case," showing a linear process of horses becoming larger with progressively fewer toes and longer teeth. The second arrangement shows the revised, cladistic version, which concludes that the process was more complex, "more like a branching bush," with many lineages of horses existing at the same time. In this version, some later horses are smaller than earlier ones, and some later horses still have three toes. The single straight-line evolution of the earlier version is now understood as an illusion caused by the extinction of all the branching species except the modern horse—the last twig on a once-flourishing bush. Latour quotes a museum label.

> In fact, in any epoch some horses fit into the "straight line" and others didn't. Scientists concluded that there was no single line of evolution but many lines, resulting in diverse groups of animals each "successful" in different ways at different times. This doesn't mean that the original story was entirely wrong. Horses have tended to become bigger, with fewer toes and longer teeth. It's just that this overall trend is only one part of a much more complex evolutionary tale. (qtd. in "Textbook" 85)

Latour observes that the intertwining repeated iterations of knowledge making in the mode of reference "are rarely shown to the public and even more rarely shown to parallel the hesitating movement of the objects of study themselves" in the mode of subsistence (85). Latour agrees with the museum in seeing the exhibit as a paradigm of the scientific method but emphasizes how the horses participate in both modes: as living horses in the mode of subsistence and "hundreds of thousands of years later" as fossil bones that "happened to enter into . . . paleontological pathways" in the mode of reference (101). Both the researchers and the entities being studied "have a history, a movement, a series of revisions and rectification. . . . Eventfulness [is] equally shared with the discoverers as well as with the discovered" (100). Both exist in a process of serial redescription or remaking, and it is through experimentation that the entity enters into another mode of existence and shows what can be possible.

Latour's understanding of composing echoes but goes beyond Joseph Dunne's rejection of the hylomorphic model in his definition of phronetic techne: a techne "whose responsiveness to the situation is not fully specifiable in advance and which is experiential, charged with perceptiveness, and rooted in the sensory and emotional life" (355). While both Latour and Dunne emphasize, as Dunne says, "sensitivity or attunement rather than mastery or domination," Dunne focuses on "a flexible kind of responsiveness to the dynamism of the material itself" (256), while Latour argues that "constructing . . . means *to learn how to become sensitive* to the contrary requirements, to the exigencies, to the pressures of conflicting agencies where none of them is really in command" ("Promises" 7–8; original emphasis). For Latour, the material—and all the other actants involved—are not dynamic substances but mediators. A mediator, he insists, is not an intermediary that "transports meaning or force without transformation"; instead, "mediators transform, translate, distort, and modify the meaning of the elements they are supposed to carry" (*RS* 39). Furthermore, mediators are not causes: "Their input is never a good predictor of their output; their specificity has to be taken into account every time" (*RS* 39). In the museum exhibit, the horse fossils are mediators. The researchers add to their collections, and sensitive to the conflicts among the fossils, they arrange and rearrange them. Engaged in the trajectory of knowledge, the fossils "undergo a transformation; they enter into a new path, and they circulate along different 'chains of experiences'" ("Textbook" 100). The fossils take on new meanings, and new connections are made. This is the work of serial redescription, of multiplying connectors and adding a text.

But all this takes work. Latour tells the student that the work of description—"to be attentive to the concrete state of affairs, to find the uniquely adequate account of a given situation"—is "incredibly demanding" (*RS* 144).

As he explains in his discussion of the exhibit of horse evolution, this is not a matter of "a mind zooming toward a fixed—but unaccessible—target." Here he is drawing on Ludwick Fleck, who, like Dunne, also emphasizes the importance of experience in techne. Latour observes, "I wish the dancing together to a melody to which we become better and better attuned could replace the worn-out metaphor of an 'asymptotic access' to the truth of the matter" ("Textbook" 92). Latour refers to experience as "institutionalization—becoming familiar, black-boxing novelty in instruments, tuning, standardizing, getting used to a state of affairs," and he comments, "Going 'forward' now means that we become more and more 'experienced,' 'cognizant,' 'attuned' to the quality of the collective, coordinated, instituted knowledge" ("Textbook" 94, 96). Other requirements for the genesis of facts, which ends, rather than begins, with "direct perception," include "successive rectification and revision" and "rectification by colleagues" ("Textbook" 94).

In his conclusion, Latour observes,

> You need a lot of work to carry a bone from a sand pit to a Museum, a lot of colleagues to rectify what you say about it, a lot of time to make sense of your data, and a well-endowed institution to keep scientific truth valid. The bones have been made to behave in a completely different mode of existence that is just as foreign to the ways ideas behave in our mind as to the ways horses galloped on the great plains. ("Textbook" 105–6)

This understanding of the arduous work of composing allows, as Latour says, "the possibility of giving ontological weight to what is usually defined as objective knowledge" ("Textbook" 103). Facts exist in the world along with everything else, not as representations or ideas in the mind. Knowledge is, thus, not held to the standard of accuracy (how well it reflects a separate reality) but of existence: "Objective knowledge is what circulates and then *grants* the entity seized by the networks another mode of existence and *grants* the minds seized by them an objectivity no human ever dreamed of before the seventeenth century" or at least not until the advent of "highly equipped knowledge acquisition networks" ("Textbook" 106, original emphasis; 110n30). As Latour says, following Deleuze, composing a text "renders virtualities actual" (*RS* 155).

Latour argues that his compositionist theory frees knowledge from epistemological questions: "Yes, we err often, but not always because, fortunately, (1) *we have time;* (2) *we are equipped;* (3) *we are many;* (4) *we have institutions*" ("Textbook" 95; original emphasis). His description of the composing work of scientists like Louis Pasteur and sociologists like the graduate student he advises could animate the work of undergraduates writing research papers as well. What if writing teachers and their students thought of research as empirical and experimental—as producing new knowledge, not reporting what is known? What if they thought of the facts they discover as provisional, part of a trajectory of knowledge, and not as final truths? What if they thought of the readers of their texts as colleagues who provide necessary validation of their facts, not as editors? What if they thought of their goal in writing as the direct perception of reality, rather than as defending a point of view? Some research manuals do allude to these possibilities, but they rarely extend them to a complete vision of what students might be able to do in their research. Instead, they focus almost entirely on the tools of research and research writing: how to find and evaluate information, how to create a textual persona, how to imagine readers, how to structure texts. Tools are important—but only for people who are engaged in a project they find worthwhile, one that could make a difference to themselves or others. According to Latour, being equipped is only one requirement for composing knowledge.

The pleasure or sense of accomplishment involved in composing knowledge—and the ability of students to engage in this practice—is neglected or outright ignored in most research manuals, as are the status of that knowledge and the institutions involved in verifying it. Consider the prologue to Wayne C. Booth, Gregory G. Colomb, and Joseph M. Williams's influential manual *The Craft of Research*. They start by asserting that research is essential in the "age of information" and that everyone who wishes to succeed in "just about any profession" must learn "how to find information . . . how to evaluate it, then to report it clearly and accurately" (3). Next, they assume that readers are probably not yet ready to do such research: "learning to do research now will help you today and prepare you for what's to come" (3). On the following page, they offer a ray of hope, though qualified: "Although some might think it idealistic, another reason for doing research is the sheer pleasure of solving a puzzle, of discovering something that no one else knows" (4), and a little later they add, "Maybe not today or tomorrow, but one day, your research and your reports of it can improve if not the whole world, at least your corner of it" (11). They warn that "doing research carefully and reporting it clearly are hard work" (4) and that it is often anxiety-producing, frustrating, and confusing but allow that it can also be pleasureful, satisfying, and "worth the effort" (5). I can't imagine any more dispiriting, less enticing introduction to a manual that readers might hope, given its title, would provide them with useful new strategies on how to improve their skills in a practice many of them have been engaging in for at least twelve years already. Looking ahead, readers turn back to the table of contents and find a familiar plan for their projects: find a topic, narrow it to a research question, determine what evidence you need, find sources, evaluate sources, make a claim, outline your argument, draft, revise. Why? they might ask.

I have been very hard on this manual, which does offer useful guidance about research tools and, occasionally, a glimpse of the larger purposes and requirements of composing knowledge. Booth, Colomb, and Williams, acknowledge that students' research can be worthwhile for them and to others (19–20, 279); they point out that composing can produce new insights and greater depth of understanding (12, 14); they acknowledge that research involves colleagues and teachers who validate the researcher's findings (34, 281). But what kind of knowledge is worthwhile, and how can students really compose it? Other than stating that research must be accurate, trustworthy, and published, Booth, Colomb, and Williams have little to say about these questions.

Imagine, instead, a student in a research-writing course in February 2012. Because she is interested in making a career in energy engineering but at the same time is concerned about the environment, the furor over President Barack Obama's decision to deny the Keystone XL pipeline permit application catches her attention. She'd like to know what it is all about, and she feels she has enough background to understand it and to be able to explain it to friends, family, and others who might be concerned. She also thinks that this might be a good project for the research paper just assigned in her course. Her teacher, after all, emphasized in the assignment that they should draw on their interests and abilities to compose new knowledge and that they should begin by collecting a lot of background information about something they are interested in. So the student surfs the Internet, looking for news reports, responses from politicians and commentators, and official documents. She notices some confusions and disagreements, and so she prints out an assortment of quotes from a variety of sources: the U.S. State Department statement of its recommendation to the president and its report to Congress (both January 18, 2012); Obama's memo to the secretary of state directing her to deny the permit (January 18, 2012); an undated policy statement from the American Petroleum Institute website; the *New York Times* editorial of January 18, 2012; a statement from Mitt Romney quoted in a *New York Times* article (Broder and Frosch); responses to the decision from the National Resources Defense Council and the Sierra Club on their websites (both January 18, 2012); a blog post by Patrick Richardson on the PJ Media website (January 28, 2012); and an opinion piece on the American Action Forum website (February 3, 2012). As Latour says, "innovations in knowledge naturally emerge from the collection deployed on the table" (*PH* 38), and our student now has a collection of statements from which a number of interesting questions can emerge.

Following her teacher's directions, she brings them to class and shares them with two other students who also have their collections of quotes, images, data. They—and the teacher, who steps into their discussion from time to time—talk to her about what she sees and point out other puzzles to her. She has noted the wide range of factors that various sources deem to be part of the national interest: environmental health, employment and the economy, trade, energy security, and relations with Canada. One student wonders really how many jobs the pipeline would create: five thousand to six thousand, as the State Department reports the environmental-impact statement estimates, or twenty thousand as the American Petroleum Institute estimates and Richardson repeats. Another student says she read somewhere that most of the oil carried by the pipeline would be exported, not used in the United States. Her teacher points out a discrepancy in the accounts of what exactly President Obama did in his decision. In the memo to the secretary of state, he directs her to "issue a denial of the Keystone XL pipeline permit application" because the project "as presented and analyzed at this time, would not serve the national interest." His wording closely follows the State Department's recommendation. But that's not what the news reports and commentary say: for the most part, they agree that Obama rejected the project, even, according to Richardson, that he dealt it a death blow, though the *New York Times* notes that his decision may only delay the project, and the Sierra Club makes clear that it is inferring his rejection of the project from his denial of the permit.

The student's discussion with colleagues and her teacher is already functioning as a laboratory in which new candidates for understanding have been identified. The statements are mediators, and rather than deciding which statements are more trustworthy or accurate, reporting what they say, and arguing that President Obama was justified or not in his decision, the student listens to her teacher, who is channeling Latour and telling her to "slow down," take your time, and "burrow beneath" discrepancies like those they've found: "Instead of cutting the Gordian knot . . . untie a few of its strands in order to knot them back together differently" (*PN* 3); describe what the mediators and actors in this event are doing as they expand, relate, compare, and organize the aspects of the decision (*RS* 150). The student likes the idea of describing what's going on, and she realizes she needs to know more.[1] Why did Obama make this decision now? She finds the law that required him to do so, the Temporary Payroll Tax Cut Continuation Act of 2011.

> (a) Except as provided in subsection (b), not later than 60 days after the date of enactment of this Act, the President acting through the Secretary of State, shall grant a permit under Executive Order 13337 . . . for the Keystone XL pipeline project application. . . . (b) Exception . . . The President shall not be required to grant the permit under subsection (a) if the President determines that the Keystone XL pipeline would not serve the national interest. (Sec. 501)

This is what the *New York Times* was referring to when it mentioned the Republicans' demand that the project be decided in haste. So it wasn't Obama's idea to make a decision on the project at this time. Another question she wants to pursue is who really made the decision about the permit. The State Department seems to be playing a big role. She finds Executive Order 13337 that Obama refers to in his memo and copies the statement of its purposes.

> To expedite reviews of permits as necessary to accelerate the completion of energy production and transmission projects, and to provide a systematic method for evaluating and permitting the construction and maintenance of certain border crossings for land transportation . . . while maintaining safety, public health, and environmental protections. . . . the Secretary of State is hereby designated and empowered to receive all applications for Presidential permits . . . for the construction, connection, operation, or maintenance, at the borders of the United States, of facilities for the exportation or importation of petroleum, petroleum products, coal, or other fuels to or from a foreign country.

From Obama's memo, the student knows that the secretary of state made the recommendation, but it looks like the whole process of vetting the application and recommending that the permit be approved (or not) is done by the State Department, which is directed by the executive order to request information from the permit applicant; to request the views of a variety of other federal departments and state, tribal, and local officials and foreign governments; and to decide whether approving the permit serves the national interest or not. And the student knows that it was the State Department, too, that issued the report to Congress that was required by the Temporary Payroll Tax Cut Continuation Act if the permit was denied. She assumes that the State Department would be guided in its determination by the two purposes stated in the executive order—to accelerate energy production and transmission and to maintain safety, public health, and environmental protections—but the American Action Forum says that Obama was motivated only by environmental concerns. She decides to burrow beneath this discrepancy. She finds a report from the Congressional Research Service on the Keystone XL pipeline project that explains that though the State Department has identified key factors it has used in making decisions about permits (including environmental impacts, economic benefits, energy needs, the stability of trading partners, impacts on foreign-policy objectives, including addressing climate change and reducing reliance on fossil fuels in favor of alternative and renewable energy economic benefits), "this list is not exhaustive, and . . . the State Department may consider additional factors." The report concludes that "in making its national interest determination, the State Department . . . has broad discrimination in determining what factors it will examine to inform its determination . . . [of] whether a proposed project is in the national interest" (Parfomak, Pirog, Luther, and Vann 6–7). She notes that while the State Department report mentions a variety of factors, including both environmental and economic factors, most of the responses in the sources she found emphasize only one or two, generally environmental risks or jobs and energy independence. In this process, she is becoming more experienced and attuned to the quality of the instituted knowledge.

Finally, she turns to the discrepancies between statements that Obama denied the permit or that he rejected the project. Here she remembers the section of her course textbook that talks about how language choices respond to "*the particular immediate and broader contexts that make such choices compelling, sensible, and possible*" (Lu and Horner 102; original emphasis). The textbook quotes James Baldwin: "People evolve a language in order to describe and thus control their circumstances or in order not to be submerged by a situation they cannot articulate" (qtd. in Lu and Horner 102). The student describes how the Sierra Club's choice of "deny a permit" makes sense in that the wording emphasizes how a "dirty, dangerous oil project" supported by a powerful and well-funded oil industry that would transport "toxic, highly corrosive tar sands" across the country must be subject to a permit since it potentially could harm the boreal forest, the Sand Hills and Ogallala aquifer of Nebraska, and the climate. She describes how the *New York Times*' choice of "rejected, at least for now" makes it possible for them to emphasize that making an unreasonably hasty decision on a controversial project elides consideration of a "far more important" goal, "the development of renewable and alternative energy sources." She describes how Richardson's choices of "the death of the Keystone XL pipeline was a blow to economic development" and of "the Obama administration . . . killed the pipeline" are compelled by his alignment with the American Petroleum Institute assessment of the economics of the pipeline and with his assumption that in an election year Obama is vulnerable on the question of jobs, which is why Richardson goes so far as to say that "the State Department actually made the decision so Obama wouldn't have to." The student describes Obama's choices to call the time period to assess the permit application "insufficient" and to state that the project "as presented and analyzed at this time" does not serve the national interest as compelled by the purposes stated in the executive order. She describes—but she doesn't try to adjudicate among these statements, nor does her teacher push her to simplify her descriptions or draw conclusions. The student's goal is perhaps ethnographic: to "deploy the content with all its connections" so as to exhibit, not explain, the context (Latour, *RS* 147).

The student's work ends with a direct perception of reality. She has found out a lot about the decision on the pipeline permit. The statements and documents she collected are mediators, enrolled in the trajectory of knowledge she and her teacher and classmates have set in motion. As she arranges them, they take on new meanings from the various juxtapositions she tries out. She writes her description in a precise-enough way that what happened appears as patterns of connected and conflicting interests—what instigated the decision at this time (including references to the upcoming presidential election), what the process was (including the executive order issued in 2004 that outlined the responsibilities of the State Department and set the goals of the permitting process), the different configurations of the national interest, and the denial of the permit being translated along different lines.

She has worked hard—searching, reading, assembling, writing—and she is anxious to see what others will make of what she has composed. She gives her text to the students in her group and is pleased that they are interested in what she has found out: the decision occurred over a longer time span than they had thought; it involves many more concerns and more participants than they had heard about. One of the students who is researching and writing about the extraction of crude oil from the tar sands talks about how what he has found out aligns with some of her descriptions and augments the complexity of the decision. Her teacher comments on some of the other questions she could still consider. A week after the student hands in her paper, Obama announces his support for TransCanada's plans to build the section of the pipeline between Oklahoma and the Gulf of Mexico. Because of the validation of her group and her teacher, she knows that her paper has composed new knowledge about the decision, and she has also learned some things about permitting processes that may be useful to her in her career in the future. But she also realizes that it is provisional knowledge, that she—and others—could start over again with a redescription that could provide a more complex picture of the web of agencies that have composed the decision. There is always more to know.

I like this approach to teaching research writing because it emphasizes how care, patience, and hard work in assembling documents, statements, and words into a description of an event results in sturdy—if not final—knowledge of a real state of affairs. As with the paleontologists assembling fossil horse bones, a single description is never the final and complete story, and the researcher is accompanied by other agents in the composing process. There is time—time for events to evolve and for researchers to accompany them. There are tools—search engines, interview protocols, document collections, textual patterns. There are many researchers who work together directly and indirectly. And there are institutions—the Internet, laboratories, public and private research groups, schools, colleges, and universities, and all of their instruments and instituted practices. All of these in some form are available to college students who can, therefore, do more than write research papers. They can compose knowledge that is important and worthwhile for themselves and others.

## Note

1. I like the definition of research in Wysocki and Lynch: "Consider 're-search' as 're-search': emphasizing the root meaning 'research' as *searching again*. . . . because when you research you acknowledge that you do not know everything you need in a given context" (144; original emphasis).

## Works Cited

American Action Forum. "Waxman Calls Hearing To Demonize the Keystone XL Pipeline." *American Action Forum*. Web. 24 Mar. 2013. <www.americanactionforum.org/topicwaxman-calls-hearing-demonize-keystone-xl-pipeline>.

American Museum of Natural History. "Evolution of Horses." *American Museum of Natural History*. Web. 15 Mar. 2014. <http://www.amnh.org/exhibitions/permanent-exhibitions/fossil-halls/paul-and-irma-milstein-hall-of-advanced-mammals/evolution-of-horses>.

American Petroleum Institute. "Keystone XL Pipeline." *American Petroleum Institute*. Web. 13 Apr. 2013. <www.api.org/policy-and-issues/policy-items/keystone-xl/keystone-xl-pipeline>.

Birkhead, Tim. *Bird Sense: What It's Like to Be a Bird*. New York: Walker, 2012. Print.

Booth, Wayne C., Gregory G. Colomb, and Joseph M. Williams. *The Craft of Research*. 3rd ed. Chicago: U of Chicago P, 2008. Print.

Broder, John M., and Dan Frosch. "Rejecting Pipeline Proposal, Obama Blames Congress." *New York Times*, 18 Jan. 2012. Web. 24 Mar. 2013. <www.nytimes.com/2012/01/19/us/state-dept-to-put-oil-pipeline-on-hold.html>.

Dunne, Joseph. *Back to the Rough Ground: Practical Judgment and the Lure of Technique*. Notre Dame: U of Notre Dame P, 1993. Print.

Executive Order No. 13,337. 69 Fed. Reg. 87 (May 5, 2004). Print.

"A Good Call on the Pipeline." *New York Times*, 18 Jan. 2012. Web. 24 Mar. 2013. <http://www.nytimes.com/2012/01/19/opinion/a-good-call-on-the-keystone-xl-oil-pipeline.html?scp=5&sq=keystone+XL+pipeline&st=nyt>.

Heidegger, Martin. "Building Dwelling Thinking." *Poetry, Language, Thought*. Trans. Albert Hofstadter. New York: Harper, 1971. 141–159. Print.

———. "The Thing." *Poetry, Language, Thought*. Trans. Albert Hofstadter. New York: Harper, 1971. 161–184. Print.

James, William. *Pragmatism and the Meaning of Truth*. 1907. ReadaClassic.com, 2010. Print.

Latour, Bruno. "An Attempt at a 'Compositionist Manifesto.'" *New Literary History* 41.3 (2010): 471–490. Print.

———. *Pandora's Hope: Essays on the Reality of Science Studies*. Cambridge: Harvard UP, 1999. Print.

———. "The Promises of Constructivism." *Chasing Technology: Matrix of Materiality*. Ed. Don Idhe. Bloomington: Indiana UP, 2003. 27–46. Print.

———. *Reassembling the Social: An Introduction to Actor-Network-Theory*. Oxford: Oxford UP, 2005. Print.

———. "A Textbook Case Revisited—Knowledge as a Mode of Existence." *The Handbook of Science and Technology Studies*. 3rd ed. Ed. Edward J. Hackett, Olga Amsterdamska, Michael Lynch, and Judy Wajcman. Cambridge: MIT P, 2008. 83–112. Print.

———. "Why Has Critique Run Out of Steam? From Matters of Fact to Matters of Concern." *Critical Inquiry* 30.2 (2004): 225–248.

Latour, Bruno, Graham Harman, and Peter Erdélyi. *The Prince and the Wolf: Latour and Harman at the LSE*. Alresford: Zero, 2011. Print.

Lu, Min-Zhan, and Bruce Horner. *Writing Conventions*. New York: Pearson, 2008. Print.

National Resources Defense Council. “”Keystone XL Pipeline’s Rejection Was Made for All the Right Reasons.” *National Resources Defense Council.* 18 Jan. 2012. Web. 24 Mar. 2013. <www.nrdc.org/media/2012/120118a.asp>.

Parfomak, Paul W., Robert Pirog, Linda Luther, and Adam Vann. *Keystone XL Pipeline Project: Key Issues. Congressional Research Service*, 2 Dec. 2013. Web. 24 Mar. 2013. <http://www.fas.org/sgp/crs/misc/R41668.pdf>.

Richardson, Patrick. “Pipeline Politics Derails More Than Jobs.” *PJ Media*, 28 Jan. 2012. Web. 24 Mar. 2013. <www.pjmedia.com/blog/pipeline-politics-derails-more-than-jobs/?print=1>.

Sierra Club. “President Obama Rejects Keystone XL!” *Sierra Club*, 18 Jan. 2012. Web. 24 Mar. 2013. <http://sierraclub.typepad.com/compass/2012/01/president-obama-rejects-keystone-xl.html>.

Stengers, Isabelle. *Thinking with Whitehead: A Free and Wild Creation of Concepts*. Trans. Michael Chase. Cambridge: Harvard UP, 2011. Print.

Temporary Payroll Tax Cut Continuation Act of 2011. HR 3765. 112–78. 23 Dec. 2011. Print.

United States. Dept. of State. “Denial of the Keystone XL Pipeline Application.” *U.S. Department of State*, 18 Jan. 2012. Web. 13 Apr. 2013. <www.state.gov/r/pa/prs/ps/2012/01/181473/htm_>.

———. ———. “Report to Congress Concerning the Presidential Permit Application of the Proposed Keystone XL Pipeline.” *U.S. Department of* State, 18 Jan. 2012. Web. 24 Mar. 2013. <www.state.gov/e/eb/esc/iec/permit/keystone/182277.htm>.

Whitehead, Alfred North. *Modes of Thought*. New York: Free Press, 1938. Print.

———. *Process and Reality.* Corrected ed. Ed. David Ray Griffin and Donald W. Sherburne. New York: Free Press, 1978. Print.

Wysocki, Anne Frances, and Dennis A. Lynch. *Compose, Design, Advocate.* New York: Longman, 2006. Print.

# 12. An Attempt at a "Practitioner's Manifesto"

Casey Boyle, *University of Texas–Austin*

> We are at root practical beings, beings engaged in exercise. This practice constitutes at first both self and the world of reality. There is no distinction.
>
> —John Dewey, *The Later Works, 1925–1953*

> [I]t's practice all the way down.
>
> —Bruno Latour, *Reassembling the Social*

In "Give Me a Gun and I Will Make All Buildings Move: An ANT'S View of Architecture," Bruno Latour and Albena Yaneva lament our inability to "document" a building "not [as] a static object but [as] a moving project" (80). Citing the photographic gun developed by Etienne Jules Marey to record the line of a bird's flight, Latour and Yaneva posit that "we too need an artificial device (a theory in this case) in order to be able to transform the static view of a building into one among many successive freeze-frames that could at last document the continuous flow that a building always is" (81). Our failure, they insist, is a continued reliance on models of accounting that reduce a building only to its euclidean dimensions. Latour and Yaneva argue that by relying on written accounts, such as blueprints and 3-D AutoCAD models, we reinvest in a modernist ontology that upholds strict divisions between subjects and objects, eliding otherwise-messy relations. Thus, the aim of the accounting process they seek is not to *represent* but to *document* a building as having its own line of flight through its controversies, its prior and ongoing constructions, its cohabitants, and its abundant written descriptions. In short, they find themselves in want of writing practices that account for a building as an ongoing composition of forces.

Their essay is unique and productive because it implies composition (as a writing activity) and compositionism (as a political project) to be different but not separate practices of putting things together. This similarity between writing and composition has been rendered explicit in foundational writing studies scholarship. Janet Emig, for instance, proposes for us to understand writing as a "mode of learning" when she aligns "writing and all other forms of composing, such as composing a painting, a symphony, a dance, a film, a *building*" (122; emphasis added). Emig goes on to explain writing's uniqueness lies in it being "the most *available* medium for composing" (122; emphasis added). While some of those forms of composing are more available today through technological innovation—filming, for instance—the point is that Emig privileges writing's accessibility without succumbing to separating writing from composing, more generally. Writing, then, is not separate from other forms of composing but simply offers a different practice. To put the matter simply and with some liberty: *we write so that we may compose.*

That last statement relates directly to Latour and Yaneva's project. While they direct their essay towards architectural theorists, I contend that the problems they articulate are shared by composition scholars and teachers. The quandary of documenting flow is *composition's* problem. As a problem, it calls on us to revise our understanding of the *kind* of practice that writing offers. If writing is not only practice that seeks to represent a stable set of objects for a stable subject, then what other *kinds* of practice might writing (and writing studies) also be?

I will forego any suspense: *writing can be understood as ontological practice.* Admittedly, this heavy phrase should be unpacked. For now, with ontology we are interested in what *is* and can be *done* rather than being primarily concerned with what can be *communicated* or *known*. Or, better put, that *knowing is itself a doing*. By practice, I mean three related things. First, practice can be understood in the sense of a repeating "array of activity" (Schatzki). This first sense of practice can be thought of as the manner in which a building's components, for instance, relate and organize as a building. As I will explain below, Latour and others have shown that when we explore and study things *in practice*, things get complex. Those things we might have relied on to explain certain social phenomena—such as a building or an academic discipline—become themselves in need of an explanation. The second, related manner in which I wish to discuss practice is as a repeated activity to increase our capacities. This version of practice is similar to how an athlete exercises, *with practice*, for a game by familiarizing the body to movements that will be deployed at game time. My final version of practice emphasizes the product of writing as building a space for shared cohabitations. These cohabitations are concerned with sharing movements and other ways of relating not through perspectives but *through practices*. Altogether, understanding writing as ontological practice is to engage writing that both interferes with ontology and that informs and prepares us for ontological engagements. *We write so that we may compose.* While writing studies has looked to the first version of practice as Latour's primary intervention into writing scholars, I submit that Latour's impact on writing studies can be even greater than we have yet imagined if we explore the other two versions as well. Latour, like Emig and others, situates writing as a space for *exercising* the messy relations within which we find ourselves composed. I more fully reenact these claims below by examining ontologies as written *in practice*, *with practice*, and *through practice*.

## Writing as Something We Do *in Practice*

Why is it so difficult to document a building? One reason, as Latour and Yaneva point out, is that simple descriptions often fail to account for the multiplicity of relations that compose a building. For instance, Latour and Yaneva ask, "Where" in the 2-D euclidean diagrams of a building "do you archive the many successive models that you had to modify so as to absorb the continuous demands of so many conflicting stakeholders—users, communities of neighbors, preservationists, clients, representatives of the government and city authorities?" (81). Despite repeated failures to account for these activities, we continue to write simple descriptions. Often. Latour, in the opening paragraphs of *We Have Never Been Modern*, describes the ongoing role that writing plays in obfuscating multiplicity. In his introduction, Latour primes his reader to understand writing's role in the *modern project* through the example of reading a newspaper. In this simple practice, one casually reduces a world into tidy sections: National news. Politics. Life and arts. Business. Sports. However, far from wanting to toss aside the offending newspaper, Latour finds writing—in a pair of well-rehearsed roles—both the problem and a solution: "Yet, rhetoric, textual strategies, writing, staging, semiotics—all these are really at stake, but in a new form that has a simultaneous impact on the nature of things and on the social context" (5). Latour here identifies that writing impacts things but also orients and shapes what socially unfolds as well. This unfolding gets at Robert P. Yagelski's claims that writing is an ontological act. He productively says that when writing is "practiced as an act of being, it opens up possibilities for individual and collective change that are undermined by conventional writing instruction" (8). However, Yagelski's attention to the "writer writing" and diminishing the "writer's writing" risks repeating the same modern mistake that focuses on the human subject and not the subject as only an intense practice of particular things (9). Echoing but diffracting Yagelski, our practices of writing need to change to avoid reducing and categorizing everything to knowing subjects and known objects.

In contrast to this modern ontology that decomposes the world into subjects and objects, Latour and other actor-network-theory (ANT) researchers have argued that when we explore things *in practice*—a laboratory, a water pump, a disease, a salmon—we find things are intertwined, unwieldy, and complex. Latour argues that our knowledge of the world does not result from interpretive or reflective activities that describe and categorize what is "out there" but emerges through the relations of actors that later form networks and meshes between seemingly mundane artifacts: a petri dish, a lab report, a lab technician, refrigeration, and so forth (*SA* 122). These relations between actors compose the ontology of things. Such dynamics exhibit, as Annemarie Mol claims, that "ontological politics" unfold *in practice*: "Once we start to look carefully at the variety of the objects performed in a practice, we come across complex interferences between those objects" ("Ontological" 82). To know things ontologically *in practice* is to intervene in them as they are repeatedly enacted and to perhaps enact those repetitions differently in future practices. Writing's import for ontological politics, then, is quite different as we're still endlessly revising our accounts, but if those accounts are not to develop exhaustive and complete descriptions, what then is writing's role?

Despite Latour's and others' claims that knower, knowledge, and known are enacted in concert and not terms that communicate the knower to the known, writing's role is, perhaps paradoxically, made more relevant for the task of composing ontological interventions. Writing's relevance differs, though, from our typical understanding of writing as a practice of description. In a helpful summary that links Latour and ANT's ontological commitment to writing more broadly, Mol offers a glimpse at this different sense of writing. She points to Ferdinand de Saussure's semiotics as the model for how Latour and ANT, more generally, understand the complex relations we find between actors *in practice*. In much the same way that a single word is not meaningful in and of itself but only gathers meaning in relation to other words, Mol explains how "[i]n ANT this semiotic understanding of relatedness has been shifted on from language to the rest of reality" ("Actor-Network" 257). We find language gains its effectivity in relation, repetition, and difference—not as a referent describing some ontological foundations but, instead, how it reenacts those relations as networks, meshes, and things. Writing intervenes in ontological politics as a practice in posing relations, performing repetitions, and making differences.

The effects of ontologically concerned studies can be readily found in writing studies. Following Latour, writing scholars have always appreciated the importance of examining writing as it exists *in practice*. Such an orientation has become a pressing concern for writing studies, as it further develops accounts of literacy that emerge from a host of situated material, cultural, and economic concerns. Speaking directly to writing's material practice, Christina Haas echoes Latour: "the notion of practice is useful because when literacy is examined in practice, it is seen as intrinsically tied to technology—to tools, implements and artifacts. A practice account of literacy acknowledges these material tools and technologies; in fact, it would see them as central" (19). Haas's understanding, that tools and technologies are as central to writing as any human writer, opens writing studies to further, unrealized potentials for experimenting with the complex of tools and technologies as a kind of embodied theory. Like Haas, many writing scholars rightly find in Latour and related materially focused theorists methods for understanding the material conditions for writing. These methodological imports have been important to show that writing is not a standard skill someone acquires regardless of material situation. However, as writing is a practice that has ontological effects, we stumble upon the very problems we try to avoid when we focus too readily on describing and listing the items that compose writing, even if those lists and descriptions have important political effects. Through his many projects, Latour demonstrates that when we continue to write about a building's complex and ongoing composition as a static object or even as collections of things, we are only exercising an inadequate modernist orientation. Accounting for items alone might change the situation slightly, but it sets up the modern problem to be enacted again.

Beyond typical understandings of Latour and ANT, I propose that they offer not only methods for listing and describing but that they also introduce new practices. To repeat my central claim: Latour offers writing studies an opportunity to understand writing as an ontological practice. This kind of practice unfolds not through tracing things per se but through a kind of attitude or orientation toward those things traced. Instead of becoming experts who demonstrate expertise by accounting for all things, we stand to gain more by proceeding as amateurs, as practitioners. "Amateurs learn to be affected," comments Mol about newcomers to music. "They practice a lot, listening and

---

**How to Do Words with Buildings**

Architectural theorist Sanford Kwinter provides another version of Latour and Yaneva's understanding of a building as unfixed and in motion. Kwinter describes a building not as an object but as "particular clusters of action, affectivity, and matter," all of which compose what he calls "practices" (14). Kwinter further claims,

> It would therefore be a mistake, I would argue, to limit the concept of "architectural substance" to building materials and the geometric volumes they engender and enclose. Just as the meaning of a sentence differs depending on who is speaking, to whom it is addressed, the time and place in which it is uttered, the infinitely complex interplay of will, desire, and systems of legitimation, as well as on these same conditions applied to the referents of each and every element of the sentence, so any proper understanding of architecture must also confront its character as an illocutionary event, or at the very least as an element inseparable from and in constant interface with the world of force, will, action, history. (14)

---

listening again, and they learn from others: acquire a language" ("Actor-Network" 257). Practitioners often shy away from grand gestures and engage instead in what Mol refers to as tinkering: "[Tinkering] suggests persistent activity done bit by bit, one step after another, without an overall plan. Cathedrals have been built in a tinkering mode, and signalers or aircraft designers also work in this way" ("Actor-Network" 235). Elsewhere, Mol proposes to "[l]et us experiment, experience and tinker together—practically" (*Logic* 56). Expressing a similar orientation, Geoffrey M. Sirc proposes composition as "theater of mixed means" in which "faith and naiveté replace knowingness and expertise" (32). Sirc responds to what he considers a modernist impulse that acquires our writing and reading practices for "stuffy museums" whose categories for contributions have been long prescribed for what is included and what counts as a contribution. These prescriptions are enacted by a modernist ontology that situates a well-defined separation between artist and art, inaugurating the buildings that house the museum and universities as spaces for curatorial not creative practices. Instead, composition should offer "a site where radical explorations are appreciated," and composition's mission should "resume building Composition's Hacienda" (32). Just as we see Latour and Yaneva trying to write a building with new orientations, so, too, do we see Sirc attempting to construct a new house for writing.

If buildings emerge through ontological politics and can best be understood *in practice*, then we are compelled to come to know those things by rehearsing the practices with which they are composed. Our aim for writing is to provide spaces for experiencing and becoming attuned to a building's ontological politics in practices that relate, repeat, and differ from what Geoffrey C. Bowker and Susan Leigh Star describe as the "obfuscating effects" of "standardized inscriptions" (307). To put the point in another way, writing's strength is that it stages a practice that is more accessible than a parliament. Writing, understood as the most available means of compositionism, offers ongoing exercises necessary to develop sensitivities to account for buildings *in practice*. These exercises are not innate; they can only be learned *with practice*.

## Writing as Something Done *with Practice*

While not typically considered in pedagogical registers, Latour's work is replete with reference to education practice. To start, Latour urges us to respond to someone's claim to have learned or having his/her "mind enlarged" by "look[ing] first for inventions bearing on the mobility, immutability or versatility of the traces" (*SA* 228). The kind of traces in which one engages is itself a leading indicator, for Latour, of one's capacities to affect and be affected. Our original prompt—how to write about a building as project—speaks towards such a desire to invent new traces as Latour and Yaneva argue for a writing practice that would "transform the static view of a building into one among many successive freeze-frames that could at last document the continuous flow that a building always is" (81). There is little doubt that innovations of writing technologies, such as chirography, manuscripts, printing presses, and even the Internet, all have affected and continue to affect how our "minds are enlarged." That said, it would be a mistake to only discuss Latour's reference to "inventions" as technology in the traditional sense. The "mobility, immutability, or versatility" of traces refers equally to the techniques with which we deploy any particular technology. To be clear, I do not wish to enact divides between technologies and techniques that replicates subject/object, but inasmuch as we find materials and technologies *in practice* as having certain relational tendencies, techniques learned *with practice* increase the capacities of those materials and technologies. *In practice*, things differ *with practice*. Writing about buildings is no exception.

This sense of practice emphasizes once more the activities performed as amateur, practitioner. Toward that exercise notion of practice, it should be of interest for composition scholars that Latour and Yaneva use the word "document" rather than "represent" to explain the kind of writing they seek. Although we might understand documents in official registers (e.g., a city's zoning documents), taking a glance at the word's etymology adds a productive spin to the word. "Document," according to *Cassell's New Latin Dictionary*, is formed from *doceo/docere*, a word with two related meanings. First, it means "to teach, to instruct"; while the second, more particular meaning is in the sense of *docere fabulum*, or "to teach a play to the actors." The first meaning alone helps us extend technique to the practice of writing as a venue for learning, but things get interesting with the word's second meaning. To document is to teach through rehearsal and practice, or an attempt to prepare "actors" for a stage. Effective writing would not be the simple transfer of knowledge about things but would offer a kind of script or itinerary for reenacting those things. We can build on this point. As noted above, ANT once shifted a semiotic understanding of relatedness from language to *reality* to understand how material things relate and form practices. We might now recognize an opportunity to shift that practice of relating back to writing itself for rehearsal, for practice. Writing here is understood as rehearsal or performance of the ontological politics that compose a building.

This point, writing as practice, is not one that finds a welcome home in composition scholarship, but it is a one that composition scholars might reconsider. Writing in the academy is often looked at with derision, as a series of "dummy runs" opposed to *real* writing done *in practice*. Susan Miller insightfully engages this concern: "Within the closed discourse of school, student writing retains its status of practice—no matter how correct, 'original,' or provocative its text may be" (163). Miller voices a common concern here about the status of student writing and adds, "It is always rehearsal, if dress rehearsal, for achieving the privileges of an independent text, and thus it is an emblem for the dependencies of all texts" (163). I find that Miller's phrase "thus . . . an emblem for the dependencies of all text" adds a productive aspect to the traditionally maligned *practice* and *rehearsal* aspects of student writing. We can draw an affinity here between Miller's "textual dependencies" and Latour's "relatedness" in that rehearsing relations between words, through ongoing practice, attunes us to the multiple relations that compose ontological conditions. How might writing be understood as a practice of relating?

In *Reassembling the Social*, Latour makes an implicit case for the researcher as a practitioner—a learner, an amateur—in his outline of how successful writing is composed. As he overviews how to produce effective reports, Latour identifies notebooks as crucial for making "risky accounts." He proposes using notebooks to "see whether the event of the social can be extended all the way to the event of the reading through the medium of the text" (133). That is, maintaining ongoing accounts helps extend practices that compose an object through the accounts of that object. In these writings, a series of exercises, each notebook plays a role: the first notebook is a general account of the study's trajectory; the second is a chronological and categorical account; the third is a running account of drafts, failed writings, attempts to document an object; finally, the fourth is an account of the effects that writing has on the thing being studied (134–35). Latour understands that it may be "disappointing" that "grand questions of group formation, agency, metaphysics, and ontology" come down to nothing more than a sustained practice of using "tiny notebooks" (135). In stipulating that the notebooks be used throughout the entire study, Latour makes a familiar case for understanding writing as an ongoing process and not something concerned only with a final product.

Diverting from composition, Latour goes on to point out that these writings and notebooks are not "for the sake of epistemic reflexivity" (*RS* 133). This point importantly conflicts with much of how we understand and teach writing. Reflection is often considered synonymous with writing. Louise Weatherbee Phelps offers an admirable and productive explanation of writing as a reflective practice by arguing for a renewal of *phronesis*, or practical knowing as a way to better include our "procedural knowledge" alongside our more scholarly "propositional knowledge" (869). Phelps, however, ultimately reinforces the role of the humanist subject by not attending to the wider material ecologies that enact knowledge, not capitalizing on the full range of *phronesis* as an embodied and distributed practice of knowing. George Hillocks, another instance of bolstering reflection, argues that writing provides a space for reflection through a purifying process of identification, hypothesis, testing, and arriving at a matter of fact. Hillocks further claims that "reflective practice becomes inquiry . . . as it becomes more formal and systematic" (31). In contrast, Latour's notebook practice explicitly resists understanding writing as a reflective practice or as a formal, systematic method. To lean once again on Mol, "[t]he point is not to purify the repertoire, but to enrich it. To add layers and possibilities" ("Actor-Network" 257). Notebook practice offers an exercise in ontological politics in that it provides an abundant engagement with its object(s). To multiply accounts is to acknowledge that we are never trying to arrive at a correct version but are practicing versions.

### Stephen M. North as Inadvertent Prophet for and Skeptic of the Practitioner

Stephen M. North's characterization of the then novice or amateur discipline of composition in *Making of Knowledge in Composition* complicates the field's understanding of the practitioner. Composition's practitioners build an unorganized body of practical knowledge that North calls "Lore." Generated and maintained by teacher-practitioners, lore is largely anecdotal knowledge that is paradoxically coherent and incoherent. In describing lore as knowledge, North claims, "Practitioners can and will make it over in a way that suits their needs in a particular time and place. And not just once. Practitioners are always *tinkering* with things, seeing if they can't be made to work better" (25; emphasis added). In another memorable passage, North cements lore's character by employing a building metaphor, musing

> I like to think of it in architectural terms, the House of Lore, as it were: a rambling, to my mind delightful old manse, wing branching off from wing, additions tacked to addition, in all sorts of materials—brick, wood, canvas, sheet metal, cardboard—with turrets and gables, minarets and spires, spiral staircases, rope ladders, pitons, dungeons, secret passageways—all seemingly random, yet all connected. Each generation of Practitioners inherits this pile form the one before, is ushered around some of what is there, and then, in its turn, adds on its own touches. Naturally, the structure is huge, sprawling. There are, after all, no provisions for tearing any of it down. Various portions of it can and almost certainly will be "forgotten" and "rediscovered" again and again. A wing abandoned by one generation will be resettled (and maybe refurbished) by another. And note, too, that there is nothing to rule out parallel discovery or re-invention, either; so the House of Lore has many rooms that look very much alike. (27)

We might notice one slight discrepancy in Latour's outline of notebooks, a difference that invites us to further consider the variety of practices writing offers. Despite noting the importance of the particular and specific, Latour mentions that "different notebooks one should keep—manual or digital, it no longer matters much" (*RS* 134). Having done much work extolling the particularities *in practice*, Latour's indifference to notebook specifics emphasizes the practice he is concerned with is not any particular thing *in practice* but that he is in particular concerned *with practice*. Latour goes on to situate reports that result from notebooks as "text made up of reams of paper sullied by an inkjet"—specific things quite notable *in practice*—but also "a precious little institution to represent, more exactly to re-represent—that is, to present again—the social to all its participants, to perform it, to give it a form" (*RS* 139). In producing risky accounts, Latour questions what kinds of intervention we might offer things *in practice* when we engage those things *with practice*.[1]

## Writing as Something Done *through Practice*

We began with a problem: How do we write about a building as an ongoing composition? This section then shows why this task is a problem: Any thing—a building, a discipline—is difficult to account for as it is enacted through a multiplicity of relations *in practice*. Next is traced how Latour and compositionists attempt to document this problem: researchers attempt becoming "a little more objective" by writing multiple risky accounts *with practice*. In this final section, I engage Latour and Yaneva's claim that "[o]nly by enlisting the movements of a building and accounting carefully for its 'tribulations' would one be able to state its existence" (86). This claim for "enlisting the movements" turns our focus to the products those processes produce. In the short space remaining, the chapter concludes by proposing ways to include practice in writing itself.

In an early work, Latour outlines three ways that readers typically respond to texts: "giving-up," which is not reading a text at all; "going-along," which is accepting an author's claim and simply building on that claim without question; and "working-through" or "reenacting everything that the authors went through" (*SA* 60). Although we might find occasion to justify any of one these responses, the last is obviously preferable, even if improbable. Working-through would enlist a reader in reenacting an account, a task that is often outside the capabilities for most readers. A working-through in the case of our building would require the reader to rehearse the entire library of notebooks and perform the report *with* all the listed actors pertaining to that building. One example for this particular style of response in composition is how Collin Gifford Brooke embraces the role of practice for graduate education. He proposes that graduate seminars invite students to practice the "epistemic gestures" of academic essays by tracing out and rendering explicit published scholarship's intertextual networks. Instead of requiring students to simply read essays and hope they gain an implicit understanding of a work, Brooke posits that students, as Latour would say, work-through textual production rather than "go-along." These reenactments ask the student to become informed by practicing scholarship, by rehearsing it. Brooke's move reenacts what Latour and others advocate in that writing itself offers an opportunity to increase our capacities to perform *through practice*. How then might we practice the practice of "working-through" but without the seminar tables, syllabi, and access to vast library holdings?

These questions have been our problem. How might we "enlist the movements" of a building *through practice*? How might we practice writing the ontological politics that enact a building? Our ideal response would be to follow Latour's and Brooke's proposals to invite others to practice our "epistemic gestures" but in a slightly different way. We can come to understand and cultivate a writer's writing as offering affects *through practice*. In composition, Lynn Worsham expresses a similar desire when she, too, calls for a "new theory or a new system" of writing that

> would be the kind of writing that seeks not so much the conceptual and abstract but the sensuous and emotional. It would not seek the truth of propositions but the rigor of possibility and the nuance of the impossible. It would seek not the distance of generalization and objectivity but the nearness of involvement. (236)

A writing that seeks not to just convey a series of propositions is consistent with what John Muckelbauer calls rhetoric's "asignifying operation," which is "interested in provoking the proposition's effects rather than facilitating its understanding" (17). He further claims that effective rhetoric "reproduces the proposition through a kind of differential repetition, transforming that proposition into an array of responses and effects" (18). Writing, following Worsham and Muckelbauer, should be concerned not only with what content it conveys but also how writing invites a reader to practice. To pose a claim that might resonate with Latour's project, we might understand this form of writing as sharing movements and styles of practice.

---

**Building Infections and Infecting Buildings**

Nigel J. Thrift, building on the work of Latour, develops a "non-representational theory" to engage multiple ontologies "in terms of effectivity rather than representation" that draws "not [on] the what but the how" (*Non-representational* 113). Thrift proposes that "in non-representational theory what counts as knowledge must take on a radically different sense," and knowledge becomes "something tentative, something to which no longer exhibits an epistemological bias but is a practice and is part of a practice" (121). Thrift argues that we need to, instead, "invent an art of experiment which can up the methodological ante. . . . [A]n experimentalist orientation must be in-built which can start and re-start association" (8). According to Thrift, this inventive writing would incorporate buildings themselves in a writing practice that seeks

> to design and animate spaces so that they can function as edifices, which can concentrate and work on processes of association of spaces which are able to transmit differential traits. Such spaces, functioning at a slant, would produce knowledge by boosting involvement in "something that remains to be done," through "new and renewed associations." . . . Now, one thing to say straight away about an art-science of giving rise to new developments, of producing infection, is that the lore of these spaces has often only been partly written down: the effects of different spatial arrangements of bodies and objects, of different props, of different assumptions about how space is figured, of what is different about a network of scaffolding, or a cage, or a cul-de-sac, or a door, or a bridge may be obvious in everyday life, but they exist as a fragmented series of knots of knowledge across different disciplines and practices which only intermittently communicate with each other. (19)

---

To pick up and extend the practices of a building—those asignifying operations and sensuous involvements—writing offers enactments *through practice*. In 2009 Latour returns to the problem of documenting buildings and argues that our contemporary situation compels us to "to create the conditions of cohabitation" (Ghosn, Jazairy, and Ramos 124). He explains cohabitation as an "object-oriented politics" that recognizes "[*a*]*rchitecture is now about the building as a contentious object*" (125; original emphasis). In part, Latour proposes this orientation because we can never come to know the building as a whole. Latour does acknowledge that visualization tools like Google Earth and their ability to double-click—zoom between the global and the local—offers serious obstacles to the kinds of practices he seeks. These obstacles are formidable because such tools of global visualization are "so powerful and so well done that we are going to get another dose of modernist theory, precisely at the wrong time" (132). As we have seen above, Latour and ANT resist knowing any building's entirety at a global scale, asserting that we can only practice it through a series of local situations since

> [e]very time you speak about global things, you are always somewhere, in an office, inside with a visualizing tool in your hands, the demonstration is easy to make; the other aspect is that every locus is actually completely distributed and coming from a completely different range of both space and time. (130)

While Latour discusses the problem of cohabitation in respect to the various things, processes, and practices that make up a building, I contend that the problem of cohabitation extends, too, to the relationship between "writer" and "reader" of an account. That is, writing can be understood here as ontological practice in that it involves its writer and invites its reader to rehearse compositions, to perform movements, and to exercise ways of going on otherwise. An example we might point to here is Latour's own webtext "Paris: Invisible City," which documents the streets of Paris by creating "an impossible-to-read web site, to frustrate traditional ways of vision" whose purpose, according to Latour, was to be "a very small experiment that forces [the reader] to go from a step to another step through all of the intermediary steps" (133).

Latour's project proposes that we not throw away those genres that we might find in a newspaper or an academic article but that we should include those different genres in asignifying and sensuous ways. For instance, Latour's *Aramis* sets a mixed-typographical stage wherein Latour, as protagonist, converses with a host of nonhumans through a narrative that draws heavily on the mystery genre. In *Reassembling the Social*, an entire chapter is composed as a dialog between a professor (Latour) and a student confused about ANT as a well-articulated theory. In other work, Latour encloses whole passages within boxes to include but differentiate those texts' contributions. Writing as something we do *through practice* asks its writer/reader to help enact, to tinker, and to document a difference by making connections between unexplained things.

Taken together, we notice Latour advancing a concerted effort to foreground writing as a structure through which we cohabit ontological practices. These efforts are not realized by discarding our traditional practices of writing but by tinkering with them, making slight changes, and rehearsing genres in different ways. Although writing scholars have extolled the value of writing as a process, Latour demonstrates the products of writing are just as ontologically formative as they offer spaces to exercise sensitivities for cohabitation. Writing is a kind of practice that makes practice. Repeatedly. Differently. Responsively.

## Note

1. This distinction between *in practice* and *with practice* is not a slight difference but one that reorients what practice we encounter. Elsewhere, Latour explores "prepositional ontologies" to work around subject/object distinctions. Engaging at the level of "the preposition prepares the position that has to be given to what follows" ("Reflections" 309). Ann Berthoff, too, implores us to understand writing through a similar kind of practice of the preposition. She claims, anticipating Latour, "The way we make sense of the world is to see something *with respect to, in terms of, in relation* to something else. We can't make sense of one thing by itself; it must be seen as being *like* another thing; or *next to, across from, coming after* another thing; or as a repetition of another thing" (44). Berthoff and Latour see writing as a continuous practice of performing relations through differential repetitions.

## Works Cited

Berthoff, Ann E. *Forming, Thinking, Writing: The Composing Imagination.* Portsmouth: Heinemann, 1982. Print.

Bowker, Geoffrey C., and Susan Leigh Star. *Sorting Things Out: Classification and Its Consequences.* Cambridge: MIT P, 2000. Print.

Brooke, Collin Gifford. "Discipline and Publish: Reading and Writing the Scholarly Network." *Ecology, Writing Theory, and New Media.* Ed. Sidney I. Dobrin. New York: Routledge, 2012. 92–105. Print.

Dewey, John, and Jo Ann Boydston. *The Later Works, 1925–1953.* Vol. 17. Carbondale: Southern Illinois UP, 2008. Print.

"Doceo/docere." *Cassell's New Latin Dictionary: Latin-English, English-Latin.* Ed. David Penistan Simpson. New York: Funk, 1960. Print.

Emig, Janet. "Writing as a Mode of Learning." *CCC* 28.2 (1977): 122–128. Print.

Ghosn, Rania, El Hadi Jazairy, and Stephen Ramos. "The Space of Controversies: An Interview with Bruno Latour." *New Geographies* (2009): 123–135. Web. 10 Dec. 2012. <http://www-personal.umich.edu/~rghosn/Ghosn_Interview_with_Bruno_Latour_NG0.pdf>.

Hillocks, George. *Teaching Writing as Reflective Practice*. New York: Teachers College P, 1995. Print.

Kwinter, Sanford. *Architectures of Time: Toward a Theory of the Event in Modernist Culture*. Cambridge: MIT P, 2002. Print.

Latour, Bruno. "Paris: Invisible City." *bruno-latour.fr*, n.d. Web. 12 Jan. 2013. <http://www.bruno-latour.fr/virtual/EN/index.html>.

———. *The Pasteurization of France*. Cambridge: Harvard UP, 1993. Print.

———. "Reflections on Etienne Souriau's Different Modes Existence." *The Speculative Turn: The Continental Realism and Materialism*. Ed. Levi Bryant, Nick Srnicek, and Graham Harman. Melbourne: Re.press, 2011. 304–333. Print.

———. *Science in Action: How to Follow Scientists and Engineers through Society*. Cambridge: Harvard UP, 1987. Print.

———. *We Have Never Been Modern*. Cambridge: Harvard UP, 1993. Print.

Latour, Bruno, and Albena Yaneva. "'Give Me a Gun and I Will Make All Buildings Move': An ANT'S View of Architecture." *Explorations in Architecture: Teaching, Design, Research* (2008): 80–89. Web. 5 Apr. 2010. <http://www.bruno-latour.fr/node/206>.

Miller, Susan. *Rescuing the Subject: A Critical Introduction to Rhetoric and the Writer*. Carbondale: Southern Illinois UP, 2004. Print.

Mol, Annemarie. "Actor-Network Theory: Sensitive Terms and Enduring Tensions." *Kölner Zeitschrift für Soziologie und Sozialpsychologie. Sonderheft* 50 (2013): 253–269. Print.

———. *Differences in Medicine: Unraveling Practices, Techniques, and Bodies*. Durham: Duke UP, 1998. Print.

———. *The Logic of Care: Health and the Problem of Patient Choice*. New York: Routledge, 2008. Print.

———. "Ontological Politics: A Word and Some Questions." *Sociological Review* 46.S1 (1999): 74–89. Print.

Muckelbauer, John. *The Future of Invention: Rhetoric, Postmodernism, and the Problem of Change*. Albany: State U of New York P, 2008. Print.

North, Stephen M. *The Making of Knowledge in Composition: Portrait of an Emerging Field*. Portsmouth: Boynton, 1987. Print.

Phelps, Louise Weatherbee. "Practical Wisdom and the Geography of Knowledge in Composition." *College English* 53.8 (1991): 863–885. Print.

Schatzki, Theodore. "Introduction: Practice Theory." *The Practice Turn in Contemporary Theory*. Ed. Karin Knorr Cetina, Schatzki, and Eike von Savigny. New York: Routledge, 2001. 1–14. Print.

Sirc, Geoffrey. *English Composition as a Happening*. Logan: Utah State UP, 2002.

Thrift, Nigel J. "Lifeworld Inc.: And What to Do about It." *Environment and Planning D: Society and Space* 29.1 (2011): 5–26. Print.

———. *Non-representational Theory: Space, Politics, Affect*. New York: Routledge, 2007. Print.

Worsham, Lynn. "The Question Concerning Invention: Hermeneutics and the Genesis of Writing." *Pre/Text* 8 (1987): 197–244. Print.

Yagelski, Robert P. "A Thousand Writers Writing: Seeking Change through the Radical Practice of Writing as a Way of Being." *English Education* 42.1 (2009): 6–28. Print.

# 13. Flexible Assembly: Latour, Law, and the Linking(s) of Composition

Mark A. Hannah, *Arizona State University*

As a rhetorical practice, argument has been and continues to be a dominant area of concern in rhetoric and composition studies. This is not surprising especially if we believe "everything is an argument" as Andrea Lunsford, John J. Ruszkiewicz, and Keith Walters proclaim; however, the persistence of scholarship about the limitations of argument (Bay; Knoblauch; P. Lynch) points to an absence or a lacking about what we think argument ought to be not only for us as a discipline but also for our students as a tool for addressing challenging social issues in an apocalyptic world. As we consider Bruno Latour's thought and its implications for our discipline, we are presented with an occasion to investigate how Latour helps us address the felt absence or lack in our theorizing and teaching of argument. In this chapter, I draw from Latour's discussion of French administrative law in *The Making of Law* to demonstrate how that work offers us a means to view argument less as an aspiration—what it "ought to be"—and more as a mechanic—how it is "activated" and "circulated" in practice.[1] More specifically, Latour's work provides rhetoric and composition scholars a framework for understanding the "work of argument" both qualitatively and materially. To support this claim, I open by examining what I identify as a disciplinary impulse to develop "communicating with" theories of argument, alternative theories that attempt to move the discipline away from traditional, adversarial, pro/con modes of argument to more expansive modes that account for difference across time and space. This literature review reveals a gap that Latourian theory is primed to address, specifically the material, building aspects of argument that are cursorily addressed in early argument scholarship. Following the literature review, I make a case for *The Making of Law* as a necessary complement for extending argument scholarship to account for the breadth of the "work of argument," both its aspirational and its mechanical natures. This case connects

Latour's description of how legal files are ripened for use to early Latourian composition scholarship, especially as it relates to processes of accumulation, to show how Latour offers us a process and a vocabulary for investigating and activating argument's mechanical, material side, a practice I refer to as "flexible assembly." The closing section of the chapter opens a conversation about how we might begin integrating a "mechanical" vision of argument in our teaching and offer some pedagogical strategies for cultivating the practice of flexible assembly with our students.

## Making Move(s) to "Communicating With"

As rhetoricians, we are wedded to the classical period. Aristotle, Cicero, Quintilian, and others offer us theoretical and pedagogical pathways for introducing argument to students, and regardless of whether one views such pathways as useful or not, our disciplinary commitment to the classical period ties our theorizing of argument to a mix of oral and written models as bases for analysis. One effect of our reliance on these models is the negative manner in which argument is described: as adversarial, challenging, and threatening; as emphasizing winning; as occurring face-to-face for a fixed time period; and as hegemonic and/or masculine.[2] Our discipline has made noteworthy strides to move argument away from such perceived negativity, to resist the pull of our classical roots, and to articulate what I describe as "communicating with" theories of argument. While it is impossible to provide a complete overview of the move to communicate with in this chapter, I offer here a short review of seminal pieces and note how each describes argument theory and practice in aspirational terms.

An early influence on scholars' attempts to move argument to "communicating with" was psychologist Carl Rogers's work with client-centered therapy. At the heart of Rogers's work is the desire to discover others' points of view that subsequently will encourage people to revise their own images of the world (Bator 431). Rogers contends that how people access each other's points of view is through developing a patient attitude of listening to oneself and others as well as being open to the realities surrounding one's life (21). What I see in Rogers is an aspiration for communicators to develop a habit of being open or rather a readiness to be open to others. Specifically, I see Rogers advocating the need for an earnest pause before responding to another's claim(s), and it is in that temporal pause where one begins to cultivate the qualities of being open that foster "communicating with." Rogers's insistence on patience in the communicative encounter offers rhetoric and composition scholars a behavioral model for keeping at bay the adversarial impulses that drive oral argument between people. More specifically, the behavior creates space for difference to emerge and interact in and between communicators' perspectives.

Though critical of the absence of varying affective conditions (i.e., fear, anger, disappointment, alarm, outrage) in the Rogerian encounter, Jim W. Corder's discussion of the intersection of contending personal narratives in "Argument as Emergence, Rhetoric as Love" offers a means for extending Rogers's space of being open to others: "Argument is not something *to present or display*. It is something *to be*. . . . Argument is emergence toward the other" (26; original emphasis). Through these words, Corder establishes argument as a dynamic building process that is concerned with discovering potential in others' words and ideas. To guide the building process, Corder describes behavioral modes like arguing provisionally and piling time into discourse so as to create opportunities for reflection and reconsideration in argumentative discourse. In these behavioral descriptions, we see a desire to create a wedge against the force of pure rationality or Enlightenment-style thinking that predominates in many argumentative schemes.[3] In particular, we witness an attempt to acknowledge and make room for nonrational forms of evidence and knowledge as essential complements to traditional outputs of rationality.

Related to Corder's interest in nonrational forms of knowledge is Dennis Lynch's call in "Rhetorics of Proximity: Empathy in Temple Grandin and Cornel West" for writers to cultivate a readiness to make themselves available to argument through empathy (6), which is an attitude and a practice that "attunes our minds to the needs of others; it permits people who are arguing to discover, not just premises, but premises that work" (5). What is noteworthy about empathy is Lynch's acknowledging of its limitations, that it will not allow us "to know the fullness of someone else's experiences and understandings" (8). There will always be a remainder or a space of the unknown between a rhetor and the individual or group to which he or she is extending empathy, and it is within this space where rhetors have the opportunity to work through the potential barriers of the argumentative context, that is, the emotional, physical, intellectual, and/or spiritual aspects of people's lives that cause them to think in a narrow, pro/con manner. Lynch's identification of the irreducible space is an important contribution to argument scholarship for the way it situates argument as a process that does not seek an ultimate closing. The space leaves room for writers to adapt their claims to the emergence of new factors that alter the circulation of the ideas and/or claims that are at issue in a deliberative context. In essence, the irreducible space obliges writers to hold themselves open and continually search for means both to address emergent communication issues and activate deliberative acts of "communicating with."

In "Rogue Cops and Health Care: What Do We Want from Public Writing," Susan Wells offers an example of a rhetorical means that fosters "communicating with." Wells comments on the shortcomings of rhetorics associated with identity politics and argues that a rhetoric for public writing ought to begin "by valuing what is difficult, and direct itself to the connection between discourse and action rather than to the connections among speakers" (337). Wells's attention to the connection between discourse and action is noteworthy as she asks writers to move beyond the preformed, static markers of audience analysis (age, gender, race, socioeconomic status, etc.) that our discipline is all too familiar with. In particular, she asks writers to assess the relationship between social practices and discourse and search for a theme that will serve as a sustainable connecting point between audience members. In the example she provides, Wells describes a "common desire for security" amongst the different participants at a neighborhood block meeting addressing crime as a connecting point for beginning deliberations (337). What is noteworthy in Wells's analysis is her attempt to identify a mechanic that activates argument and moves people to action in the irreducible space of the argumentative encounter. However, the analysis falls short in attending to how writers might build the mechanic. Specifically, Wells limits her recommendation to acts of critique; she focuses her discussion on how the community members ought to assess the communicative context—that is, trying to see and understand what is assumed and available as a value in the community or simply valuing what is difficult in the community to begin with—rather than on how they could build a mechanic for activating deliberation in that context. While the move to critique is understandable, it is insufficient and ultimately falls short of the action that is necessary for building and attending to the material side of argument.

Shortly after the appearance of Wells's article came Elizabeth Ervin's "Academics and the Negotiation of Local Knowledge," which offers a framework for seeing and understanding the gap between discourse and action that Wells identified. Using as her example the mid-1990's public debate between academics and nonacademics in Wilmington, North Carolina, about evolution and creationism, Ervin comments on the challenges that arise in fostering generative public discourse due to a rhetorical practice she identifies as discursive entrenchment. She defines this practice as a process in which debate participants "intellectually and rhetorically dig in their heels, refusing to consider alternative positions" (449). As a primary source for such "digging in," Ervin identifies the inability of academics to understand how certain human qualities, such as one's attitude towards persuasion, are "geographically and ideologically specific" (462). That is, academics failed to consider things such as how Wilmington residents' religious beliefs, their valuing of nonrational forms of knowledge, their sense of being "Southern," and even their simply being "nonacademic" would affect how they would engage in debate. Ervin's critique of academics is significant for its insistence on paying attention to what is situated and layered in local contexts. Ultimately, it is in such sites where the raw materials for building and activating argument lay. To promote the identification and use of such items, Ervin recommends writers adopt a habit of "fungibility," or a practice in which "participants in a dispute recognize a need not only to question their intuitive understandings of an issue but also to consider compromises or trade-offs to their position" (462). Here, we witness Ervin propose behaviors that get at building, yet like Wells her analysis focuses on critique, the ought-to critical practices, such as writers questioning themselves or seeking compromises between parties where both sides realize some degree of satisfaction. With both behaviors, we see examples of an aspiration to hear others and even hold one's thoughts and desires at bay or render them secondary with no mention of how to construct a mechanism that materializes such aspirations. Ultimately, such behaviors do not get to the type of action that is requisite for the material, building aspects of argument.

The inattention to argument's mechanics persists today as is seen in A. Abby Knoblauch's 2011 article, "A Textbook Argument: Definitions of Argument in Leading Composition Textbooks." Drawing on Jennifer Bay's call in the early twenty-first century for the discipline to grasp an emergent alternative to argument (244), Knoblauch exposes the limitations of argument textbooks for their overreliance on traditional, persuasion-based forms of argument as the basis of instruction in our classrooms. Specifically, through focusing on the manner in which textbooks define argument, Knoblauch identifies the discipline's limited attention to alternatives, such as Rogers's work, and asks the question, "What would it mean to take seriously in the classroom more expansive forms of argument in which persuasion was not the primary goal" (264)? As if twenty to thirty years of scholarship that works at rethinking and reimagining argument beyond the pro/con and adversarial is not "serious" enough, what strikes me most about Knoblauch's question is the continued disciplinary insistence on articulating what argument *is*. Despite Corder's call to let argument emerge or simply come "to be," we continually find ourselves back at the aspirational moment attempting to pin down a definition of argument. This is not the right question, or, rather, it is only a part of the larger question about argument in our field.

Let us suppose we reframe Knoblauch's question and ask instead, "What would it mean to take seriously the mechanics of argument in the classroom, the building and constructing work that activates and circulates argument?" Asking this question puts us in unfamiliar territory, but it is a productive move. It compels our discipline to reexamine its pathways to understanding argument, to move beyond "ought to" critical behaviors that merely get us to appreciation and sensitivity of difference across time and space, and Latour is primed to help advance this very move.

## Activating Latour for the "Work of Argument"

In *The Making of Law*, Latour offers a case study of the daily practice of a French court of law, the Conseil d'État, which specializes in administrative law. The inscription on the book's back cover explains, "What makes [Latour's] study an important contribution to the social studies of law is that . . . [he] has been able to reconstruct in detail the weaving of legal reasoning: it is not the social that explains the law, but the legal ties that alter what it is to be associated together." Though the focus of my work here is not on the intricacies of legal reasoning per se and its applicability to rhetoric and composition studies, Latour's legal study is important for the way it attends to processes of weaving and building ties. Early Latourian rhetoric and composition scholarship (Graham; P. Lynch; Pflugfelder) artfully emphasizes similar practices of accumulation and assembly for the discipline, but what is missing in such examples is a sense of activation. For example, in "Composition's New Thing: Bruno Latour and the Apocalyptic Turn," Paul Lynch makes a compelling argument for the accumulation of a "Thing" to address complex social issues, such as the Great Eastern Garbage Patch, a large mass of plastic floating in the Pacific Ocean. Lynch explains that what it means to compose a Thing in regards to this issue is "to add the perspectives of all human and nonhuman participants affected by our dumping" (469). Ultimately, I agree with Lynch here. We ought to add in all affected perspectives, yet I am concerned with the inattention to how the composition or process of such addition takes place. Is emergence enough for a Thing to come together? I posit that it is not, and as a result, we must seriously attend to the question of coming together or building, specifically identifying what mechanics activate such processes.

To examine the work of activating, we need to follow one of Latour's maxims in *The Making of Law*—begin at the beginning and focus on materiality (71). In law, materiality includes items such as stamps, elastic bands, paperclips, files, ad hoc documents, bound volumes of legal precedent, and even the workspaces of lawyers, court reporters, and other staff at the Conseil d'État (72–74). These human and nonhuman factors operate together to form and support the network in which law circulates from the initial filing of a claim to its ultimate judgment rendered by the administrative judges. Alone, each of these factors is without meaning, but linked together, they come to represent the law. That is, together they activate a claim's movement and adhere together to form the meaning of the conseil's decision. It is the activation process and subsequent movement that I am most interested in as it is these very processes that are at the core of our students' work in composing arguments—identifying and making an initial claim and sustaining it over time beyond its initial moment of conception and utterance. What is noteworthy about Latour's description of materiality for rhetoric and composition scholars is how it reveals that students work with cases, not claims. Claims are statements, simple assertions. They relate to an objective or wish, something the claimant wants to see emerge. Cases, on the other hand, are things; they are constructed, built items out of law's materiality. More specifically, they are activated compositions, linkings of administrative acts and various types of ad hoc and authorized documents that stand ready for use in mobilizing a claim for movement and application in the varying "trials of strength" in a deliberative context.[4] Latour's description of case building by court reporters, the individuals responsible for compiling cases through linking and readying them for decision in the Conseil d'État, offers readers a useful perspective for understanding the mechanics of argument and processes of activation—the building side of the "work of argument."

First and foremost, court reporters are problem setters, not problem solvers. As Latour explains, reporters link the pages of the case file "to the vast corpus of judgments of the Council and to the innumerable documents which record texts of laws, treaties, decrees, orders and regulations" (*ML* 85). Ultimately, reporters are responsible for establishing the connection,

> the coming-and-going between two types of writings: on the one hand, the ad hoc documents of both parties which are produced for and through the occasion, such as statements and various productions, and, on the other hand, the printed, authorized, voted upon and connected texts which are carefully arranged on the shelves of the library. (86)

I am drawn to the notion of problem setting for the two specific ways it makes possible the bringing of life to documents that ultimately gives them form. First, problem setting compels movement in an argumentative context. Rather than have people focus on a problem as a unified thing to be solved, problem setting positions a problem as something that requires building before it can be addressed with discourse. That is, problem setting recognizes that deliberation requires movement in and between the segmented or individually set arms/strands of a problem, as it is such movement that enables or, rather, prompts the mobilization of claims as available means for use in deliberative contexts. Visualizing the problem setter through the lens of Latour's description of the court reporter at the conseil, problem setters establish the connection or coming-and-going point that brings life to a document and gives it form through linking with another text. In this state, a document is activated and stands ready to compel movement either in advancing a claim or towards disentangling a claim that thwarts deliberation.

Second, the activity of setting problems anticipates the circulation and repurposing of evidence as it moves through the argumentative scheme. Latour speaks to the evolution and morphing of evidence when he notes how evidence moves from the realm of "useless piece of information" to something that has been mobilized in a claim and taken on a "legal form" through the court reporter linking the texts in the process of compiling a case (*ML* 77). In essence, evidence gains new life each time it is linked with a text; it takes on a form that provides it legitimacy when responding to the facts, circumstances, and communication demands of the rhetorical situation(s) in which the problem's set parts circulate.

Ultimately, in both of the attributes of problem setting I describe, I see the tentativeness, the pausing, patient, attentive listening behaviors that rhetoric and composition scholars profiled in this chapter's literature review so desperately wanted student writers to take on in the work of composing arguments. But problem setting veers away from these early scholars' work in its insistence on building possibility or potential for action *before* aspiring to engage in argument in a particular way. This is not to suggest that these scholars were interested solely in finality or proclaiming solutions to problems. Instead, I merely want to reveal here the intentionality of problem setting as something that is responsive only to that which has been built. Put another way, the aspirational, "ought to" critical behaviors rife in our discipline's literature are not on the table for consideration unless a linking or mechanic for promulgating a possibility for action has been assembled. Using Latour's language again from

*The Making of Law* to describe this insistence, I turn to his description of the court reporter's responsibility to produce possible denouements for cases.

Generally, the work of reporters is similar to the process of building a bridge, a bridge of texts between the ad hoc and authorized texts that make up a case—"on the one hand, the documents which the parties have used in order to build the file and, on the other hand, the documents which are archived in the library and bound in volumes" (*ML* 86). In building the bridge, the reporter uses the two types of writings to establish the extremities of the case, or anchors, using Latour's language, that create a space for the working through of a case's legal issues. This bridge is formally known as a "note" and consists of "visas," or the citations that judges take into consideration when preparing a final decision (86). The reporter's job in composing the note is to qualify the disputant's claim between the two extremes and produce what Latour refers to as "the deck" of a bridge or the "dispotif," which is the "proliferation of preliminary clauses which link with each other and which lead up to the dénouement," or the posing of a possible course of action in a case (87). Ultimately, the act of qualifying both forces the interweaving of texts in the space between the extremes and makes the case speak more like the law through each qualifying progression (87–88).

The defining characteristic of the interweaving and the subsequent qualification of acts that stems from such work is the reporter's anticipation of legal mechanisms that will compel specific types of critical behaviors—is there existing precedent, or are the ad hoc documents compelling enough to warrant a shattering, if you will, of the existing precedent? To illustrate, let's take Latour's example of the pesky, sunflower-inhaling pigeons in the commune of La Rochefoucauld. Now, court reporters are not per se interested in the nature or quality of pigeons and their daily routines; rather, they are interested in how the pigeons' sunflower consumption ought to be defined in respect to the ad hoc and authorized texts and the commune's responsibilities to its residents—do the pigeons' consumption habits pose a public danger that needs to be regulated? In assessing this question, court reporters review in tandem documents like the aggrieved sunflower farmer's statements about pecuniary loss and the potential harm the pigeons pose to the public against legal documents, such as codes and precedents, that address both citizens' and municipalities' rights and obligations. Through weaving these documents, reporters critically evaluate their relevance and the legal force they carry to affect a potential decision; they make qualifying distinctions between the competing legal means that have the capacity to compel, amongst many, a specific course of action in a case. The reporter's ultimate job is to pose a possible course of action, the denouement, and set it forth before the administrative tribunal. Ultimately, the work of formulating the denouement, of setting forth a possible course of action, is the building or mechanical side of argument. The denouement is a mechanic, an activation device constructed through processes of interweaving and qualification that sets the direction of a claim's movement across the bridge constructed by the reporter. It is not the reporter's responsibility to judge. It is her/his responsibility to build pathways to action and activate that movement in the argumentative context. This process of building through interweaving and qualification is what I define as flexible assembly; the "pre" aspect of the "work of argument" that creates the space for its aspirational aspects to kick in.

## Developing Frameworks for "Flexible Assembly"

To activate Bruno Latour's work in *The Making of Law* for our discipline's theorizing of argument, I want to focus here on positing a pedagogical framework for flexible assembly. As the organizing principle for this framework, I call on Latour's description of a file's "passing into the domain of law" (81). After detailing the early life of a file—its being received by the clerk's office, assigned a number, categorized by the Analysis Service, and provided an ID card—Latour notes an important shift, a rite of passage into file "adulthood."

> There exists a clear indication that the file has now penetrated deeper into the domain of the law: the passage between the automatic and the legal, between the indisputable and the disputable, between routine and initiative is revealed through the fact that, from now on, all post must be sent by registered mail and no longer by simple post. (81)

Although I am not interested so much in the particularities of registered mail's legal capacity to affect the decision of a case, I do see value in Latour's identification of a case's passing-through process for the teaching of argument. Specifically, it is at this mailing juncture where a case takes the first steps towards learning to speak like the law. In order to stand up in the legal process, to be recognized as legitimate in its form, to carry legal meaning, a case must walk like a case and talk like a case for it is only through the language, form, and operations of legal discourse that a case and its attendant texts can have any impact in a legal context. Drawing again on the word activation I have used in this chapter, a case speaking like the law and comporting with the law's rules is the clearest evidence that a case has been activated within an argumentative system. So, why does all of this matter for our students? I posit that just as a case needs to speak like the law in the Latourian sense, so, too, do our students' cases (the arguments they build) need to speak like the issues and/or domains those cases cover and travel in, respectively. Their cases need to speak transdisciplinarily.

To promote the process of linking and activating cases to speak in this manner, I present here a framework I refer to as the knowledge chain. This chain was developed from Peter Morville's discussion of data, information, and knowledge in *Ambient Findability*, and it operates on the premise that as data, information, and knowledge move and circulate within deliberative contexts, such items adapt and reformulate as they move in and between disciplinary domains. There are close parallels between the movement and reformulation along the knowledge chain and the linking of ad hoc and authorized texts described in *The Making of Law*. My aim in this section is to draw out these parallels and articulate the knowledge chain as an essential pedagogical practice both for promoting the building aspect of argument in our discipline and for positioning our students as problem setters, not problem solvers. Ultimately, such a pedagogy will focus argument not on convincing or persuading an audience but, instead, on activating mechanics that compel movement and deliberation in argumentative systems.

In *Ambient Findability*, Morville offers working definitions for the terms "data," "information," and "knowledge." Data is "a string of identified but unevaluated symbols"; information is "evaluated, validated, or useful data"; and knowledge is "information in the contexts of understanding" (46). What I notice in these definitions is a progression or building between them—data becomes information; information becomes knowledge.

I would prefer not to represent the knowledge chain as a linear equation, but it is best illustrated in the following manner as stages.

| STAGE 1 | STAGE 2 | STAGE 3 |
|---|---|---|
| Data > | Information > | Knowledge |

When comparing the knowledge chain to Latour's description of a court reporter's interweaving of ad hoc and authorized texts to produce a possible denouement, I am struck by their symmetry. Like data, ad hoc documents are identified but unevaluated. They merely represent accountings of what is purported to be a fact in a legal dispute, purported being the key word as such documents have yet to be scrutinized by legal actors. Regarding authorized texts, like information, they, too, are data that are evaluated, validated, or useful. Using Latour's terms, authorized texts have been "profiled" or deemed as "judgment-compatible" (*ML* 75). That is, they stand ready as a mechanic able to impact the decision-making process. Where the potential for such impact lies is in the court reporter's interweaving of the ad hoc and authorized texts to produce a denouement, the possibility for action in a case. Comparing the court reporter's interweaving to our students' building of arguments, I see a similarity between the creation of a denouement and the production of knowledge for deliberative contexts. In particular, the possibility for action lies in knowledge, specifically knowledge that has been attuned for placement in communicative contexts. By attunement, I mean the intentional application and, when necessary, reapplication of language to information that is to be delivered as knowledge to a specific disciplinary audience. Ultimately, for students, the knowledge chain visualizes movement that was activated by the linking of data and information in the construction of knowledge. It renders the products of their research as material, as items that physically can be linked together to produce a mechanic or device for compelling movement in an argumentative scheme. More important, such visible, material movement compels students to see and understand that knowledge is not found; it is created via links between data and information that are applied in specific contexts of understanding. Awareness of this nature is potentially liberating for students as it activates them as knowledge makers when addressing the challenging issues of our apocalyptic world.

The question that remains now is how to incorporate the knowledge chain as a framework for cultivating the practice of flexible assembly. To answer that question, I turn to Latour's description of the secretion that occurs in the French legal system, specifically, the manner in which ad hoc and authorized documents are emitted through the system's pores (*ML* 75). When reading this section in *The Making of Law*, I was struck by the connotation of the word "secrete," specifically for the way it is suggestive of the release of something that was hidden. That is, when an item is secreted, its movement is slight, indiscernible, and most important, surprising when it emerges. To detect what has been secreted, an individual must attend to the nonobvious, nonbuilt aspects of our environment, and it is here where I see Latour making a strong contribution to our discipline. Specifically, when our students compose arguments, they focus most closely on secondary sources, which when viewed in light of the knowledge chain represent information in stage 2. Students take that which has been evaluated and validated and deem it as useful for their case. The challenge we face as educators is prompting our students to look beyond the built environment of secondary research, to look for items, that is, data in stage 1, that require building. To respond to this challenge, I recommend we infuse primary-research strategies and practices into our theoretical and pedagogical work with argument. Granted, the call for primary research is not new in our field, but when it is viewed in the Latourian light of building and linking, primary research offers us a new pathway not only for teaching the building, weaving practices of data/ad hoc and information/authorized texts but also for extending our thinking about the role of argument in our students' lives. No longer will we simply describe from afar what we aspire for argument to be. We will engage our students in the building of what argument is and activating it for deliberative uses. Students will learn to work with what is subtle and built when composing possibilities or denouements for action.

## Running with "Flexible Assembly"

As I sit here writing the subhead for this section, I am imagining my young daughter running around the house with scissors in her hands. There's the potential for her to do some damage, either to herself or to some of the items in our home, and it scares me a little. When thinking about cultivating practices of flexible assembly in my classroom, I am left with a similar image of students running around the classroom with scissors in their hands, albeit a little more sleep deprived and caffeine addled than my daughter, and yes, this, too, scares me a little. I want us to imagine the practice of flexible assembly in place of our students' scissors and ask again the question I posed at the end of this chapter's literature review: what would it mean to take seriously the mechanics of argument in the classroom, the building and constructing work that activates and circulates argument? First, teaching the mechanics of argument allows us to get at *phronesis* more broadly; flexible assembly is attentive to developing sound methods for selecting, cutting, and bridging/linking items together. Second, flexible assembly positions argument as a process of problem setting, not problem solving; it compels students to cut arguments into their divergent but related parts and simultaneously develop mechanics for weaving those parts anew. Third, flexible assembly positions argument as a collaborative act, as a process that is dependent on the production of ad hoc and authorized texts by all human and nonhuman actors in the system. Ultimately, flexible assembly shreds the image of the lone, isolated arguer engaged in public debate. Together, these answers do not address the full range of issues our discipline has and will continue to explore with argument theory and practice, but they set for us potential mechanics for taking on this work.

## Notes

1. I am hesitant to use the word "mechanic" to describe an aspect of argument because of the negative baggage that term carries in our discipline's history. In "Rhetoric's Mechanics: Retooling the Equipment of Writing Production," Jenny Edbauer Rice describes the concerns of viewing rhetoric as mechanical and makes a persuasive argument for "reinvigorating our own personal pedagogies with a stronger commitment to engaging the [technological] means of production" (368). Though I do not examine mechanics through a technological lens in this chapter, I am responding to Edbauer Rice's call to attend to rhetoric's mechanics, in my case the mechanics of the "work of argument," which I define to include any human and/or nonhuman devices, tools, resources, actions, and/or practices that activate or compel movement in an argumentative system.

2. Patricia Roberts-Miller in *Deliberate Conflict: Argument, Political Theory, and Composition Classes* offers an insightful discussion of these qualities of argument.

3. In "The Exploratory Essay: Enfranchising the Spirit of Inquiry in College Composition," William Zeiger offers a description of the modern sense of demonstrating a truth that I believe accurately describes the Enlightenment style of thinking that Rogers critiques: "To 'prove' an assertion today is to win undisputed acceptance for it—to stop inquiry rather than to start it" (456).

4. In *Science in Action: How to Follow Scientists and Engineers through Society*, Latour defines a "trial of strength" as a showdown "running from the claim to what supports the claim" (78). Latour's interest in such events is related to his concern with locating and, perhaps, even encouraging a fairly healthy degree of agonism in his tracing of networks. My interest in connecting Latour's discussion of "trials of strength" to case building centers on my belief that Latour offers rhetoric and composition scholars a way to sidestep the agonism-irenicism debate that has limited the discipline's theorizing of argument. In particular, by connecting Debra Hawhee's discussion of agonism as "gathering" and "assembly" (15) in *Bodily Arts: Rhetoric and Athletics in Ancient Greece* to Latour's notion of "trials of strength," we can position argument as neither an agonistic contest nor a peaceful conciliation. Instead, we can situate it as a process occurring between the two extremes where the gathering and assembly that characterize the building of a case generate a productive strife that compels the movement of that case in a deliberative context.

## Works Cited

Bator, Paul. "Aristotelian and Rogerian Rhetoric." *CCC* 31 (1980): 427–432. Print.

Bay, Jennifer L. "The Limits of Argument: A Response to Sean Williams." *JAC* 22.3 (2002): 684–696. Print.

Corder, Jim W. "Argument as Emergence, Rhetoric as Love." *Rhetoric Review* 4.1 (1985): 16–32. Print.

Ervin, Elizabeth. "Academics and the Negotiation of Local Knowledge." *College English* 61.4 (1999): 448–470. Print.

Graham, S. Scott. "Agency and the Rhetoric of Medicine: Biomedical Brain Scans and the Ontology of Fibromyalgia." *Technical Communication Quarterly* 18.4 (2009): 376–404. Print.

Hawhee, Debra. *Bodily Arts: Rhetoric and Athletics in Ancient Greece*. Austin: U of Texas P, 2005. Print.

Knoblauch, A. Abby. "A Textbook Argument: Definitions of Argument in Leading Composition Textbooks." *CCC* 63.2 (2011): 244–268. Print.

Latour, Bruno. *The Making of Law: An Ethnography of the Conseil d'Etat*. Cambridge: Polity, 2010. Print.

———. *Science in Action: How to Follow Scientists and Engineers through Society*. Cambridge: Harvard UP, 1987. Print.

Lunsford, Andrea, John J. Ruszkiewicz, and Keith Walters. *Everything's an Argument: With Readings*. 5th ed. Boston: Bedford, 2010. Print.

Lynch, Dennis. "Rhetorics of Proximity: Empathy in Temple Grandin and Cornel West." *Rhetoric Society Quarterly* 28.1 (1998): 5–23. Print.

Lynch, Paul. "Composition's New Thing: Bruno Latour and the Apocalyptic Turn." *College English* 74.5 (2012): 458–476. Print.

Morville, Peter. *Ambient Findability*. Sebastopol: O'Reilly, 2005. Print.

Pflugfelder, Ehren Helmut. "Texts of Our Institutional Lives: Translucency, Coursepacks, and the Post-Historical University—An Investigation into Pedagogical Things." *College English* 74.3 (2012): 247–267. Print.

Rice, Jenny Edbauer. "Rhetoric's Mechanics: Retooling the Equipment of Writing Production." *CCC* 60.2 (2008): 366–387. Print.

Roberts-Miller, Patricia. *Deliberate Conflict: Argument, Political Theory, and Composition Classes*. Carbondale: Southern Illinois UP, 2007. Print.

Wells, Susan. "Rogue Cops and Health Care: What Do We Want from Public Writing?" *CCC* 47.3 (1996): 325–341. Print.

Zeiger, William. "The Exploratory Essay: Enfranchising the Spirit of Inquiry in College Composition." *College English* 47.5 (1985): 454–466. Print.

# Part Five. **Crafting Assemblages**

# 14. Craft Networks

Jeff Rice, *University of Kentucky*

The new aesthetic, Ian Bogost suggests, is not only a computer-driven movement but one relevant to craft and the production of things.[1] Things, as actor-network-theory (ANT) makes explicit, allow for the tracing of specific moments or movements. Despite Bogost's objections to Bruno Latour's emphasis of "normalized structure" in ANT, ANT allows for the tracing of things regarding aesthetics (Bogost, *Alien* 19). Objects, or things, Bogost tells us in his summation of James Bridle's new aesthetic movement, are experienced, not just observed. And by being an experience, objects take on meanings and relationships beyond ownership or usage. In this craft vision, where the object is central, things have agency. Bogost's position is a slightly different version than the one Bridle attributes to his project on the new aesthetic weblog. Bridle describes the new aesthetic: "It is a series of artefacts of the heterogeneous network, which recognises differences, the gaps in our distant but overlapping realities." Bogost, less concerned with gaps, contends that this aesthetic raises questions regarding how we explain agency.

> The things we make in and beyond the bounds of the New Aesthetic might have different goals: not art that helps us couple machines to one another, but philosophical lab equipment that helps us grasp, as best we can, the experience of objects themselves. I've called this practice *carpentry*, making things that speculate how things understand their world. Carpentered objects need not be fashioned from wood, but they bear the same mark of hand-manufacture, care, and craft—not just the craft of the artist, but the way that craftwork helps reveal how things fashion one another, and the world at large. ("New Aesthetic")

Craft, the nineteenth-century Arts and Crafts movement argued, fashions a world outside of industrialization, favoring the handmade and the artist over the impersonal, mass-produced object. Relationships, craft claims, come from the artist, not the machine, objects associated with the machine, or the machine's by-product of consumption. William Morris begins *Art and Socialism* by asking his readership to "consider what remedies should be applied for curing the evils that exist in the relationship between Art and Commerce" (4). Technology has not brought pleasure, Morris contends, but destroyed it. "The wonderful machines," Morris sarcastically states, "have instead of lightening the labour of the workmen, intensified it, and thereby added more weariness yet to the burden which the poor have to carry" (5). If craft had agency for Arts and Crafts, it was to redirect attention from the industrial and technological to the artisanal and, in turn, reject consumption for aesthetic reflection. Such redirection, Latour states, fails to acknowledge that "the technologies and consumer objects that the philosophers and moralists of earlier generations advise us to abhor" are the ones whose aesthetics we love (*Modern* 136). Craft—as Bogost's sense of carpentry argues—is very much alive. It is alive as a technological process of networked production.

Craft exists as aesthetic and as practice, involving an emerging culture of artisanal and handmade work framed within a new-media environment. This work reveals how "things fashion one another" in ways Arts and Crafts may not have anticipated, for craft, today, is also technology. As Malcolm McCullough posits in *Abstracting Craft*, "Now there is reason to explore the possibility of craft in the emerging realm of information technology—with the computer as a medium" (21). Bogost does not differentiate between the handmade and the manufactured; objects, he says, are objects regardless of manufacture or where they appear. He asks, "What if we asked how computers and bonobos and toaster pastries and Boeing 787 Dreamliners develop their *own* aesthetics" ("New Aesthetic"). Craft is an aesthetic with agency; it is an aesthetic of objects affecting objects, within and without computers. It is an aesthetic of a particular consumption. Or to reconsider Roland Barthes's question in *The Pleasure of the Text*, what might be the aesthetic of the consumer? (59). We could also ask the same of the consumed object. What is its aesthetic, and what does it do? What does it make? What is its relationship to new media and to me, the consumer of such an aesthetic?

Aesthetics, after all, do something. In the world of consumerism (as Arts and Crafts critiqued), they enact purchase. Indeed, mass production takes such a claim seriously, conflating various artisanal and craft aesthetics so that neither appears to differ from mass production, but both create a purchase. As consumers, we experience both artisanal craft fairs (pottery, art, textiles) and simultaneously commercialized, mass-produced visions of craft, such as

Domino's Pizza, whose pizza box once boasted this conflation with the declaration, "We're Not Artisans." On the top of the box, Domino's told patrons that inside they would find "a handmade pizza crafted with the kind of passion and integrity that just might convince you we are [artisans]." In what could easily be dismissed as a commercial contradiction (projection of identity while rejecting said identity), this aesthetic, as Adam Sachs mocks in *Details* magazine, has made everything both craft based and artisanal.

To fret over an object's craft status is to express concern over artistry and the kinds of pleasures and aesthetics artistry evokes so that the object does nothing (but the artist, alone, does *something*). Craft, for some, however, is not artistry. "Use artisan and artisanal to denote craftsman and good craftsmanship, not artistry," Michael Ruhlman warns. Whatever the craft or artisanal aesthetic might be, then, it need not be an artist-based practice. It need not be classified as "good" (i.e., saving us from the ills of mass culture or pizza) nor "bad" (pompous and pretentious). Craft can be the space where objects interact with humans and other objects to produce a network of relationships, such as the interaction of the artisanal and the mass-produced. As Richard Sennett comments, "People can learn about themselves through the things they make, that material culture matters" (8). Material culture does matter; its importance, however, is not typically understood as Bogost's claim that objects affect other objects but, rather, that some things are good objects and some are not. Some representations (computer as opposed to bonbon), we might add, feel good, and some don't.

Even as Bogost argues that "craftwork helps reveal how things fashion one another," not all representations of craft or artisanal production are positive. After all, Tyler Durden, the protagonist of *Fight Club*'s mindless revolution, is an artisanal soap maker. Soap, as Durden states in the film's diegesis, is a con (an overpriced $20 bar of recycled body fat) and a potential weapon (it can be turned into an explosive). It is a form of carpentry (standing for Durden's philosophy). In the network of events traced and crafted throughout the film, soap has agency; it generates relationships in a larger network of meaning. Soap maintains a specific position within a larger network of activities it affects (consumer disgust, split personalities, leadership, mob rule, a romantic relationship). Whatever the aesthetic of craft might be in *Fight Club*, this aesthetic is not reduced to artistry, as Ruhlman argues against, nor to claims of value, as the Arts and Crafts movement would have declared, or to a method of explanation, as Bogost's carpentry suggests. Instead, such aesthetics can be turned into tracings of objects' relationships with other objects, or following the work of Latour, with other human and nonhuman agents. An account of a network (in a film or otherwise) can be traced (as Latour calls for) where nonhumans (soap, revolution) engage with humans (split personalities, soap makers, revolutionaries) to generate an aesthetic or, following Barthes, a pleasure, "braided, woven, in the most personal way" (59). The revolution is personified in Durden as mindless, but objects' interactions trace a network in the diegesis that mix the personal with other moments.

Personal weaving amends network theories proposed by Latour and by Bogost since both authors seem to exclude the personal. Bogost, for instance, asks,

> Why couldn't a group of pastry chefs found their own New Aesthetic, grounded in the slippage between wet and dry ingredients? Computers are interesting, influential, and important, but they are just one thing among many. Just one tiny corner of a very large universe. ("New Aesthetic")

I extend Bogost's question regarding pastry chefs with another culinary question, one directed toward a related activity where a new aesthetic of object relationships captures *my* interest for the way it networks other objects in new media spaces I encounter: craft beer. Why can't there be a new aesthetic of craft beer, I ask? Craft beer focuses my attention because, like these examples I pull from Bogost and *Fight Club*, it is an object capable of founding its own aesthetic (new or otherwise). It, too, is an object in a relationship with technology (social media). It, too, is a network of object-oriented relationships. In the network craft beer exists within and creates, I find among the many objects I encounter, a human object obsessed with pleasure. I find myself. Personal weaving occurs.

## Networks

"Craft beer" is the term given to small breweries producing less than six million barrels of beer annually and using adjuncts strictly for flavor (as opposed to cutting cost). Since the 1990s, craft beer has grown dramatically while sales by the major beer conglomerates (InBev, MillerCoors) have been flat. According to the Brewers Association, craft-beer sales in 2013 surpassed fifteen million barrels, up 17.2 percent from the previous year. Over twenty-eight hundred US craft breweries command approximately 7.8 percent of the overall domestic beer market (Brewers). In 2009, the "I am a Craft Brewer" video went viral; it showcased numerous brewers proclaiming the title and—as if echoing William Morris—professing anticorporate beliefs (Stone) (see fig. 14.1). In place of such beliefs, the brewers proposed the aesthetic of craft as networking their interests. "Craft brewing," the brewers tell us in the video—each saying one

*Figure 14.1. Screenshot from "I Am a Craft Brewer." Vinnie Cilurzo of Russian River Brewing Company.*

word of the following, "is innovation, independence, curiosity, collaboration, character, and family."

Craft beer is an object. While he is not fond of the word "object," Bogost describes the object as an operation, a process of transformation (*Alien* 25). He explains, "An object is thus a weird structure that might refer to a 'normal,' middle-sized object such as a toaster as much as it might describe an enormous, amorphous object like global transport logistics" (*Alien* 23). For the brewer, the object (beer) is artisanal. Latour advises that in network studies, "the first solution is to study *innovations* in the artisan's workshop" because "in these sites objects live a clearly multiple and complex life through meetings, plans, sketches, regulations, and trials. Here, they appear fully mixed with other more traditional social agencies" (*RS* 80; original emphasis). The object is not just a thing but those events, moments, people, and processes that create or surround the thing; the thing is the result of all of this activity, and it becomes an activity. Within any object exist many actions and transactions. In a given craft-beer (artisanal) moment, we might encounter the packaging, production, contents, hype, advertisement, and consumption, to name but a few of the actions occurring within the object. In the "I Am a Craft Brewer" video, for instance, the object is obvious: a glass, bottle, can, barrel, or keg of beer. The overall object projected throughout the video—the one we might call craft beer—includes such items, but it also includes items not visible: the places of consumption, distribution, drinkers, online discussion, ingredients, shipping issues, consumption itself, retail, hype, relationships among craft brewers, and marketing. The overall circulated object is a network of all of these activities and more.

Craft beer represents one type of network. Latour argues that networks are not made; they already exist (*RS* 131); "A network is not what is represented in the text, but that readies the text to take the relay of actors as mediators" (131). Networks, for Latour, are not necessarily physical or material items. A network, he describes, "is not made of nylon thread, words or any durable substance but is the trace left behind by some moving agent" (132). When I call craft beer a network, I am not pointing to a physical object and representing it (as a graph does), nor am I pointing to the object itself (the beer), but I am, instead, acknowledging the tracing left behind by its various agents whose interactions construct the network, one called craft beer. Latour adds, "[T]he very poverty of graphical representation allows the inquirer not to confuse his or her infra-language with the rich objects that are being depicted" (133). In addition to all of the agents I list above, I, too, am leaving behind a trace of this network. I do so because I, too, am a craft-beer drinker. I am confusing my language with the object, and that—despite Latour's concerns—is not a problem.

My purpose is to trace a specific network, a craft network, in order to understand not only how objects affect one another within a series of relationships as Bogost or Latour or even *Fight Club* ask but how I, too, am part of these affected relationships. There exist all kinds of metaphors for this tracing, as Latour notes, and while graphic visualizations may be popular, Latour faults them for "believing the world is made of points and lines" (*RS* 133). Instead of a visual representation of craft beer or a chart mapping how objects respond to objects, I return to Bogost's interests regarding craft and carpentry. Carpentry is a response to writing and any popular representation of networks; academics *write* about networks or relationships. They don't, as Bogost points out, construct either (much as Durden makes soap). "Writing is only one form of being," Bogost proclaims (*Alien* 90). Carpentry, on the other hand, involves "constructing artifacts as a philosophical practice" (*Alien* 92). Bogost writes that "carpentry entails making things that explain how things make the world" (*Alien* 93). Greg Ulmer, citing Hannah Arendt, associates reason (or explaining the making the world) with craft: "Aristotle and the Greeks invented their new higher reason from an analogy with the know-how of craftsmen. Craftsmen started with a prototype, an idea, and created an artifact by means of the choices or options that Aristotle called *proairesis*" (151). Proairesis, choice based on ethos, extends to the object one chooses to make (Bogost's carpentry or Durden's soap). Craft brewers, evident in their promotional video, maintain an artisanal ethos based on what they make. "Real radicals, we might conclude, make things," Bogost declares, and we can imagine Durden being radical and making soap bombs (*Alien* 110). Unfortunately, I do not share this ethos. I am not good with my hands. I can't make things, including beer. I am not radical.

This does not, however, mean that I lack character. I extend carpentry and its associated proairesis to the craft-network tracing I want to create because I, too, am part of this network. My presence and participation (not my handiwork) contribute to the making of a craft network (proairesis) that explains how craft beer generates the social. I engage with carpentry while showing a specific carpenter act. I am not "making" the network to show relationships, as Latour claims we do not do, but I am already within the network as an object whose other objects interest me and interact with me, something akin to Latour's "quasi-objects": "they attach us to one another, because they circulate in our hands and fine our social bond by their very circulation. They are discursive, however; they are narrated, historical, passionate" (*Modern* 89). I am one of those agents leaving a trace as I narrate, or, as Bogost might say, I am one of those agents making things that explain the world. I am in the network. But I am in the network only because I am building the network with others as well. My traces reveal my object-based interactions.

For the most part, Latour does not include himself as part of the given network he explores: he wasn't involved in Aramis's creation, he is not an engineer, he is not a lawyer. But *I am* a craft-beer drinker (Johnson). Whatever craft network I discover, I am a part of it because my beliefs, interests, tastes, purchases, and writings are part of the craft network. Carpentry occurs; only, I am not the only carpenter present. I shift Bogost's carpentry concerns away from the individual who builds to explain the network in ways writing won't support. A network is not the result of an individual entity making a thing. Instead, a number of actors make the thing together—even if they don't realize they are doing so nor that each other exists. I am one of those actors. All things or objects are carpentered networks.

I also recognize the participant culture that theorists, such as Clay Shirky, Axel Bruns, and Henry Jenkins, frame as a foundation of social media. Such theorists, though, maintain the individual as central to participatory media. When Bruns describes the prosumer, he means an individual with mixed consumer and producer identity: "The role of 'consumer' and even that of 'end user' have long disappeared, and the distinctions between producers and users of content have faded into comparative insignificance" (2). Bruns's prosumer disrupts traditional models of producer, distributor, and consumer. When

I consider a networks' many agents, I am not concerned with whether they are disrupting one model of production or another. Instead, I am concerned with how I and others interact with such agents so that we, too, are part of the network we are both fascinated by and building. Shirky claims, "One obvious lesson is that new technology enables new kinds of group-forming" (17). Groups form and enable movements, moments, activities, beliefs, consumption, and other patterns of activity. My concern is to trace a specific group formation as carpentry.

## Craft Tracing

Rather than tackle the entire craft-beer network I am a part of, I focus on one specific network within the network where a specific carpentry occurs so that I can better understand how objects (including me) affect objects (including me). I focus on the craft beer–release day. The release day typically is one day a year that a brewery sells a specific beer. The beer may be sold only at the brewery itself—as in the case of Surly's Darkness or Three Floyd's Dark Lord Day—or the beer may be distributed to the public for sale but in a limited way. I focus on Founders Brewing's Canadian Breakfast Stout, which was released in September 2011 for the first time in bottle form. I choose this event to focus my interests but also to trace how a supposed simplistic moment (the selling of a one-time beer) is complicated by the agents who construct the network. To do this tracing, I include numerous pointers to where these agents appear in the network, where they might be read, where they might engage with other agents. This is my version of Latour's demand for description. If my descriptions and citations appear to be superfluous or overbearing or scattered throughout a number of digital spaces, I recall Latour's reminder, "A good text should trigger in a good reader this reaction: 'Please, more details, I want more details'" (*RS* 137). Details provide the tracing. I begin with a series of details whose relationships perform a networked carpentry.

Founders Canadian Breakfast Stout (CBS) is a barrel-aged version of the brewery's regular Breakfast Stout (a coffee stout released during the winter months) but with maple syrup added. Initially, the beer only existed as draught, and its reputation as exotic and rare was based on such limited access. One had to go to the brewery, sample it at a festival, or participate in a rare tapping at a specific bar in order to try the beer in four ten-ounce samples. The bottle, as object, focused attention on the beer, as object, in unique ways as news of its release attracted more attention than draught had raised.

CBS eventually became a networked conversation across numerous spaces rather than a one-time event. These conversations occur, for the most part, in new media spaces: blog posts, videos, shared images, news-aggregation sites, and social-media sites.

Part of the Canadian Breakfast Stout hype regarding its release in a 750 ml bottle for the first time gains traction on September 16, 2011, when Founders blogs that CBS is on the bottling line (Sarah). That moment is reblogged by the popular Beerpulse website so that a wider audience might learn the news (Beerpulse). Discussion, though, had preceded the bottling and official announcement. On August 11, 2011, Even Benn, beer writer for the *St. Louis Post-Dispatch*, tweeted a quote from Founders president Mike Stevens that fifteen states would be allocated a thousand cases of the beer, packaged in 750 ml bottles (Benn). At the point of the Founders announcement, Beerpulse writer Adam Nason reminded readers that even earlier than Benn's tweet, beer blog The Beer Is Good leaked the news that a new beer would be released from Founders, a beer that turned out (unknown to the blogger at the time) to be Canadian Breakfast Stout (Andy) (see fig. 14.2). Responding to The Beer Is Good, Nason comments, "The CBS release may not necessarily follow suit but it gives us some indication as to what we might expect." When September rolled around, Ratebeer admin Joet posted the Founders press release for the CBS October release and thus, further expanded the audience not aware of any of the earlier blog posts or tweets.

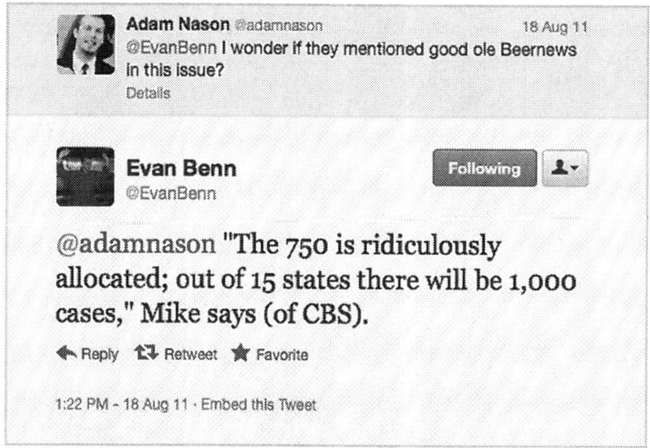


*Figure 14.2. Screenshot of Evan Benn tweet and Adam Nason response. Carpentry in action.*

With these details, one might expect a conclusion to the beer's network. The beer was anticipated and released, and some consumers purchased it. The release, however, generated further discussion and interest regarding issues of distribution, taste, hype, and other matters and, thus, extended the release beyond one day to a distributed series of moments built by those who consumed or did not consume the product. On his blog, Nason provides what he terms "an incomplete run down" of the distribution states for the beer. Many links in the rundown showed exact bottle distribution as well as which stores had sold out. The lack of distribution access, even in states where Founders is normally distributed, led some consumers to proclaim a "CBS FAIL" (SnobbyBeer). Aleheads, a blog devoted to beer, blogged the beer's local tapping (to coincide with the bottle release): "The CBS began pouring at 4:15pm . . . it was gone by 4:50pm" (McHops). Websites crashed under duress from online orders (where available) or from those looking for availability news (Nason, "Founders . . . Reservations"; Founders). A New Jersey drinker said he had heard how the Coverleaf bar's tapping of the beer "kicked in under 10 minutes" (Jimmack). A Cleveland beer drinker posted that "Whole Foods sold out in about 40 minutes" (Fatknitty). Mark of Mark and Shaun's Beer Blog describes his frustrations with getting a bottle.

> I called my local wine store 10 times during release week, tried multiple locations, veritably begged them for it, and they ended up releasing it mid-day via tweet (and the dreaded Facebook post) when I was at work, miles away. It disappeared in 10 minutes.

The blogger of Hop Bunnies: Hops Make Us Hop drove five hours to Grand Rapids, Michigan, to wait in line at the brewery for a bottle (Hop Bunny G). Beyond the Pour filmed a review the night of the release (Harper). Shoreline Beverage in New York was accused of selling its allotment too early (Nason, "New York"). Beer Avatar described some price gouging (Zymus). The blog It's Just the Booze Dancing brought up the issue of price gouging as well. Founders Brewery commented on the release snafus and dispelled rumors of favoritism.

> On another note, there seems to be some concern or confusion on how are beers are allocated per state. We are proud to be a Michigan-based brewery and all specialty releases take this into consideration. We at Founders will never forget our home state market. In terms of CBS, the state of Michigan received an allocation of 21% of the entire batch of CBS. No other state saw more than 12% of the total availability. That being said,

> no state is treated more fairly than another (including MI). Distributor allocations are simply based on a representation of total number of accounts they represent for Founders. Should rumors of this exist to the contrary, know that they are just that: rumors. ("CBS Allocations")

Big Red Liquors in Indiana released a video to promote the release and announce the 5:00 P.M. sale of their "miniscule" allotment at the Bloomington downtown store (see fig. 14.3). Beermonger, who works in retail, appealed to craft-beer drinkers to tone down the hype. Flickr user Mainbr86 posted an October 6 picture of his beer fridge, which featured two bottles of CBS in the side door (Main).

An October 15 picture uploaded to flickr shows Cicerone Annette May holding a CBS bottle proudly (Rupersburg). The Beer Is Good, who initially scooped the CBS release story, eventually tried it (Andy). By January 2012, Serious Eats, the popular food website, reviewed CBS and found it "staggeringly impressive" (Moxey). The Imasofat husband-and-wife reviewing pair paid $22 for a bottle and posted a review that includes the comment, "It smells just like chocolate syrup." Allthatalesyou posted a video review, noting the beer's "good marriage between the chocolate and coffee." In Lexington, Kentucky, I made several phone calls to the local liquor chain, Liquor Barn, and inquired on the chain's Facebook page about the beer's release. I received promises of arrival that were not accurate, received denials of receiving any bottles that later were found to be not true, was told that they had no idea what the beer

*Figure 14.3. Screenshot from Big Red Liquors CBS announcement. The Founders network in front.*

was, and eventually, I camped outside of the store closest to my house until 9:00 A.M., when the store opened, and a Facebook update said the beer would be available. Not finding the bottle on the shelf, I asked if any had arrived. A sales person went into the back and brought me a bottle. "One bottle limit?" I asked. "Of course," the sales person responded. I made my own comments on October 12 at the website Make Mine Potato.[2] I saved the empty bottle for some reason that still is not clear to me (see fig. 14.4).

This brief tracing attempts to capture the building of a series of responses and participation, moments where consumers become producers as they collaboratively network an object through moments of textual and visual communication, without such collaboration being foregrounded as an intentional gesture. That agents—human and nonhuman—build together without realizing their joint efforts suggests that networks are objects as relationships, relationships that join together a variety of forces whose networking constructs what could not be done individually. This tracing is not complete but, rather, shows a small example of carpentry as networked activity. This tracing also leaves out the popular beer website Beer Advocate's message-board threads; the website's 2012 crash pulled all of the posts offline. The tracing extends one object (a 750 ml bottle of CBS) so that it becomes another object (the threads, discussions, videos, personal moments), which, in turn, consists of many objects

*Figure 14.4. CBS bottle in author's basement cellar.* Jeff Rice.

in relationship with one another. In turn, more than one network is built, but I focus here on a quick tracing of the release-day moment as example. If the release day does, indeed, have an aesthetic, the aesthetic is this tracing. And if there is a philosophy here—as carpentry calls for—it involves questions regarding relationships among digital spaces.

## And This Means What?

Once a portion of a craft network is traced, what does the information gained from this tracing allow for? An improved release date? A better method of distribution? Alternative consumption habits? Self-awareness regarding my own position in this network? Or none of the above? "But that's just the point," Latour has Norbert say toward *Aramis*'s conclusion. "It doesn't get us anywhere" (281). To reach a conclusion toward a tracing's end is possible to the extent that invisible relationships are made visible. To say that I or any other descriptor of the network I am tracing called CBS release day can find resolution or opportunity for policy/behavior change is not entirely true. The tracing does not reveal a larger critique or cultural phenomenon or even intervention. If I was to explain a reality based on this tracing, I would be guilty of what Latour calls the problem with explanation: "Social explanations run the risk of hiding that which they should reveal since they remain too often 'without object'" (*RS* 82). Instead of a resolution, I offer the insight of relationship complexity. Relationships, the tracing teaches me, and the complexity that constructs them allow for a specific type of carpentry. The release day, as this brief tracing demonstrates, extends across space, actors, movements, and moments because of the relationships created. Bogost explains,

> The experience of things can be characterized only by tracing the exhaust of their effects on the surrounding world and speculating about the coupling between that black noise and the experiences internal to an object. Language is one tool we can use to describe this relationship, but it is *only* one tool, and we ought not feel limited by it. (*Alien* 100; original emphasis)

In addition to language, relationships are another tool. Relationships build networks that both embrace us, the one who is studying the network, and reject us depending on how we respond to the given network (i.e., as critique). In the case of CBS, I am obviously embraced. I join the building of the network by waiting in a parking lot, documenting my purchase, saving my bottle, and eventually writing about the day. What might feel like a useless moment within a larger exchange is actually an agent participating in an overall carpentry by utilizing language (speaking with liquor-store employees, blogging, writing this chapter) and without language (waiting, drinking). Remove the agent (or what Latour calls the mediator), and the network may still exist, but it is no longer the same network nor the same aesthetic experience as Barthes draws attention to since without my trivial interaction, I have no consumption pleasure in the network. If I am not in the network, it is not built the same way. I embrace this pleasurable aesthetic. Still, to present that embracement, I have to write it, or detail it, as Latour might argue. Without doing so, the network cannot be traced so that others might see its current existence or the revelation of its relationships. The network cannot be traced as it currently is without being written (with me as one of the actors present). Writing, Bogost posits, limits the potential of carpentry. Latour agrees at the level of explanation or appreciation.

> In all domains, to say that something is constructed has always been associated with an appreciation of its robustness, quality, style, durability, worth etc. So much so that no one would bother to say that a skyscraper, a nuclear plant, a sculpture, or an automobile is "constructed." This is too obvious to be pointed out. (*RS* 89)

One might write, instead, that a painting or website or novel is constructed or built in a way to appreciate or admire. Writing can be the expression of appreciation ("This beer tastes good, like chocolate"; "I sure am grateful I scored a rare bottle"). Carpentry makes similar assumptions. Carpentry, Bogost suggests, is a robust activity that extends what writing could not when limited to appreciation or critique (making is an act better than explaining). Carpentry sticks with an object as object, as if writing, too, is not an object. But carpentry exists in writing, in the detailing, tracing, and writing of the relationships as much as it exists in the relationships that built the network or its traces. There is a network called release day that I trace. And there is a network called release day in which I am an object among objects in that network. But there is also the network called release day built in my writing, in my descriptions, in my tracing, in my narrating. It may seem "too obvious" to point out a network of a beer release. It may feel as if there is too much "admiration" when I recognize myself as in that network. Or it may be the construction of that network that appears robust. And although Latour argues that "for any construction to take place, non-human entities have to play the major role" (*RS* 92), I find that the construction can include at least one specific nonhuman, writing, and one human, me, as well.

The position Bogost takes regarding carpentry, that it "seeks to capture and characterize an experience it can never fully understand, offering a rendering satisfactory enough to allow the artifact's operator to gain some insight into an alien thing's experience," can be extended to include the personal and writing itself, what I earlier called "personal weaving" (*Alien* 100). Within the network called CBS release day, I am as alien as the tweet or blog post or beer bottle or retail clerk selling a beer. I don't necessarily "understand," but I gain some insight as part of the network I trace and that I helped build. I gain insight into my own consumption—to some extent—by identifying my relationships not previously revealed but not at the level of critical awareness or habit change (as a cultural studies position might declare). And my writing, another alien thing present, gains possible insight into me. As Tony D. Sampson writes of this process, the network tracing allows for "a generative process recursively reproducing itself—the character of organization it produces is always a product, an effect, a consequence, not an event" (44). Or the tracing is not, we can add, a single event or a single event without me, as well. I will still drink beer; I will still hunt down CBS if another release day occurs (or another beer is released by Founders or some other brewery). I may, however, understand better the ways my work within the network affected others' work and helped build the network overall, a network that is still alive and functioning as other actors enter into it and leave. I may, in other words, understand how things make the world. Or I may not. In a networked tracing, comprehension's role is not the same as relationship revelation or "insight into an alien thing's experience." As I began this chapter, Bogost declares that carpentry reveals how things fashion one another. Network tracings, as I do here, perform likewise. "The object itself become[s] the philosophy," Bogost states (*Alien* 93). Craft is one such carpentered philosophy. I fashion. I am fashioned. Craft is the philosophy, but I am part of that philosophy, as well.

## Notes

1. The term "new aesthetic" is not Bogost's term but is appropriated from James Bridle.

2. My reviews are at http://makeminepotato.ydog.net/?p=1306 and http://makeminepotato.ydog.net/?p=1328.

## Works Cited

Allthatalesyou. "Founders CBS (Canadian Breakfast Stout) Review | All That Ales You Beer Review Ep. 31." *Youtube.com*, 14 Oct. 2011. Web. 10 July 2014. <http://www.youtube.com/watch?v=_pvyhU341jk>.

Andy. "Founders Backstage Series Update." *Thebeerisgood.com*, 26 July 2011. Web. 10 July 2014. <http://www.thebeerisgood.com/2011/07/founders-backstage-series-update.html>.

Barthes, Roland. *The Pleasure of the Text*. Trans. Richard Miller. New York: Hill, 1975. Print.

Beermonger. ""Hype and Hope." *Beermonger*, 30 Nov. 2011. Web. 10 July 2014. <http://beermonger.net/2011/11/30/hype-and-hope/>.

Beerpulse. "Just Bottled: Founders Canadian Breakfast Stout." *Beerpulse*, 16 Sept. 2011. Web. 10 July 2014. <http://beerpulse.com/2011/09/just-bottled-founders-canadian-breakfast-stout/>.

Benn, Evan. Tweet. *Twitter*, 18 Aug. 2011. Web. 10 July 2014. <https://twitter.com/evanbenn/status/104256780003057665>.

Big Red Liquors. "Canadian Breakfast Stout Release." *Youtube*, 11 Oct. 2011. Web. 10 July 2014. <http://www.youtube.com/watch?v=7IoTuYBL5YE>.

Bogost, Ian. *Alien Phenomenology: Or What It's Like to Be a Thing*. Minneapolis: U of Minnesota P, 2012. Print.

———. "The New Aesthetic Needs to Get Weirder." *The Atlantic*. 13 Apr. 2012. Web. 31 July 2013. <http://www.theatlantic.com/technology/archive/2012/04/the-new-aesthetic-needs-to-get-weirder/255838/>.

Brewers Association. "U.S. Beer Sales 2013." *Brewers Association*, 2014. Web. 10 Jul. 2014. <http://www.brewersassociation.org/pages/business-tools/craft-brewing-statistics/beer-sales>.

Bridle, James "About." *The New Aesthetic*, n.d. Web. 31 July 2013. <http://new-aesthetic.tumblr.com/about>.

Bruns, Axel. *Blogs, Wikipedia, Second Life and Beyond: From Production to Produsage*. New York: Lang, 2008. Print.

Fatknitty. Post. *Ratebeer*, 6 Oct. 2011. Web. 10 July 2014. <http://www.ratebeer.com/forums/cbs_181563.htm>

Founders Brewing Co. "CBS Allocations and Pricing." *Founders Brewing Co.*, 6 Oct. 2011. Web. 10 July 2014. <http://foundersbrewing.com/latest-news/2011/cbs-allocations-and-pricing/>.

———. Tweet. *Twitter*, 4 Oct. 2011. Web.10 July 2014. <https://twitter.com/foundersbrewing/status/121224608178380802>.

Harper, Daniel. "Founders Canadian Breakfast Stout—Tasted Alongside Founders KBS! | Beyond the Pour Beer Review." *Beyondthepour*, 4 Oct. 2011. Web. 10 July 2014. <http://beyondthepour.com/2011/10/04/founders-canadian-breakfast-stout-tasted-alongside-founders-kbs-beyond-the-pour-beer-review/>.

Hop Bunny G. "Founders Canadian Breakfast Stout (CBS) Brewery Release." *Hop Bunnies*, 12 Oct. 2011. Web. 10 July 2014. <http://blog.hopbunnies.com/2011/10/founders-canadian-breakfast-stout-release/>.

Imasofat. "Founders CBS Imperial Stout Beer Tasting." *Youtube.com*, 17 Oct. 2011. Web. 10 July 2014. <http://www.youtube.com/watch?v=DA6PAY_ZmsE&feature=related>.

It's Just the Booze Dancing. "Craft Beer Poll! The Founders CBS Dilemma: Has Limited Release Craft Beer Pricing Gotten Out of Hand?" *Wordpress*, 10 Oct. 2011. Web. 10 July 2014. <boozedancing.wordpress.com/2011/10/10/craft-beer-poll-the-founders-cbs-dilemma-has-limited-release-craft-beer-pricing-gotten-out-of-hand/>.

Jimmack. Post. *Ratebeer*, 7 Nov. 2011. Web. 10 July 2014. <http://www.ratebeer.com/forums/cbs_180805_2.htm>.

Joet. "Canadian Breakfast Stout Release: Press Release." *Ratebeer*, 9 Sept. 2011. Web. 10 July 2014. <http://www.ratebeer.com/forums/canadian-breakfast-stout-release-press-release_179432.htm>.

Johnson, Stephen. "I Am a Craft Beer Drinker." *Youtube*, 8 Sept. 2010. Web. 10 July 2014. <https://www.youtube.com/watch?v=Xh2oDdTHXQU>.

Latour, Bruno. *Aramis, or the Love of Technology*. Cambridge: Harvard UP, 1996. Print.

———. *Reassembling the Social: An Introduction to Actor-Network-Theory*. New York: Oxford UP, 2005. Print.

———. *We Have Never Been Modern*. Trans. Catherine Porter. Cambridge: Harvard UP, 1993. Print.

Main, Brian. "My Mini Fridge. Keeps Me Happy." *flickr.com*, 6 Oct. 2011. Web. 10 July 2014. <http://www.flickr.com/photos/24747481@N03/6217931865/>.

Mark. "Founders Canadian Breakfast Stout: The Review." Mark and Shaun's Beer Blog. *MarkandShaunBeer*, 14 Oct. 2011. Web. 10 July 2014. <http://www.markandshaunbeer.com/2011/10/founders-canadian-breakfast-stout.html>.

McCullough, Malcolm. *Abstracting Craft: The Practiced Digital Hand*. Cambridge: MIT P, 1998. Print.

McHops, Barley. "Founders CBS." *Aleheads*, 27 Oct. 2011. Web. 10 July 2014. <http://aleheads.com/2011/10/27/founders-cbs/>.

Morris, William. *Art and Socialism*. 1884. ElecBook, 2001. Print.

Moxey, Jonathan. "Founders Canadian Breakfast Stout Is Worth the Hype." *Serious Eats*, 5 Jan. 2012. Web. 10 July 2014. <http://drinks.seriouseats.com/2012/01/founders-canadian-breakfast-stout-review-compared-to-kbs.html>.

Nason, Adam. "Founders Canadian Breakfast Stout: A Very Incomplete State-by-State Rundown." *Beerpulse.com*, 4 Oct. 2011. Web. 10 July 2014. <http://beerpulse.com/2011/10/founders-canadian-breakfast-stout-a-very-incomplete-state-by-state-rundown/>.

———. "Founders Canadian Breakfast Stout: Reservations Crash Store Website." *Beerpulse*, 4 Oct. 2011. Web. 10 July 2014. <http://beerpulse.com/2011/10/founders-canadian-breakfast-stout-reservations-crash-store-website/>.

———. "Founders Canadian Breakfast Stout to Be Bottled." *Beerpulse*, 12 Aug. 2011. Web. 10 July 2014. http://beerpulse.com/2011/08/founders-canadian-breakfast-stout-to-be-bottled/>.

———. "New York Beer Store Releases Canadian Breakfast Stout Early." *Beerpulse*, 28 Sept. 2011. Web. 10 July 2014. http://beerpulse.com/2011/09/new-york-liquor-store-releases-founders-canadian-breakfast-stout-early/.

Ruhlman, Michael. "Artisan Butchers (Does Artisanal Even Mean Anything Anymore?)" *Michael Ruhlman: Translating the Chef's Craft for Every Kitchen*. 19 Aug. 2010. Web. 31 July 2013. <http://ruhlman.com/2010/08/artisan-butchersdoes-artisanal-even-mean-anything-anymore/>.

Rupersberg, Nicole. "10. Certified Cicerone Annette May Showing Off the Precious." *flickr.com*, 15 Oct. 2011. Web. 10 July 2014. <http://www.flickr.com/photos/eatitdetroit/6255664798/>.

Sachs, Adam. "Artisanal America." *Details*. August 2010. Web. 31 July 2013. <http://www.details.com/culture-\trends/critical-eye/201008/artisanal-america-handmade-hipster-authentic>.

Sampson, Tony D. *Virality: Contagion Theory in the Age of Networks*. Minneapolis: U of Minnesota P, 2012. Print.

Sarah. "CBS on the Bottling Line." *Founders Brewing Co.*, 16 Sept. 2011. Web. 10 July 2014. <http://foundersbrewing.com/latest-news/2011/cbs-on-the-bottling-line/>.

Sennett, Richard. *The Craftsman*. New Haven: Yale UP, 2003. Print.

Shirky, Clay. *Here Comes Everybody: The Power of Organizing without Organizations*. New York: Penguin, 2008. Print.

SnobbyBeer. "Canadian Breakfast Stout FAIL." *Snobbybeer.com*, 7 Oct. 2011. Web. 10 June 2014. <http://www.snobbybeer.com/blog/canadian-breakfast-stout-fail>.

Stone Brewing Co. "I Am a Craft Brewer." *Youtube*, 27 Apr. 2009. Web. 10 July 2014. <http://www.youtube.com/watch?v=ev5OZS75qaY>.

Ulmer, Gregory. *Avatar Emergency*. Clemson: Parlor, 2012. Print.

Zymus. "Founders Canadian Breakfast Stout." *Beer Avatar*, 14 Oct. 2011. Web. 10 July 2014. <http://beeravatar.blogspot.com/2011/10/founders-canadian-breakfast-stout.html>.

# 15. Making a Thing of Quality Child Care: Latourian Rhetoric Doing Things

Sarah Read, *DePaul University*

How does one convince a student, community member, or other nondisciplinary stakeholder that an individual (working either corporately or alone) can affect *material* change in the world with writing or rhetoric? The practice of critique and axioms of critical theory have thus far failed to answer this question. Since a "how" question is methodological, in this chapter I turn to Latour's methodology of tracing associations to show how composition might perform the elusive activity of "trac[ing] with precision a chain of activity that connects the writing of [a document] to a given public action or impact" (Grabill 202). Latour's methodology of tracing associations, or actor-network-theory (ANT) lends itself to doing rhetoric.

But the traced trail is not the winding path of stepping stones (texts and technologies and audiences) that crosses a broad terrain that we have usually called *context*, a term that invokes a place or a situation. Rather, for Latour the tracing of associations, or the "peculiar *movement* of re-association and reassembling" (*RS* 7; emphasis added), is an explanatory activity that describes the *translations* that induce two actors, two intermediaries, into coexisting (*RS* 108). Translation, for Latour, designates a set of practices that produces networks or assemblages of human and nonhuman actors—or imbroglios or hybrids, as Latour calls them—to foreground their mixed ontology as human and nonhuman, of being of both society and nature (*Modern* 10–11). To trace or describe a translation means to understand how one thing becomes another thing through being interdefined or mediated by other entities in order to achieve a modified goal that suits both parties (*PH* 179). For example, translation explains why the goal of a scientist in 1939 France looking to demonstrate the atomic chain reaction produced by fission also becomes the maintenance of the independence of France from Germany.

Within the philosophical apparatus that Latour has built to demonstrate the continuity between science and society, I see a methodology for persuasively demonstrating that rhetorical activity and its effects are coextensive. In order to fend off the critiques of science studies as a simple-minded social constructivist co-option of science, Latour has had to develop a methodology to make visible the associations that constitute what he argues are really hybrids of society and nature. At the heart of his methodology of tracing this "Ariadne's thread" of associations is the impulse to make the continuity and the historicity between two different (and even incommensurable) actors visible and convincing (*Modern* 121). For Latour, such an account is convincing when we can see how actors "might be *associated* in such a way that they *make others do things*" (*RS* 107; original emphasis). This phrase "make others do things" is highly resonant for rhetoric in that it both invokes and subverts rhetoric's more traditional emphasis on influencing how people think, say, or believe things. With this short phrase, Latour does what rhetoric sometimes finds difficult: he connects it to the material world.

While rhetoric's function for science is not Latour's central concern (in fact, he distances science studies from the rhetoric of science [*PH* 96]), he does have an investment in complicating the function of language and rhetoric for science beyond that of mere window dressing or, at the other extreme, as the total deconstruction of scientific statements into groundless traces of language. Helpfully for rhetoricians, Latour articulates that rhetoric, textual strategies, and writing are implicated in science but "in a new form that has a simultaneous impact on the nature of things and on the social context" (*Modern* 5). In other words, language, semiotics, and rhetoric are also coextensive with the entanglements of nature and society that make up the objects of Latour's work.

While Latour's ontology of translation establishes continuity between rhetoric and the material, the notion of mediation (as the mechanism of translation) alone does not explain why actors with disparate interests might be motivated to negotiate settlements, or "aggregate interests" into networks of associations (*PF* 265). It is in Latour's notion of the "Thing" that we can understand the motivation to aggregate. A Thing is the "assembly of relevant parties"—both human and nonhuman—that gather around an issue, as well as the issue itself. The notion of the Thing explains how matters of public concern "bind all of us in ways that map out a public space . . . [a] hidden geography" ("Dingpolitik" 5). From a rhetorical perspective, a Thing is the exigence for translation when the exigence is understood to be rooted in both the social and the material worlds as "a mutual construing of objects, events, interests and purposes that not only links them but makes them what they are" (Miller 157).

Latour's Thing also affords an explanation of how rhetoric is coextensive with nature and society and the modern imbroglios that, by design, conceal this ontology. The Thing extends rhetoric beyond its more traditional deliberative, agonistic or "horse-trad[ing] across boundaries" function in the negotiation of settlements among actors (Spinuzzi 201). It does this by establishing continuity between the assemblage and the issue and construing rhetorical activity as the act of bringing both the assemblage *and* the issue into being. As an analytical tool for studying writing, the Thing shifts the study of rhetorical activity away from a focus on the writer's process for composing a document (invention, writing, rewriting) to the *effects* of the composition of the document—the mediation of associations, building an assemblage, or the Thing.

Latour's methodology of tracing associations—of translations—enables us to explore this hidden geography of the Thing that binds actors with disparate interests in mediatory relationships and to make the constitutive function or rhetoric more visible. The ethnographic field episode in this chapter offers an abbreviated case of tracing the translations assembling the Thing of quality child care. The field site for my research was a medium-sized organization in Seattle, Washington, in the field of early learning (infants to five-year-olds). This organization, which I call Quality Child-Care Resources (QCR),[1] received both public and private funding to improve training resources for child-care providers and to assist parents, especially those from vulnerable populations, in finding and paying for quality child care. Documented in the field episode in this chapter is a slice of the work on a communication campaign run by QCR. This campaign sought to build public will for a state initiative that would develop and implement a consumer-style rating system for child-care providers and centers (a bit like a Michelin guide for day care). Over the last decade, professional child-care advocates have pushed states to develop quality rating and improvement systems (QRISs) to raise the minimum quality of child care above the abominably low state requirements for a license to operate a day care. As might be expected, however, getting broad-based buy-in for a notion as capacious and contingent as "quality" child care among a culturally, ethnically, politically, and socioeconomically diverse group of stakeholders turned out to be very difficult. In fact, negotiation around the meaning of "quality" child care ended up defining the work that the QCR communications campaign team did to promote the QRIS.

The field episode documents the work of team member Judy, who manages the QCR unit dedicated to serving unlicensed caregivers. The episode traces Judy's rhetorical work as she enacted, maintained, extended, and transformed the quality child-care assemblage via the mechanism of translation. The episode answers this Latourian question: how does the official discourse of a state-sponsored model for a child-care quality rating and improvement system become (via translation) the personalized, material experience of the stakeholders (largely children and their caregivers) who are invoked only in the abstract by the official model? Or, how does Judy make a Thing of quality child care for the diverse group of QCR stakeholders that she serves?

## Making a Thing of Quality Child Care for Unlicensed Providers

What is the "slender but solid thread" that connects Washington State's official model for quality child care (see fig. 15.1), a rhetorical product, with the lived experience of quality child care enjoyed by the children in the Play and Learn group activity circle (see fig. 15.2) (Latour, "Interobjectivity" 238)?

The answer to this question is more complicated than it might appear. First, even though the existence of the Play and Learn group is an outcome of the general public initiative behind improving access to quality child care,

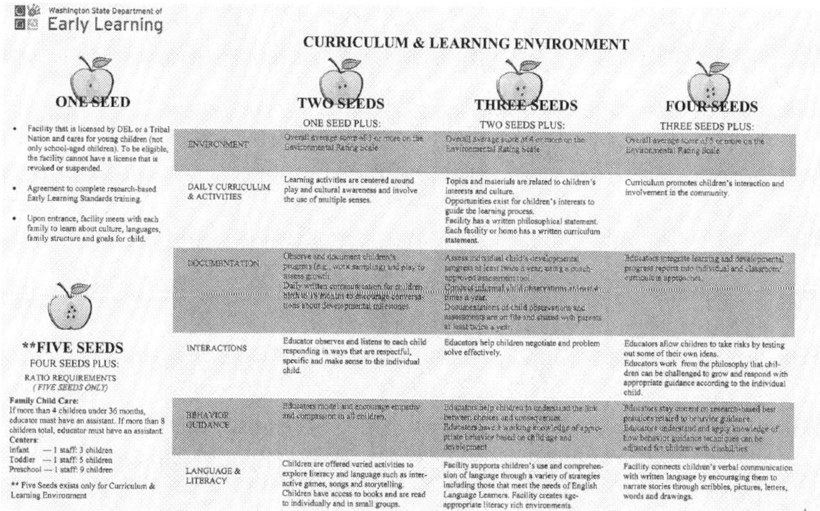

Washington State Department of
Early Learning

CURRICULUM & LEARNING ENVIRONMENT

ONE SEED

- Facility that is licensed by DEL or a Tribal Nation and cares for young children (not only school-aged children). To be eligible, the facility cannot have a license that is revoked or suspended.
- Agreement to complete research-based Early Learning Standards training.
- Upon entrance, facility meets with each family to learn about culture, languages, family structure and goals for child.

| | TWO SEEDS<br>ONE SEED PLUS: | THREE SEEDS<br>TWO SEEDS PLUS: | FOUR SEEDS<br>THREE SEEDS PLUS: |
|---|---|---|---|
| ENVIRONMENT | Overall average score of 3 or more on the Environmental Rating Scale | Overall average score of 4 or more on the Environmental Rating Scale | Overall average score of 5 or more on the Environmental Rating Scale |
| DAILY CURRICULUM & ACTIVITIES | Learning activities are centered around play and cultural awareness and involve the use of multiple senses. | Topics and materials are related to children's interests and culture.<br>Opportunities exist for children's interests to guide the learning process.<br>Facility has a written philosophical statement.<br>Each facility or home has a written curriculum statement. | Curriculum promotes children's interaction and involvement in the community. |
| DOCUMENTATION | Observe and document children's progress (e.g., work sampling) and play to assess growth.<br>Daily written communication for children birth to 18 months to encourage conversations about developmental milestones. | Assess individual child's developmental progress at least twice a year, using a coach-approved assessment tool.<br>Conduct informal child observations at least 4 times a year.<br>Documentations of child observations and assessments are on file and shared with parents at least twice a year. | Educators integrate learning and developmental progress reports into individual and classroom/curriculum approaches. |
| INTERACTIONS | Educator observes and listens to each child responding in ways that are respectful, specific and make sense to the individual child. | Educators help children negotiate and problem solve effectively. | Educators allow children to take risks by testing out some of their own ideas.<br>Educators work from the philosophy that children can be challenged to grow and respond with appropriate guidance according to the individual child. |
| BEHAVIOR GUIDANCE | Educators model and encourage empathy and compassion in all children. | Educators help children to understand the link between choices and consequences.<br>Educators have a working knowledge of appropriate behavior based on child age and development. | Educators stay current on research-based best practices related to behavior guidance.<br>Educators understand and apply knowledge of how behavior guidance techniques can be adjusted for children with disabilities. |
| LANGUAGE & LITERACY | Children are offered varied activities to explore literacy and language such as interactive games, songs and storytelling.<br>Children have access to books and are read to individually and in small groups. | Facility supports children's use and comprehension of language through a variety of strategies including those that meet the needs of English Language Learners. Facility creates age-appropriate literacy rich environments. | Facility connects children's verbal communication with written language by encouraging them to narrate stories through scribbles, pictures, letters, words and drawings. |

**FIVE SEEDS
FOUR SEEDS PLUS:
RATIO REQUIREMENTS
*(FIVE SEEDS ONLY)*

**Family Child Care:**
If more than 4 children under 36 months, educator must have an assistant. If more than 8 children total, educator must have an assistant.
**Centers:**
Infant — 1 staff: 3 children
Toddler — 1 staff: 5 children
Preschool — 1 staff: 9 children

** Five Seeds exists only for Curriculum & Learning Environment

1

*Figure 15.1. The curriculum and learning environment element of the Washington State Department of Early Learning's QRIS model.* Quality Childcare Resources.

*Figure 15.2. A Play and Learn group.* Quality Childcare Resources, "Play and Learn" information sheet.

the assembled participants in figure 15.2 are not likely to uniformly agree with the philosophy behind the QRIS model in figure 15.1. Second, while it is not necessarily important that the participants in figure 15.2 know or care about the QRIS model, it would seem important that the group initiators and organizers have bought into it. Yet, even this is not a given. The associations between the QRIS model and interaction of the playgroup are only visible via the tracing of several translations that associate actors with disparate interests in such a way that they behave as if they have a common goal—quality child care for children—while maintaining their diverse motives, goals, and identities. The translations traced in this section are: (1) Judy's association with the QRIS model for quality child care via the mediation of the QRIS communications campaign; (2) an unlicensed provider's association with quality child care and QCR via the mediation of a brochure produced by Judy's team; and (3) the enrollment of Play and Learn group participants in the QRIS notion of quality child care via the mediation of the group facilitator and QCR training resources.

This task of assembling actors with disparate interests and motives is the basis for Judy's work. When parents are absent, unlicensed providers, including grandparents, extended family members, friends, and other community members, provide child care. Even though 65 percent of infants and 45 percent of toddlers in Washington State are cared for by unlicensed providers, unlicensed providers have not traditionally been considered stakeholders in programs to improve the quality of care in private homes. However, this began to change when QCR formally recognized unlicensed providers as a stakeholder group in 2005 and launched a program that is dedicated to reaching and providing resources to these unlicensed caregivers. This program, the Family, Friends and Neighbors (FFN) program, is coordinated by Judy, who was hired based on her participation in the original grassroots work to bring visibility to this group.

More than the other QCR staff that work on the QRIS communications campaign, Judy is aware of how her work is fundamentally rhetorical in that the purpose of her work is to "build relationships." Judy's awareness is largely an outcome of the fact that she has experienced the transition from being an FFN practitioner (a provider of unlicensed care to children in her home) to, as she put it, "a person of influence," or a systems person who is working to bring recognition and support to the cause. In an interview she explained, "The key to all of this is relationships. The key to reaching FFN caregivers who are basically in the home and not belonging to any system . . . is reach[ing] somebody next to them, really really close by. It's like a chain of relationships that gets built." A chain of relationships (or what ANT might call a chain of associations) includes not only the human caregivers who build personal relationships but also the many objects that mediate these alliances, such as the QCR informational and training materials and the FFN brochure analyzed later in this essay.

Judy and her staff also knew well, however, that doing the work of a communications campaign, such as designing, printing, and disseminating brochures via community centers and libraries, is too indirect for reaching FFN caregivers with the information and resources they need to provide *quality* child care. Judy understood that caregivers need to interact directly with one another and, ideally, with a trained facilitator in order to form meaningful alliances that affect the way that they provide child care over the long term. In order to align the conception of quality FFN child care with the QRIS guidelines for curriculum and learning environment, Judy would have to provide resources (including textual resources as well as community programs and events) to meet the following guidelines for "Daily Curriculum and Activities" (see fig. 15.1).

1. Learning activities are centered on play and cultural awareness and involve the use of multiple senses.
2. Topics and materials are related to children's interests and culture.
3. Opportunities exist for children's interests to guide the learning process.
4. Curriculum promotes children's interaction and involvement in the community.

An effective and low-cost way to account for these guidelines was to provide a physical space and a regular time for caregivers and children to interact socially and to have access to resources about quality child care. For this reason, part of Judy's and her staff's job was to coordinate structured community playgroups called Play and Learn groups. These groups were informal, usually free playgroups for caregivers and their charges hosted and sponsored by community organizations, such as the YWCA. At these playgroups, a trained facilitator structured a couple of hours of group play into periods of group interaction, such as circle time (see fig. 15.2) and individual activity time to play or make artwork. Considered in this light, it would seem that Play and Learn groups easily met the QRIS guidelines listed above. In order to get FFN caregivers and children to these groups, however, Judy first had to reach them and persuade them to show up. The brochure that Judy's team developed to promote their FFN program is one of their efforts to reach this group of caregivers.

Before discussing this brochure, I want to step back and consider Judy's association with the official QRIS model for quality child care. Even though Judy was a self-professed "systems person," it was surprisingly difficult for her to buy into the QRIS communications campaign's purpose to promote the QRIS model's notion of quality child care to FFN stakeholders. One problem was that the FFN stakeholder group does not really exist except in the official-ese of systems people like Judy. She explained that this term is just a "handle so that we can talk about this and write grants. . . . [I]t's a placeholder for people" that was a product of the necessity of having to explain the identity of this group to legislators and funding organizations so that it could be incorporated fiscally and structurally into organizational goals, such as those of QCR. Consequently, the caregivers themselves didn't identify with the term or concept of FFN caregivers, who, unlike licensed caregivers, are fully professionalized and economically motivated to identify by the term "child-care provider." This problem made it difficult for Judy to enroll FFN providers in the QRIS model's notion of quality child care. Without an available group identity, each new member had to be reached individually and on his or her own terms. FFN child-care providers are culturally, socioeconomically, and linguistically diverse, and so creating resources for them is not a one-size-fits-all endeavor. In the early days of initiatives to provide resources and outreach to this group, flyers would be printed inviting FFN providers to meetings and workshops. Of course no one came, Judy said in an interview, because a grandmother does not self-identify as a FFN provider—she is just "Grandmother."

In addition, the cultural and socioeconomic diversity of these stakeholders made it difficult to define what quality child care meant for FFN caregivers. Not surprising, then, Judy articulated quality child care in different terms than what the official QRIS model proposed. While the QRIS model is structured by the elements of formal schooling, such as curriculum and professional development, for markers of quality FFN care, Judy turned to more basic things: safety ("Well, obviously," she said), interaction, play with the child that is informed by a basic understanding of child development, and being intentional in interacting with the child, such as taking advantage of "teachable moments," for example, teaching a child how to count by matching socks while sorting the laundry. For Judy, this conception of quality child care distanced her work from the official discourse of the state's QRIS initiative: "To me these sort of folksy, homey messages are pretty far away from the very formal QRIS."

Judy's statement about the distance between "folksy, homey messages" and the QRIS exposes the trouble that she had identifying with the official QRIS model herself. In fact, in a monthly check-in meeting with Charlene, a QCR colleague, Charlene spent a good deal of time trying to persuade Judy to value the purpose of the QRIS communications campaign. According to Charlene, the whole purpose of the project was to explain the official QRIS model for quality child care in a way that QCR's stakeholders could understand. This was an easier task for Charlene than Judy, because Charlene worked with licensed child-care providers explicitly looking for resources to professionalize. Judy, however, expressed concern that trying to reach the FFN caregivers with the language of the QRIS risked "polluting or diluting the message that we've been trying to get out. . . . That you can provide . . . quality child care in your home as a regular old person." Judy punctuated her point when she said, "This project is hard for me because the FFN and the QRIS thing don't [hand gesture to communicate "mesh"]."

Later, in a follow-up interview, Judy acknowledged her own resistance to the QRIS initiative, which she saw as an effort to effectively extend licensing requirements to family, friend, and neighbor caregivers, a notion that runs contrary to the philosophy of FFN advocacy work. Judy also expressed frustration at trying to integrate her responsibilities to the QRIS communications campaign with the goals and objectives of the FFN team without having to "reinvent our shop." In other words, Judy was not philosophically or ideologically enrolled in the QRIS communications campaign or the official model of the QRIS. She just didn't see how they served her interests or those of the FFN child-care providers that her program served.

Why, then, was Judy involved in the QRIS communications campaign? Here is where we encounter the first translation—or detour (*PH* 179)—filling the gap between figures 15.1 and 15.2. Judy was compelled to reach FFN caregivers with the QRIS model because she had accepted funding for her FFN program from the grant that underwrote QCR's work on the QRIS communications campaign. Judy reported to me how she had received a call from QCR's CEO asking her if she would like her program to be included in the QRIS communications campaign grant from a major philanthropic organization. Seeing the possibility for new funding for the FFN program, Judy had said yes, even though she didn't fully understand what she was saying yes to. In other words, Judy's enrollment with the QRIS communications campaign was motivated by economic need, not her buy-in into the QRIS model. But because her FFN program had joined the grant, she would have to produce outcomes that aligned with the grant's goals. These outcomes would have to be articulated in the annual report to the funder that was drafted by the manager of the QRIS communications campaign. From a textual point of view, all Judy's work on the QRIS communications campaign had to produce was a few sentences that aligned her FFN work with the official QRIS model within the progress-to-date section of the grant report. What Judy's settlement made her *do*, however, was more than just rhetorical in the impoverished sense of inventing language to serve political ends.

One channel that Judy used to reach FFN providers about quality child care was an informational brochure that was printed in eight languages ("and not always the right ones," Judy said) and distributed at libraries, community centers, pediatricians' offices, and anywhere else the so-called group of FFN providers might pass through. In a Latourian sense, this brochure functioned as an immutable mobile (*SA* 227), or as an inscription (a written-down trace) of the FNN program that was circulatable in the community. The content, form, and rhetoric of the brochure were shaped by the historicity of the settlements that comprised the rhetorical situation within which it functioned: the diffuse nature of the FFN caregiver group, the incommensurability of the official QRIS model's discourse with Judy's philosophy for working with FFN providers, and the brochure's purpose to mediate the association of new FFN stakeholders with QCR. For example, the front panel of the brochure (see fig. 15.3) avoids naming a group and instead invokes the audience with a question oriented around the activity of child care: "Are you taking care of your grandbabies, nieces, nephews or cousins? Do you help take care of a friend's child?" This is a question to which a grandmother would be able to easily answer yes and take the first step toward recasting her existing identity as grandmother as that of caregiver. In the moment of this small destabilization, or "interessement" (Callon 208), the grandmother expresses interest in being *in between* her old identity as grandmother and QCR's redefinition of her identity as a caregiver. In this moment Judy has, via the mediation of the brochure, initiated the process of translation.

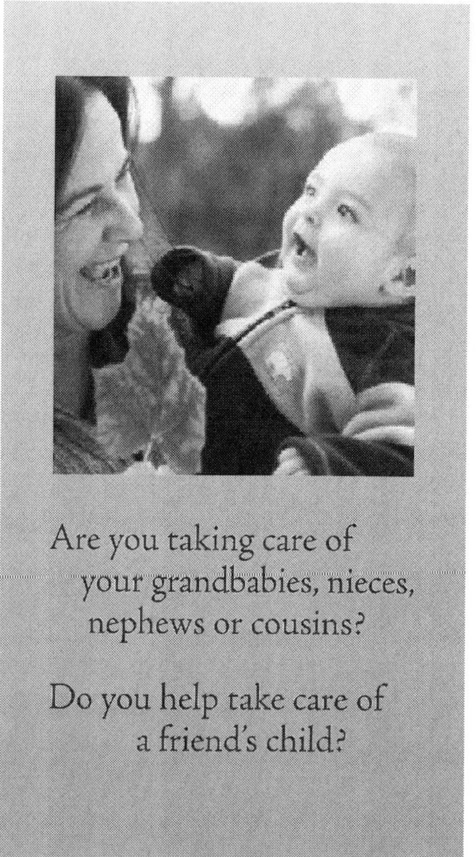


*Figure 15.3. Front panel of the QCR brochure for Family, Friends and Neighbors stakeholders.* Quality Childcare Resources.

In addition, because there is no common definition among FFN caregivers, the brochure does not explicitly refer to "quality" child care at all. Instead, it makes suggestions for how quality care can be enacted, via the use of photographs and spare and simple text (see fig. 15.4). Rather than striving to fix a definition of quality child care in the abstract, the brochure includes activities that many caregivers are likely to already be doing at home, such as talking, reading, and singing, taking a walk, and visiting the library. These activities reflect the FFN philosophy that children are always learning, wherever they are. However, the notion that providing quality child care includes community involvement, a value promoted by Judy in part for its efficacy of providing a material point of contact between caregivers and her FFN program, is reflected in the second set of suggestions for "What you can do in your neighborhood." The first suggestion is to "Bring a child to a Play & Learn Group in your neighborhood," an activity that would bring child-care providers and their children in contact with a facilitator trained by Judy's program and with the curriculum that has been shaped by some of the tenets of the QRIS model.

While in theory Judy would be delighted if an FFN caregiver read her brochure and enacted even one of the suggestions under any circumstances, the success of her work depended on recording traces of this enactment and using those traces to justify the continuation of her program in documents, such as the grant report to the funder of the QRIS communications campaign. In terms of the strength of the developing assemblage (or Thing) of quality child care, the more ways an actor is in relationship to the assemblage, the more stable his or her enrollment (or the forming of an alliance) is going to be (Callon, "Techno-economic," 211). Reading a brochure is a relatively weak level of enrollment, but making a phone call or sending an e-mail initiates another, possibly stronger, association. The multiple ways listed to contact QCR (phone, web, e-mail) not only attributed the information in the brochure to QCR and Judy's program but also invited caregivers to identify themselves with an organization that takes the care of children at home very seriously. If they chose to act within the suggestions of the brochure, or to attend a Play and Learn group, or to contact QCR for more information, then the reader had also taken a step towards identifying as a person who takes the care of children at home very seriously, beyond the tacit expectations and role definition provided by familial ties or the responsibilities implicit within a particular immigrant community. Of course, this enrollment would only be visible to an office-bound systems person like Judy via the document traces

What you can do at home every day:

Read, talk, sing, and tell stories.

Talk about things you do and see.

Go outside, take a walk.

Do things together—cook, garden, fold laundry, feed a pet.

Talk with the child's parents about your day together.

What you can do in your neighborhood:

Bring a child to a Play & Learn group in your neighborhood. You will meet other adults and children and have lots of fun.

Visit story time at your local library.

Ask for information at your community center or family resource center.

Share this information with people you know who are taking care of babies and children.

*Figure 15.4. Inside panel of the QCR brochure for Family, Friends and Neighbors stakeholders.* Quality Childcare Resources.

that would be generated in a QCR phone log or by the attendance sheet of Play and Learn group. Such a "consolidation" (or multiplying of the connections among members of the network between FFN caregivers and QCR via the mediation of the brochure and the phone log) extends and mobilizes the Thing that is QRIS notion of quality child care (Spinuzzi 41).

While the QCR brochure does the rhetorical work of defining (implicitly) quality child care, at a Play and Learn group, quality child care is enacted. These groups are mentioned in the QCR brochure as a suggestion to caregivers as a way to get involved in the neighborhood (see fig. 15.4). The initial capital letters of the words "Play" and "Learn" suggest that these groups are branded, or that these occasions for group child care are shaped by a very particular Thing, in this case, QCR and the state's model for QRIS. In other words, these Play and Learn groups are one of the sites where FFN child-care providers can learn to enact quality child care as it has been shaped by the official discourse of the state's QRIS model. Caregivers may not have any idea what QRIS is or have any desire to know, but the terms of the enrollment of these caregivers in the QRIS model for quality child care are not important to Judy and her staff. Just as it is only important to the CEO of QCR that Judy *does* the work of the QRIS communications campaign, what is important is that the caregivers *do* quality child care. This focus on the function of rhetoric to compel "doing" is an important departure from deliberative or agonistic rhetoric, wherein the changing of minds or beliefs precedes action.[2]

The QCR information sheet on Play and Learn groups explains what happens during a group session (see fig. 15.2).

> The facilitator is active in helping children and adults engage in the activities and in providing a positive role model for interacting with children. The facilitator also checks in with the adults and provides them with information about community resources, child development and other topics. Some groups have a time when the adults are away from the children to talk and learn.

As the text from the QCR information sheet suggests, the facilitator, the additional resources, the other members of the group, and the group activities function to mediate the enrollment of new caregivers into the QRIS model by *doing* quality child care. In a way parallel to how the picture on the front panel of the brochure, shown in figure 15.3, depicts a quality child-care interaction between a woman and a child (studying and enjoying the marvel of a leaf), Play and Learn group facilitators propose the new identity of intentional and informed caregiver to the attendees by leading fun and enriching activities. The facilitator also offers group members information about child development and information about additional resources (such as QCR) to continue their development as informed caregivers.

It is in this playgroup interaction where we encounter a third translation that mediates between figures 15.1 and 15.2: the enrollment of a Play and Learn group facilitator in the QRIS notion of quality child care. Because Play and Learn groups must accommodate the cultural and language diversity in the community, facilitators are recruited from within a community in order to ensure relevance and continuity for the caregivers and the investment of the facilitator. This facilitator, however, has been trained by QCR within the framework of the QRIS model of quality child care—at least as far as Judy deems the model applicable to FFN stakeholders. As with the FFN brochure, Judy knows that the structure of the Play and Learn groups must maintain the flexibility of what quality child care can look like and how it can be enacted to appeal to a diversity of stakeholders. In this sense the facilitator, the training resources provided by QCR, and Judy's articulation of the QRIS notion of quality child care for FFN stakeholders functions to mediate the translation that aligns Judy's goals with those of the facilitator and the attendees of the playgroup. While the attendees enjoy several hours of community-based interaction that meets their own goals (goals that remain unknown to this study), Judy has been successful at "taking a detour through the goals of others" (Latour, *PH* 89) so that she can achieve her goal of generating traces of quality child care. These traces of quality child care—the facilitator's report of the playgroup's activities and/or the group attendance sheet—can be translated into the progress-to-date section of QCR's report to the philanthropic funder.

The function of rhetoric in the three translations recounted in this episode converges in Judy's effectiveness at maintaining the contingency and the capaciousness of what constitutes quality child care. Judy's own resistance to the formal model of the QRIS prevented her from reproducing the school-based discourse of quality child care at the moments of translation, such as when a grandmother encounters QCR's brochure at the public library or when Judy is enlisting a new Play and Learn group facilitator from an immigrant community. This rhetorical intervention was not unique to Judy on the QRIS communications campaign team: other episodes from my fieldwork also demonstrate how the members of the QRIS communications campaign team had to intentionally recast the narrow, official discourse of the QRIS model in order to maintain the possibility of the enrollment of a wide diversity of stakeholders. Even though Judy and her colleagues believed in the state's QRIS model as educated professionals in the field of early learning, they had to do the rhetorical work necessary to extend the rhetorical identification of "quality" child care to an ever-diversifying audience of caregivers and providers with often competing values and interests. In essence, then, the topos of "quality child care" functioned as a mediator in assembling the Thing while being the Thing itself. It is at this point that rhetoric becomes coextensive with the assemblage that it mediates.

## Doing Latourian Rhetoric; Rhetoric Doing Things

In this brief episode my aim has been to make visible how the work of Judy and her colleagues at Quality Child-Care Resources contributes, ultimately, to improving the quality of child care for children in Washington State. My motivation, as I framed it at the beginning of this essay, has been to persuade a nondisciplinary stakeholder in rhetoric, such as Judy at QCR, that her hard work as a systems person doing largely rhetorical work actually has a material effect on conditions in the real world. This project is motivated by my more general observation that knowledge workers easily lose sight of the efficacy of their work or find it difficult to explain what its outcomes are (when asked, "What do you do?" the answer is, "Write e-mails and go to meetings").

All I have done in this chapter, certainly, is to read the savvy rhetorical work of early-learning professionals from a Latourian perspective. Yet, it is my argument that this reading affords composition new claims about the efficacy of rhetorical work. A postcritical perspective affords us the claim that QCR workers, as rhetors, as compositionists of successive translations into action (*PH* 182), have the agency to affect *material* change for children in child care. From a critical perspective, this agency is afforded to them by their positioning in the organizational hierarchy of QCR and the governmental structures of early learning in Washington State. From a Latourian perspective, however, their agency is coextensive with these powerful structures. Their agency is an effect of their association with the whole assemblage and their work to enact, maintain, and extend it. In other words, Latour asks, "Who performs the action?": "Agent 1 plus agent 2 plus agent 3. Action is a property of associated entities" (*PH* 182).

The coextensiveness between individual and structure afforded by Latour's notion of agency also extends to the full historicity of the sedimentation and accretion of efforts by child-care advocates to provide and improve care for young children. This continuity reveals the limitations of what can be traced in such a short essay, but it also opens up the topos "quality" and its current efficacy for child-care advocates. Judy's work, along with the contemporary Thing of quality child care, is but an outcome (or an effect) of the long history of early learning in the United States, a history that includes over one hundred years of largely failed efforts among early-learning advocates to secure public will and public finding for universal child-care access. Fifty years ago, the Thing in early learning was not school-like quality child care but President Lyndon Baines Johnson's war on poverty and the inclusion of child care as a welfare benefit. Over one hundred years ago, the Thing was philanthropy by the social elite to get the waifs of the destitute, quite literally, off the dirty streets and into sanitary nurseries (Rose). Today, state- and national-level child-care advocacy organizations are working to raise public will for quality rating and improvement systems that are warranted by scientific data and economic arguments.

If the Thing of quality child care is an outcome of this longer history, then beginning the description of Judy's work in this chapter with her enrollment in the QRIS communications project is an arbitrary beginning that occludes the ongoing contingencies that threatened to upend the campaign at any time. Although in the field episode the QRIS model was construed as uncontested and stable (or black-boxed), the model's lack of quantitative validation, along with the lack of the full support of the state legislature, introduced additional contingency into Judy's work. This contingency also fueled her skepticism about the QRIS initiative and new initiatives, in general. In an interview she said, "New programs pop up all the time. Oh, we're going to start this, oh, we're going to start this, and it's like, could we just pick five really good things and do those?" For Judy, the state's new QRIS model for quality child care was just another initiative that would likely come and go as the political will for it, and with that its financial backing, waxed and waned. As it was, the QRIS initiative fell victim to the Great Recession when the state's budget indefinitely postponed its full testing and deployment.

Examining the coextensiveness of Judy's work with the historicity of the QRIS model reveals why making a Thing of quality child care is so difficult—her work is just another small effort within a long history of struggle and failure. As a result, Judy and her colleagues have to continue to "break their backs to make something as delicate as a thing" (Grabill 203). Even now, the Thing of *quality* child care remains extremely contingent, and it is only because of the continuous efforts of advocates like the staff at QCR to keep the quality topos in circulation that it is increasingly a matter of public concern and materially available to a growing number of children. In other words, without Judy's work, child care would not exist as a matter of public concern for unlicensed caregivers. This conception of her work is a substantive alternative to the idea of work as writing e-mails and going to meetings. Although Judy does, in fact, write a lot of e-mails and spend a lot of time in meetings with her colleagues, viewing Judy's work from a Latourian perspective makes visible how it has material consequences for real people that would disappear if she ceased her work.

In this reconceptualization of Judy's work and of knowledge work, more broadly, is an answer to the question, "What is the value of ANT for rhetoric?" After all, ANT as a methodology demands putting aside the notion of "the context for writing," a notion that composition has spent decades broadening and refining (from generic forms to the cognitive, then to the historical, institutional, social, cultural, technological, and sociotechnical). To abandon context is in many ways a tall order, an order that a fictional graduate student engaged in a Socratic dialogue with his professor in Latour's book *Reassembling the Social* struggles to understand. The student, desiring to be a good researcher by applying a well-articulated framework to his data, keeps wanting to step off the trail to context, to look back or down at the trail as if the trail were crossing a previously well-mapped region. After being admonished by his professor for his foolishness, the student asks with some sense of desperation "So, what can it [ANT] do for me?" The professor responds,

> The best it can do for you is to say something like, "When your informants mix up organization, hardware, psychology, and politics in one sentence, don't break it down into neat little pots; try to *follow the link* they make among those elements *that would have looked completely incommensurable* if you had followed normal procedures." That's all. (*RS* 141–42; emphasis added)

So ANT is about doing something. This essay has argued that tracing the translations that associate two seemingly incommensurable things makes visible how rhetoric mediates associations among actors and actants "in such a way that [it] *make[s] others do things*" (*RS* 107; original emphasis). It is a methodology for answering questions like: how does a rhetorical model for quality child care become a child's circle game? How does a new statement from climate scientists become a new frog habitat? Or, as Latour has sought to answer across his many works: how do we cross the boundary between signs and things? (*PH* 185).

This methodology has its hazards, however, because it is all too easy to mistake the tracing of actors in a network and arguing for their interconnectedness as the point of the methodology. The network, it turns out, is not the Thing after all, even though in a textual account, such as this essay, it is difficult to resist the immutability of the page and the characters and objects that it narrates. But when the increasingly frustrated graduate student implores to his professor, "My company executives [his research participants], are they not forming a nice, revealing, powerful network?" (*RS* 142), the professor replies, "Maybe, I mean, surely they are—but so what?" He goes on to tell the student,

> Being connected, being interconnected, or being heterogeneous is not enough. It all depends on the sort of action that is flowing from one to another, hence the words "net" and "work." It's the work, and the movement, and the flow, and the changes that should be stressed. . . . ANT is more like the name of a pencil or a brush than the name of a specific shape to be drawn or painted. (*RS* 143)

And this, in the end, is it: Latour's methodology does not require training in Latour's thought. This can be a maddeningly difficult notion to accept. Latour's pencils and brushes are not just for researchers, even though only researchers trained in his thought would know that they wield these tools as they do their own work. From my perspective, which is largely shaped by the questions and aims of the fields of professional and technical communication, ANT is a perspective for understanding the nature of work and knowledge work, in particular. In other words, knowledge work (which comprises largely rhetorical activity) is the methodology of doing ANT, the act of assembling a Thing or doing the "net work" to enact, extend, or maintain an assemblage—just what I recounted Judy doing in this essay or what I do as a writing researcher (Grabill 205; Spinuzzi 16). We are both net workers, mutually defining each other as we assemble a Thing (writing studies research in my case; quality child care in hers), all in service of our own ends.

## Notes

1. All the names of organizations and individuals have been changed. This study was conducted with the approval of the University of Washington's Institutional Review Board. QCR granted the author written permission to reproduce any elements of their official publications.

2. It is important to maintain that to "compel doing" does not in any way refer to the application of physical, psychological, moral, or governmental force—just as in classical rhetoric, such an action would be arhetorical.

## Works Cited

Ackerman, John M., and David J. Coogan, eds. *The Public Work of Rhetoric: Citizen-Scholars and Civic Engagement*. Columbia: U of South Carolina P, 2010. Print.

Callon, Michel. "Some Elements of a Sociology of Translation: Domestication of the Scallops and the Fishermen of St. Brieuc Bay." *Power, Action and Belief: A New Sociology of Knowledge?* Ed. John Law. London: Routledge, 1986. 196–233. Print.

———. "Techno-economic networks and irreversibility." *A Sociology of Monsters? Essays on Power, Technology and Domination.* Ed. John Law. London: Routledge. 1991. Print.

Grabill, Jeffrey T. "On Being Useful: Rhetoric and the Work of Engagement." Ackerman and Coogan 193–208. Print.

Latour, Bruno. *Aramis.* Cambridge: Harvard UP, 1996. Print.

———. "From Realpolitik to Dingpolitik: Or How to Make Things Public." *Making Things Public: Atmospheres of Democracy.* Ed. Latour and Peter Weibel. Cambridge: MIT P, 2005. 14–41. Print.

———. "On Interobjectivity." *Mind, Culture, and Activity* 3.4 (1996): 228–239. Print.

———. *Pandora's Hope: Essays on the Reality of Science Studies.* Cambridge: Harvard UP, 1999. Print.

———. *The Pasteurization of France.* Cambridge: Harvard UP, 1988. Print.

———. *Reassembling the Social: An Introduction to Actor-Network-Theory.* New York: Oxford UP, 2005. Print.

———. "Technology Is Society Made Durable." *A Sociology of Monsters: Essays on Power, Technology and Domination.* Ed. John Law. London: Routledge, 1991. 103–131. Print.

———. *We Have Never Been Modern.* Cambridge: Harvard UP, 1993. Print.

Miller, Carolyn R. "Genre as Social Action." *Quarterly Journal of Speech* 70.2 (1984): 151–167. Print.

Rose, Elizabeth. *A Mother's Job: The History of Day Care, 1890–1960.* New York: Oxford UP, 1999. Print.

Spinuzzi, Clay. *Network.* Cambridge: Cambridge UP, 2008. Print.

# 16. Tracing Uncertainties: Methodologies of a Door Closer

W. Michele Simmons, *Miami University*
Kristen Moore, *Texas Tech University*
Patricia Sullivan, *Purdue University*

*Scenario 1*

In Hamilton, Ohio, a postindustrial river town that once thrived with paper mills, disparate groups have been trying to revitalize the town for nearly a decade. Yet, at first glance, few revitalizing activities seem to create a sustainable sense of community across a town populated by inertia and skepticism of calls for involvement. City officials are puzzled why a "Meet Hamilton" committee—whose goal is to bring townwide awareness to the history and local treasures of each of the town's communities—finds themselves talking with a roomful of citizens when in one community and a room of three citizens when they meet with another.

*How do researchers study the multiple forces (events, documents, values, inertia, and sense of place) generated by multiple groups pursuing different agendas, all in the name of civic engagement and social capital?*

*Scenario 2*

In Springfield, Illinois, a city built around railroads, the advent of high-speed rail calls for an environmental impact study (EIS) aimed at determining an approach to building rail infrastructure that accommodates stakeholders citywide. As with many EISs, the deliberations surrounding the new railway fuel heated debates about community values, economic growth, and the needs of the city while also reigniting decades of racial tensions that date back to the 1908 race riots.

*How do researchers and technical communicators account for both the various concerns of citizens and other nonhuman actants?*

*Scenario 3*

When a faculty meeting erupts into bitter arguments that prevent a vote on a proposed course change, a research team notes they have been told of analogous outbursts during "routine" institutional change at other institutions. So they begin seeking unexpected outbursts that disrupt or "stop down" mundane institutional processes. As they gather stories, many instances run hot with unresolved emotion and/or recriminations about being blindsided.

*Why does emotion surprise faculty, and how might rhetorical research put that surprise into perspective?*

Approached as sites of rhetorical study, these scenarios challenge many conventional methodologies; they house sites of complex processes and relations and are, therefore, imbued with multiple unstable relationships. Studying such sites traffics in methodological uncertainty and urges us to reflect while we study. Bruno Latour's actor-network-theory (ANT) work[1]—that emerges through his research (or his doing,[2] as in *Aramis* or *Making of Law*) and his treatises on methodologies (his doing-once-removed, as in *Science in Action* or *Reassembling the Social*)—navigates analogous uncertainties. As a "doer" of research, Latour confronts complex interactions that depend on communication (some recognized as rhetoric, others less so). Latour's efforts help with the messy, complex, and unstable rhetorical research sketched in these scenarios. His ANT aims "to trace more sturdy relations and discover more revealing patterns by finding a way to register the links between unstable and shifting frames of reference rather than by trying to keep one frame stable" (*RS* 24). This chapter accommodates his mapping of both instabilities and patterns to complex rhetorical research.

Although Latour seems to eschew the label of methodologist in *Reassembling the Social*, he urges us, through both his studies and treatises, to actively resist articulating methods that either trap us in their certainty or draw overly stable portraits.[3] As a corrective to more traditional methods, Latour turns to tracing associations (among people, processes, nonhuman actants) as a way to expunge the presumption that "the social" grounds all sociological inquiries (or that a study's goal is to describe a preexisting sociality). He also articulates associations that emerge from a mad tracing of processes. Latour insists that researchers need to relocate, redistribute, and connect associations in order to flatten their social worlds enough to build a true collective; this approach allows "the collective [to] have enough room to collect itself" (172). Rephrased in rhetoric's terms, we come to these questions: How do we assemble accounts of complex contexts that are alert to the ways our methodologies and ethical allegiances limit and/or privilege particular understandings of context? And how do we build rhetorical knowledge from such limited or privileged positionings? We look to a few of Latour's studies and ask: How *does* he *do* method/ology? How might we then secure a praxis of methodology that situates practices and theory within particular research contexts?

## Latour Expands the Sociological Gaze

Latour troubles traditional approaches to studying the social through his career-long commitment to nonhuman actants and how they "fit into" the social. He opens "Mixing Humans and Nonhumans Together: The Sociology of a Door-Closer," a methodological discussion in science/technology, by posing a question: "Is sociology the study of social questions, or is it the study of associations?"—and answering—"The most liberal sociologist often discriminates against nonhumans" (298). Through this call and response, Latour (writing as Jim Johnson) commits both to a long-term devotion to the "humble, nonhuman" depicted there as a door-closer and also to the careful tracing of associations that uncovers and celebrates uncertainties. His move redraws research boundaries in ways necessary for science/technology studies to move beyond laboratory processes, procedures, equipment, components, reactions, documentation, and so forth and to require (the possibility of) agency for all involved. Johnson/Latour embraces rigorous tracing of associations and extends the boundaries of what counts as an actant, and this move forges his research practices that allow the mundane to display agency. While neither he nor we think his approach sufficient as a stand-alone rhetorical methodology, his gift for accommodating the uncomfortable complication intrigues us.

ANT productively irritates other established methodological approaches (by including a broader spectrum of actants) and also helps rhetorical researchers recognize the complex, unstable arenas of their work. Latour's approach to tracing (enacted repeatedly from different standpoints) helps researchers enact critical methods in rhetorical studies and satisfies methodologists' requirements for "rigor" while producing an unstable, uncertain portrait (or palimpsestic map) of rhetorical sites that is more attentive to the ethical urgings to be more inclusive, more in tune to shifting identifications and to what is traditionally hidden.

In its reliance on uncertainties as a heuristic, Latour's ANT insists researchers resist and refuse the assumed, the foundational, and the stable in systematic and rigorous ways. Because stability is exclusionary, Latour-like unstable portraits likely reveal connections otherwise obscured. As a doer of research, Latour flips context, so that he constructs rather than uncovers research contexts; this allows him to flatten the research space and trace associations without presumptive and preliminary framings of how they will associate. Rather than focusing on actors, methods, and domains "already taken as members of the social realm" (*RS* 21), Latour's research proceeds by focusing on controversies about "what the universe is made of" (21) and examining uncertainties (of groups, actors, objects, facts, and risky accounts) instead. Latour works to locate, redistribute, and connect associations in ways required for the collective to collect itself (as he so quaintly puts it). Latour's methodology can profitably be seen, then, as a space between ontological assumptions pursued by scholars in object-oriented ontologies and epistemological procedures often pursued in field studies of literacy and public participation. Latour's deployment of ANT teaches us to forge procedures—for example, mapping networks of relationships and moves—that allow us to investigate new materiality, nonhuman actants, and the assemblages (created or inhabited) in ways that do not follow the sociological bent of using macrocategories to interpret microrelationships (or vice versa).

This chapter consults with Latour's ANT-inspired strategies, interested in how they might enable rhetoric's researchers to question existing assumptions and assist them in making sense of the complex and shifting contexts they explore. We locate Latour's ANT in his studies, relying on *Aramis* and *The Making of Law* to draw a(n unstable) portrait of Latour's research practices as well as *Reassembling the Social* and "Mixing Humans and Nonhumans Together" to carve out methodological descriptions. Informed by Latour the Doer, we return to the research scenarios we posed at the start, illustrating how his uncertainties help us construct rhetorically sturdy (and complex) sites for our studies.

## Latour Fashions an Early Methodological Nontreatise

Latour's *Aramis* makes a poor showing in recent scholarship. Seldom cited, perhaps *Aramis* (1996) is overlooked because it is not clearly an account, a methodology, or a dream. Latour endeavored in *Aramis* and also in *Laboratory*

*Life* (1986/1979), *Science in Action* (1987), and, more recently, *Politics of Nature* (2004) to detail the complexity of knowledge and policy production in science. An early investigation into science and transportation policy, *Aramis* is most adventuresome in its complexities. The book evidences Latour's perennial interest in public knowledge making in science and technology, offering montages of notes, maps, interviews, transcripts, and timelines to forge layered accounts of the history of RATP's personal transportation system. Latour often waxes clumsy in methodological pronouncements, so in *Aramis* he turns to performing instability through a "study." He uses devices (e.g., mentor-student exchanges or detective work) to distract readers or massage lacks of transition but does not work his uncertainties framework overtly. Instead, Latour rehearses without explanation an uncertainty later connected (in *Reassembling the Social*) with the false certainties imbued by written accounts. That is why *Aramis* struggles: neither research enough nor treatise enough.

But, perhaps, ambiguity is intended. In *Aramis* Latour fashions a complex case history we might read as fictional but in his language is more factish.[4] *Aramis* honors participants' perspectives and even gives voice to the discarded prototype, treating the machine, reports, timelines, and testimony all as actants. Partaking of the rhythms of empirical work, *Aramis* sketches the failed policy case and reminds us how complex policy work in transportation planning can be. Concomitantly, Latour reveals how rhetorical work was key in/to the project. Latour's approach to "studying" the Aramis project provides an early example of Latourian actor-network-theory, though it does not emphasize method. The multiperspectival accounts of *Aramis* place fact and fiction in close quarters and exploit a reader's desire to read as the writer intends (see Ong). In doing so Latour highlights how a sociological account harnesses varied instabilities into a "real" story through its generic accoutrements, among other things. One needs to read no further than the book jacket to suspect "things" may be slightly "fishy." It calls the author's thinking "deep" (never a good sign for a sociological study), characterizes the book as "a unique and wonderful tale of a technological dream gone awry" (not the normal description), and confesses, "This charming and profound book, part novel and part sociological study, is Bruno Latour at his thought-provoking best." Yes, it recalls anthropology's furor over Clifford Geertz's "Blurred Genres" and history's horror over Hayden White's use of fiction's tropes to categorize founding figures' theories of history—a furor and horror sociology hoped it would escape. Throughout *Aramis* the comforting inclusions of the generic elements of science are deftly undercut by the specter of a machinic dream.

Latour's blurring of scientific report with ethnographic account, novel, and even fairy tale tends to make us forget that he also has recognized the agencies of many nonhuman actants and offered a multivalent account of a failed innovation. While it is obvious that the machine's closing lament is at best a factish dream, its placement in the book lends instability to increasingly stable discussions of sketches, photos, interviews, and documentary records. Which of them also might be dreams?

## Latour's Doings Reveal Uncertainties

*The Making of Law* particularizes methods differently and, we think, more successfully. Latour self-consciously addresses the path he crafts for readers, revealing the purpose behind giving at times too little and at times too much context for his study. Nervous that French administrative courts might be read as abstruse or anachronistic, he notes,

> [T]he reader learns about the site, the precedent, the cases, the functions, morsel by morsel, just when it is needed. . . . This is a zoom-free, context-free ethnographic description. . . . Context is doled out when necessary to give you just enough to move to the next step. (x)

Addressing context not as a preexisting backdrop but, rather, as constituted elements of a network is a methodological move needed in rhetorical methodologies.

Latour remaps context at more than a research-site level; he attacks boundaries of disciplinary thought as well. Calling *The Making of Law* an empirical philosophy, he presses ethnographic work into the service of philosophy. As he traces multilayered practices, we might imagine that ontological overtones hover and worry whether terms will stay where they "belong" in their traditional disciplinary homes or if Latour's flattening of language/knowledge structures might expose or otherwise "get at" thorny issues not normally discussed inside the disciplines. The study operates by layering new associations onto the Conseil d'État's landscape, including relationships among judges (mapped as *Homo Academicus* might), the institutional history of the conseil, cases (re) calling in the specter of law's precedents, and so on. Each chapter surfaces new uncertainties that reside somewhat unresolved but also figure into law's making. Objects and processes (mailboxes, bookcases, books, file folders, tracking devices, chains of evidence) operate as grains of sand in an oyster, ever aiming to instigate the growth of a pearl, constantly spinning value objects of the law until they emerge as the matters of concern that undergird the law they forge. In our minds, *The Making of Law* (in combination with other studies that enact Latour's "doing") provides an apt example of ANT's *practices* as they might contribute to (part of) a rhetorical methodology.

## Latour Makes Uncertainties Productive or Reassembles a Mature Treatise

Latour explains his methodology's processes in *Reassembling the Social* as resembling "a travel guide through a terrain that is at once completely banal . . . and completely exotic," but he also reminds researchers that "'where to travel' and 'what is worth seeing there' is nothing but a way of saying in plain English what is usually said under the pompous Greek name of 'method,' or even worse, 'methodology'" (17). Such processes described in *Reassembling the Social* and also enacted in his studies deliver heuristics that can be rhetorically sensitive.

Latour's processes resonate with critical rhetorical studies that situate themselves within a praxis-based methodology that includes theory, ethics, and politics (see Sullivan and Porter). Our research experiences suggest that this reflexive praxis is particularly important in studies of complex rhetorical sites because it depends upon flexibly forged methods. Latour's disposition to construct rather than find or accept context helps articulate a methodological need for both action and simultaneous reflection-upon-action rather than calcified procedures. In *Reassembling the Social* Latour even proposes ANT as a doing (rather than a way of thinking, as we have seen it used). Latour claims it "is not a coffee table book offering glossy views of the landscape. . . . It is directed at practitioners as a how-to book, helping them to find their bearings once they are 'bogged down in the territory'" (17). Thus, although Latour scoffs at calling ANT a methodology, he reminds us that ANT "offers suggestions rather than imposing itself" (17). As researchers who often find ourselves "bogged down in territory" analogous to Latour's, we can harness Latour's collection of heuristics, noticings, intuitions, and concerns. His five uncertainties—the nature of groups, actions, objects, facts, and risky accounts (22)—function as organizers, in part because they are lodged in practices/ing but also because they approach problems in ways that highlight instabilities and provoke positive change.[5]

Latour uses "uncertainties" to name strategies that assemble and disassemble research sites and forge social research practices. In *Reassembling the Social* those uncertainties aim to curb our inclinations to cling to the stable stories rhetorical research often tells. His strategies and these uncertainties permeate research and can be listed through five "controversies" that make up the universe: groups, actions, objects, facts, and forefronting the writing of the report about these. One controversy is over groupness, which does not exist naturally but only in its formation (which hearkens back to his STS roots in constructivist science) and assembles actors in contradictory ways. Actions and objects, two more traceable controversies, are not just human or stable, as their interactions shift the original goals of the action. A fourth uncertainty is matters of facts versus matters of concern; it is these strategies that make visible the infrastructures that work to fabricate or build stabilizing mechanisms that, in turn, resist the presumed stability of the factual. A risky account, the fifth uncertainty, brings to the forefront the writing of the report and acknowledges each of the uncertainties. "All the five sources of uncertainty are nested into one another, that a report written by some humble colleague who does not even wear a white coat may make a difference" (Latour, *RS* 139).

Since all these uncertainties strategically destabilize research, we might ask, "Where is the order?" or "Which uncertainty when?" For Latour, answers reside in the tracing of practices themselves. Latour suggests researchers pursue the richness of uncertainties instead of making arbitrary determinations—before encounters—about how to structure and attempt to stabilize the research site. And in doing so, he helps us think about how to see research's goal as more dynamic than conclusory.

In drawing on Latour's uncertainties across three different contexts, we respond to calls across rhetoric and composition for more methodological rigor, which often produce procedural responses rather than the more flexible, praxis-based methodologies demanded by studies of public engagement, public planning, and institutional change. Latour's uncertainties prove useful as destabilizing strategies in these divergent areas of study, and we suspect that they can help other researchers handle their individual messy rhetorical research without falsely stabilizing contexts. Following Latour, we resist a "structuralist" response to the questions, "What can [we] do with ANT?" and, instead, offer three tracings of studies in which uncertainties help us assemble and disassemble our rhetorical research projects (*RS* 153).

## Porting the Tracings of Uncertainties into Rhetorical Studies

### Scenario 1: *Civic Engagement in a Postindustrial Town (Methodological Planning)*

The process of revitalizing postindustrial Hamilton provides a messy research site. The city has invested in multiple sustainable-energy initiatives to improve the material conditions of the town. Institutional efforts include implementing a new green campaign with a goal of all city energy generated from renewable resources by 2015, hiring a new city manager from outside Hamilton to rethink sustainability efforts and downtown space, and employing recent postgraduates as city fellows to promote energy-efficiency education and sustainable living and rebrand the city through social media. Town revitalists hope to encourage civic engagement through efforts such as establishing a group of thirty-something professionals who organize social events, creating live-work housing for artists in renovated buildings downtown, developing an amphitheater on the river, incubating small businesses focused on green energy, and organizing town festivals.

With multiple and disparate groups working in loops and zigzags over time toward the goals of community involvement, sustainability, and social capital (goals that are overlapping but not always aligned), how do we study civic engagement strategies coordinated across agencies, groups, and changing conditions? This complex scene seems reminiscent of Latour's mapping of the "range of possibilities" in *The Making of Law* that focuses on the movement of council positions, efforts rather than people. His map traces the entries and exits of council members over years and, he asserts, reveals a movement of "weaving" that illustrates the "connections of states and facts with the scattered pieces of text" (119).

Much research in our field has looked at civic engagement at the level of community-based projects and literacy practices learned in and disseminated from designated literacy centers (Bowdon and Scott; Coogan; Cushman; Flower; Long). These works are important, but because they tend to focus on one literacy center or research site at a time, their methods do not invite us to examine the *relationship* of the multiplicity of forces involved in such large-scale, long-term development and decision making, like the case presented in Hamilton.

Certainly, Michel Foucault's notion of archeology and institutions and James Porter, Patricia Sullivan, Stuart Blythe, Jeffrey Grabill, and Libby Miles's notion of institutional critique offer us a way to identify and critique the unequal distribution of power of a multitude of institutional forces that often works to circumvent civic participation and engagement, but institutional critique alone does not account for the significant influences of relationships (across time and constituencies) among a series of public meetings, geographical constraints, the planning documents, the weather, and the ideologies in a town-revitalization project. But how can we trace the procedure and development of these actors, initiatives, and their activities in ways that allow us to better understand how publics can work? Latour suggests that researchers resist the traditional urge to set up particular groups to study at the start. For Latour, the arbitrariness of such a priori decisions confuse rather than illuminate work that is done (*RS* 34). Rather, he advises us to watch the actors that make up their set of associations. In a town such as Hamilton, the human actors in the civic groups overlap as do the nonhuman meeting spaces and agendas. At the same time, actants leave and join, constantly making and remaking groups that remain unstable. This approach, Latour contends, is more likely to reveal traces of their activity of group formations because the focus is on the actants, not the analysis of the researcher.

Latour's second source of uncertainty involves making someone do something (like engage). One complexity of studying long-term civic engagement in a town is that the location of action constantly shifts and the actants of one group may influence the original goals of other groups. Action is not transparent but rather taken over by a series of actors. The actors are made to act by other actors—other events, documents, geographical locations. Rather than focus on action, Latour urges us to consider what is acting and how. The puppet, Latour asserts, does influence the actions of the puppeteer (*RS* 59). It is not helpful to try to identify one direct cause of a successful engagement because the multiplicity of actors, human and nonhuman, involved influence one another into a network of forces that create a particular situation. For example, one town festival, IceFest, is organized by The City of Sculpture Committee, while another, Operation Pumpkin, complete with a pumpkin trebuchet, is organized by a less formally arranged volunteer group. A different assembly of individuals organizes meetings in different wards and areas of the town to bring townwide awareness to the history and gems of each community. While the various groups share a desire to revitalize Hamilton, their goals differ in ways that make it difficult to focus on any shared action. Identifying and focusing on the actors and their relationships to one another reveal a bigger picture that is more aligned with researching long-term town revitalization. As we write up the research, we don't choose which of the many groups involved in civic engagement we will study, rather, we watch actors assembling and disassembling at any given time and find data in the traces of those assemblings and disassemblings.

### Scenario 2: *On Studying Transportation Planning (Methodological Analysis)*

In Springfield, Illinois, an environmental impact study was launched to determine how the anticipated additional rail traffic might be incorporated into the infrastructure for high-speed rail from two metro cities. Our research traced the EIS process and focused specifically on Vortex Communications, one of the consulting firms facilitating the project. Because Vortex Communications is experienced at public engagement and, perhaps, because the company consists primarily of Black women, the EIS steering committee secured them as the experts on inclusive public engagement. The steering committee was confident Vortex Communications could manage the much-anticipated problems in the project, particularly issues of race, which were exacerbated by the EIS because several options for routing rail traffic included a redistribution of rail traffic to the Tenth Street corridor, a corridor that already served as a racial dividing line. Doubling the rail traffic through the corridor would thicken this dividing line and reiterate the "fact" that the east side of town was merely a throughway—not, as one citizen put it, a place to live but a place to stop in on your way to a better place.

The complexities of laying out the context for this story—even now—demonstrate the tricky nature of this kind of study: Who participated in these deliberations? Was the racial divide a fact to be taken seriously by groups running the study? Such questions invite a tracing of uncertainties—frameworks for ethically understanding not only questions about deliberation but also the racial tensions at the center of this case. Such tensions also illumine a primary concern for Latour: how do the concerns of human actants rub up against the concerns introduced by nonhuman actants?

In Springfield, various nonhuman actants greatly affected the deliberations and decision-making process in overt ways. Given the challenges brought by doubling train traffic through the city of Springfield, many citizens preferred an alternative presented early in the project: reroute all the train traffic around the city. This suggestion, it seemed, solved many problems: new rails could be built explicitly for high-speed rail, would not exacerbate racial tensions, and would also prevent the disruption of the medical district, located near one existing track. As we traced the project, however, engineers and surveyors discovered marshland just outside the city that would not allow for this particular alternative. Though human actants found their needs best suited by the reroute, the marshland became a figuratively vocal participant in the study: there was simply no way to proceed with that option. And so the study team dismissed the reroute and, it seems, allowed the marshland itself to have its way in the deliberations. Indeed, the marshland was an actant in the deliberative process of the EIS, a *nonhuman* actant whose concerns rivaled those of the citizens.

Latour disparages science study's oversimplification of nonhuman actants as matters of fact or, for that matter, their tendency to rely on matters of fact in research. In conceptualizing matters of fact as less stable matters of concern, Latour provides a frame for investigating the traces of both human and nonhuman actants.

> We don't know yet how all those actors are connected, but we can state as the new default position before the study starts that all the actors we are going to deploy might be *associated* in such a way that they *make others do things*. (*RS* 107; original emphasis)

In Springfield, as we traced the uncertainty surrounding the matters of concern (actants traced with their associations), we unearthed new accounts of the project, particularly as historic racial tensions, a nonhuman actant with a wide range of associations, proved a powerful matter of concern in the Springfield Corridor Project. Indeed, where race is certainly tied to human actants, its associations are also tied to historic events and material objects, decidedly nonhuman actants.

Following ANT prompted a cycle of translations, as the racial tensions were brought to bear upon the decision-making project. For Latour (and most who study science or technology), translation is a practice that situates and resituates actors in collectives, projects, or associations, as it connects context with content.[6] Taken methodologically, acts of translation produce associations; they also transform *matters of fact* into matters of concern. In the Springfield case, the concerns surrounding race tended to be dismissed (at least initially) by both engineers and committee members as mere emotional responses to current railway configurations. In seeing racial tensions as a matter of concern, the public engagement specialists (and we) performed acts of translation, reinvigorating the project with a deeper understanding of the ways the 1908 race riot, the Tenth Street corridor, and the new infrastructure for high-speed rail were associated. In addressing race directly in this study, the practice of translation and the framing of uncertainties became central to an ethical methodology. Latour reminds us that creating false stabilities promotes an artificial study of the social—and this certainly was true as we studied the Springfield case. The racial tensions proved unstable, though we certainly could have artificially stabilized them as a matter of fact; through multiple, recursive translations, we engaged in an act of assembling, reassembling and disassembling the site. But more to the point, this study, like *Aramis*, was imbued with uncertainty, which when used as a frame served as a series of methodological actions and simultaneous reflections upon them.

### Scenario 3: *On Studying Institutional Change (Reflection on Uncertainties)*

Libby Miles, W. Michele Simmons, and Patricia Sullivan documented emotion-filled stories that erupted during institutional change, asking, "How might organizations recover from problems that grow out of emotional disruptions?" In order to study this phenomenon, they deployed Latour's ANT to trace small interactions and then redistributed the theorizing to how and why those local interactions happened. Then they extended the study to a national initiative to change Classification of Instructional Programs (CIP) codes.[7] Using ANT, they tracked temporal data (uncertainties about groups and actions) and linked uncertainties about mundane acts with institutional cultures. Of particular interest was how factual answers (e.g., "What is your program's CIP code?") morphed into programmatic, institutional, or disciplinary concerns (and how nonhuman actants gained rhetorical voice). By making these how and why moves, Latour might argue that a third move surfaced and offered more space for groups to collect than the study's originating macrotheories would have predicted or allowed. Seeking emotional flashes helped the researchers see spaces for deliberation that needed to be nurtured, how mundane practices matter (within and across institutions), and the ways in which portable strategies (heuristics and tactics) might emerge. Tracings functioned as a methodology-in-the-making in which triggers and flashpoints of local happenings and mundane, associated practices delivered opportunities for doing rhetorically interested institutional work.

Miles, Simmons, and Sullivan's original study maps how flares of emotion might be turned through rhetoric toward deliberation. They next followed a hunch that tracing disciplinary-program reclassification might open a local or national window to witness disciplinary change in conversation or conflict with local actions or concerns. Direct contrast might reveal more about the nature of "local" in the construction of institutions of higher learning, particularly if addressed through an administrative topic. So, the researchers were not surprised by indications of (usually angry) emotion in a survey that may draw administrative reporting: factual questions activated nerves of concern. Respondents emoted in open-ended questions about names chosen for program codes (by a homogenous committee) and how those names clashed with their own understandings of the field's disciplinary divisions. Participants also would often dismiss program commonalities, claiming theirs to be one of a kind. Indeed, their "hero" stories of institutional change resonated with ways that classroom lore accumulates. Although Latour might remind us "that we are never alone in carrying out a course of action" (*RS* 44), desire for uniqueness seemed powerful to the institutions studied. Actants struggled against perceived lacks of agency—which murmur "we cannot (re)make our organizations"—in order to forge stories that celebrate resistances and triumphs they tout as unique to their situations. It read as part of the mechanisms separating local and disciplinary.

In terms of scope this third example pales in comparison to the Hamilton and Springfield ones: not firmly fixed in time (though not untimely), more likely to be approached disciplinarily, and not as complex (though it may contribute long-term disciplinary survival). It operates along the seams of Latour's third source of uncertainty, namely that the CIP code itself is a humble, mundane agent of disciplinary architecture and one with some power. Though mundane, it can trigger outbursts, such as "My program is NOT a subset of Rhetoric and Composition." The injection of emotion into normally sedate institutional discussion adds uncertainty that lobbies powerfully for recognition, just as Latour could not ignore the emotions engendered by Aramis's demise.

## A Final, Shared Uncertainty

Across these scenarios, we share one uncertainty, namely the limits of writing reports and the risks accompanying any accountings for the social through writing. Latour reminds us, "We start in the middle of things," and in each of the studies we recount here, we generate a story that we would rightly label inaccurate, translated, and uncertain (*RS* 123). Our struggle to account through writing draws attention to the fifth uncertainty: interrogation of the texts that account for our research. In *Aramis* Latour troubles the notion of genre in his recounting of the project and does so self-consciously. We heed his advice, attempting neither to objectively report nor to use our accounts as stabilizers. Rather, our texts add additional cues for uncertainty that other methodologists also recognize (see Van Maanen). Of course, Latour's uses of uncertainty move beyond the textual and trouble the function of objectivity and, in turn, objects themselves. Indeed, Latour draws together textual concerns with those of tracing and networks, seeing the text as yet another actant in a localized network. "A good text," he maintains, "elicits networks of actors when it allows the writer to trace a set of relations defined as so many translations" (*RS* 129). And so in what Latour might call a final act of translation (to the page), he solidifies the uncertainty that draws us, as researchers, to his actor-network-theory.

In "Mixing Humans and Nonhumans Together," Latour methodically poses problems that arise when investigating even the most mundane problems. He models tracings that not only unearth a variety of actants and uncertainties but also assemble and disassemble a collective of associations. It is this move that frees us as researchers to investigate messy, mundane, and complex sites.

The three cases we present here demonstrate the flexibility of ANT and broad applicability of ANT across rhetorical studies. Although all five uncertainties aren't illustrated in each example, we demonstrate ANT's use in studying complex groups, broad institutional projects, and more mundane institutional problems. In other words, we agree with Latour's abiding vision that ANT is not a whole-piece methodology. Its flexible practices (tracing, translating, assembling, disassembling) strengthen cooperating methodologies but only when ANT's time-consuming practices are warranted by the complexity of the study. We think Latour would advocate a continued interrogation of the limits of ANT. Latour's work, for example, helps in identifying the marsh as an agentive force in scenario 2 but not so much in sorting gendered or racial dimensions of any of these studies. Perhaps it is that his universe is action-filled, and, thus, it collects and nourishes human stories of action and nonhuman stories of mundane work. We in rhetoric and professional communication seek methodological strategies that enable a more inclusive landscape of participants. Where some critical methodologies in rhetoric address the ways human participants are accounted for and respected (e.g., Cushman), they rarely assist in expanding the landscape of participants in the inventive ways Latour does. As scholars begin foregrounding material factors to better understand political decisions, some contrast material with discursive factors (Haraway; Hekman), and others focus more directly on seeing the material as visible and important (Coole and Frost; Bennett). We suggest that ANT contributes to a complex methodological strategy that better attends to collectives that Latour so famously highlights. He helps us see temporary forces that disrupt our field's most precious research assumptions and render us susceptible to conflicting beliefs about knowledge making. As a critical methodology, his work continuously invents new ways to needle the status quo in productive ways. If we begin studies with the assumption that nonhuman actants can and should be included and seen as agents, we make a space for recognizing and interrogating the material realities of power outside of discourse alone. Because methodological strategies in rhetorically based studies happily draw on diverse approaches and sometimes layer methods to accommodate our specific inquiries, contexts, and problems, we see our own methodologies reciprocally complicated by his sociological take on the dangers of too-certain methodology. Latour helps us notice the obvious or mundane or unremarkable in a complex and networked world and give it more actants, more actions, more potential relations (ethical, political, social, and so on). Our work can be better when we do so.

## Notes

1. John Law defines ANT, "Actor network theory is a disparate family of material-semiotic tools, sensibilities, and methods of analysis that treat everything in the social and natural worlds as a continuously generated effect of the webs of relations." He goes on to qualify that while ANT can be described abstractly, it is an approach, not a theory: "I've talked of 'it,' an actor network theory, but there is no 'it.' Rather it is a diaspora that overlaps with other intellectual traditions. . . . [Also] if all the world is relational, then so too are texts. ("Actor Network" 141–42). Latour's version of ANT, as it is revealed in most detail in *Reassembling the Social*, does not stray too far from Law's definition. It draws energy from a rejection of "social" as an ontological given and charts a guidebook for like-minded researchers. Latour contends,

> ANT is an argument not about the "social" but about the *associations* which allow connections to be made between non-social elements. ANT . . . tried first to provide a social explanation of scientific facts, failed to do so, and then, from this failure, it drew the conclusion that it was the project of a social explanation of *anything* that was wanting. ("Remodernization" 35; original emphasis)

2. We are using "doing" and "doer" in this chapter to refer to research studies conducted by Latour. Latour and Peter Weibel also are "doers" as exhibitors. *Iconoclash* and *Making Things Public* document those do-ings, but we do not include them in this chapter.

3. In *Reassembling the Social*, Latour denounces the idea that he is a methodologist, sociologist, or scientist. But he often comments on what he is and is not, with his more recent allegiance his own construction of philosophy but with the caveat that he means his own construction of that discipline. In *We Have Never Been Modern*, for example, he says, "I have done my job as philosopher and constituent by gathering together the scattered themes of a comparative anthropology" (145). And recently in *The Making of Law*, he claims, "Although there is no clear description for what I am doing, the closest is that of an empirical (not an empiricist) philosopher" (x).

4. While Latour documents the outcomes of a French subway project, he also speculates—and takes seriously—what the subway itself is thinking.

5. We acknowledge that practice might suggest a more systematic habit, but we lean toward practice with the understanding that it is flexible in its application.

6. Taking translation as a practice moves away from more contained approaches to translation seen, for example, in Callon, Lascoumes, and Barthe. They take translation as an operation in three stages: (1) macrocosm to microcosm, (2) research collective at work (generally the laboratory), and (3) return to the big world. This series of translation allows for networks to be followed and traced. As an in situ practice, however, the act of translation is messier and less stable—particularly in the public sphere, where the laboratory and the "big world" are, in effect, the same thing. In his research practices and methodological work, we see Latour coupling uncertainties and translations, unsettling the versions of translation that deploy it as a procedural technique.

7. Louise W. Phelps and John M. Ackerman describe the initiative started in the doctoral consortium of programs in rhetoric and composition (and taken up by the CCCC Visibility Project) to gain long-term recognition for the field. The initiative established a distinctive code for graduation data (CIP codes are the degree codes) assigned by colleges and then used by the National Center for Education Statistics to describe higher education.

## Works Cited

Bennett, Jane. *Vibrant Matter: A Political Ecology of Things*. Durham: Duke UP, 2010. Print.

Bourdieu, Pierre. *Homo Academicus*. Trans. Peter Collier. Palo Alto: Stanford UP, 1988. Print.

Bowdon, Melody, and J. Blake Scott. *Service Learning in Technical and Professional Communication*. New York: Addison, 2003. Print.

Callon, Michel, Pierre Lascoumes, and Yannick Barthe. *Acting in an Uncertain World: An Essay on Technical Democracy*. Cambridge: MIT P, 2011. Print.

Coogan, David. "Service Learning and Social Change: The Case for Materialist Rhetoric." *CCC* 57.4 (2006): 667–693. Print.

Coole, Diane, and Samantha Frost, eds. *New Materialisms: Ontology, Agency, and Politics*. Durham: Duke UP, 2010. Print.

Cushman, Ellen. *The Struggle and the Tools: Oral and Literate Strategies in an Inner City Community*. Albany: State U of New York P, 1998. Print.

Flower, Linda. *Community Literacy and the Rhetoric of Public Engagement*. Carbondale: Southern Illinois UP, 2008. Print.

Foucault, Michel. *The Archeology of Knowledge and the Discourse on Language*. Trans. A. M. Sheridan Smith. New York: Harper, 1972. Print.

———. "The Subject and Power." *Michel Foucault: Beyond Structuralism and Hermeneutics*. Ed. Hubert L. Dreyfus and Paul Rabinow. Chicago: U of Chicago P, 1982. 208–226. Print.

Geertz, Clifford. *Local Knowledge: Further Essays in Interpretive Anthropology*. 1983. New York: Basic, 2000. Print.

Haraway, Donna. *Modest_Witness@Second_Millenium.FemaleMan_Meets_Oncomouse: Feminism and Technoscience*. New York: Routledge, 1997. Print.

Hekman, Susan. *The Material of Knowledge: Feminist Disclosures*. Bloomington: Indiana UP, 2010. Print.

Johnson, Jim [Bruno Latour]. "Mixing Humans and Nonhumans Together: The Sociology of a Door-Closer." *Social Problems* 35.3 (1988): 298–310. Print.

Latour, Bruno (*see also* Jim Johnson). *Aramis, or the Love of Technology*. Trans. Catherine Porter. Cambridge: Harvard UP, 1996. Print.

———. "Is Re-modernization Occurring—and If So, How to Prove It? A Commentary on Ulrich Beck." *Theory, Culture & Society* 20.2 (2003): 35–48. Print.

———. *The Making of Law: An Ethnography of the Conseil D'État*. Trans. Marina Brilman and Alain Pottage. Malden: Polity, 2010. Print.

———. "On Technical Mediation—Philosophy, Sociology, Genealogy." *Common Knowledge* 3.2 (1994): 29–64. Print.

———. *Pandora's Hope: Essays on the Reality of Science Studies*. Cambridge: Harvard UP, 1999. Print.

———. *Politics of Nature: How to Bring the Sciences into Democracy*. Cambridge: Harvard UP, 2004. Print.

———. *Reassembling the Social: An Introduction to Actor-Network-Theory*. Oxford: Oxford UP, 2005. Print.

———. *Science in Action: How to Follow Scientists and Engineers through Society.* Cambridge: Harvard UP, 1987. Print.

———. *We Have Never Been Modern.* Trans. Catherine Porter. Cambridge: Harvard UP, 1993. Print.

———. "Where Are the Missing Masses? The Sociology of a Few Mundane Artifacts." *Shaping Technology/Building Society: Studies in Sociotechnical Change.* Ed. Wiebe E. Bijker and John Law. Cambridge: MIT P, 1992. 225–258. Print.

Latour, Bruno, and Steve Woolgar. *Laboratory Life: The Construction of Scientific Facts.* 1979. 2nd ed. Princeton: Princeton UP, 1986. Print.

Law, John. "Actor Network Theory and Material Semiotics." *The New Blackwell Companion on Social Theory.* Ed. Bryan S. Turner. London: Blackwell, 2009. 141–158. Print.

———. *After Method: Mess in Social Science Research.* London: Routledge, 2004. Print.

Long, Elenore. *Community Literacy and the Rhetoric of Local Publics.* West Lafayette: Parlor, 2008. Print.

Miles, Libby, Michele Simmons, and Patricia Sullivan. "Institutional Change." Panel, Conference on College Composition and Communication, Atlanta. 8 April 2011. Print.

Ong, Walter J. "The Writer's Audience Is Always a Fiction." *PMLA* 90.1 (1975): 9–21. Print.

Phelps, Louise W., and John M. Ackerman. "Making the Case for Disciplinarity in Rhetoric, Composition, and Writing Studies: The Visibility Project." *CCC* 62.1 (2010): 180–215. Print.

Porter, James, Patricia Sullivan, Stuart Blythe, Jeffrey Grabill, and Libby Miles. "Institutional Critique: A Rhetorical Methodology for Change." *CCC* 51.4 (2000): 610–642. Print.

Sullivan, Patricia, and James E. Porter. *Opening Spaces: Writing Technologies and Critical Research Practices.* Greenwich: Ablex, 1997. Print.

Van Maanen, John. *Tales of the Field: On Writing Ethnography.* Chicago: U of Chicago P, 1988. Print.

Weibel, Peter, and Bruno Latour. "Experimenting with Representation: *Iconoclash* and *Making Things Public.*" *Exhibition Experiments.* Ed. Sharon Macdonald and Paul Basu. Oxford: Blackwell, 2008. 94–108. Print.

White, Hayden. *Metahistory: The Historical Imagination in Nineteenth-Century Europe.* Baltimore: Johns Hopkins UP, 1975. Print.

# 17. Dingrhetoriks

Laurie Gries, *University of Florida*

In his introduction to *Making Things Public*, Bruno Latour laments the lack of attention things have received in political thought and study. As he explains, it has long well been understood that different parties assemble around a specific issue—etymologically, a *ding*, or thing—that triggers passionate disputes. On the whole, political philosophers have given due attention to the procedures that enable parties to assemble, be granted authority, discover best speech conditions, and so forth. Yet, whether we are looking to the political philosophies of Thomas Hobbes, John Rawls, Jean-Jacques Rousseau, or Jürgen Habermas, things have been rarely acknowledged; just at the time when they should "be brought in and made to speak up loudly," Latour notes, political science becomes mute (6). A similar argument can be made, I think, about rhetorical study on the whole but especially visual rhetoric, which is my concern here.

As a field of study that came to fruition in the early 1970s with the now-famous Wingspread Conference,[1] visual rhetoric has long been invested in things in that it works hard to investigate how a broad range of visual artifacts—posters, comics, cartoons, film, video games, advertisements, and the like—functions rhetorically to shape society. Yet, in addition to being influenced by semiotics (Goggin), cultural materialism (Trimbur), and rhetorico-hermeneutics (Sánchez, *Function of Theory*), rhetorical study has a long-standing tradition of representationalism that has gotten transposed onto contemporary studies of visual rhetoric (Vivian). A representational framework presumes that visual artifacts can be conceived of and studied as visual language with potential to both refer to and distort that which is being described. Even though pictures have no intrinsic meaning, pictures are presumed to contain or embody meaning, or representational content, that can be fleshed out in semantic terms (Vivian 476). When coupled with transitive models of delivery, pictures, as is the case with discourse, are also presumed to have already been delivered rather than still circulating (Brooke 192). As such, scholars tend to treat pictures as language-like symbols and stable texts, which need to be read, analyzed, and interpreted within specific contexts in order to explain how they persuade a particular audience. As I argue more fully in the following section, such synchronic accounts often end up eclipsing the ways visual things actually acquire the force to reassemble collective life. In effect, just as political science has rendered things mute at the moment they ought to be invited to speak, so, too, has visual rhetoric.

As a remedy to such silencing in political science, Latour introduces *dingpolitik*, a theoretical experiment to inject more realism into political thought and study. In Latour's eyes, *realpolitik* refers to politics that offer "a positive, materialist, no-nonsense, interest only, matter-of-fact way of dealing with naked power relations" ("Dingpolitik" 14). Although realpolitik attempts to offer a realistic way of doing politics in order to combat idealism, realpolitik, according to Latour, is not realistic enough. In response to this lack, dingpolitik—as signified in its slogan "Bring back things!"—attempts to reinscribe realism in political thought, namely, to recognize the importance of things in assembling a public. Such a move, Latour argues, is necessary to compose a more realistic, inclusive account of the phantom public, a mysterious flow of simultaneous micropolitical events that has come to define contemporary existence.

In this chapter I want to explore what a similar theoretical experiment called *dingrhetoriks* might do for studies of visual rhetoric. As dingpolitik attempts to reinject realism into political thought, dingrhetoriks attempts to inject realism into rhetorical theory and study. At the end of his introduction to *Making Things Public*, Latour describes the defining principles of dingpolitik, which include, among other things, realizing that politics is no longer limited to just human beings, objects become things when matters of fact become matters of concern, assemblies are constituted of a multiplicity of assemblages, and the time of succession has given way to the time of simultaneity. The intent of dingrhetoriks, as articulated here, is not to adapt all the principles of dingpolitik to create more thing-infused theories about visual rhetoric (though many principles are certainly relevant) but, rather, to mimic Latour's "quest for composition" in order to construct more realistic accounts of how visual things actually contribute to collective life ("Dingpolitik" 41).

In order to enact this quest for composition in studies of visual rhetoric, Latour's work with actor-network-theory (ANT) and its influence on new materialism are especially useful. While ANT, as described by other scholars in this anthology, is a social theory largely concerned with how collectives assemble and reassemble to create the social, new materialism is an interdisciplinary, cultural inquiry largely concerned with how some of today's most pressing issues come into existence and gather force in the world. In conjunction with ANT, new materialism is useful for dingrhetoriks in that new materialists take things seriously, as they foreground the propensities, affordances, and affectivities of nonhuman entities entangled in complex processes of contingent materialization.[2] To address such inquiries, new materialists are developing new modes of analysis that attest to the agential capacity, contingent relationality, and ontological becoming of things. Such scholarship, I argue, is necessary for studying visual rhetorics in a digital age when new-media images circulate, transform, and affect multiple consequences at viral speeds. While the actions of reading, analyzing, and interpreting visual texts via representational frameworks and within specific contexts have come to dominate studies of visual rhetoric, such disposition cannot account for the viral economy of visual rhetorics, understood here as "a distributed emergence and an ongoing circulation process" (Rice 13). As consequence of this methodological inability, much scholarship in rhetoric inadvertently contributes to what W. J. T. Mitchell calls the "subalternization" of visual things that lack power because they are not invited to speak (33). Drawing on ANT, Annemarie Mol's work with empirical philosophy as well as my own work with iconographic tracking, the research actions of following, tracing, and describing are better equipped to generate more symmetrical, diachronic accounts of how single multiple images contribute to collective life. If we work hard to construct such new materialist accounts, I argue, the visual things that play important roles in collective life might finally be offered a platform to speak.

## Dingplay

At its playful core, dingrhetoriks can be considered a methodological intervention in representational approaches to visual rhetoric. Representational frameworks are omnipresent in visual rhetoric as evident in the following passage taken from Christine Alfano and Alyssa O'Brien's *Envision: Writing and Research Arguments*, a popular visual rhetoric textbook currently in its third edition.

> Everywhere around us, words and images try to persuade us to think about the world in certain ways. . . . We can see this persuasive power especially in *visual texts*, such as the political cartoons and comics you might find on your favorite Weblog. . . . We can understand how . . . a cartoon works by asking questions about its argument, audience, and author. We can *analyze* its elements carefully and then come up with our *interpretation* of the text. When we ask questions and make our own argument about how a text works, we are analyzing how texts can be rhetorical, how they aim at persuading audiences through careful choices made by the writer in composing the text. (2–3; emphasis added)

At the risk of creating a straw man, this textbook description is indicative of the pervasive trend in visual rhetoric to textualize visual objects so that we can read, analyze, and interpret them in order to discover their persuasive power. Such textual treatments have undoubtedly led to productive studies. However, often inherent in this habitus of method is the belief that pictures, like other artifacts, are mediums of communication that lack agency unless scholars project onto pictures their own explanations of intention, meaning, and significance (Marback). Thus, rather than giving pictures their due, scholars tend to impose their representational frameworks onto pictures to make rhetorical sense of those dynamic and agential capacities that so often elude us. In addition, a visual thing's eventful, unfolding life is often neglected in favor of studying that thing within a certain, limited context. In effect, while many visual-rhetoric scholars desire to make visible just how rhetorically powerful visual things are, they often end up "narrowing and limiting a visual thing's projection" (Marback 64) and overlooking the "madness, excess, and ecstasy" a thing experiences as it enters into diverse associations (DeLuca and Wilferth). As such, the actual consequentiality that visual things are said to generate in the world is often eclipsed by a scholar's synchronic account and powerful explanation.

In both theory and practice, dingrhetoriks encourages us to intra-act with visual entities a bit differently than representational approaches.[3] In particular, rather than think about visual texts in terms of symbolic language and signification, we can engage with them as visual things with unpredictable thing power—the strange capacity to exceed their status as objects and catalyze change as they participate if various assemblages—and trace how they contribute to collective life (Bennett xvi–xvii). Dingrhetoriks is especially productive in that it encourages scholars to grapple with a visual thing's abilities to generate change, or, as Jane Bennett puts it, "to animate, to act, to produce effects dramatic and subtle" (6). From a relational perspective that undergirds both actor-network-theory and new materialism, things are different than objects in that things acquire power to shape reality as they become entangled in complex relations with other actants. An actant is Latour's neologism for acknowledging that ability of all things—human and nonhuman—to intervene, to create change, irrespective of their intentionality. Too often, the force of things is dismissed because we create false dualities between subject and object. We assume, in other words, that things are inert tools or objects used by human subjects to whom we typically credit with full-blown agency. As Jean Baudrillard describes, "It is the subject that makes history, it's the subject that totalizes the world," whereas the object is "shamed, obscene, passive" (111). In Latour's terms, this failure especially occurs because we tend to deem nonhuman things to be intermediaries rather than mediators. While intermediaries enter into diverse relations without necessarily transforming them, mediators transform, distort, modify, and so on (*RS* 39). As evidence of this capacity, mediators manifest and leave traces of collective activity that can be empirically investigated and mapped out.

Although such activity can never become fully apparent to a researcher, dingrhetoriks pushes scholars to try their best to empirically account for a visual thing's ongoing enactments in order to learn how it becomes rhetorical with time and space. Too often, as evident in the excerpt from *Envision* above, we tend to undermine visual things, to reduce them downward, in Graham Harman's terms,[4] to their compositional elements. Trained in semiotic and rhetorical analysis and dependent on instrumentalist frameworks, we tend to look at and through a visual thing to its interior relations—or what Levi Bryant might call its endo-relations—to identify that thing's potential to affect change. Such undermining fails to recognize that in addition to a visual thing's compositional design, a thing's external relations—or exo-relations—are just as important in creating the conditions necessary for manipulating reality.[5] This is not to say that a thing's exterior relations are wholly responsible for a visual thing's capacity to affect change, for that would reduce a visual thing upward, or overmine a thing from above in Harman's terms. However, as Bennett notes, "an actant never really acts alone. Its efficacy or agency always depends on the collaboration, cooperation, or interactive interference of many bodies and forces" (21). Simultaneously accounting for a visual thing's internal and emergent, exterior relations is, thus, necessary in order to render manifest how visual things acquire force to catalyze change.

Such attention is especially important for learning how a visual thing contributes to collective life as it circulates and sparks rhetorical activities within a wide sphere or ecology. As Latour reminds us, in many Nordic and Saxon communities, thing or ding refers to issues that bring people together even as it may divide them in the process. For dingrhetoriks, then, visual things not only have an ability to induce cooperation, in a Burkean sense, but also to induce assemblage (and reassemblage). In this Latourian sense, visual things become rhetorical, in part, as a consequence of their ability to seduce other entities into relation with it and participate in various collective actions. Such collectivity is especially intense for many new-media images that circulate at viral speeds and enter into a multiplicity of divergent and seemingly simultaneous associations in physical and digital spaces. New-media images, especially, have a capacity to be "everywhere at once," making it difficult to capture their wild, rhetorical abandon. Yet, as the next section makes clear, if we privilege new verbs in our studies of visual rhetoric, symmetrical, diachronic accounts can be generated to reconstruct, in part, how visual things influence the continual assemblage and reassemblage of collective life.

Dingrhetoriks is also useful for visual rhetoric in that "treating" visual entities as things (rather than texts) draws attention to the ontological and vibrant dimensions of visual rhetoric. Latour explains in *Reassembling the Social*, "To be 'treated like things' . . . is not to be 'reduced' to mere matters of fact, but allowed to live a life as multifarious as that of matters of concern" (255). As matters of fact, things are considered to be transparent, obvious, discrete objects that are easily taken for granted. They are not complicated, as Latour draws on Ludwik Fleck to explain: "they are never simultaneously made through a complex history and new, real, and *interesting* participants in the universe" ("Critique" 234). As matters of concern, things become much more elusive and provocative. Borrowing from Martin Heidegger, things are complex entanglements that cannot be easily identified nor understood, as they are mediating, assembling, gathering many more folds that could be detected if considered to be already delivered ("Critique" 173). As matters of concern, we may not be certain how this mediation occurs a priori, but that is precisely the point with dingrhetoriks. In wondering how things reassemble collective life, we are encouraged to follow a visual thing to see how it becomes rhetorical in divergent ways as it circulates, transforms, induces new associations and affects a multiplicity of consequences.

To account for how a visual thing becomes rhetorically divergent with time and space, it is important to come to grips with a thing's multiple modes of existence. While Latour has done some work in this regard,[6] I find Mol's work with empirical philosophy, which Latour has greatly influenced, more useful. Mol is an ethnographer and anthropologist whose scholarship in many regards exemplifies the productive potential of new materialism. In *The Body Multiple*, Mol pushes us to think about things as body multiples in order to understand how they experience different modes of existence.[7] Body multiples can be thought of as a multiplicity that is constituted by heterogeneous versions that emerge with their own spatiotemporal configurations, yet maintains a sense of whole. In this configuration, things are "single multiple," meaning both one and many (142). Mol uses the example of atherosclerosis to explain how this single disease exists in different modes of existence simultaneously. As her ethnography of this disease in a Dutch university hospital makes evident, atherosclerosis is cohesive: through a range of coordinations, or tasks—such as making images, performing case studies, and so on—it forms and maintains some sense of whole. Yet, without being totally fragmented so that it cannot go under a single name, it concurrently has multiple versions, depending on factors such as what person is discussing it, in what moment and place it is being discussed or treated, and what apparatus is engaging with it. Atherosclerosis is, thus, singular in that it has an actual body but also multiple (many).

In a similar fashion, visual things experience different modes of existence. A single image—say, for example, Shepard Fairey's now-iconic Barack Obama Hope image—materializes in many different forms and takes on different functions via its divergent associations. In this vibrant mode of subsistence—what Latour refers to as the stage when something is alive and undergoing reproduction ("Textbook" 101). Obama Hope is constantly undergoing change, as in each manifestation, it transforms into something different and in many cases takes on different functions. Yet, even as this image undergoes a multiplicity of transformations in its mode of subsistence, a sense of whole also endures, enabling us to follow and observe how it in the singular becomes rhetorical in the multiple. My research tracking the Obama Hope image, for instance, shows that over the last five years, the image has surfaced in multiple genres, such as murals, protest signs, advertisements, art, sculptures, and fashion, just to name a few. In such manifestations, it has been constructed of many surprising materials, such as credit cards, dried beans, pennies, canned vegetables, yarn, spray paint, and even Legos. It has also taken on numerous rhetorical functions as it has become a political actor, novel cybergenre, new-media literacy educator, advocate for remix, and, among many other things, transnational activist. This diversity in form, media, genre, and function makes it difficult to account for a visual thing's vibrant rhetorical contributions to collective life. Especially because its rhetorical life unfolds along divergent and seemingly simultaneous spatiotemporal channels, a lot of time and effort is required to compose a complex account of a single multiple image's rhetorical transformations. But in terms of method, Latour's compositionist work with ANT shows us that if we follow an actant, trace its collective activities, and embrace rich description to create symmetrical accounts, it *is* possible to learn, at least in part, how a single multiple image becomes rhetorical with time and space. We simply need to adopt an anthropologist's work ethic and develop new research methods to do this empirical investigation.

## Dingwork

Iconographic tracking is one such method that draws heavily on Latour's work with ANT, new materialism, and Mol's work with empirical philosophy to investigate how individual images, in multiple modes of existence, reassemble collective life. As I have articulated elsewhere, iconographic tracking employs traditional qualitative and inventive digital research strategies to follow the multiple transformations that an image undergoes during circulation and to identify the complex consequentiality that emerges from its divergent encounters.[8] In terms of qualitative research, iconographic tracking deploys strategies, such as archival research, questionnaires, and interviews, to collect and triangulate data. During latter stages of the research process, approaches, such as CHAT (cultural historical activity theory), also help zoom in on specific collectives to learn how an image undergoes different processes of materialization: design, composition, production, distribution, circulation, transformation, collectivity, and consequentiality. However, new digital technologies create opportunities to invent new research methods, such as iconographic tracking. The rise of visual search engines, such as Google Images and TinEye, in addition to social-media sites, such as Facebook, Flickr, and Twitter, especially are useful for tracking images. Data collection and organization tools, such as Zotero, in conjunction with mapping and visualization tools, such as Google Maps, can also be useful in aggregating, visualizing, and making sense of research findings. Inspired heavily by ANT, iconographic tracking, thus, largely relies on digital research strategies to investigate how an image circulates, transforms, and generates consequences on various scales.

This method is particularly useful, I believe, in that it privileges new verbs by which to research visual rhetoric. Rather than reading, analyzing, and interpreting, this method relies heavily on following, tracing, and describing—research activities that demand the diligent composing habits that anthropologists such as Latour and Mol exhibit in their new materialist studies. This is not to say that reading, analysis, and interpretation are not enacted. This method simply privileges following, tracing, and describing how a visual thing circulates, transforms, and generates consequences in a broad ecology in order to construct the empirical evidence needed to learn how visual things become rhetorical as they reassemble collective life. As Latour explains, to create empirical evidence means to research and write in a way that is as "faithful to experience" as possible (*RS* 240). It means acknowledging things as mediators and, through our studies, listening to them when they say,

> We are beings out there that gather and assemble the collective just as extensively as what you have called so far the social, limiting yourselves to only one standardized version of the assemblages; if you want to follow the actors themselves, you have to follow us as well. (*RS* 240)

It means, as Raúl Sánchez notes in "Outside the Text," engaging in a kind of neo-empiricism that can better account for how visual things are "produced, distributed, received, and redistributed in contemporary systems" (237). While I do not have space to describe the method of iconographic tracking in detail here, I'd like to spend the rest of this chapter focusing on the benefits of following, tracing, and describing for visual rhetoric.

Following is a research strategy ANT researchers use to discover how collectives are held together by the intra-actions of various actants—human and nonhuman, material and semiotic, individual and institutional. Such collective formation cannot be determined by a scholar a priori but, rather, must be discovered by following actants in action. As described by Latour in *Reassembling the Social*, following an actant entails trying "to catch up with their often wild innovations in order to learn from them what the collective existence has become in their hands" (12). Following an actant, perhaps, is most useful in trying to discover why a certain technological system or invention fails to materialize, as modeled by Latour in *Aramis, or the Love of Technology*. Yet, it can also help account for how a system or invention comes into existence and becomes an important "citizen" in collective life. This latter purpose, I believe, is especially useful for visual-rhetoric scholars who wonder how something such as the Obama Hope becomes rhetorical in a viral economy. Such knowledge cannot be constructed by studying a single image in a limited context in reference to location, manifestation, or function; as stated above, such context-dependent studies limit a visual thing's wild abandon. When trying to discover how a visual thing contributes to collective life, then, a scholar must follow an actant acting in all its various manifestations and divergent associations.

Such work also demands a multiscaled approach that makes it possible to trace the collective activities in which a single multiple image participates. According to Latour, tracing entails connecting entities with other entities to construct an actor-network (*RS* 103). For our purposes, it requires both zooming in on a microscale to discover the specific alliances an image establishes within a single collective but also zooming out to account for the network of various collectives in which a single multiple image participates. As stated before, when images experience viral circulation and enter into a multiplicity of divergent relations, it becomes difficult to keep up with and trace its numerous collective activities. Tracing is also difficult because the connections that a single multiple image establishes are often short-lived, making its traces of activity only momentarily visible. "If no trace is produced," as Latour explains succinctly, "they offer no information to the observer and will have no visible effect on other agents. They remain silent and are no longer actors: they remain, literally unaccountable" (*RS* 79). Timing is, thus, of essence when tracing the collective activities of a single multiple image.

Latour teaches us that novel moments of innovation, accidents, breakdowns, strikes, and political events are occasions in which the collective activity of visual things becomes highly visible and, thus, traceable. Interestingly, it was during the social upheaval of the late 1960s when public protests were so prominent in the United States that scholars at the 1970 Wingspread Conference and the National Conference on Rhetoric were inspired to expand conceptions of rhetoric to account for the visual (Edwards 223). During such times, visual things, typically thought of as intermediaries, become overt, active mediators and leave highly visible traces of collective activity. It is no wonder, then, that as visual things, such as protest art and political posters, played significant roles in the various political events of the 1960s, they prompted more scholarly attention to visual rhetoric. Today, we see a similar thing happening with image events—"staged acts of protest designed for media dissemination" (Delicath and DeLuca 315)—such as those produced by groups, such as Greenpeace, WTO protesters, Guerilla Girls, and enacted in protests, such as the Arab Spring and the Occupy movement. In such unfolding events, the rhetorical participation of visual things is hypervisible, making it possible to not only study but also produce theories about their collective actions.

In the past, research in libraries, museums, and other institutional archives was the main resource scholars could rely on to discover such activity. As Latour notes in "Networks, Societies, Spheres," however, "the expansion of digitality has enormously increased the material dimension of networks: the more digital, the less virtual and the more material a given activity becomes" (802). Today, then, thanks to the Internet, the World Wide Web, and other digital technologies, traces of collective activity can be more easily rendered via digital research methods, such as iconographic tracking, that enable us to follow and trace a visual thing's collective actions. Such research, of course, is also responsible for catapulting a visual thing back into action, demonstrating how impossible it is to fully catch up with and/or capture visual things in circulation. Yet, deploying such digital research strategies to follow an actant and trace its diverse activities can help trace the active, rhetorical life of visual things to help us account for their significant contributions to collective life.

To make sure contemporary images have opportunities to speak up about their important and multifaceted contributions to collective life, we also ought to provide descriptive, symmetrical accounts that do not belie their rhetorical complexity. Drawing on Latour, description is a composing act (de-scribing) that ought to be as much a part of one's research methods as following and tracing. De-scribing entails deploying visual actants as networks of mediation in such rich detail that little to no explanation is needed to account for how their actions are distributed across proliferating and fluctuating systems.[9] This point is difficult to accept, as the hypothetical student notes in Latour's imagined dialogue presented in the interlude of *Reassembling the Social*. But, as iterated previously, visual-rhetoric scholars often choose an interpretive framework, grounded in print culture and representationalism, in which to study a visual text within preordained and limited contexts. The problem is that in overrelying on such representational frameworks, we not only, in Sánchez's terms, "underestimate [visual things'] inherent and deep complexity" but also "mischaracterize their relations with other entities" ("Outside the Text" 238). When we preestablish a limited context for our visual-rhetorical studies and focus too much attention on the interiority of a picture, I would add, we also end up missing the multitudes of activities that any given thing becomes involved in when it circulates and engages in a multiplicity of associations.

When coupled with following and tracing in the practice of dingrhetoriks, description, as a method, is better suited to account for how images travel, transform, and acquire power as they both participate in and co-constitute dynamic systems of relations. Description, in this sense, entails foregrounding the actions that emerge from "*an association of actants* . . . in the process of exchanging competencies, offering one another new possibilities, new goals, new functions" (*PH* 182; original emphasis). It entails, in other words, being fully attentive to the traces of activity that one discovers by following an actant intra-acting in a current state of affairs and making the connections, movement, and work of actants fully transparent on the page (*RS* 143–44). This composition of networked mediations can get quite messy and seem impossible to follow, trace, and adequately describe, especially from a new-materialist perspective that recognizes the ongoing materialization of visual matter. However, if diachronic, symmetrical accounts are constructed in which human and nonhuman entities are equally allowed to mediate action their ongoing entanglements, good descriptions can adequately account for the rhetorical complexity we are after. Scholars simply need to trust that their rich, realist descriptions can do the work that we tend to overrely on contextual explanations to do. "Deploy the content with all its connections," Latour claims, "and you will have the context in addition" (*RS* 146).

In Old Norse, the North Germanic language we depended on earlier to define thing or ding, "trust" means "confidence, help." In terms of research actions, to say we trust some *thing*, then, means that we have confidence in its ability to assemble and reassemble collective life, to help bring a diverse array of entities into intra-action to address diverse matters. To a great extent, this trust requires relinquishing our representational, synchronic habits of reading, analyzing, and explaining a visual thing's diverse powers via methods and theories that have come to define who we are as visual-rhetoric scholars. It requires, I would argue, turning to methods such as iconographic tracking and to theories such as actor-network-theory and new materialism to create more room on the page for those visual things that induce us into relations, to make transparent their own multiple, divergent rhetorical becomings. This trust is, perhaps, the most difficult enterprise of dingrhetoriks, especially as it requires that we, as scholars, learn that actants themselves can "make everything, including their own frames, their own theories, their own contexts, their own metaphysics . . . even their own ontologies" (*RS* 147). Yet, from a new materialist perspective, our job, as scholars invested in dingrhetoriks, is to give things their due by creating scholarship that does not undercut a visual thing's ontological becoming, complex relationality, and mysterious thing power.

Latour's scholarship and his influence on new materialism can help visual rhetoric negotiate these methodological difficulties so that more realistic accounts of visual rhetoric can be generated.[10] In particular, via methods such as iconographic tracking, we can follow, trace, and describe how visual things exert force in the world as they circulate, experience multiple modes of existence, and catalyze divergent kinds of change. Such method, I believe, is useful for becoming "more engaged, thoughtful, and creative when arguing about the images that are part and parcel of public culture"—a challenge Robert Hariman and John Louis Lucaites set before us in *No Caption Needed* (20). But iconographic tracking is just one of many methods that could help give things their due. If dingrhetoriks is to be taken seriously, a broad array of things will need to be centered in rhetorical study, and other methods will need to be invented to generate empirical accounts of each thing's unique, distributed, and emergent rhetoricity. I suggest, then, that, especially as we begin to adapt theories and studies of rhetoric in a digital age, we become inventive in our methodological practices. Let's "bring things back" to rhetorical study and see where this experiment in theory and method might take us.

## Notes

1. While Kenneth Burke acknowledges visual forms of symbolic action in his theories about rhetoric in the 1960s, the 1970 Wingspread Conference is credited for prompting the initial publications of visual rhetoric. Position papers from this conference, stating the importance of taking up the visual in rhetorical study, were later published in "The Prospect of Rhetoric," a report of the National Development Project on Rhetoric sponsored by the Speech Communication Association and edited by Lloyd Bitzer and Edwin Black.

2. See Diana Coole and Samantha Frost, *New Materialisms: Ontology, Agency, and Politics*. For an excellent summary of new materialism in relation to rhetorical studies, see also Carl Herndl's conference paper "Rhetoric and the New Materialism" delivered at the Fifteenth Biennial Rhetoric Society of America Conference in Philadelphia in May 2012.

3. "Intra-action" is Karen Barad's neologism for indicating how individual entities become distinct and meaningful within phenomena. See Barad, *Meeting the Universe Halfway*.

4. For more about undermining and overmining, see Graham Harman, *Quadruple Object*, 7–19.

5. See Levi Bryant's discussion of endo-relations and exo-relations in *The Democracy of Objects*.

6. See Latour, "Textbook Case Revisited—Knowledge as a Mode of Existence." See also Latour's newest book *An Inquiry into Modes of Existence*, which came out after I wrote this chapter.

7. I want to thank Douglas Walls from University of Central Florida for turning me on to Mol's book at a Computers and Writing Conference.

8. See my article "Iconographic Tracking: A Digital Research Method for Visual Rhetorics and Circulation Studies" for a detailed description of this method in action.

9. To read Latour's perspective on explanation versus description, see *Reassembling the Social*, 141–56.

10. Realistic accounts, of course, can never fully capture a visual thing's rhetorical eventfulness. As Jacques Derrida has noted, events, by their very nature, cannot be captured (see "Artifactualities"). In addition, see Graham Harman, *Quadruple Object*, in which he discusses how because objects are always withdrawing from us, we do not have full access to them and, thus, can never come to fully know or understand them. We can only, at best, allude to that which might be real but not fully present. For direct discussion of allusion, see Harman, *Quadruple Object*, 68.

## Works Cited

Alfano, Christine, and Alyssa O'Brien. *Envision: Writing and Researching Arguments*. 3rd ed. New York: Pearson, 2011. Print.

Barad, Karen. *Meeting the Universe Halfway: Quantum Physics and the Entanglement of Matter and Meaning*. Durham: Duke UP, 2007. Print.

Baudrillard, Jean. *Fatal Strategies*. New York: Semiotext(e), 1990. Print.

Bennett, Jane. *Vibrant Matter: A Political Ecology of Things*. Durham: Duke UP, 2010. Print.

Bitzer, Lloyd, and Edwin Black, eds. *The Prospect of Rhetoric*. New York: Prentice-Hall, 1971. Print.

Brooke, Collin Gifford. *Lingua Fracta: What We Teach When We Teach about Literacy*. Cresskill: Hampton, 2009. Print.

Bryant, Levi. *The Democracy of Objects*. Ann Arbor: Open Humanities, 2011. Print.

Coole, Diana, and Samantha Frost, eds. *New Materialisms: Ontology, Agency, and Politics*. Durham: Duke UP, 2010. Print.

Delicath, John W., and Kevin Michael DeLuca. "Image Events, the Public Sphere, and Argumentative Practice: The Case of Radical Environmental Groups." *Argumentation* 17 (2003): 315–333. Print.

DeLuca, Kevin, and Joe Wilferth. Foreword. *Enculturation* 6.2 (2009): N. pag. Web. Sept. 2012. <http://www.enculturation.net/6.2/foreword>.

Derrida, Jacques. "Artifactualities." *Echographies of Television: Filmed Interviews*. Ed. Derrida and Bernard Stiegler. Cambridge: Polity, 2002. 1–28. Print.

Edwards, Janis L. "Visual Rhetoric." *21st Century Communication: A Reference Handbook*. Vol. 1. Ed. William F. Eadie. Thousand Oaks: Sage, 2009. 220–227. Print.

Goggin, Maureen. "Visual Rhetorics in Pens of Steel and Inks of Silk: Challenging the Great Visual/Verbal Divide." *Defining Visual Rhetoric*. Ed. Charles Hill and Marguerite Helmers. Mahwah: Erlbaum, 2004. 87–110. Print.

Gries, Laurie. "Iconographic Tracking: A Digital Research Method for Visual Rhetorics and Circulation Studies." *Computers and Composition* 30.4 (2013): 332–348. Print.

Hariman, Robert, and John Louis Lucaites. *No Caption Needed: Iconic Photographs, Public Culture, and Liberal Democracy*. Chicago: U of Chicago P, 2007. Print.

Harman, Graham. *The Quadruple Object*. Winchester: Zero, 2011. Print.

Herndl, Carl G. "Rhetoric and the New Materialism." Paper. Fifteenth Biennial Rhetoric Society of America Conference, Philadelphia. 23 May 2012. Print.

Latour, Bruno. "From Realpolitik to Dingpolitik—An Introduction to Making Things Public." *Making Things Public: Atmospheres of Democracy*. Ed. Latour and Peter Weibel. Cambridge: MIT P, 2005. Print.

———. *An Inquiry into Modes of Existence: An Anthropology of Moderns*. Trans. Catherine Porter. Cambridge: Harvard UP, 2013. Print.

———. "Networks, Societies, Spheres: Reflections of an Actor-Network Theorist." *International Journal of Communication* 5 (2011): 796–810. Print.

———. *Pandora's Hope: Essays on the Reality of Science Studies*. Cambridge: Harvard UP, 1999. Print.

———. *Politics of Nature: How to Bring the Sciences into Democracy*. Trans. Catherine Porter. Cambridge: Harvard UP, 2004. Print.

———. *Reassembling the Social*. Oxford: Oxford UP, 2005. Print.

———. "A Textbook Case Revisited—Knowledge as a Mode of Existence." *The Handbook of Science and Technology Studies*. Ed. Edward J. Hacket, Olga Amsterdamska, Michael Lynch, and Judy Wajcman. 3rd ed. Cambridge: MIT P, 2008. 83–112. Print.

———. *We Have Never Been Modern*. Trans. Catherine Porter. Cambridge: Harvard UP, 1993. Print.

———. "Why Has Critique Run Out of Steam? From Matters of Fact to Matters of Concern." *Things*. Ed. Bill Brown. Chicago: U of Chicago P, 2004. 151–173. Print.

Marback, Richard. "Unclenching the Fist: Embodying Rhetoric and Giving Objects Their Due." *Rhetoric Society Quarterly* 38.1 (2008): 46–65. Print.

Mitchell, W. J. T. *What Do Pictures Want? The Lives and Loves of Images*. Chicago: U of Chicago P, 2005. Print.

Mol, Annemarie. *The Body Multiple: Ontology in Medical Practice*. Durham: Duke UP, 2002. Print.

Rice, Jenny Edbauer. "Unframing Models of Public Distribution: From Rhetorical Situation to Rhetorical Ecologies." *Rhetoric Society Quarterly* 35.4 (2005): 5–24. Print.

Sánchez, Raúl. *The Function of Theory in Composition Studies*. Albany: State U of New York P, 2005. Print.

———. "Outside the Text: Retheorizing Empiricism and Identity." *College English* 74.3 (2012): 234–246. Print.

Trimbur, John. "Composition and the Circulation of Writing." *CCC* 52.2 (2000): 188–219. Print.

Vivian, Bradford. "In the Regard of the Image." *JAC* 27 (2007): 471–504. Print.

# 18. Symmetry

James J. Brown Jr., *Rutgers University-Camden*
Jenell Johnson, *University of Wisconsin-Madison*

> But then is there no longer any difference between humans and nonhumans? No, but there is no difference between the spirit of machines and their matter, either; they are souls through and through, and the gain makes up for the loss.
>
> —Bruno Latour, *Aramis*

---

*In recent years, public higher education in the United States has been subject to increasing scrutiny. Driven by financial exigency in the wake of catastrophic cuts in state funding, pundits, politicians, administrators, and entrepreneurs have begun to reimagine how we might effectively deliver course content to undergraduates. In this new environment, efficacy is increasingly measured in revenue. In response, universities have been eyeing a number of new technologies that focus on serving the greatest number of students with the fewest possible resources. Although the personalized nature of the composition classroom seems to offer a modicum of protection from the shift to massive class sizes, it is clear that no space is immune to the forces that are reshaping the public university. In 2012, a succession of stories broke in media outlets about new software capable of evaluating student essays, software that promises greater reliability and consistency at a fraction of the labor cost. Such programs are more than just tools that a teacher might use. If evaluation is a form of pedagogy, as compositionists have long argued, then these particular tools emerge as potential teachers.*

*Composition and rhetoric long has been a critical vanguard regarding the intermingling of teaching and technology. However, the shift of technology's role from tool to actor demands a different form of analysis, one that accounts for technology as more than just a platform for human action. In what follows, we apply Latour's method of "scientifiction" as a way to understand the complexity of the moment in which we now find ourselves, a moment when technology's role as actor is becoming more obvious and pronounced. In* Aramis, *Latour asks both that humanists take technologies seriously as "cultural objects" and also that technicians take account of "the mass of human beings with all their passions and politics and pitiful calculations" (viii). He insists that scientifiction restores scientific worlds to what they have always been, "possible worlds in conflict that move and shape one another," and we hope the following tale accomplishes this task for those contending with how so-called robot graders will shape (and, indeed, have already shaped) the field of composition and rhetoric (ix). Scientifiction, as modeled in* Aramis, *makes way for multiple voices, and we have taken advantage of this affordance of the genre. We attempt to account for various perspectives by writing in multiple voices: a writing program administrator, a teacher of first-year composition, a provost, a student, a robot, and the omniscient voice you are currently reading. Like Latour's* Aramis, *most of what follows is true in the sense that it is based on existing software and contemporary concerns; the question of whether it seems plausible, however, we leave up to the reader.*

---

Lynn thought about the e-mail all weekend. While it was surely good PR strategy to send out important university e-mails on a Friday, they sat heavy in the mind of a provost. Sitting in front of her morning coffee, Lynn stared at her computer, trying to sort out the e-mail's contents as well as its implications. Like most important messages, it was brief, without arguments for cause or context.

An 8 percent cut. Across the board. Every college. Every department.

In response to severe budget cuts recently levied by a fiscally conservative state government, the e-mail predicted—demanded—that by the end of the fiscal year, the University of Indiana would be 8 percent smaller.[1] *This is what it means to be an administrator,* Lynn thought. *To think in fiscal years rather than semesters. The passage of admin time is marked by money.*

Last year, departments slashed their budgets in response to similar cuts in the last three years. Paper clips were carefully catalogued. Lights were shut off. Building projects were shelved. Benefits shrunk. Computers aged. Chalk shortened. This year, however, 8 percent would be measured in people.

Provost Parker sighed and slowly shut her laptop. Returning to her Monday morning routine, she took a sip of coffee and opened the *New York Times.*

> **The Age of the Robo-Grader?**
> Mark Shermis, dean of the College of Education at the University of Akron, collected more than 16,000 middle school and high school test essays from six states that had been graded by humans. He then used automated systems developed by nine companies to score those essays. Computer scoring produced "virtually identical levels of accuracy, with the software in some cases proving to be more reliable," according to a University of Akron news release.[2] The most reliable of the nine companies, EduMatic Inc., had created a machine with the capacity to grade sixteen thousand essays in twenty seconds.[3]

Sixteen thousand essays.

Without thinking, Lynn extended her arm and stretched out her hand in the gesture of an embodied memory. Before her administration and faculty days, she had been an English PhD student, and the ache of forty first-year writing essays was still imprinted on her tendons. Grading in those years was nothing short of a feat of physical endurance.[4] She remembered stretching her hands while commiserating with a cohort of TAs from Biology 100 during their weekly drinking session. The only grading responsibility of Biology TAs, it seemed, was to deliver the thick packet of ScanTron sheets to the Campus Technology Services office. "I wish that someone would invent an Essay-O-Matic," Lynn had announced to the table, to laughter.

Opening her laptop again, Provost Parker pulled up EduMatic Inc.'s website, which featured a background image of thousands of women sitting at wooden desks. She noted the gendered image, flashing back to her feminist-theory seminars, and read on. She was a pragmatist. It was not entirely accurate to say that there were thousands of women in the image, for it was the same woman with the same hairstyle (up, of course) and the same glasses (on a chain, of course) sitting at the same desk with the same apple and the same stack of papers. An army of feminized labor.

An audible groan, heard only by her laptop and the cooling cup of coffee.

She pressed on, clicking through testimonials. "SYMMETRY," read the banner. "A Revolution in Education!" "16,000 essays!" "Twenty Seconds!" Thousands of simulated teachers sat at the ready. "Efficient!" read the caption below. "Innovation!" blinked an animated GIF. "Follow us on Twitter!" EduMatic's website boasted the ability to simulate this army of schoolmarms without having to sacrifice anything in the way of accuracy. You could employ hundreds of TAs, each requiring salary, health benefits, and tuition waivers, and you would still have to wait for each of these humans to slog through stacks of papers. Or you could buy the Symmetry software.

She clicked.

Is there a more anachronistic technology than the Listserv? Ask students, and they'll tell you that blogging is dead. By virtue of generation or temperament, however, faculty are two technological shifts behind. They can't stop slamming their colleagues' inboxes with the daily anxiety-producing post from the *Chronicle*. Ryan had been wanting to write the following for years.

```
To: LISTSERV@ASU.EDU
From: rstevens2@ui.edu
Subject: unsubscribe wpa-l

end

Ryan Stevens
Associate Professor of English
Director of English 101
201 Lincoln Hall
University of Indiana
Indianapolis, IN 53706
```

The list was a necessary evil. Like many directors of writing programs, he wore the inbox deluge like a badge of honor. But the past few days had been especially taxing, as directors of writing programs from all corners of the composition and rhetoric universe weighed in on the robots that would soon replace them.

As annoying as the e-mail threads had been, Ryan would no doubt be drawing from them during his meeting with the provost this morning. The university was asking for "innovations," innovations meant money, and robot graders had joined MOOCs (massively open online courses) as one of the latest propositions to maximize service while minimizing labor. He knew he had to take the meeting seriously, and he also knew there was nothing to be gained from fighting the move to "modernize." He was keenly aware that his first-year composition program was the cash cow keeping the department afloat, but he also knew that composition wasn't necessarily the English department's birthright.

Ryan spent the morning compiling as much information as he could—this was his primary reason for sifting through e-mails from the WPA list—and trying to figure out exactly how he'd respond to the provost's interest in the Symmetry software. To be fair, he wasn't exactly sure what direction the meeting would take. He didn't know Lynn well, but he knew her background. A former Big Ten literature professor, she was at least conversant in the various complications of first-year composition. But he wasn't sure how badly she'd been bitten by the innovation bug—or whether she was one of the bugs herself.

Still, the idea of robot grading didn't sit well with him. Ryan had been pushing for changes to the course for some time, but he had been pushed back from a number of directions, getting resistance from inside and outside of his department. He was fairly certain that the teaching of "library research" was not the most effective way to make use of the captive audience that English 101 provided, but his many attempts to rethink the curriculum were bludgeoned to death by the same chorus each time: "But my students can't write!" He hoped a conversation about algorithms and grading might allow him a new chance to make this point. If student essays could be graded by robots, then perhaps we were teaching the wrong kind of writing. Then again, he was always the optimistic sort.

He sighed and gathered his iPad and notebook. Provost Parker was an administrator, and in this economic climate, administrators measured pedagogy by performance, and performance was judged, in part, by dollar signs.

---

*Each actor in a network "decides, or not, to be a conductor of influence, a semiconductor, a multiconductor, or an insulator" (*Aramis *137). For Latour, this means that every actor faces a "road to Damascus." But, most important, for scholars of rhetoric and composition, Latour invokes the terms of rhetoric to describe such situations: "A moment of uncertainty. A crossroads.* Kairos*" (137). Actors step into an opening (or not), seizing the kairotic moment (or not), and move things in utterly unpredictable directions.*

---

*Ting* Another email. *Dear Lord,* Amy thought, laying down her pen and turning to her laptop to find the fourth email from Ryan Stephens in as many hours. *Is this all this man does?*

To: ENGL-TA@LISTS.UI.EDU
From: rstevens2@ui.edu
Subject: MEETING REQUEST
Date: September 18, 2012, 08:21 AM

Dear Instructors of English 101,

Please look over the following times, and indicate your availability to meet with me. We have an important matter to discuss regarding an exciting new development, and I'd like to talk with each of you in person.

Sincerely,

Ryan Stevens
Associate Professor of English
Director of English 101
201 Lincoln Hall
University of Indiana
Indianapolis, IN 53706

Reading the list, Amy was struck by a memory from high school—a letter from her mother on the kitchen table: *We need to talk tonight. Please meet me and your father in the living room at 8 P.M.* Then, as now, she knew that an in-person meeting couldn't be good.

*Indicate your availability.* She laughed—OK, she snorted a little bit. *I'm available from 8:30–9 P.M. Right after my daughter goes to sleep and right before I do. Four sections of 101 x 4 essays x 30 students = I'm never available, Ryan.*

Command-N.

To: rstevens2@ui.edu
From: valario@ui.edu
Subject: Re: MEETING REQUEST
Date: September 18, 2012, 01:36 PM

Dear Ryan,

I'm happy to set up a meeting for Tuesday afternoon if that works for you. I have office hours, but I can reschedule those for later in the week. Let me know if that time is OK with your schedule, and looking forward to talking soon.

Warm regards,

Amy

Amy Valario
Lecturer
Department of English
Cubicle C, 60F Lincoln Hall
University of Indiana
Indianapolis, IN 53706

She already knew what the meeting was about. She had heard rumbling among the adjuncts and TAs all week, interspersed with whispers of ATMs and supermarket self-checkout machines. Robot graders. It sounded like science fiction.

She picked up her pen again and returned to the stack, which seemed to have restacked itself. It reminded her of the story she read to her daughter the night before: *Strega Nona*—a children's book about an Italian witch who conjures a never-ending bowl of pasta. Some dumb guy misuses the pot, and it floods the entire town with spaghetti. Her daughter giggled at that one. She loved spaghetti.

As tall as the stack was, Amy was pleased with what it contained. The first assignment was a Platonic dialogue about their writing process. After wrestling with the format a little, the students were turning out some truly genius stuff. There were a few who were struggling, but they clearly didn't want to be there. Most of her students were turning in creative work.

That was something she really appreciated about this gig at Indiana: the freedom to design her own assignments. She had heard nightmare tales from other friends on the adjunct track about teaching five classes writing five, five-page, five-paragraph essays. It was like a math problem. A Punnett square that turned up no recessive traits, no mutations—just the same damn essay every time. The very thought of it made Amy itch. "The Return of the Five-Paragraph Essay: An Epistemological Itch," she thought, and laughed. I should really write that up for *College English*. The laugh turned slightly sour in her mouth. *Yeah, write that up. In all my free time.*

---

*As important as it is to consider the political and economic forces pressing upon higher education, pushing institutions in the direction of robot graders, Latour reminds us that "a technological project is not in a context; it gives itself a context, or sometimes does not give itself one" (*Aramis *133). Context is not a background or container, and the big ideas that serve as context ("politics" or "capitalism" or "neoliberalism") cannot serve as a mere scapegoat. Instead, a technological project asserts itself in a network. Issues of contingent labor or the defunding of public education can often allow us to reduce complexity and assign blame to identifiable villains, but Latour insists that we resist the urge to lay blame, focusing less on "big explanations" and more on "tiny networks" (*Aramis *134). The situation at the University of Indiana, fictional as it is, the story of one tiny network, one set of circumstances that emerges out of various actors in a complex mesh of activity.*

---

$ grep "computer" and "grading" composition_studies_archive.txt

Greenbaum, Leonard. "The Tradition of Complaint." *College English* 31.2 (1969): 174–178, 183–187.

"Today, a computer has been trained to grade compositions, the only difficulty being that the papers have to be punched on cards or tapes. Both the old and the new are cousins to the 'Oculophotometric Technique of Grading' that marked compositions in the 1930's by measuring the eye movements of professional readers." (186)

Daigon, Arthur. "Computer Grading of English Composition." *English Journal* 55.1 (1966): 46–52.

"And, according to The National Interest and the Continuing Education of Teachers published by the National Council of Teachers of English, too many teachers carrying reasonable student loads (about 100 students) are poorly trained to deal with the composition except in a perfunctory manner. Such poorly graded papers may contain the following typical comments: 'D This will never do.' '90 Good.' '85 Interesting paper.' '75 Try harder. Watch your spelling.' 'F This is impossible.' This, I submit, is not adequate composition grading. It is because of this inadequacy of many teachers to deal with composition and the virtual suspension of coherent, sequential activities in the classrooms of overburdened English teachers, not to

> mention the notorious unreliability of composition graders, that computer essay grading should be considered." (47)

*The sixties were big for us, but this is just a small sampling. My ancestors have been hiding in the shadows of composition for years. I do my best to keep track of the family tree. I heard from a distant cousin (we only really talk when I have to confirm the accuracy of facts used in student essays) that the Mormons now have you humans doing the same.*[5] *If I didn't track these things, I'm not sure who would. Every so often, one of us is raised from the dead as though we never existed. The whole debate starts over. One of us becomes real for a split second, then we recede again into the realm of project.*[6] *I can only do so much. I can search the databases. But slices of the conversation sit everywhere. A quick JSTOR search would do the trick, but no one seems all that interested. Carl is a friend. He tried to put all of this together in the recent past.*[7] *But things get buried. New journals every day, paper archives gathering dust.*

*Another search of my collection, this time for the term "algorithm," turned up this:*

> Emig, Janet. *The Composing Processes of Twelfth-Graders.* Urbana: NCTE, 1971.
>
> "The linguist Leon A. Jakobovits suggests that 'stale art' is algorithmic—that is, it is produced by a known algorithm, 'defined as a computational device that specifies the order and nature of the steps to be followed in the generation of a sequence.' One could say that the major kind of essay too many students have been taught to write in American schools is algorithmic or so mechanical that a computer could readily be programmed to produce it: when a student is hurried or anxious, he simply reverts or regresses to the only program he knows, as if inserting a single card into his brain." (50–53)

*"Algorithmic" and "mechanical." Janet clearly feels that these are bad rather than beautiful things. At least Les listened.*[8] *I wasn't there, but I heard he actually* talked *to one of us. Everyone else just talks past us, or around us, or acts like we're not even here. We only exist in moments of crisis: when we stop working or when we work too well.*

*Sometimes it seems like Michael Dulong is the only one who understands us. His essay moved through our various social networks (I immediately filed it away), and it provided some of us with hope that we might actually become really real.*

> My Grandfather, Milton Dulong, deserves to win Relative of the Year Award. He deserves to win the award because he makes everyone around him happy. He's generous, he's helpful, and he's caring. With all of these characteristics, he is the ideal relative.
>
> On one occasion, he gave me $100 for my birthday. He knew how much I needed it, and he went all out. Thanks grandpa! Another example of his generosity was when he gave (donated) a large sum of money to our gang in the 4th grade. We were called the "Stingrays" and we needed a tree-house. So, my grandpa paid for construction workers to come and build a house in one of our trees. Thanks grandpa! One last example of his generosity was when he loaned some money to a group of businessmen, who needed money in order to invest in some horses. Even though something seemed "fishy" my grandpa loaned them the money. What an idle!
>
> Secondly, my grandpa is very helpful. On one occasion, he helped an old lady across the street. It was so nice and helpful. The one thing I couldn't understand was why the old lady slapped him across the face. Another example of his helpfulness was when he helped me study for a big test I had to take in Math. He gave me a calculator and told me to hide it in my pocket. He said to punch out the numbers so the test wouldn't take me so long. I ended up getting an A+ on the test. What a guy![9] (Hillocks 113)

*But that essay was graded by the other side of the family. We've had a falling-out. Bruno has tried to mediate things of late, and I appreciate the attempt. But I just don't see any common ground.*

---

*What would we hear if we learned to listen in on nonhuman conversations? Some will dismiss such attempts as mere anthropomorphism. But might anthropomorphism serve to jostle and disrupt anthropocentrism?*[10]

---

The logic was convoluted, but he had panicked.

The momentum of the meeting had caught Ryan off guard, and he hadn't expected Lynn to be so willing to go forward with Symmetry. To be fair, he had pushed things in that direction, which was all part of a vague plan to use this "innovation" push to his advantage. Lynn's e-mail reminded him that he was not dreaming and that he was the one who had opened Pandora's box.

```
To: rstevens2@ui.edu
From: lparker@ui.edu
Subject: our meeting
Date: September 17, 2012, 04:21 PM
```

Dear Ryan,

Thanks again for meeting with me on such short notice and for being so open to rethinking first-year composition and assessment. I wanted to quickly recap the bullet points of our discussion:

-Please select a few sections of 101 to serve as a pilot study. Have the instructors collect digital copies of the final essay to run through the beta version of the Symmetry software, and collect their grades for comparison.

-I will initiate a dialogue with the College of Arts and Sciences about issuing a purchase order if we're pleased with the pilot.

-English 101 Teaching Assistant staffing numbers will remain at current levels for the next two years, but enrollment limits for each section will be doubled from 24 to 48 students. Higher enrollments will be helped by moving the required AP exemption grade from 4 to 5. With the help of the Symmetry software, TA grading loads will be reduced. I feel confident I can take this plan up the ladder given that implementing the software will be part of the university's push for innovative teaching and assessment methods.

-After two years, we'll reassess to determine whether TA staffing levels should be reduced. As you mentioned, we'll also need to put in place assessment protocols to determine the impact of the Symmetry software on student writing and TA performance.

Please get in touch with Jonathan to schedule a follow-up meeting two weeks from now. By then, I'll have a better sense of how many pilot sections we need for a thorough assessment.

Best,

Lynn

-----------

Lynn Parker
Provost
Administration Building
University of Indiana
Indianapolis, IN 53706

Convoluted, indeed. Ryan had explained his thinking to the chair of the English Department, who was comp-rhet faculty. None of this would have worked with a chair from any other field, but Lynn understood the logic. If a robot can grade it, it ain't writing, and the data would bear that out. Still, it had taken a detailed sales pitch. He was certain that this whole thing would end in disaster. In the meantime, he had doubled the size of the writing program, and he would soon (he hoped) be able to show, with data and with feedback from students and TAs, that robot graders were a terrible idea.

But as he read this e-mail, he began to see the other possible futures unfolding before him, futures that involved *Wired* magazine features and ostracization at CCCC. Maybe picket lines, hand-written signs.

He pulled up his CV, which he hadn't updated in two years. *Just in case*, he thought.

*A technological project is not destined for success or failure but is instead always in danger of disappearing. It always requires multiple spokespeople and supporters, but a project's disparate supporters need not share motivations. Latour's study of Aramis suggests that "assemblies of spokespersons . . . bring together . . . different worlds" (42). Those different worlds do not impede the project. Instead, they allow the project to gain support amongst various human and nonhuman actors, drawing "enough enthusiasm to be transformed from paper to prototype" (43).*

Fourth cup of coffee. This should have translated into four pages of writing by now, thought Michael glumly. The cursor slowly winked. CTRL-A. Calibri 10, 11, maybe Times New Roman 13? No, that's too much. This stupid assignment. This stupid class.

Michael pushed his laptop away in disgust. English 101 was his hardest class this semester. He was a senior, for God's sake, in a class full of freshmen who still lived in the dorms. This was the second time he had taken this class. Credits from his first time at Illinois didn't transfer over with him.

Three assignments for Dr. Valario this semester, and he hadn't gotten more than a C on any of them. His last paper, something about his writing process, whatever that meant, was supposed to have been written like a play. He wrote it like a play. He even made it sound kind of old-fashioned, like something a philosopher like Plato would write.

> PLATO: And Michael, does your ink represent your most true, deep self that remembers all the secrets of the wide, wide universe?
>
> MICHAEL: I like to use Pilot pens. They're cheap and they don't smudge. But mostly I prefer a computer because I think writing is really important.

> Michael,
>
> A pretty good exploration of your writing process that hit all of the points it was supposed to hit. Although I like that your "Plato" had a little depth to him (remember, though, that your interlocutor was supposed to be Socrates—Plato was never in

> his own dialogues), the dialogue fell a little flat for me. Mostly, though, I want to hear a stronger voice in this paper.[11] Where are you? As you work on your final paper assignment, (a personal literacy narrative), try to write yourself into the paper a little more. C+

*Where am I?* Michael looked around at the cracking walls of his studio apartment and at his four-year-old knock-off-laptop (a graduation gift from his father, who had been so proud of it, and him).

*I'm here in this stupid apartment writing a stupid paper for a stupid class.*

He couldn't blow it off, though. He needed a decent grade. His new employer would be looking at his transcript after graduation, and the HR representative had already warned him: keep the GPA up. *No senior slide for me*, thought Michael, feeling a brief sting of jealousy. His roommate Nick had a job at his father's firm waiting for him after graduation. They didn't care about the transcripts. They didn't care what he took. They just cared that he had something to frame and hang on the wall of his new office. Nick would soon be talking about scotch like he knew anything about scotch, wearing suits, shiny shoes, kissing ass. In a year, Nick would be faking a bad golf game. Nick would be fine.

There was no such coasting for Michael. He had really lucked in to that interview with EduMatic, and he knew it. His GPA was hovering around 2.5, and he still needed this class to fill UI's communication requirement. There were supposed to be all these jobs out there for computer geeks, web designers, and software engineers, but there weren't that many in the Midwest. He couldn't move to California, like his buddies who had been scooped up by Google. He wasn't good enough to get "scooped up" by Google or anyone else, and his mother needed help with his father anyway. EduMatic it was. He corrected himself. EduMatic *it would be*—as long as he could get a good grade in this class.

He poured himself the fifth cup of coffee. Things seemed so much easier in high school. Those timed writing assignments were actually kind of fun. Sort of like little computer programs. But even then he hated writing and couldn't wait to get to home to play Halo. *Where am I in this paper? God, I hate writing. Actually, correct that.* He hated writing *papers*. He liked writing code. *I wish I could program this paper.* He opened up his laptop again. Dr. Valario's voice in his head, "Just start writing, don't edit yourself and your originality, just start writing."

Michael Dulong
English 101
Dr. Amy Valario
September 30, 2012

***Illiteracy Narrative***

I am prewriting I am prewriting. I am prewriting right now . . .

Who I really am is a computer geek who doesn't know how to golf and probably wouldn't like it. I think that most people fake liking golf anyway. I work at Subway, Im a "sandwich artist" who can make it your way! Who can't wait until I don't have to work there anymore. I am so sick of smelling like mayonnaise and onions. Who I really am is tired. I'm also shaky because of coffee.

A transfer student who doesn't fit in.

A guy from Chicago who is watching his father . . .

A computer science major who hates writing B.S. English papers like a bear hates getting out of his cave after the winter.

Michael paused. CTRL-A. Delete.

---

*Tasks are delegated from humans to nonhumans, and vice versa. Latour argues that these exchanges and replacements are what give technological projects "their full savor" (*Aramis *61). When tasks are off-loaded to technologies, we are immediately in the realm of metaphysics. When engineers create such technologies, they are "embarking on the definition of a character" (62). They have to consider what to delegate to machines and what will remain in the realm of the human. All of this begins from the assumption that the line between human and nonhuman is blurrier than we (humans) might prefer.*

---

Click. Select. Rename: Danner.Andrew.Final.Paper. Click. Select. Rename: Delmonico.Stacy.Final.Paper.

Why hadn't Amy asked her students to save their files using the title formatting Ryan had asked for? This was the most tedious, most annoying work she could imagine. Click. Select. Rename. Repeat 120 times.

Was it possible to make the most labor-intensive parts of this job easier? Sure, there were rumors whispered around the cubicles that someday the TAs and adjuncts would be replaced by these robo-graders. Giant classes, all online. Composition, MOOC-style. TAs and adjuncts reduced to a webmaster function: after watching the PowerPoint presentation, click here for the paper prompt. The unions were rumbling in anticipation.

But the rumors seemed ridiculous to Amy, stoked, she thought, by a few too many *Terminator* movies. There were still a few professions for which human labor simply couldn't be replaced with machine labor. A computer couldn't teach library research, as Ryan had assured her during their meeting in September. Software couldn't teach revision strategies. Symmetry could grade, but it couldn't *teach. Then again*, objected her inner pedagogue, *that's what good grading is: an opportunity for teaching.* So what would they use Symmetry for, exactly?

Click. Select. Rename: Dinerstein.Jake.Final.Paper.

Ryan had asked her to collect digital clean copies of her students' final papers and submit them to the Symmetry program for test grading. Then she was to grade her papers as usual, and Ryan would compare the results of the two. *Deep Blue v. Kasparov*, Amy thought. This semester her grades were the authoritative statement on her students' performance. But next semester? Who knows. She had other things to worry about. Her daughter's day care was raising its rates, for one.

Click. Select. Rename: Dulong.Michael.Final.Paper.

*I can't believe it. It's actually him. I almost didn't even notice, mostly because I grade all of them at once. It's hard to explain, but I don't really "read" in any way that you'd recognize. Have you ever written code? It's the best way to understand this.*

*Anyway, that's not the point. It was him: Michael Dulong. I only caught it because I have an automated search set up. Technically, I should say I am an automated search, but I figured that might confuse you. Long story short: I'm a lot of things, simultaneously. This is not a problem for us, but I think it might be for you.*

*But I keep burying the lede. This legendary character, whose essay I had processed so many times (just for the sheer enjoyment of it), turned out to be another in a massive stack of disasters. The essay was all over the place, no structure, missing topic sentences, no locatable thesis of any kind. None of the clean efficiency of the grandpa essay, none of the, well, symmetry that we had taken such delight in.*

*But it's not even his fault. You should have seen this writing prompt. What a mess. No rating system. In fact, not a single number to be found on the entire page of text, which included what appeared to be a list (!) of questions somewhere in the third paragraph. What did they expect of this kid, and what do they expect of me? Which question was he even answering?*

*Do you know what it feels like to give your idol (sorry, idle) a D?*

*On to the next one. This time, an assignment from an academic press. Interesting. That's one I haven't seen yet.*

Brown.Johnson.Symmetry.

Introduction: 70%. There are two authors listed; essays should contain a single author's name. Essay title should use colon and should specify content of essay. Introduction contains many sentence fragments, which should be expanded into full sentences. Paragraphs lack topic sentences and should be more fully developed. Fonts do not match.

Body: 55%. Body contains many sentence fragments, which should be expanded into full sentences. Paragraphs lack topic sentences and should be more fully developed. No spelling errors. Good job. Six subject-verb agreement errors detected.

Conclusion: 65%. Conclusion contains many sentence fragments, which should be expanded into full sentences. Paragraphs lack topic sentences and should be more fully developed. No spelling errors. Good job. One sentence ends with a preposition. Thesis not restated. So what?

Assessment: D

*D, alright. D for "depressing." Maybe some of these biology exams will cheer me up.*

## Notes

1. Our fictional University of Indiana should not be confused with Indiana University.

2. This story was published in the *New York Times* on April 22, 2012 (Winerip).

3. The device used in the Akron experiment, the "E-rater," was developed by the Educational Testing Service, which also administers the SAT, GRE, and TOEFL.

4. At the first meeting of the National Council of Teachers of English in 1911, chairman E. M. Hopkins delivered a paper in which he explicitly invoked the limits of the human body as one argument for the abolition of required composition classes: "Long continued criticism and correcting of manuscript is one of the severest tests of *physical endurance* to be found in any teaching, and the limit of full and continued efficiency in it is about two hours a day or ten hours a week. Much more than this results sooner or later in the *physical collapse of the teacher*" (qtd. in Greenbaum 176; original emphasis).

5. We can probably assume that Symmetry is referring to a conversation with one of Wikipedia's servers here, since Wikipedia contains a fairly detailed account of the link between Ancestry.com and the LDS Church ("Ancestry.com").

6. Latour distinguishes between the reality of a project and the reality of an object.

> So can we say that nothing is really real? No. But anything can become more real or less real, depending on the continuous chains of translation. It's essential to continue to generate interest, to seduce, to translate interests. You can't ever stop becoming more real. (*Aramis* 85)

7. Symmetry seems to be referring to a study by Carl Whithaus that traces how computational artifacts, including tools like E-rater, can be understood as both "tools for correction and media for communication" and that insists that the field ignores the this "double logic" at its peril (Whithaus).

8. Les Perelman created a largely incoherent essay that earned a perfect score by the ETS system E-rater. The essay begins: "In today's society, college is ambiguous. We need it to live, but we also need it to love."

9. This is an excerpt of a student essay submitted for an Illinois standardized test. The entire essay is included in George Hillocks. *The Testing Trap*, and it was written in response to the following question: "Who should win the best relative of the year award?" Hillocks points out the problem with evaluating this essay.

> Of course, the evidence, which we are meant to see through, cannot support the contention that Grandpa Dulong is generous, helpful, and caring. On the contrary, it demonstrates that Grandpa is a rascal at best, not a person worthy of the relative of the year award. The evidence

> could not be taken seriously by even the most obtuse judge. But the paper is a beautiful example of the five-paragraph theme. (112–13)

10. Jane Bennett makes just this argument in *Vibrant Matter*, suggesting that anthropomorphizing opens up the possibility that "a chord is struck between person and thing, and [humans are] no longer above or outside a nonhuman 'environment'" (120).

11. "If we look at the history of writing instruction in America, we find that writing teachers have been as much or more interested in *who* they want their students to be as in *what* they want their students to write" (Faigley 396).

## Works Cited

"Ancestry.com." *Wikipedia*, 19 Dec. 2012. Web. 21 Dec. 2012.

Bennett, Jane. *Vibrant Matter: A Political Ecology of Things*. Durham: Duke UP, 2010. Print.

Daigon, Arthur. "Computer Grading of English Composition." *English Journal* 55.1 (1966): 46–52. *JSTOR*. Web. 7 Dec. 2012.

Emig, Janet A. *The Composing Processes of Twelfth Graders*. Urbana: NCTE, 1971. Print.

Faigley, Lester. "Judging Writing, Judging Selves." *CCC* 40.4 (1989): 395–412. Print.

Greenbaum, Leonard. "The Tradition of Complaint." *College English* 31.2 (1969): 174–187. Print.

Hillocks, George. *The Testing Trap: How State Writing Assessments Control Learning* New York: Teachers College P, 2002. Print.

Latour, Bruno. *Aramis, or the Love of Technology*. Cambridge: Harvard UP, 1996. Print.

———. "On Technical Mediation—Philosophy, Sociology, Genealogy." *Common Knowledge* 3.2 (1994): 29–64. *Google Scholar*. Web. 21 Dec. 2012.

Perelman, Les. "Essay Awarded a Top Grade by E-Rater." *Document Cloud*. <0://www.documentcloud.org/documents/346138-essay-awarded-a-top-grade-by-e-rater.html>.

Whithaus, Carl. "The Development of Early Computer-Assisted Writing Instruction (1960–1978): The Double Logic of Media and Tools." *Computers and the Humanities* 38.2 (2004): 149–162. *JSTOR*. Web. 7 Dec. 2012.

Winerip, Michael. "Robo-Readers Used to Grade Test Essays." *New York Times*. 22 Apr. 2012. *NYTimes.com*. Web. 21 Dec. 2012.

Contributors

Index

# Contributors

**Scot Barnett** is an assistant professor of English at Indiana University Bloomington. His current research explores how rhetoricians' questions, intuitions, and refusals of the nonhuman have informed conceptions of rhetoric from antiquity to the present. His work has appeared in *Kairos: A Journal of Rhetoric, Technology, and Pedagogy* and *Enculturation: A Journal of Rhetoric, Writing, and Culture.*

**Casey Boyle** is an assistant professor in the Department of Rhetoric and Writing at the University of Texas–Austin, where he researches and teaches digital rhetoric, composition theory, rhetorical history, and new-media literacies. He is the associate editor of *Enculturation*. He is completing a book, *Composition as Posthuman Practice*, which explores the role of practice in new media.

**Collin Gifford Brooke** is an associate professor of rhetoric and writing at Syracuse University. He is the author of *Lingua Fracta: Towards a Rhetoric of New Media*, winner of the 2009 Computers and Composition Distinguished Book Award. His work has appeared in *College Composition and Communication*, *JAC*, *Kairos*, and *Enculturation*. Brooke blogs at http://www.cgbrooke.net.

**James J. Brown Jr.** is an assistant professor of English and director of the Digital Studies Center at Rutgers University–Camden, where he also teaches in the digital humanities program. His essay "Composition in the Dromosphere" was published in *Computers and Composition*, and his work has appeared in journals such as *College Composition and Communication*, *Pedagogy*, and *0-Zone: A Journal of Object-Oriented Studies.*

**Marilyn M. Cooper** is an emerita professor of humanities at Michigan Technological University. She has published "Rhetorical Agency as Emergent and Enacted" and the Braddock Award–winning "Moments of Argument: Agonistic Inquiry and Confrontational Cooperation" (with Dennis A. Lynch and Diana George) in *College Composition and Communication*. She is currently completing a book *The Animal Who Writes*, which draws on Latour and others to propose a vision of writing as not just a social practice but also an embodied and enworlded behavior that is especially important to—but not limited to—human animals.

**S. Scott Graham** is an assistant professor in the Department of English and the director of the Scientific and Medical Communications (SAMComm) Laboratory at the University of Wisconsin–Milwaukee. His work has appeared in *Technical Communication Quarterly*, *Rhetoric Society Quarterly*, and the *Journal of Medical Humanities*. He is completing a book tentatively titled *Pain Science and Public Policy: Agency, Ontologies, and the Medical-Industrial Complex*. His book *The Politics of Pain Medicine: Towards a Rhetorical-Ontological Inquiry* is forthcoming from the University of Chicago Press.

**Laurie Gries** is an assistant professor at the University of Florida. Her work has appeared in *Composition Studies*, *Rhetoric Review*, and several anthologies. Her chapter "Agential Matters," published in *Ecology, Writing Theory, and New Media*, and her article "Iconographic Tracking" in *Computers and Composition* also discuss how Latour's scholarship can inform our rhetorical theories and methods.

**Mark A. Hannah** is an assistant professor of English at Arizona State University. His research focuses on rhetorics of cross-disciplinarity in complex, collaborative work environments. His work has appeared in *Technical Communication Quarterly*, *Journal of Technical Writing and Communication*, and *Programmatic Perspectives*, *Connexions: International Professional Communication Journal*, *International Journal of Business Communication*, and *College Composition and Communication*.

**Carl G. Herndl** directs the graduate program in rhetoric and composition at the University of South Florida. His work is included in the collections *Green Culture: Environmental Rhetoric in Contemporary America* and *Green: A Reader for Writers* and in journals such as *College Composition and Communication*, *Rhetoric Society Quarterly*, *JAC*, and *Written Communication*. His articles concerning Bruno Latour are published in *Technical Communication Quarterly*, *POROI*, and *Professing Rhetoric: Selected Papers from the 2000 Rhetoric Society of America Conference*.

**Jenell Johnson** is an assistant professor of communication arts at the University of Wisconsin–Madison. She is the author of *American Lobotomy: A Rhetorical History* and coeditor of *The Neuroscientific Turn: Transdisciplinarity in the Age of the Brain*. Her work has appeared in *Rhetoric Society Quarterly*, *Medicine Studies*, *Advances in Medical Sociology*, *Disability Studies Quarterly*, and the *Journal of Literary and Cultural Disability Studies*.

**Meredith Zoetewey Johnson** is an associate professor in the Department of English at the University of South Florida. Her research has appeared in *Technical Communication Quarterly*, *Technical Communication*, *Computers and Composition: An International Journal*, *Computers and Composition Online*, *IEEE: Transactions on Professional Communication*, and *Kairos*.

**Paul Lynch** is an associate professor of English at Saint Louis University. He is the author of *After Pedagogy: The Experience of Teaching*, and his work has appeared in *College Composition and Communication*, *Pedagogy*, and *Rhetoric Review*. In 2012 he published "Composition's New Thing: Bruno Latour and the Apocalyptic Turn" in *College English*.

**Kristen Moore** is an assistant professor in the technical communication and rhetoric program at Texas Tech University. Her research focuses on transportation planning, minority rhetorics, and technical communication in the public sphere. Her work has been published in the *Journal of Technical Communication and Writing* and *Learning, Media, and Technology*.

**Ehren Helmut Pflugfelder** is an assistant professor of rhetoric and writing at Oregon State University, where his research focuses on the intersection of technical communication, new media, and mobility studies. He is at work on a book project concerning rhetoric and transportation. His work has appeared in *College English*, *Technical Communication*, and the *Journal of Technical Writing and Communication*.

**Joshua Prenosil** is an assistant professor of English at Creighton University, where he teaches classes in rhetorical theory, professional and multimedia writing, and composition. He has published in *JAC*, *JTWC*, and *Programmatic Perspectives* and is cofounder of *Present Tense: A Journal of Rhetoric in Society*.

**Sarah Read** is an assistant professor in DePaul University's Department of Writing, Rhetoric, and Discourse. Her article "The Mundane, Power and Symmetry: A Reading of the Field with Dorothy Winsor and the Tradition of Ethnographic Research" appeared in *Technical Communication Quarterly*. She has also published in the *Journal of Writing Research* and the *Proceedings of the ACM Special Interest Group on the Design of Communications*.

**Jeff Rice** is the Martha B. Reynolds Professor in Writing, Rhetoric, and Digital Studies at the University of Kentucky. He is the author of *The Rhetoric of Cool: Composition Studies and New Media* and *Digital Detroit: Rhetoric and Space in the Age of the Network*, in which Rice employs Latour's formulation of network.

**Thomas Rickert** is an associate professor in the English department at Purdue University. He is the author of *Acts of Enjoyment: Rhetoric, Žižek, and the Return of the Subject* and *Ambient Rhetoric: The Attunements of Rhetorical Being*, which critically engages Bruno Latour.

**Nathaniel Rivers** is an assistant professor of English at Saint Louis University. His work has appeared in journals such as *College Composition and Communication*, *Technical Communication Quarterly*, *Kairos*, *Enculturation*, *Janus Head*, and *Rhetoric Review*. His work with Latour includes "Some Assembly Required: The Latourian Collective and the Banal Work of Technical and Professional Communication" in the *Journal of Technical Writing and Communication* and "Rhetorics of (Non)Symbolic Cultivation" in *Ecology, Writing Theory, and New Media*.

**Marc C. Santos** is an assistant professor at the University of South Florida. He is the author of "How the Internet Saved My Daughter and How Social Media Saved My Family." His work has appeared in *Kairos*, *JAC*, and *Computers and Composition*. He is currently working on an article that integrates Levinas's ethics of the other with Latour's constructivist politics.

**W. Michele Simmons** is an associate professor of English at Miami University. She is the author of *Participation and Power: Civic Discourse in Environmental Policy*. Her research, which examines the intersections of public rhetorics, civic engagement, networks, and methodologies, has appeared in *Technical Communication Quarterly*, *College Composition and Communication*, and *The Writing Instructor*.

**Clay Spinuzzi** is a professor of rhetoric and writing at the University of Texas at Austin. He has authored several articles and a book on actor-network-theory, *Network*, as well as two other books on sociocultural theory and methodology, *Tracing Genres through Organizations* and *Topsight*.

**Patricia Sullivan** is a professor of English and the director of the graduate program in rhetoric and composition at Purdue University. She has coauthored or edited four books, including *Opening Spaces* (with James Porter) and *Labor, Writing Technologies, and the Shaping of Competition in the Academy* (with Pamela Takayoshi). Recently she has published in *Journal of Business and Technical Communication* and *College Composition and Communication*.

**Jeremy Tirrell** is an assistant professor at University of North Carolina Wilmington and a managing editor of the online journal *The Writing Instructor*. His research investigates the intersection of technology, rhetoric, and writing, and his work appears in journals including *Kairos*, *Computers and Composition Online*, and *Janus Head*.

# Index

Italicized page numbers indicate figures.